W9-AGO-386

Civic Engagement in a Network Society

edited by

Kaifeng Yang
Florida State University

and

Erik Bergrud
Park University

Information Age Publishing, Inc.
Charlotte, North Carolina • www.infoagepub.com

Library of Congress Cataloging-in-Publication Data

Civic engagement in a network society / edited by Kaifeng Yang and Erik Bergrud.
    p. cm. — (Research on international civc engagement)
  Includes bibliographical references.
  ISBN 978-1-59311-557-9 (pbk.) — ISBN 978-1-59311-558-6 (hardcover)
1. Political participation. 2. Internet—Political aspects. I. Yang, Kaifeng. II. Bergrud, Erik.
  JF799.C58 2008
  323'.042—dc22

                                                                    2007046230

ISBN 13: 978-1-59311-557-9 (paperback)
ISBN 13: 978-1-59311-558-6 (hardcover)

Copyright © 2008 IAP–Information Age Publishing, Inc.

All rights reserved. No part of this publication may be reproduced, stored in a retrieval system, or transmitted in any form or by any electronic or mechanical means, or by photocopying, microfilming, recording or otherwise without written permission from the publisher.

Printed in the United States of America

CONTENTS

PART III.
THE INTERNET AND CIVIC ENGAGEMENT

CHAPTER 1

CIVIC ENGAGEMENT IN A NETWORK SOCIETY

An Introduction

Kaifeng Yang and Erik Bergrud

Network governance has become a prominent phenomenon among and across public, private, and nonprofit sectors in contemporary democratic societies (Agranoff, 2007; Koppenjan & Klijn, 2004; O'Toole, 1997). In particular, government decision making and public service delivery are conducted with increasing involvement of nongovernmental organizations and citizen groups. As many practitioners and researchers observe, businesses, nonprofits, neighborhood organizations, and other citizen groups have become essential partners of government and supporters of citizen engagement, contributing resources, skills, and capacities to community problem solving. Moreover, network participants and community stakeholders are increasingly connected with advanced information and communication technologies (ICTs) such as the Internet. Successful governing networks (formal or informal) and communities are often enabled by powerful online networks or virtual communities (Day & Schuler, 2004).

Civic Engagement in a Network Society
pp. 1–12
Copyright © 2008 by Information Age Publishing
All rights of reproduction in any form reserved.

Such fundamental changes manifest the shift from a mass society to a network society in which a combination of social and media networks shapes its primary mode of organization and most important structures at all levels. The term network society was coined by Jan van Dijk (2006) and Manuel Castells (1996, 2006). For Van Dijk, the mass society is characterized by collective units (groups, organizations, and communities), homogeneity, extended scale, local scope, high connectedness within units, high density, high centralization, high inclusiveness, unitary community, vertically integrated bureaucracy, and face-to-face communication. In contrast, the network society is characterized by individuals (linked by networks), heterogeneity, extended and reduced scale, *glocal* (global and local) scope, high connectedness between units, lower density, lower (polycentric) centralization, lower inclusiveness, diverse community, horizontally differentiated infocracy, and mediated communication. For Castells (2006), the basic units of our societies have changed to networks— "the network society, in the simplest terms, is a social structure based on networks operated by information and communication technologies based in microelectronics and digital computer networks that generate, process, and distribute information on the basis of the knowledge accumulated in the nodes of the networks" (p. 7). That is, networks constitute the new social morphology of our societies (Castells, 1996).

Those changes pose both opportunities and challenges to civic engagement and democratic participation. It becomes important to conceptualize citizen participation based on a network model, taking into account not only governments and citizens as two extremes but also a series of community stakeholder and network participants (Innes & Booher, 2004; Yang & Callahan, 2007). The changes require public managers to rethink their roles, responsibilities, and values; develop new skills on networking, negotiation, collaboration, and deliberation; solve community problems by building, managing, and improving networks of stakeholders and supporters; utilize new technologies to facilitate citizen engagement; and integrate citizen engagement with other strategic issues communities face.

As those changes unfold, theoretical and empirical inquiries regarding civic engagement in network settings have begun to be published in leading academic journals. Still, more systematic efforts are necessary to move forward this line of research, to identify best practices, and to offer feasible strategies. With this in mind, we invited an international group of leading scholars and practitioners to fill this lacuna, and we started by asking the following questions:

- What do networks mean to civic engagement? What challenges, opportunities, problems, and controversies do they bring both theoretically and practically?

- How can public managers respond to those opportunities and challenges? What knowledge, skills, and competencies are necessary? How and where can they obtain those qualities? Are there successful stories from which they can learn? Are they any pitfalls they should avoid?
- How does a network for civic engagement look like? Who are the participants? How does it evolve? Should it be managed? By whom? How should it be managed? What is the relationship between civic engagement networks and other networks?
- Do such networks pose any potential problems or threats to democratic institutions? How do they affect community politics and government accountability?
- How do such networks use ICTs, particularly the Internet, to conduct their work, enhance their capacity, and create their identity? Does the Internet improve civic engagement in terms of both quantity and quality?

Our international group of contributors comes from different disciplines or areas of study such as public administration, policy analysis, urban planning, political philosophy, and political science. Their contributions form an insightful picture of civic engagement from a network perspective. They are organized into three sections, as described below.

NETWORKS, PUBLIC MANAGEMENT, AND CIVIC ENGAGEMENT

The first section includes four chapters that provide theoretical perspectives on the transition to network governance and the shift of responsibilities and roles of public administration and public managers. In the first chapter, "It Takes Two to Tango: When Public and Private Actors Interact," Annika Agger, Eva Sørensen, and Jacob Torfing provide a succinct overview of the background, merits, problems, and dilemmas of network governance. The chapter starts with a description of the broader context of network governance in the European Union (EU) countries, which are confronted with growing expectations, limited public resources, increasing fragmentation, wicked problems, democratic disengagement, declining trust in government, and globalization. It continues with a list of the potential merits of civic engagement in governance networks, while recognizing the major obstacles to achieving the potential—such as the ideology of market and the political apathy of many citizens. Consequently, the three authors argue that the future of network governance and civic engagement depends on to what extent and how the involved actors will redefine their respective roles.

The authors propose that public officials should become metagovernors who not only provide vision and framing but also directly engage themselves in the governance processes through network management and network participation. In doing so, public officials must maintain an optimal level of control, a high level of democratic legitimacy, and a clear recognition that they are only one out of many cogovernors of public governance. In the meantime, the authors contend that citizens and stakeholders should become responsible and capable producers of public governance, while acknowledging the concerns about cooptation, the governmentalization of society, and social justice. Finally, rejecting the tendency of equating network governance with consensual decision making, Agger, Sørensen, and Torfing call for an agnostic perspective that views governance networks as arenas for power struggles, where mutual dependence forces network actors to find compromises despite their conflicts.

Agger, Sørensen, and Torfing's view is echoed by Eran Vigoda-Gadot, who agrees that civic engagement has to be understood in the big picture of partnerships and different actors have different roles in the process. In his chapter, "Collaboration Management in Public Administration: A Theoretical and Empirical Exploration of Mutual Challenges of Governance, Citizens, and Businesses in Modern Network Societies," he asserts that collaboration among citizens, the private sector, and government agencies is imperative for governance in a network society, and it is important to know how, when, and why they should share information, knowledge, and resources. After developing a framework to show the potential of collaborative management for public administration, Vigoda-Gadot presents an empirical examination of attitudes toward collaboration based on a survey of 244 public-sector and private-sector managers, which offers an optimistic view about intersectoral collaboration. He emphasizes that effective managerial collaboration in public administration depends on authentic involvement and participation in decision making. The arguments and discussions are nicely weaved into an interdisciplinary perspective that integrates politics, sociology, and management at three levels of analysis: state level, management level, and community level. Linking together network actors, activities, levels of analysis, and disciplinary knowledge, Vigoda-Gadot develops a unique theoretical typology that differentiates among integration, partnership, cooperation, coordination, and association. He posits that cooperation works at the state level; coordination, integration, and partnership are at the management level; and association occurs at the community level.

Myrna Mandell, after a nice review of current research in civic engagement and community networks, aims to clarify the links or similarities between the two lines of inquiry in her chapter "New Ways of Working: Civic Engagement Through Networks." She observes that although the literature on networks and citizen engagement compliment each other, there are few articles that actually discuss both at the same time. This is unacceptable as relations with community members and voluntary sector organizations have shifted from the periphery to the center of government policy and practice. To illuminate the relationship between civic engagement and networks, Mandell differentiates two tiers of citizen involvement. The lower tier relates to cooperative networks with involvement techniques such as public hearings, citizen advisory councils, citizen juries, and local issues forums. The higher tier relates to collaborative networks with involvement techniques such as town hall meetings, multi-stakeholder negotiations, policy consensus process, and neighborhood councils. She then illustrates that civic engagement processes and collaborative network processes are similar on five aspects: the equality of all participants in the process, an overriding commitment to the whole, an emphasis on meshing different values, using results to impact public policy, and the importance of trust.

Robert Agranoff, in "Conductive Public Organizations in Networks: Collaborative Management and Civic Engagement," agrees that network governance requires the change of roles and responsibilities of public officials and citizens. Taking an organizational perspective and focusing more narrowly on public agencies, he is concerned with two fundamental questions: where do public organizations fit in a networked society? In what ways do public agencies promote and participate in civic engagement through their networks and partnerships? Using the concept of *conductive organization*, coined by Saint-Onge and Armstrong (2004), Agranoff emphasizes the importance of creating partnerships, building alliances, forming teams, and managing interdependencies. He outlines nine rules of conductive engagement: diverse partners, learning together, lateral organizational design, information-based strategies, knowledge employees, building community relations, knowledge strategy, taking advantage of ICTs, and accounting for values added by partnering. Agranoff then offers 10 observations about civic engagement in collaborative management, calling for public agencies to work together with their various partners to create public dialogue over problems of mutual concern.

CASE-BASED PERSPECTIVES ON CIVIC ENGAGEMENT AND NETWORK SOCIETY

The second part of the book includes four chapters that are based on experiences of real engagement projects. The inclusion of case materials does not make the chapters less theoretical; rather, the cases are carefully chosen to illustrate the unique perspectives or arguments of the authors. David Booher's chapter, "Civic Engagement as Collaborative Complex Adaptive Networks," provides a powerful illustration of the role, outlook, and conditions of civic engagement in rescuing the democracy crisis and confronting the challenge of network society based on the experience of CALFED, a network of 25 state and federal agencies and more than 35 major stakeholder groups in the area of water policy. Drawing from the work of Castells (1996), Booher places greater emphasis on networks, rather than individual citizens, as unit of analysis. In his view, civic engagement occurs through interconnected networks of interest and geography. The chapter is based on three related sets of literatures: democracy theory (particularly theories of deliberative democracy), collaborative planning, and complexity theory (particularly complex adaptive networks). Booher starts with the observation that current democratic institutions do not enable engaged citizens, and then reviews various proposals of deliberative democracy and asserts that an appropriate conception is a more activist approach to deliberative process, which converges with the practice of collaborative planning. Hence, he introduces the five typical phases of a collaborative planning process: assessment, convening and organization, joint fact finding, deliberation and negotiation, and implementation. Following that, Booher shows how the understanding of civic engagement can be enhanced by concepts of complex adaptive systems, such as agents, interactions, nonlinearity, system behavior, and robustness and adaptation.

Based on the complexity theory, Booher correctly realizes that it is probably overambitious to propose a specific design for democratic institutions that integrate civic engagement in the governing process. He makes it clear that his purpose is to "suggest conditions by which democratic institutions may evolve to integrate civic engagement and provide more meaningful and sustainable governance for the network society." Similar to the authors in the first part of the book, Booher believes that public agencies play a significant or pivotal role in fostering those conditions because issue-driven policy networks will connect other networks or clusters of networks where citizens engage with one another. In order to play this role, Booher writes, public managers have to change their management styles and pay attention to 11 managerial dimensions: structure, source of direction, goals, origin of system behavior, role of manager, managerial tasks, managerial activities, leadership style, criteria for success, organizational context, and source of democratic legitimacy. Booher shows that traditional management and complex adaptive network management are very different on the dimensions.

Jean Hillier and Joris Van Wezemae, in their chapter "Opening Up What May Yet Come: Performing Civic Engagement in a Complex

World," critically analyze an empirical case of civic engagement in the development of a local strategic area action plan in North-East England. Observing that few authors have discussed the importance of place meaning and place attachment for citizens, the authors outline a theoretical framework to conceptualize the relational complexities and multiplicities, nonlinearities, nonfixities and contingencies embodied in civic engagement processes. Based on the unique literature on "geophilosophy," they consider space as a multiplicity bringing together characteristics of externality, simultaneity, contiguity or juxtaposition and qualitative and quantitative differentiations. In line with Agger, Sørensen, and Torfing (chapter 2), Hillier and Van Wezemae find that citizen engagement in strategic spatial planning performs in agonistic tension between different interests. The chapter calls for attention to the connectivity of human and non-human networks and to the ways in which different realities of time and space interrelate or clash.

For Hillier and Van Wezemae, a place is not a given. What is more important is how it is produced and maintained by the connection of physical and mental, relational networks. Therefore, a place can no longer be seen as a distinct, unitary physical entity. It is materially experienced as a significant but fluxing conjunction of multiple networks. Therefore, key research questions for them become: Do collaborative processes of civic engagement produce different outputs than noncollaborative processes? How does this particular network for civic engagement perform? How has it evolved? What underlying mentalities, perceptions and assumptions exist and develop, with what impacts on performance? And what challenges and opportunities can be discerned both theoretically and practically? The authors try to address these questions based on their case analysis.

The concept of network society relates closely to the increasing globalization and connectedness among nations, whose "distance" has been significantly reduced due to modern ICTs. Communication and information sharing across national boundaries become easier than ever before, which means that the possibility for policy transfer becomes greater. According to Castells (2006), "what we call globalization is another way to refer to the network society, although more descriptive and less analytical than what the concept of network society implies" (p. 5). As the trend of decentralization and participation sweeps the world, an important question is whether civic engagement techniques can be shared among nations with different historical, political, social, and cultural contexts. In the chapter "A Comparative Study of Citizen Engagement in Infrastructure Planning in Japan and the United States: A Look at Legal Frameworks and Two Successful Cases," Shunsaku Komatsuzaki and Hindy Lauer Schachter compare the growth of citizen engagement in infrastructure planning in the United States and Japan, and point out that the two counrties face similar demands for citizen participation in infrastructure planning and are part of a global trend toward an expanded public policy role for networks of nongovernmental organizations.

By describing two successful cases—the development of a 25-year statewide transportation plan coordinated by the Florida Department of Transportation and the use of citizen participation in planning for a city road, the "Onda-Motoishikawa Line," in the city of Okohama, Komatsuzaki and Schachter show that six similar factors led to successful engagement experiences in both cases. The six factors are: the involvement of a diverse and representative group of people from organized interest groups and individuals; the establishment of frequent and varied engagement forums; the adoption of advanced information technologies (particularly the Internet) to distribute information; the use of technology to link citizens to networks of organizations; the development of appropriate procedures for multiple engagement forums; and the creation of deliberation opportunities. The two authors conclude that civic engagement techniques may be transferable in a globalized networked society.

Carolyn Lukensmeyer and Lars Hasselblad Torres, in their chapter "Citizensourcing: Citizen Participation in a Networked Nation," argue that effective policymaking open to robust citizen participation is the hallmark of good governance in the twenty-first century based on their experience from AmericaSpeaks, which uses the 21st Century Town Meeting to improve public-sector transparency, participation and accountability. They use the term "citizensourcing" to represent the type of governance that is based on sustained dialogue and interaction between citizens and the public officials. The term is adapted from "crowdsourcing," which was used by *New Yorker* staff writer James Surowiecki in his 2004 book. Crowdsourcing, or tapping the wisdom of crowds, refers to emerging practices from the private sector where companies get amateurs and professionals outside traditional organization boundaries to design products, create content, and even tackle corporate research and design problems in their spare time. Lukensmeyer and Torres believe that this can also be realized in the public sector through the design and application of new governance mechanisms.

Their experience with the 21st Century Town Meeting, which includes a combination of face-to-face discussion and networked technology that enables very large groups to interact effectively, shows some important success factors including carefully produced scripts, small group dialogue, table reporting, real-time data theming, video projection, keypad polling, and instant reporting. They identify four principles of engagement: involve decision makers, achieve representation, provide balanced information, and ensure transparency. To invent and promote new governance mechanisms that support authentic engagement, Lukensmeyer and Torres propose that the U.S. federal government should appoint a cabinet-level position responsible for transforming the way agencies and the legislature engage citizens. The position may not be permanent, but it should have sufficient powers, resources, and duration to push through important reforms.

THE INTERNET AND CIVIC ENGAGEMENT

Communication networks are inseparable from the concept of network society (Castells, 1996; Van Dijk, 2006). As Castells (2006) writes, "digital communication networks are the backbone of the network society, as power networks (meaning energy networks) were the infrastructure on which the industrial society was built" (p. 4). Castells (1996) asserts that "without its technological tools, society cannot be understood or represented" (p. 5). He depicts ICTs as one of the prime elements of the space of flows that underline the concept of network society. However, ICTs such as the Internet do not automatically lead to better governance or democracy. Castells (2006) acknowledges that "diffusing the Internet or putting more computers in the schools does not in itself amount to much social change. It depends on where, by whom, for whom, and for what communication and information technologies are used ... we need to know the dynamics, constraints and possibilities of the new social structure associated with it" (pp. 5-6).

In a similar way, Day and Schuler (2004) conclude,

> Many forms of community technologies are emerging as communities seek to achieve a diverse range of social goals. Social movements across the world are utilizing ICTs to support and sustain their communication, organization, mobilization, and activation processes. Just how solid, durable, effective, equitable, and socially meaningful the local action and global interaction of community practice and social movements in the network society will be in shaping our social environments is as yet unclear. (p. 19)

The three chapters in this section generally support the arguments above. In their chapter "Does Internet Use Really Facilitate Civic Engagement? Empirical Evidence from the American National Election Studies," Hun Myoung Park and James Perry investigate the relationship between Internet use and civic engagement in the public sphere. They observe that direct causality is often posited for the relationship between Internet use and engagement, but empirical research has produced inconsistent results that raise many theoretical and methodological issues. In order to reconcile conflicting evidence, they first try to clarify the meaning of engagement by differentiating four types of civic engagement: electoral deliberative engagement (people talking to any people and showing why they should vote for or against a candidate), nonelectoral deliberative engagement (talking about politics with family or friends), electoral action-oriented engagement (attending political meetings, rallies, speeches, or dinners and giving money to a political party and candidate), and nonelectoral action-oriented engagement (contacting government officials to express personal views on public issues and working with other people to deal with community issues). In terms of methodology, Park and Perry employ the propensity score matching method and the recursive bivariate probit model, and analyze longitudinal data compiled from the American National Election Studies in 1996, 1998, 2000, and 2004. Findings suggest that Internet use for political information positively influences civic engagement in the public sphere, but its impact differs by the type of civic engagement. Internet use appears to be more influential for deliberative and nonelectoral engagement than for electoral action-oriented engagement. Endogeneity matters in deliberative engagement such as discussion of politics but not much in action-oriented engagement. They conclude that since the potential of the Internet is not automatically realized in daily life, the question is how to effectively use the Internet in the networked society.

In a similar vein, Jason MacDonald and Caroline Tolbert, in the chapter "Something Rich and Strange: Participation, Engagement and the Tempest of Online Politics," confirm the positive impact of the Internet on civic engagement. Also unsatisfied with the mixed results about the relationship between Internet use and civic engagement, the two authors use data from the 2000 and 2002 American National Election Studies and 2004 primary elections, and show that use of online campaign news produces citizens who are more interested in the election, have more to say about the candidates, and are more knowledgeable about politics. They find support for an Internet news effect on engagement using two-stage causal models to control for endogeneity problems. Additionally, they find partial support for the hypothesis that given the young are more likely to use online election news, they are more politically engaged via online communication. The results suggest that whereas younger people are more likely to be knowledgeable, no such relationship exists for political interest. They conclude that the Internet, as the major feature of modernization in the early twenty-first century, fosters, rather than impedes, civic engagement. The online consumption of political information increases political knowledge, fosters political discourse, and engages political interest.

In the final chapter, "Opportunity for Civic Engagement: An Online Assessment of Worldwide Municipal Web Sites," Marc Holzer and Aroon

Manoharan show that many municipalities do not place much emphasis on citizen participation practices online while simultaneously upgrading other features of e-government. The chapter is based on two international surveys conducted in 2003 and 2005 through a collaboration between the E-Governance Institute at Rutgers-Newark and the Global e-Policy e-Government Institute at Sungkyunkwan University in Seoul, which evaluated the practice of e-governance in large municipalities worldwide. The top 100 municipalities selected were the most populated cities in 98 countries. The two authors find that the potential for online citizen participation is still in its early stages of development. Only one of the top overall cities is among the top five in citizen participation. Cities in Europe ranked the highest on citizen participation among the continents, while cities in South America scored the lowest. Cities in OECD (Organization for Economic Cooperation and Development) countries place more emphasis on citizen participation than do other cities. Holzer and Manoharan write that for the Internet to significantly enhance citizen participation, the e-government portal needs to be sufficiently equipped with tools like bulletin boards, feedback forms, policy forums and performance reporting systems. They call for developing a comprehensive e-government policy that also considers transitioning to citizen participation online.

While the chapters of this book contribute significantly to our understanding of civic engagement in a network society, there are still questions waiting for more discussions and clarifications. After all, both civic engagement and community networks are social practices that face constant changes due to environment uncertainties and human agency. This book serves as a call for more research in this line. We thank the contributors for their wonderful work and we look forward to working with more authors on this book series on international civic engagement.

REFERENCES

Agranoff, R. (2007). *Managing within networks: Adding value to public Organizations*. Washington, DC: Georgetown University Press.

Castells, M. (1996). *The rise of the network society.* Oxford, England: Blackwell.

Castells, M. (2006). The network society: From knowledge to policy. In M. Castells & G. Cardoso (Eds.), *The network society: From knowledge to policy* (pp. 3-22). Washington, DC: Johns Hopkins Center for Transatlantic Relations.

Day, P., & Schuler, D. (Eds.). (2004). Community practice: An alternative vision of the network society. In *Community practice in the network society* (pp. 3-20). New York: Routledge.

Innes, J., & Booher, D. (2004). Reframing public participation: Strategies for the 21st century. *Planning Theory and Practice, 5*(4), 419-436.

Koppenjan, J., & Klijn, E. -H. (2004). *Managing uncertainties in networks*. New York: Routledge.

O'Toole, L. J. (1997). Treating networks seriously: Practical and research-based agendas in public administration. *Public Administration Review, 57*(1), 45-52.

Saint-Onge, H., & Armstrong, C. (2004). *The conductive organization*. Amsterdam: Elsevier.

Van Dijk, J. (2006). *The network society*. Thousand Oaks, CA: Sage.

Yang, K., & Callahan, K. (2007). Citizen involvement efforts and bureaucratic responsiveness: Participatory values, stakeholder pressures, and administrative practicality. *Public Administration Review, 67*(2), 249-264.

PART I

NETWORKS, PUBLIC MANAGEMENT, AND CIVIC ENGAGEMENT

CHAPTER 2

IT TAKES TWO TO TANGO

When Public and Private Actors Interact

Annika Agger, Eva Sørensen, and Jacob Torfing

INTRODUCTION

Governments at different levels increasingly recognize the urgent need to mobilize and utilize the knowledge, resources, and energy of empowered citizens in the governing of our complex, fragmented, and multilayered societies. Hence, they frequently use and experiment with user surveys, public consultations, citizens juries, and institutional mechanisms of co-governance in order to reinforce the link between government and civil society. In this chapter we argue that civic engagement through the participation of individual or organized citizens in different kinds of governance networks might help to improve both the effectiveness and the democratic performance of public governance. Governance networks bring public and private actors together in relatively self-regulated negotiations that contribute to the production of public value. As such, the production of effective and democratic network governance depends on a high level of committed interaction between public and private actors. Both parties must carefully reconsider their roles and strategies and

Civic Engagement in a Network Society
pp. 15–39
Copyright © 2008 by Information Age Publishing
All rights of reproduction in any form reserved.

reflect on how they can help facilitate effective and democratic governance through a negotiated interaction driven by the recognition of interdependency, the presence of trust, and willingness to compromise. It takes two to tango, and there are many difficult steps to learn for the public and private actors. This chapter aims to contribute to this learning by analyzing the new roles for the public and private actors engaged in network governance. It begins with a brief diagnosis of the problems and challenges that confront public authorities in their quest for effective and democratic governance. It then considers the merits and problems of an increasing use of governance networks in the formulation and implementation of public policy. This is followed by a lengthy discussion of the new roles that emerge for public authorities and private actors, such as citizens and organized stakeholders, and the dilemmas these roles bring with them. The chapter concludes with a discussion of the interaction between the public and private network actors where we warn against seeing "consensus" as the primary goal of network governance. Alternatively, we recommend that governance networks are regulated by the normative ideal of "agonistic respect" in coping with conflict.

OBSTACLES TO EFFECTIVE AND DEMOCRATIC GOVERNANCE

Europe faces tough competition from other regional powers in the global knowledge economy. In response to this challenge, the European Union (EU) has formulated the ambitious goal that Europe is to become the most competitive and dynamic region in the world and should, to that end, develop a sustainable, knowledge-driven economy that maintains a high level of social cohesion. In some parts of the world, the enhancement of structural competitiveness is obtained through autocratic rule, the suppression of democratic rights and continued emphasis on obedience and discipline. However, in the EU, it is an explicit goal that the achievement of the daunting socioeconomic goals should be combined with a reinforcement of core values about democratic participation and civic engagement. The achievement of the twin goals of enhancing competitiveness, sustainability, and social cohesion while increasing democratic participation and civic engagement puts a tremendous pressure on the public authorities at all levels, authorities which are already struggling with severe and persistent legitimacy problems. The political and administrative decision makers in local, regional, and national governments and within the EU must deliver an effective and democratic governing of the European societies, but they are facing a series of problems and challenges that may jeopardize their endeavor.

Effectiveness is hampered by the concurrence of rapidly growing expectations and limited public resources. Hence, the demand for public governance in the globalized risk society is rising, and public governance is increasingly expected to be knowledge based, proactive, strategic, responsive, flexible, and targeted. At the same time, the available public resources in the EU and the individual member states are limited and difficult to augment in a global world where rising taxes tend to hamper economic competitiveness. As such, governments across Europe suffer from serious overload problems (Peters & Pierre, 2004). In order to find a way out of this impasse, the public authorities must try to mobilize the knowledge and resources of relevant and affected actors from civil society, while trying to transform citizens and stakeholders from demanding receivers of governance to responsible coproducers of governance.

Effectiveness is also hampered by the growing fragmentation and spatio-temporal complexity of Europe and the European societies which are becoming functionally differentiated into a large number of institutionalized subsystems and sociopolitical organizations (Mayntz, 1989). The resulting fragmentation is amplified by the rise of multiculturalism, growing individualization, the prevalence of postmaterialist values, risks that tend to create horizontal lines of political conflict, the development of economic globalization and technologies that draw new vertical lines of socioeconomic inequality. At the same time, complexity is growing as a result of the multiplication and interconnectedness of different spatial and temporal horizons for strategic, sociopolitical action (Jessop, 2002). Old and new political powers and responsibilities are shifted upward to transnational authorities, downward to regional and local authorities and outward to quasi-autonomous agencies and private companies. The central decision makers at the different levels of governance devise and implement strategies affecting strategic action taking place at other levels. In addition, elected governments, public bureaucracies, private firms, interest organizations and civil society organizations tend to have different temporal horizons for their political decisions and strategic actions. The result is a mounting ungovernability of society that can only be mitigated by the formation of new forms of horizontal and vertical coordination that bring the relevant and affected actors from the public and private sectors together in processes of negotiated governance and concrete problem solving (Peters & Pierre, 2004).

Last but not least, effectiveness is hampered by a growing number of wicked, horizontal problems that create a high degree of substantial complexity (Klijn & Koppenjan, 2004). Policy problems are "wicke" in the sense that the conception of the problem is blurred, specialized knowledge is required in order to solve it, the number of stakeholders is high, and the risk of conflict is imminent. "Horizontal" policy problems cut across different policy areas and can only be solved through coordination and cooperation among public and private actors. The proliferation of wicked and horizontal problems makes it difficult for public authorities to solve the urgent problems faced by citizens and private firms and further amplifies the need for crosscutting negotiation among public and private stakeholders, experts, and citizens.

Democracy is also facing some grave problems and challenges. The good news is that democracy seems to be on the march in the sense that the number of electoral democracies has increased worldwide, the respect for the rule of law and fundamental civil and political rights is growing, and transnational polities like the EU are putting an increasing emphasis on democratic values such as participation, transparency, and account-ability (Gaventa, 2006). However, at the same time, there is a growing concern about different forms of democratic deficit. Hence, there are sev-eral from esteemed scholars that the quality of democracy is in crisis (Clarke, 2002; Putnam, 2000; Skocpol, 2003).

Democracy is undermined by democratic disengagement and apathy that shows itself to be in decline in terms of voter turnout, party member-ship and participation in community activities and public affairs (Stoker, 2006). This might be caused by a growing individualization that makes it harder for people to subscribe to large political projects and participate in collective action; an increasing professionalization of politics at all levels that tends to produce frustrations for those who feel that the gulf between their own competences and capacities and what it takes to get political influence is widening; and an increasing globalization and technification of policy problems and policy regulations that make it more and more dif-ficult for ordinary people to see how the problems can be solved and how they can influence the solution. As such, we are witnessing a worrying dis-enchantment about democracy that calls for the development of new forms of democratic participation.

At the same time, democracy is undermined by the widespread distrust in elected politicians and public bureaucracy. The European Social Survey shows that as many as 40% of the citizens in Europe have no or little trust in politicians (Stoker, 2006). One of the key explanations for this is that representative democracy, which is supposed to solve the problem of how to actively involve the people in modern mass societies in popular self-government, has turned into an impediment of democracy (Pitkin, 2004). In today's Europe, there is hardly any dialog between the voters and their elected representatives. The latter are captured by political elites and strong interest groups and the former are treated as customers, who com-municate with the elected elites through opinion polls and electronic market-research processes (Gaventa, 2006). In addition, the voters only have influence on the input side of the political system, leaving the output side to be governed by public bureaucrats who often have a considerable scope for influencing public governance, even though they often lack detailed knowledge of the policy field and are difficult to hold accountable for their decisions.

Finally, democracy is undermined at its root since the idea of a unified people defined by clear national boundaries is problematized by the current "deterritorialization" of politics and governance. Abraham Lincoln defined democracy as "government of the people, by the people, and for the people" and during the eighteenth and nineteenth centuries this "people" was increasingly defined as the adult population belonging to a particular nation state. However, today, the congruence between the level and source of public governance and the people affected by public regulations has weakened. Power and authority is displaced to international policy regimes, transnational organizations, regional and local authorities, and different sorts of cross-border regions. There are also examples of policy areas with competing and overlapping jurisdictions as well as policy problems that seem to fall in an institutional void (Hajer, 2003). At the same time, the homogenizing concept of the people is problematized by a mounting migration that increases the number of nonnational residents, migrant workers, and ethnic minorities and by postmodern sentiments that seem to spur the formation of new and multiple forms of identity. As a result, the people can no longer be taken for granted. Hence, instead of a tendentially unified *demos*, we have plurality of *demoi* that must be constructed and connected in and through participatory forms of governance (Bohman, 2005; Sørensen, 2007).

The problems and challenges listed above should be taken very seriously, not only because they prevent an effective and democratic response to the urgent needs of the European populations, but also because the European ambition of becoming the most competitive and dynamic innovation region in world can only be achieved through an effective and democratic policymaking.

Effectiveness and democracy are sometimes conceived as being antithetical to each other. However, we believe that this is not necessarily so. As such, we contend that both effectiveness and democracy can be boosted through a further development of institutionalized forms of civic engagement in the formulation and implementation of public policy. To put it bluntly, we believe that the future success of the European project is conditional on the development of governance networks that can help to facilitate a more effective and democratic policymaking through the construction of dynamic links between levels, policy areas, and sectors within in the pluricentric polity that constitutes the European Union.

THE MERITS AND PROBLEMS OF GOVERNANCE NETWORKS

Today, governance networks proliferate to an astonishing extent within different countries, policy areas, and levels of governance. Although traditional forms of top-down government are still in place, policymaking and public governance increasingly take place in and through pluricentric negotiations among relevant and affected actors from state, market, and civil society. Drawing on the extensive literature we can *define* a governance network as:

> A relatively stable articulation of mutually dependent, but operationally autonomous actors who interact through conflict-ridden negotiations that take place within a relatively institutionalized framework of rules, norms, common knowledge, and social imaginaries; facilitate self-regulated policy making in the shadow of hierarchy; and contribute to the production of public value in a broad sense which includes the definitions of problems, visions, ideas, plans, and concrete regulations.

This definition makes no claim to originality; rather, it aims at capturing the main features commonly ascribed to governance networks (Jessop, 2002; Mayntz, 1991; Rhodes, 1997; Scharpf, 1994). It highlights the interdependency of the public and private actors who retain their operational autonomy in the sense that they are not commanded by superiors. The network actors interact through negotiations that combine hardnosed bargaining with consensus-seeking deliberation. In the beginning "there are no agreed upon norms, procedures, or 'constitution' to predetermine where and how a legitimate decision is to be taken" (Hajer & Versteeg, 2005, p. 341). However, the sedimented interaction of the network actors will over time lead to the formulation of an incomplete and precarious framework of rules, norms, values and ideas. The rule-governed interaction facilitates a self-regulated policymaking that takes place in the shadow of hierarchy cast by public and/or private metagovernors and, therefore, gives rise to a kind of "bounded autonomy." The network is not only contributing to the production of concrete decisions and regulations, but also to the transformation of the entire policy discourse.

Governance networks take different empirical forms in different countries, at different levels of governance and within different policy areas. They might be self-grown or initiated and designed from above, intraorganizational or interorganizational; open or closed; tightly knit or loosely coupled; short-lived or permanent; sector-specific or societywide; and preoccupied with policy formulation or policy implementation. The multiplicity of different governance networks attests to the broad relevance of the concept for describing contemporary forms of societal governance.

Governance networks may also carry different labels. As such, they are often referred to as public-private partnerships, mechanisms of cogovernance, strategic alliances, think tanks, deliberative fora, citizen panels, or public boards, committees, and councils. The litmus test enabling us to see whether the label hides a governance network is to check if we can identify a network of interdependent and yet autonomous actors engaged in processes of governance based on negotiated interaction.

There might also be different rationales behind the formation of governance networks. In some countries and policy areas governance networks are formed in order to overcome fragmentation within the public sector. In other cases they are formed in order to facilitate coordination between quasi-autonomous public agencies and private contractors.

Finally, some governance networks are formed in order to enhance input legitimacy through participation of civil society actors or to enhance output legitimacy by expanding the knowledge basis of public policymaking. The different rationales will have a crucial impact on the composition of the various governance networks.

On the basis of the vast amount of literature on governance networks, we can compile a list of the potential merits of civic engagement in governance networks with regard to the enhancement of effective and democratic governance.

Governance effectiveness is enhanced through:

- The mobilization of the participating actors' knowledge, ideas, resources, and energies; the production of strategic, proactive, and responsive policy adjustments through continuous negotiations; and the construction of program responsibility through empowered participation and democratic ownership;
- The facilitation of negative and positive coordination among relevant and affected actors across sectors, policy areas, levels, and countries; and
- A thorough identification of needs and demands; a negotiated construction of manageable problems and challenges; the reduction, or handling, of conflicts through mutual learning and the development of trust.

Democratic governance is deepened through:

- The availability and use of different forms of individual and collective participation; the development of participatory politics for amateurs; and the empowerment of the participating actors

through an experience-based and/or deliberate enhancement of
their resources, rights, competences, and know-how and a transformation of their identity;

- The establishment of an active, informed, and continuous dialog
between politicians, civil servants, and citizens; the stimulation of
public debate and a widening of the scope for discursive contestation; and the facilitation of political participation and influence on
the output side of the political system; and

- The selective activation of particular groups of citizens; the construction of horizontal links between different *demoi*; and the
recruitment, mobilization, and education of subelites that can compete with the established elites and hold them accountable.

Despite the merits of governance networks, there are major obstacles to
the development of a networked polity where the formulation and implementation of public policy is based on negotiated involvement of relevant
and affected citizens and stakeholders. The neoliberal call for an increasing use of the market in public governance and the reinforcement of hierarchical government through new public management reforms tend to
narrow the scope for network governance. Moreover, the demolishing of
corporate network structures represents a major setback for empowered
participatory governance. Finally, the political apathy of large parts of the
population makes it difficult to see how it is possible to mobilize individual and collectively organized citizens in governance networks at different
levels.

On the other hand, local, regional, and national governments, and in
particular experts and political decision makers within the EU, tend to
recognize the limits of both hierarchical and market-based governance
and favor the formation of networks and partnerships (The European
Commission, 2000, 2001). In addition, corporatist "Iron Triangles" are in
some instances replaced by broader stakeholder networks, and perhaps
most important, local experiences show that people still want to participate in public deliberation and governance, especially in relation to specific issues, and when they are personally affected and permitted to
mobilize their passions and participate as amateurs and on an ad hoc
basis (Bang & Sørensen, 2001; Sørensen & Torfing, 2003).

In sum, the prospects for public governance in the future are uncertain. One of the central factors relating to whether or not the current
transformation of European forms of governance will develop into an
effective and democratic networked polity is to what extent the involved
actors are willing and able to redefine their respective roles in the networked governance process. This need to reinterpret traditional roles
counts both for public authorities such as politicians and public adminis-

trators, and for civil society actors among which we find individual citizens and various stakeholder organizations. Let us first focus on the need for a redefinition of the roles of public authorities.

NEW ROLES FOR POLITICIANS AND PUBLIC ADMINISTRATORS

Efforts to harvest the potential benefits of network governance are easily hampered by traditional perceptions of what it means to be a politician or a public administrator. While network governance entails a strong and ongoing interaction between state actors and civil society actors, the traditional roles of politicians and public administrators assume the presence of a sharp demarcation line between state and civil society, between the governors and the governed.

Traditionally, politicians have been seen as democratically authorized sovereign rulers, who govern society through their legitimate, monopolized right to pass laws and regulations, while public administrators have been perceived as neutral and loyal servants who loyally implement laws and regulations (Sørensen, 2006, p. 99). Seen from this role perspective, citizens and organized stakeholders are not supposed to play an active part in the governing process, and if they do so, this activity is regarded as democratically illegitimate and problematic. Not that citizens and stakeholders are expected to be completely passive. Individual citizens fulfill an important role in voting for politicians at general elections and in taking part in public debates, while organized stakeholders are regarded as in their good right to lobby and put pressure on public authorities. However, allowing them to take direct part in processes of public governance through various forms of network participation would, according to a traditional role perspective, undermine the parliamentary chain of governance, which ensures an equal distribution of political influence among the citizens processed through the institutions of representative democracy as well as these politicians' sovereign control with the implementation process through detailed legal regulation of and control with all actions performed by public administration.

As such, efforts to enhance civic engagement through governance networks that involve both public and private actors do not square well with the traditional images of what it means to be a politician and a public administrator. In other words, the surge of network governance calls for the development of new roles for politicians and administrators that allow for close interaction between public authorities and various involved and affected private actors within civil society.

Empirical as well as theoretical signs indicate that such new images of what it means to be a politician and a public administrator are on their way. *Empirically*, the doctrine of new public management (NPM), which has had a huge impact on processes of public governance in most liberal democracies, advocates for politicians and public administrators who steer rather than row. Steering, the task of politicians and executive administrators, is carried out at a distance through the framing of the conditions under which self-governing actors govern, while rowing—the actual governing—is delegated to various public and private actors who interact through a variety of marketlike and/or networklike forms of contracted and/or negotiated partnership arrangements (Osborn & Gaebler, 1992; Pollitt & Bouckaert, 2004). Hence, NPM transforms sovereign politicians and public administrators at the executive level are redefined as what could be called "framework governors" who govern at a distance through the strategic construction of the conditions that structure decentralized self-governance, while lower level public administrators are redefined as self-governing producers of public purpose in fierce competition with other producers and/or in network based cooperation with relevant and affected stakeholders.

Theoretically, an emerging body of governance theory argues that contemporary public governance is to an increasing extent carried out as metagovernance, that is, as the regulation of self-regulation (Sørensen & Torfing, 2007, p. 169). In contrast to sovereign forms of public rule, which establish a firm demarcation line between the governors and the governed, metagovernance seeks to transform the governed into cogovernors who, through their participation in self-regulating governance networks and other self-regulating bodies, contribute to the production of public governance. Seen from this theoretical perspective, the role of politicians and public administrators becomes that of the metagovernor who governs through the regulation of self-regulating actors. The new role for public authorities sketched out in the NPM-program is one out of many empirical indicators of a more general move toward metagoverned public governance.

The metagovernance of networks and other forms of self-regulation can take the form of either hands-off or hands-on metagovernance. Hands-off metagovernance is carried out at a distance through a political, economic, institutional, and discursive framing of the self-regulating actors:

- Political framing is exercised through the formulation of some overall political goals and governance objectives that self-governing actors such as networks must meet;
- Economic framing takes place through the allocation of a specific amount of resources that the self-regulating actors are authorized to govern;

- Institutional framing is carried out through the establishment of specific rules of the game; and
- Discursive framing is invoked through the construction of hegemonic storylines that give meaning to the actions of the self-regulating actors.

These forms of metagovernance are hands-off in the sense that they can be carried out without any direct interaction between the metagovernor and the self-regulating actors. Hence, hands-off metagovernance establishes a division of labor between what is governed by the metagovernor and what is governed by the self-regulating actors. However, the theoretical literature on governance, as well as numerous empirical studies, envisages that metagovernance must be supplemented by hands-on metagovernance through network management and network participation in order to be efficient (Kickert, Klijn, & Koppenjan, 1997; Klijn & Koppenjan, 2000; Rhodes, 1997; Sørensen, 2007; Sørensen & Torfing, 2007). Network management is carried out through a direct involvement of the metagovernor in the governance processes within a given network, and aims to promote network cooperation as much as possible through conflict mediation, through the promotion of trust among the actors within the network and through the enhancement of communication between the network and other actors. Network participation (Mayntz, 1991, p. 18) grants metagovernors such as politicians and public administrators a platform for interacting with the network actors in order to obtain direct influence on the negotiated policy outcomes produced by the network in accordance with procedural rules and norms defined by the network.

As noted above, NPM offers a new role for politicians and administrators. This new role strictly emphasizes hands-off forms of metagovernance by arguing that politicians should govern by setting the stage for self-regulating actors through various forms of political, economic, and discursive framing, while the task of public administrators at the executive level is to metagovern through institutional framing. As such, what NPM offers is an interpretation of metagovernance which is narrower than need be. Therefore, what is needed is the development of an alternative metagoverning role for politicians and public administrators that does not merely exchange sovereign, bureaucratic rule with hands-off metagovernance, but *perceives hands-on interaction and cooperation between metagoverning state actors and self-regulating networks of public and private stakeholders as important and necessary elements in performing political and administrative metagovernance.*

Empirical studies of actual governance processes indicate that both politicians and public administrators to an increasing extent define themselves as metagovernors, although many politicians still, to some extent, cling to the image of themselves as sovereign rulers. However, while the politicians tend to define themselves as hands-off metagovernors, public administrators tend to include hands-on forms of metagovernance as a legitimate part of the public administration toolkit (Rhodes, 1997; Klijn & Koppenjan, 2000; Sørensen, 2006, 2007; Goss, 2001). As such, we face a post-Weberian politician role consisting of a mix between a sovereign ruler and a hands-off metagovernor, and metagoverning public administrators with a well equipped toolkit.

The resistance to role changes, which is vividly illustrated by the politicians' relative reluctance to reinterpret themselves as metagovernors, is thoroughly theorized by role theory and sociological neoinstitutionalism (Powell & Dimaggio, 1991; March & Olsen, 1989). Roles give meaning to the actions of those who inhabit a given institution and the collective universe of meaning that constitutes an institution is not external to the involved individuals. They become a point of reference that gives meaning, order and rhythm to the everyday lives of institutionalized actors, and function as points of identification and reference that shape the very self-perceptions of the actors who play the roles, and thus roles are not changed easily. Actors cling to the roles they have learned to play unless there are strong and pressing reasons to exchange a sedimented role perception with another (Poulsen, in press). Why, then, should not only politicians but also public administrators give up the strong image of public authorities as sovereign rulers?

What's in it for Politicians and Public Administrators?

There are both potential costs and gains related to giving up the role as sovereign ruler for the role as metagovernor. With regard to the costs, the price that must be paid is the position as unchallenged superior step-higher authority with the monopolized and legitimate right to make binding decisions for society. This position is first and foremost to the advantage of the politicians who are placed in the position of sovereign rulers, not only vis-à-vis the citizens and organized stakeholders, but also in relation to the public administration. It also places public administrators in an advantageous position in relation to nonstate actors.

However, this role scenario places the full responsibility and workload on the shoulders of public authorities. As the pressure for public problem solving, and the complexity of the policy problems that need to be solved, increases this work load produces an overload of demands directed toward public authorities, the overload transforms the sovereign role position from the best of all worlds to a nightmare. Network governance promises a way out of this nightmare. Hence, involving citizens and organized stakeholders in governance networks transforms private resources into public resources, never ending demands into responsible modesty, and low-quality decisions into high-quality decisions. Private resources become public when citizens and stakeholders gain ownership of a certain governance ambition and choose to use their private resources in order to promote the negotiated goal set up by a governance network. Private actors adapt the demands for public services when they are involved in meeting these demands, and the knowledge possessed by the involved and affected citizens and organized stakeholders helps politicians and public administrators to perform well-informed and high-quality metagovernance.

As described above, there is both a price to pay and some gains to be won by public authorities in giving up their traditional role and reinterpreting themselves as metagovernors. However, as indicated above, the decision is not the same for politicians and public administrators. The politicians have to leave a very attractive position as sovereign rulers on top of the hierarchy, and the narrow perception of what it means to be a metagovernor offered by NPM does not have much to offer. This might explain why many politicians tend to be relatively reluctant when it comes to giving up their traditional role. Public administrators, on the other hand, are confronted with a choice between a less powerful secondary position in the traditional hierarchy and a strong position as a full-fledged hands-off and hands-on metagovernor that enhances their level of autonomy vis-à-vis the politicians. This might explain why public administrators have been more open to their new role as metagovernors than the politicians. If, however, politicians were offered the much more attractive broadly defined role as hands-off and hands-on metagovernors —we could call this role *the network politician*—that allows them to interact directly with citizens and organized stakeholders in interactive governance networks, many politicians might chose differently, since this new role offers new powerful channels of influence in a societal context that does not offer sovereign positions of rule but a plurality of more or less powerful channels of influence.

Dilemmas for Metagovernors

As noted by many governance theorists and envisaged by the harvested experiences with various forms of metagovernance in the reformed liberal democracies, the transition form sovereign rule to meta-governance does not result in a weakening of the ability of public authorities to govern society. Metagoverning authorities are indeed able to govern society—they

just have to do so differently—not through detailed sovereign bureaucratic control but through the regulation of self-regulating actors which
have a considerable autonomy. However, this new way of governing is not
easy to carry out. Like all other forms of governance, it produces dilemmas that cannot be solved, but must be handled through different coping
strategies.

One of the dilemmas that face public authorities performing metagovernance concerns the question of control. Top-down control is needed in
order to ensure coordination and give direction to the increasingly fragmented processes of public governance, but such control efforts constantly threaten to undermine the benefits obtained by means of this self-
regulated fragmentation: too tight a metagovernance reduces the willingness of citizens and organized stakeholders to invest their resources, take
responsibility for, and give away relevant knowledge that enhances the
added capacity for public problemsolving; too loose a metagovernance
threatens to undermine the ability of the metagovernor to ensure a high
level of policy coordination and general direction in the governance initiatives. Another dilemma has to do with maintaining a high level of democratic legitimacy in and around governance networks. On the one hand,
governance networks enhance the democratic legitimacy of public governance if they allow for extensive functional participation of the involved
and affected stakeholders, but on the other hand, this stakeholder participation might weaken the territorially derived democratic legitimacy
which is obtained through the traditional institutions of representative
democracy. Finally, a high level of interactive hands-on metagovernance
helps to qualify and inform hands-off metagovernance, and to reduce the
amount of demands and the level of resistance among relevant citizens
and organized stakeholders, while at the same time binding public
authorities to negotiated network agreements.

As such, metagovernance is a complicated matter that calls for the
development of coping strategies and competencies among politicians
and public administrators that deviate considerably from those relevant
for sovereign rulers. More than anything, the big challenge for politicians
and public administrators, who seek to govern through the performance
of metagovernance, is to recognize that they are but one out of a plurality
of cogovernors who, each in their own right, is an important and necessary contributor to the production of public governance. The next step is
to develop their ability to balance overregulation and underregulation in
the performance of hands-off metagovernance, to find ways to produce a
plus-sum game between representative democracy and networked forms
of democracy in order to enhance the aggregate amount of democratic
legitimacy, and to develop their capacity to perform hands-on metagover-

nance without losing their position as a step higher authority in the performance of hands-off metagovernance.

NEW ROLES FOR CITIZENS AND ORGANIZED STAKEHOLDERS

Just as governance networks challenge the traditional roles of public authorities they disturb sedimented role perceptions of what it means to be a citizen and a stakeholder organization. According to the traditional image of citizenship, citizen participation is restricted to voting, keeping informed in a free public sphere, and, occasionally, organizing themselves in voluntary associations of stakeholders who seek to make themselves heard in relation to the implementation of governance initiatives formulated and initiated by public authorities (Healey, 1996). This perception of citizenship is history. Empirical data as well as theoretical developments indicate that we are moving toward a new perception of appropriate citizenship and stakeholder involvement. *Empirically*, the NPM reform program and the many market-oriented and network-oriented public sector reforms mentioned earlier (Bouckaert & Pollitt, 2004; Rhodes, 1997, 2000) lay out a much more active role for citizens and organized stakeholders in processes of public governance: Market-oriented reform programs offer citizens the active and powerful role as *consumers* and *evaluators* of public services, just as stakeholder organizations are invited to become cogovernors in and through various contracted partnership arrangements where they compete with other stakeholder organizations. Network-oriented reform programmes invite citizens and organized stakeholders to collaborate with public authorities and with each other in providing public governance not only in the implementation phase but also in the early phases of agenda setting and policy formulation. In sum, the many reforms of the institutions and processes of public governance from the 1980s and onward have invited citizens and stakeholders into the realm of public policymaking, and called on them to give up their role as spectators to policymaking and become active coproducers of public governance.

Theoretically, the growing body of governance theory, which to an increasing extent has put its mark on the social sciences from the early 1990s and onward, stresses how the line of demarcation between the public and the private sphere, between those who govern and those who are governed, becomes more and more blurred. Governance theory outlines how citizens and organized stakeholders are increasingly made responsible for the production of public governance through various forms of self-regulated governance techniques. While rationalist theories of governance tend to regard the driving force behind this integration of private actors in processes of public governance to be a rational response to an escalating functional fragmentation of modern societies, culture oriented theories of governance tend to see the new cogoverning role for citizens and organized stakeholders as linked to a more general transition of the mentality of governance within advanced liberal democracies, which among other things expresses itself as new forms of subjectification and subjection, that is, the responsible, capable citizens who are willing to govern themselves according to certain norms of appropriate conduct (Sørensen & Torfing, 2007; Triantafillou, 2003).

The new and much more active role as coproducer of public governance implies a radical change in the way citizens and organized stakeholders perceive of themselves in relation to public authorities, just as it calls for new types of competencies and resources to be able to take active part in this game of governance. With regard to the former, citizens and stakeholder organizations must take the huge mental step from seeing themselves as voters who, most of the time, remain outside the realm of politics—a position that constitutes them as irresponsible and incapable subjects—to responsible and capable producers of public governance (Pløger, 2004; Bang & Sørensen, 1998). In addition, the new role calls on citizens and stakeholder organizations to give up the traditional image of politicians and public administrators as inapproachable and uncontestable authorities with a legitimate sovereign right to rule on their behalf.

With regard to the latter, the new role as coproducers of public governance calls for a high degree of political empowerment among citizens and organized stakeholders. With regard to the consumer role, it calls for citizens and organized stakeholders who are willing and able to play the competitive market game. With regard to the role as network participant, the close cooperation with metagoverning public authorities, which is much more interactive than public hearings, citizens committees, and so forth, calls for considerable political skills (Agger & Löfgren, 2006; Fung, 2006). Hence, citizens and stakeholder organizations who participate in governance networks with public authorities must obtain a high level of institutional capacity, know-how, efficacy and resources such as information, time, and professional knowledge (Connick & Innes 2003; Healey, 2003; Innes & Booher, 1999, 2000; Sørensen & Torfing, 2003).

Research indicates that citizens and organized stakeholders have to a considerable degree taken on the new role as responsible co-producers of public governance who cooperate closely with public authorities in different governance networks, although the tendency is stronger among organized stakeholders than among ordinary citizens (Bang & Sørensen, 1998; Marcussen & Torfing, 2007; Prakash & Selle, 2004). While organized stakeholders in many European countries have transformed themselves into highly professionalized organizations with an elaborate political know-how and a general willingness to share responsibility for the production of public governance through their participation in various governance networks, citizens are more reluctant to take on the role as responsible coproducers of public governance. This reluctance might be explained by the fact that participation in governance networks calls for considerable skills and resources which individual citizens seldom possess or are willing to invest. The limited willingness among citizens to participate in governance networks might also be explained by negative experiences with public authorities who overregulate in their efforts to metagovern governance networks. Finally, the unwillingness among some citizens to take part in network governance with public authorities might be an effect of the promotion of the consumer-oriented role perception of what it means to be an active citizen. Hence, customer are perceived as being in their good right to actively and aggressively demand choice between high quality public services without in any way taking responsibility for or contributing to the production of these services.

In conclusion, empirical and theoretical signs indicate that the perception of what it means to be a citizen and an organized stakeholder has undergone a radical transformation. From being outside politics, citizens and stakeholders are being pulled into the sphere of public policymaking, although citizens are so more reluctantly than stakeholder organizations. From voters and lobbyists they are called on to accept the role as active players on the political scene either as demanding costumers and efficient producers of public services on a public market or as resourceful and responsible co-governors who are willing and capable of participating in governance networks.

What's in it for Citizens and Private Stakeholders?

As mentioned earlier, roles are hard to change. They represent a safe haven of the well-known order of things which is not given up without a considerable contextual pressure for change that points to the insufficiency of traditional roles and the advantages related to venturing into the uncertainty of change. As we have seen, the current contextual pressure for change is considerable. The next step is to ask: What gains could citizens and stakeholders have from accepting the role as responsible co-governor? Or in other words: "what will compensate them for the responsibility and load of resources and competencies which citizens and stakeholders must possess in order to take on the demanding job as cogovernors?" In answering this question four things spring to mind: increased influence, better governance outcomes, realistic expectations and shared ownership.

With regard to *influence*, participation in networks with public authorities grants citizens and stakeholders a chance of gaining substantial influence on the problem definitions of the policy proposals and the implementation of public governance. Remaining on the outside of politics might be peaceful and less demanding but reduces the possibility of proactive political participation that has to do with setting the agenda and taking initiative and not only passively reacting to policies produced by public authorities. While stakeholder organizations get a chance to obtain influence on "high politics" through participation in elite networks, ordinary citizens gain influence through their participation in various "low politics" networks consisting of affected citizens and relevant and involved street level bureaucrats and professionals.

Participation in governance networks with public authorities is also likely to produce *better governance outcomes*. As argued by Jan Kooiman, the chains of interdependency are long in the functionally differentiated modern societies, and for that reason "No single actor, public or private, has all the knowledge and information required to solve complex dynamic and diversified problems; and no single actor has the sufficient overview to make the application of needed instruments for effective implementation" (Kooiman, 1993, p. 4). When a variety of public authorities and involved citizens and stakeholder organizations pool their information, knowledge, resources and commitment to define and solve policy problems the governance outcome is likely to become much better than when sovereign authorities with limited knowledge and resources govern by means of bureaucratic forms of rule and regulation (Agger, 2005; Booher, 2004; Pløger, 2004).

In addition, close network-based interaction with public authorities help citizens and organized stakeholders to *adjust their policy expectations* and political priorities in the light of the amount of available resources and pressing problems that face the larger political community. This paves the way for small victories rather than grand failures (Leach, 2006). This is not least relevant for organized stakeholders who need to produce victories in order to gain legitimacy vis-à-vis their members and the general citizenry.

Finally, participation in governance networks promotes a sense of ownership, shared understanding and mutual trust among public authorities and citizens and organized stakeholders which enhances the chance that all parties, including public authorities stick to negotiated agreements (Agger 2005; Lukensmeyer & Torres 2006; Marcussen & Torfing 2007; Pløger 2004). In other words, citizens and organized stakeholders enhance their ability to cooperate and set up shared goals, not only with each other within the confines of civil society, but also with resourceful public actors which makes it possible to reach for higher hanging fruits.

As such, capable, engaged and skilled citizens and organized stakeholders have plenty to gain by accepting the new role as the coproducers of public governance and by venturing into governance networks with public authorities. However, where does this leave the less qualified and resourceful and less engaged and willing citizens and stakeholder organizations? For citizens who cannot or will not take part in cogovernance, membership of strong stakeholder organizations gains in importance as a necessary supplement to the role as voter and consumer. With regard to engaged and willing citizens and stakeholder organizations that lack the necessary skills and resources, participation in governance networks represents an important means to develop such competencies and resources through learning by doing and through the network-based pooling of resources with more resourceful and skilled network participants.

Dilemmas for Coproducers

While participation in governance networks gives promise of increased influence, better governance outcomes, more realistic strategizing and shared ownership to citizens and organized stakeholders, participation in governance networks, like in all other governance schemes pose some serious dilemmas (Marcussen & Torfing, 2007). We shall mention three dilemmas.

First of all, the price of obtaining proactive influence on processes of public governance is cooptation as one loses the joyful right to criticize and protest against unsatisfactory policy outcomes. Not only the public authorities but also the involved citizens and stakeholder organizations are bound by the negotiated agreements and must recognize their ownership to good as well as bad outcomes, in other words the involved civil society actors risk losing their comfortable innocence. This basic choice between mixing with "the enemy" and maintaining one's purity by staying outside the messy world of politics is known as the Wollstonecraft dilemma.

Second, the price that must be paid for the positive gains of participating in governance networks with public authorities is that the sharp borderline between the realms of public and private rule is undermined. While citizens and stakeholder organizations gain access to the realm of public rule, public authorities gain the right to introduce governance initiatives and seek to negotiate agreements that reach far beyond the public sphere. Some might argue that network governance involving public and private actors can be seen as a part of a general governmentalization of society which means that all societal actors—public as well as private—must legitimize their actions with reference to how they contribute to the provision of public governance tasks (Dean, 1999).

Finally, while participation in governance networks tends to grant lay-people such as affected and involved citizens and stakeholder organizations a more central, active and influential position in processes of public governance, it simultaneously enhances a professionalization of civil society. In order to obtain influence in the complex negotiation processes within governance networks, citizens, and stakeholders must have something to bargain with just as they must know how to bargain. In this process, the less resourceful and skilled actors are left behind, and the ones that remain such as well-educated citizens and strong stakeholder organizations become increasingly professionalized. As such, the outcome of network governance is not so much an involvement of ordinary lay people in processes of public governance as it is the consolidation of an intermediary body of sub-elites in between lay people and public authorities.

In conclusion, participation in governance networks with public authorities is a difficult and complicated matter that calls for the development of coping strategies and competencies among citizens and organized stakeholders which were irrelevant in performing the traditional roles of being a citizen and a stakeholder organization. The first step for citizens and organized stakeholders is to recognize that politics, and the heavy obligations and battles of power that follows in its wake, has moved into civil society. The next step is to develop strategies that make it possible for them to cope with the dilemmas outlined above: to chose when to take part in governance networks and when to stay out; to find a way to draw a line between public and private that establishes some sort of barrier for a governmentalization of all aspects of social life, and to seek ways to ensure that network governance does not exclusively become a playground for subelites but is institutionalized in a way that promotes the participation and/or effective representation of affected lay people.

NETWORK INTERACTION AND AGONISTIC DEMOCRACY

The interaction between public and private actors within different kinds of governance networks is propelled by their mutual dependence on each other's resources and reinforced by a new governance discourse that tends to favor "governance at a distance" through a regulated self-regulation of partnerships and networks (Rose & Miller, 1992). Negotiated interaction between public and private actors can enhance the effectiveness of public governance and deepen our democracy, but the promises of network governance will only be realized if the governance networks between public authorities and various citizens and organized stakeholders are relatively well-functioning.

The public and private network actors can improve the functioning of governance networks by reflecting on their roles and strategies along the lines described in the previous sections. But what is a well-functioning governance network? What is the ultimate *telos* of the negotiated interaction within governance networks? Should governance networks be seen as mechanisms of smooth and consensual coordination based on common values and mutual learning, or should they be seen as arenas of political conflicts and power struggles? The academic literature on governance networks is divided on this issue. Whereas interdependency theory (Kickert et al., 1997; Rhodes, 1997) and governmentality theory (Dean, 1999; Foucault, 1991) hold a conflict view of governance networks, both governability theory (Kooiman, 1993; Scharpf, 1994) and sociological organization theory (March & Olsen, 1995; Powell & DiMaggio, 1983, 1991) hold a consensus view on network governance.

This consensus approach is adopted in some of the recent and highly influential debates on public governance in Europe, which portray governance networks as consensus-based mechanisms of pragmatic problem solving taking place in a postpolitical terrain. The British Third Way project is a case in point. The Third Way project was advanced by the New Labor government, embraced by social-democratic leaders in Germany, Spain, and Sweden, and legitimized by leading scholars such as Anthony Giddens (1994, 1998) and Ulrich Beck (1994, 1997). Although the protagonists of the Third Way project do not explicitly eliminate political conflicts and power struggles, its discourse on partnerships and network governance clearly invokes the image of a consensual policymaking based on a nonadversarial, postemancipatory life politics; a strong emphasis on a postideological, managerialist problem solving; the development of a new democratic state based on devolution, transparency and civic engagement; and the advancement of a new type of dialogical democracy based on mutual tolerance. Another example of this line of thought is the debate on multilevel governance that tends to view task-specific governance networks with intersecting memberships and many jurisdictional levels as systematically skewed toward conflict avoidance through a nonideological problem solving based on Pareto-optimal solutions (see Hooghe & Marks, 2004, pp. 28-29).

In sharp contrast to the Third Way project and the recent debate on multilevel governance, we believe that the postpolitical vision of governance networks as mechanisms of consensual coordination is theoretically unsustainable, politically untenable and democratically dangerous: it is theoretically unsustainable, because power and conflicts are ineradicable features of politics and governance (Laclau, 1990); it is politically untenable, because conflict is a major source of policy innovation (Koppenjan, 2007); it is democratically dangerous, because a vibrant democracy depends on clashes between different opinions and projects (Mouffe, 2005).

Instead of viewing consensus as the ultimate telos of network governance, we should see governance networks as arenas for power games and conflictual contestation and aim to make the antagonistic clashes compatible with a plural democracy through the cultivation of a democratic ethos of agonistic respect according to which people recognize the contingency of political positions and therefore respect other people's right to think differently. In an agonistic democracy antagonistic clashes are seen as a necessary precondition for an effective and democratic governance, but the political opponents tend to identify with democratic rules and norms that transform their perception of each other from "enemies" to "adversaries." Whereas an enemy is an opponent whom we seek to eliminate by all means, an adversary is an opponent whose views and opinions we want to engage, problematize and passionately contest, but whose right to voice and fight for their opinions we respect as a necessary conditions for a plural democracy (Mouffe, 2005).

According to Connolly (1991), the development of an agonistic democracy is conditioned by the recognition of the contingency of social and political identity. We cannot respect each other in the course of struggle if we dogmatically assert that our own and other peoples' identity is given by God, or has an ultimate foundation in reason, progress, or human nature. Respectful contestation requires that we recognize the relational, dynamic and contingent character of what our adversaries are fighting for.

In our view, governance networks are promising settings for the development and cultivation of agonistic respect. Total consensus will be hard to achieve in a governance network since the public and private network actors pursue different interests, and total war and untamed antagonism will ruin the possibility for coordination among the actors. Agonistic respect is to be found somewhere in between these polar extremes, and it is likely to be furthered by the mutual dependence that links the public and private network actors and forces them to find compromises and respect each other despite of overt and/or covert conflicts. Agonistic respect is an ethos that makes it possible for the network actors to return to the negotiation table after a fierce battle. It permits them to benefit from constructive policy conflicts and to insist that governance networks are arenas of political struggles that must be democratized.

REFERENCES

Agger, A. (2005). *Demokrati og deltagelse—et borgerperskektiv på Kvarterløft* (Democracy and participation—A citizen perspective on area based initiatives in Denmark) Copenhagen, Denmark: Statens Byggeforsknings Institut).

Agger, A., & Löfgren, K. (2006). How democratic are networks based on citizen involvement? A framework for assessing the democratic effects of networks. *Working Paper Series 2006*(1), 1-28.

Bang, H. P., & Sørensen, E. (1998). The everyday maker: A new challenge to democratic governance. *Administrative Theory & Praxis, 21*(3), 325-342.

Beck, U. (1994). The reinvention of politics: Towards a theory of reflexive modernity. In U. Beck, A. Giddens, & S. Lash (Eds.), *Reflexive modernization: Politics, tradition and aesthetics in the modern social order* (pp. 1–55). Cambridge, England: Polity.

Bohman, J. (2005). From demos to demoi: Democracy across borders. *Ratio Juris, 18*(3), 293-314.

Booher, D. (2004). Collaborative governance practices and democracy. *National Civic Review, 93*(4), 32-46.

Bouckaert, G., & Pollitt, C. (2004). *Public management reform: A comparative analysis.* Oxford, England: Oxford University Press.

Clarke, R. (2002). *New democratic processes.* London: IPPR.

Connolly, W. E. (1991). *Identity/difference: Democratic negotiations of political paradox.* Ithaca, NY: Cornell University Press.

Connick, S., & Innes, J. (2003). Outcomes of collaborative water policy making: Applying complexity thinking to evaluation. *Journal of Environmental Planning and Management, 46*(2), 177-197.

Dean, M. (1999). *Governmentality: Power and rule in modern society.* London: Sage.

The European Commission. (2000). *The commission and non-governmental organizations: Building a stronger partnership* (COM(2000)11 Final). Brussels, Belgium: Author.

The European Commission. (2001). *European governance: A white paper* (COM(2001)428 Final). Brussels, Belgium: Author.

Foucault, M. (1991). Governmentality. In G. Burchell, C. Gordon, & P. Miller (Eds.), *The Foucault effect* (pp. 87-104). Hertfordshire, United Kingdom: Harvester Wheatsheaf.

Fung, A. (2006). Varieties of participation in complex governance [Special issue]. *Public Administration Review, 66*(1), 66-75.

Gaventa, J. (2006). *Triumph, deficit or contestation?* (IDS Working Paper). Brighton, United Kingdom: Institute of Development Studies, University of Sussex.

Giddens, A. (1994). *Beyond left and right—The future of radical politics.* Palo Alto, CA: Stanford University Press.

Giddens, A. (1998). *The third way—The renewal of social democracy.* Cambridge, England: Polity Press.

Goss, S. (2001). *Making local governance work: Networks, relationships and the management of change.* Basingstoke, United Kingdom: Palgrave-Macmillan.

Hajer, M. (2003). Policy without polity? Policy analysis and the institutional void. *Policy Sciences, 36,* 175-195.

Hajer, M., & Versteeg, W. (2005). Performing governance through networks. *European Political Studies, 4*(3), 340-47.

Healey, P. (2003). Collaborative planning in perspective. *Planning Theory, 2*(2), 101-123.

Hooghe, L., & Marks, G. (2004). Contrasting visions of multi-level governance. In I. Bache, & M. Flinders (Eds.), *Multi-level governance* (pp. 15-30). Oxford, England: Oxford University Press.

Innes, J. E., & Booher, D. E. (1999). Consensus building and complex adaptive systems: A framework for evaluating collaborative planning. *Journal of the American Planning Association, 65,* 412-423.

Innes, J. E., & Booher, D. E. (2000). Planning institutions in the network society: Theory for collaborative planning. In W. Salet & A. Faludi (Eds.), *Revival of strategic spatial planning* (pp. 175-189). Amsterdam: Royal Netherland Academy of Sciences.

Jessop, B. (2002). *The future of the capitalist state.* Cambridge, England: Polity Press.

Kooiman, J. (Ed.). (1993). *Modern governance: New goverment-society interactions.* London: Sage.

Kickert, W. J. M., Klijn, E. H., & Koppenjan, J. F. M. (Eds.). (1997). *Managing complex networks.* London: Sage.

Klijn, E. H., & Koppenjan, J. F. M. (2000). Interactive decision making and representative democracy: Institutional collisions and solutions. In O. van Heffen, W. J. M. Kickert, & J. J. A. Thomassen (Eds.), Governance in modern society: Effects, change and formation of government institutions (pp. 114-124). Dordrecht, Netherlands: Kluwer Academic.

Klijn, E. H., & Koppenjan, J. F. M. (2004). *Managing uncertainties in networks: A network approach to problem solving and decision-making.* London: Routledge.

Koppenjan, J. (2007). Consensus and conflict in policy networks: Too much or too little? In E. Sørensen & J. Torfing (Eds.), *Theories of democratic network governance* (pp. 133-152). Basingstoke, United Kingdom: Palgrave-Macmillan.

Laclau, E. (1990) *New reflections on the revolution of our time.* London: Verso.

Lukensmeyer, C. J., & Torres, L. H. (2006). Public deliberation: A manager's guide to citizen engagement. *Collaboration Series 2007,* pp. 4-57.

March, J. G., & Olsen J. P. (1989). *Rediscovering institutions: The organizational basis of politics.* New York: Free Press.

March, J. G., & Olsen, J. P. (1995). *Democratic governance.* New York: Free Press.

Marcussen, M., & Torfing, J. (Eds.). (2007). *Democratic network governance in Europe.* Basingstoke, United Kingdom: Palgrave-Macmillan.

Mayntz, R. (1989). Political control and societal control problems: Notes on a theoretical paradigm. In T. Ellwein, R. Mayntz, F. Scharpf, & H. Willke (Eds.), *Yearbook on government and public administration, 1987/88* (pp. 81-98). Baden-Baden, Germany: Nomos.

Mayntz, R. (1991). *Modernization and the logic of interorganizational networks* (Working Paper). München, Germany: Max-Planck Institut für Gesellschaftsforschung, European Centre for Social Welfare Policy and Research.

Mouffe, C. (2005). *On the political.* London: Routledge.

Osborn, D., & Gaebler, T. (1992). *Reinventing government: How the entrepreneurial spirit is transforming the public sector.* Reading, MA: Addison-Wesley.

Peters, B. G., & Pierre, J. (2004). Multi-level governance and democracy: A Faustian bargain. In I. Bache & M. Flinders (Eds.), *Multi-level governance* (pp. 75-89). Oxford, England: Oxford University Press.

Pitkin, H. F. (2004). Representation and democracy: Uneasy alliance. *Scandinavian Political Studies, 27*(3), 335-342.

Pløger, J. (2004). Strife: Urban planning and agonism. *Planning Theory, 3*(1), 71-92.

Pollitt, C., & Bouckaert, G. (2004). *Public management reform: A comparative analysis.* Oxford, England: Oxford University Press.

Poulsen, B. (in press). Public administration in teams. In E. Sørensen & P. Triantaffillou (Eds.), *The politics of selfgovernance.* London: Ashgate.

Powell, W. W., & DiMaggio, J. (1983). The iron cage revisited: Institutional isomorphism and collective rationality in organizational fields. *American Sociological Review, 48*(2), 147-160.

Powell, W. W., & DiMaggio, J. (1991). *The new institutionalism in organizational analysis.* Chicago: University of Chicago Press.

Prakash, S., & Selle, P. (2004). *Investigating social capital.* London: Sage.

Putnam, R. D. (2000). *Bowling alone: The collapse and revival of American community.* New York: Simon & Schuster.

Rhodes, R. A. W. (1997). *Understanding governance: Policy networks, governance, reflexivity and accountability.* Buckingham, United Kingdom: Open University Press.

Rhodes, R. A. W. (2000). The governance narrative: Key findings and lessons from the ESRC's Whitehall programme. *Public Administration, 78*(2), 345-364.

Rose, N., & Miller, P. (1992). Political power beyond the state: Problematics of government. *The British Journal of Sociology, 43*(2), 173-205.

Scharpf, F. W. (1994). Games real actors could play: Positive and negative coordination in embedded negotiations. *Journal of Theoretical Politics, 6*(1), 27-53.

Skocpol, T. (2003). *Diminished democracy: From membership to management in American civic life.* Norman: University of Oklahoma Press.

Stoker, G. (2006). *Why politics matter.* Basingstoke, United Kingdom: Palgrave-Macmillan.

Sørensen, E. (2006). Metagovernance: The changing role of politicians in processes of democratic governance. *American Review of Public Administration, 36*(1), 98-114.

Sørensen, E. (2007). Local politicians and administrators as metagovernors. In M. Marcussen & J. Torfing (Eds.), *Democratic network governance in Europe* (pp. 89-108). Basingstoke, United Kingdom: Palgrave-Macmillan.

Sørensen, E., & Torfing, J. (2003). Network politics, political capital, and democracy. *International Journal of Public Administration, 26*(6), 609-634.

Sørensen, E., & Torfing, J. (Eds.). (2007). *Theories of democratic network governance.* Basingstoke, United Kingdom: Palgrave-Macmillan.

Triantafillou, P. (2003). Psychological technologies at work: A history of employee development in Denmark. *Economic and Industrial Democracy, 24*(3), 411-436.

CHAPTER 3

COLLABORATION MANAGEMENT IN PUBLIC ADMINISTRATION

A Theoretical and Empirical Exploration of Mutual Challenges for Governance, Citizens, and Businesses in Modern Network Societies

Eran Vigoda-Gadot

Author Note: Some sections of this chapter are based on Vigoda-Gadot, E., (2003), *Managing Collaboration in Public Administration: Governance, Business, and Citizens in the Service of Modern Society*, West Port, CT: Prager.

INTRODUCTION

Two of humankind's oldest scourges—terrorism and disease—have recently brought the idea of collaboration to the forefront of public debate. For example, the lack of collaboration among various government agencies prior to the attacks of September 11, 2001 was of such an egregious nature that a new Homeland Security umbrella department was formed to ensure a higher degree of cooperation. In China in early 2003, SARS (Severe Acute Respiratory Syndrome) was found to have spread far beyond initial reports, a discovery that led in April of that year to the unprecedented step of firing the mayor of Beijing for mishandling the sit-

Civic Engagement in a Network Society
pp. 41–64
Copyright © 2008 by Information Age Publishing
All rights of reproduction in any form reserved.

uation. Moreover, experts have said that it is no longer a case of *if* but *when* a pandemic of avian flu will hit the human population. The World Health Organization (WHO) recently urged all countries to develop or update their influenza "pandemic preparedness plans" after experts estimated anywhere between 2 and 50 million people could die if a pandemic hits and the world is not prepared.

These examples, together with several natural disasters such as Hurricane Katrina and the tsunami that caused an immense environmental disaster in various countries during 2005, are illustrative of emerging threats to modern societies that necessitate collaboration among various parties in the local, national, and international arenas. This chapter follows several calls for the interdisciplinary study of public administration (Goodwin, 1998; Kettl & Milward, 1996; Rosenbloom, 1998; Vigoda, 2002b) and suggests that collaboration must start by sharing knowledge and experience among everyone who would play a role in preventing and/ or responding to such disasters. Therefore, one of the major foci of this study is the network society in which we all live. To handle future terror attacks and outbreaks of disease or other natural disasters, as well as to maximize the results of collaboration when times are good, it is imperative for citizens, the private sector, and government agencies to learn how, when, and why they should share information, knowledge, and resources (Shui-Yan, 2005; Thomas, 2003). Furthermore, it is suggested that the power of citizens as individuals and within groups in the civic society is expected to increase dramatically and reinforce the calls for more authentic involvement and participation in decisions on which effective managerial collaboration depends (Box, 1998).

The chapter progresses on several tracks. Based on recent calls for reforms and change in public administration, especially in public management (i.e., Pollitt & Bouckaert, 2000), I first develop a theory of collaboration management in and around public institutions that is rooted in an interdisciplinary perspective (Rosenbloom, 1998; Vigoda, 2000). In this context, collaboration between citizens and the third sector, as well as with the private sector is suggested as the most fruitful way to move forward. Next, we suggest a theoretical typology among closely related concepts such as integration (i.e., Li & Hambrik, 2005), partnership (i.e., Bassett, 1996; Cloke, Milbourne, & Widdowfield, 2000), cooperation (Tang, 2005; Thomas, 2003), coordination (Nicol, 1998), and association, as well as negotiation and empowerment (i.e., Berman, 1995; Weber & Khademian, 1997). This typology leads to an empirical exploration of the need for and the potential of collaboration as perceived by 244 senior managers from both the profit and the nonprofit sectors. The findings of the survey further support our argument about the need for and feasibility of managerial collaboration across sectors and players. While current thinking in the field is rather pessimistic about the actual willingness of the concerned parties to cooperate, this chapter offers a more realistic approach to making these joint ventures a reality. Finally, the chapter concludes that cross-sectoral collaboration management is one of the greatest challenges facing free democracies. Collaboration and civic engagement in a modern network society will hinge on our ability to meet this challenge.

COLLABORATION IN THE TWENTY-FIRST CENTURY: THE SEPTEMBER 11 EFFECT AND THE THREATS FROM MOTHER NATURE

The simultaneous terrorist attacks on New York, Pennsylvania, and Washington, DC on the morning of September 11, 2001 signaled the emergence of several striking changes in the United States and throughout the world. Perhaps one of the most interesting results of these terror actions was the sharp change in American public opinion about the role of government in day-to-day life and about its size, responsibilities, and challenges. The American nation, which in times of peace is reluctant to give too much power to governmental and administrative institutions at any level, was suddenly much more willing to consider a significant expansion of these institutions' authority and power if doing so would prevent similar threats in the future. There is no doubt that that such a major change of heart was the direct effect of a serious threat to the public's sense of security and well-being. Just as the success of the attacks stemmed from the high degree of collaboration among many terrorist organizations and countries that support terrorism, such as Afghanistan, Iraq, Iran, and Syria, so too people and governments worldwide suddenly realized that comparable collaboration among free nations was needed to counter these threats.

In a similar manner, Mother Nature poses threats to the world's population that can be countered only through coordinated international efforts. Pandemics and natural disasters such as hurricanes, earthquakes, and tsunamis are too powerful and extensive for one community or even one nation to handle by itself. Public administrations in the affected areas must rise to the challenge of dealing with these problems. While we have always expected national institutions to perform this duty, the global nature of many of these events makes government involvement all the more necessary.

There are several reasons for our strong reliance on the government to deal with such crisis management. First, we simply have no other institution or body to turn to when our basic rights and needs are endangered. Second, in the last century governments and the public sector have grown larger than at any other time in the past, increasing the public's dependence on the goods and services they provide. Third, the public sector provides more goods and services for a larger, more heterogeneous population with greater demands and higher expectations than ever before (Peters, 1996b; Pollitt & Bouckaert, 2000). In sum, we depend on governments and on public administrative bodies because we believe that they can cure society's ills and meet the needs of their citizens. Put another way, citizens of modern states feel that, limited as they are, governments and public administration are the major gatekeepers of social and political order, and only they can address large-scale social pandemics and provide essential services. While these expectations are not new, what is new is the realization that doing better also means doing things together, based on growing knowledge of our societies. The crises mentioned above are not likely to be solved by competition among sectors, but rather through collaborative efforts, and especially through collaboration of knowledge.

COLLABORATION VERSUS COMPETITION: THE CALL FOR A MINDSET CHANGE IN PUBLIC ADMINISTRATION

Dreadful as they are, terrorist attacks, diseases, and natural disasters are only symptoms of the problem. As Bardach (1998) noted, getting agencies to work together is an ambitious task that calls for an extensive change in mindset by all of the concerned parties. Historically, democracies of various types have encouraged a tradition of competition for available resources. Competitive jargon is commonly used by politicians, public sector officials, and business leaders alike. Consequently, this language has also become the most common terminology to explain public policy and governmental decision making (i.e., Farnham & Horton, 1995; Weimer, 2005). In a world where competition is the "name of the game," governments are expected to fight more vigorously for their piece of the action by responding better to the public's demands and reducing the costs of services (Rouke, 1992; Vigoda, 2000). Hence, in recent decades, we have become familiar with privatization, outsourcing, contracting out, and new public management (NPM) strategies that represent a desire by policy makers to make public agencies fiscally prudent, efficient, and effective (Hood, 1991; Rainey, 1990). The transformation of old-style bureaucracies into more flexible, responsive, effective, efficient, and knowledge-based bodies has left room for other players, such as the private sector and the third sector, to move in. However, these transitions generally involved competition among these players, rather than cooperation.

While the contribution of competitive strategies, methods, and actions to our societies' well-being is not disputed, concerns have been raised about the next stage of bureaucratic reform (i.e., Peters, 1996a). Are we headed toward greater fragmentation of our societies and communities, or is there an alternative to the rising level of competition and conflict? In many respects, the terms competition and conflict are the antithesis of collaboration. In any situation where more than one person is involved, people may choose to compete or to collaborate in order to accomplish a certain goal or to fulfill a need (Nash, 1953). For example, rational-choice and game-theory approaches use elements of rational thinking, competition, and maximization of self-interests by social players as the basis for explaining human behavior and policy decisions (i.e., Axelrod, 1984: O'Toole, 1995). Other theories of conflict, power, and politics use the same rationale (i.e., Pfeffer, 1992). Thus, it seems that we know more and more about patterns and strategies of competition and conflict in public affairs but we remain unclear about the potential power of collaboration in that regard. Whereas recent essays have paid some attention to collaboration in public administration (i.e., a special issue of *Public Administration Review,* 2006, Vol 66), collaboration has remained an underdeveloped area in managerial and public administration thinking, and the literature that has developed it theoretically and empirically is to date insufficient. In a world of dominant capitalistic values, competition takes the lead, and collaboration across sectors, at least with regard to public affairs, is seen as less significant and more problematic.

Therefore, a gap must be filled in public administration thinking. What does collaboration in the public sector arena actually mean? What implications does it have for managerial concepts? Is it a reasonable solution to the ills of our societies and bureaucracies? If so, how can it be implemented wisely and what strategies will ensure its success? Where should we start applying collaborative ventures and who are the partners in this process? Indeed, we have many questions and very few answers. However, as with every scientific journey, a return to knowledge sources and to disciplinary origins can prove beneficial.

DISCIPLINARY ORIENTATIONS: KNOWLEDGE ABOUT COLLABORATION AND THE COLLABORATION OF KNOWLEDGE

The eclectic nature of public administration as a science and as a profession (Lynn, 1996; Rosenbloom, 1998), its theoretical fragility and instability, together with people's mistrust of governmental services and institutions (Berman, 1997; Nye, Zelikow, & King, 1997) are major indications of the need for change in public service. In keeping with Fredrick-

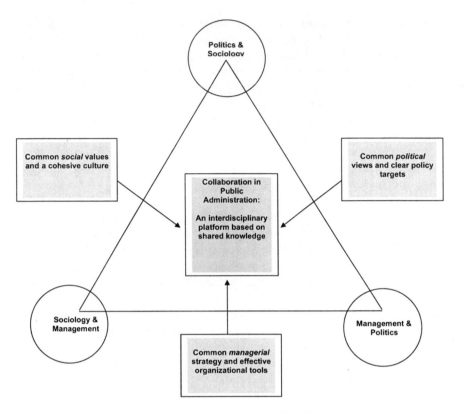

Source: Reprinted from Vigoda (2003), with permission from Praeger Press.

Figure 3.1.   An interdisciplinary spectrum of collaboration perspectives.

son (1997), I suggest that there is a demand for better management of public assets, values, and needs, and for advancing the collective idea of accomplishing these goals together rather than going it alone. Such a spirit of collaboration in no way contradicts the liberal values of pluralism or the free-market principles of self-motivation and individual entrepreneurship. It is merely an extension of its boundaries that is necessary to meet the complex challenges of modern times. The answer to environmental and manmade threats lies in entrepreneurial innovation that thrives in collaborative rather than competitive situations.

Figure 3.1 suggests a triangle of disciplines that depicts the basic essence of collaboration in public administration. Following Goodwin (1998), I believe that there is a growing need for research to reexamine the old distinctions among markets, state, and civil society. According to this view, to achieve collaboration in public administration an interdisciplinary platform should be developed, based on shared knowledge and experiences. The fields of knowledge that are most relevant are political science and policy studies (i.e., Guy, 2003), social and cultural understanding (i.e., Yanow, 2003) and managerial and organizational wisdom (i.e., Hood, 1991).

The science and craft of public administration integrates various scholarly fields (Kettl & Milward, 1996; Vigoda, 2002b). It involves politics, but not only politics. It deals with policy, but reaches much farther and deeper than policy questions. It incorporates sociological and cultural factors but it goes beyond these issues. It deals with people as workers, citizens, clients, and consumers, as leaders and managers, as well as with a variety of other human constructs that merge into a unique branch of knowledge. A multidisciplinary collaborative approach is evidently required to explain better what every scholar already knows from his or her personal perspective: that the truth about public administration has many faces.

Moreover, the application of multidisciplinary and collaborative knowledge (political, social, and managerial) to public services is essential before further practical advances can be made. I argue that some tenets of administrative culture and democratic values need to be explored in order to synthesize theory and practice and maximize the collaboration between national leaders, public officials, and the citizenry. The major challenge facing public administration in the coming years is the need to create a revitalized generation of administrators that is appreciative of creative participatory democracy, as suggested by Putnam (1993), and willing to join forces with other social players such as the private sector to advance the public good.

CONCEPTUAL FRAMEWORK OF COLLABORATION

Beyond the interdisciplinary ideology lies a need to clarify the concept of collaboration in public administration. Comparing similar concepts frequently used by scholars from three disciplines may be helpful in this regard. Figure 3.2 presents a suggested typology of criteria by disciplinary origin and a theoretical perspective that can contribute to our understanding of the meaning of collaboration. Beyond the disciplines and perspectives already mentioned in the previous sections, I have used two additional criteria: (1) old-style structure and, (2) new dynamics and interactions. The old-style structure refers to the classical arrangement and formation of power relations while new dynamics and interactions refer to the modern type of contacts, interfaces, and relations among units. Examining these two criteria in the light of the theoretical perspec-

Discipline and Perspective / Criterion	Politics and policy: State level analysis	Organization and Management: Business level analysis			Social and Cultural: Community level analysis
		Management focused	Labor focused	Business focused	
1. Old style structure	Bureaucracy	Centralization	Cohesion of work	Private money and ownership	Social power and stratification
2. New dynamics and interactions	Democracy	Decentralization, Participation in Decision Making, and empowerment	Division of work	Public money and ownership	Pluralism and communitarianism
3. Collaboration	**Cooperation**	**Coordination**	**Integration**	**Partnership**	**Association**

Source: Reprinted from Vigoda (2003), with permission from Praeger Press.

Figure 3.2. An analysis of the meaning of collaboration using three disciplinary perspectives.

tives of political, managerial, and social disciplines should give us a better insight into the meaning of collaboration.

First, a conceptual and practical conflict exists between public administration in its classic bureaucratic form and the nature of democracy in which it should operate. Some will say that this is actually an inevitable conflict between administration and politics in free societies (Gawthrop, 1996; Guy, 2003; Thompson, 1983). Others will note that bureaucracy does not necessarily contradict the democratic ethos. On the contrary, it guards democracy and makes it work (Box, Marshall, Reed, & Reed, 2001; Vigoda, 2002a). Unless a strong bureaucracy is present, democracy may lose its essence and be perceived as a weak and ineffective governance mechanism. When collaboration is brought into the discussion, things become even vaguer. Democracy proudly encourages freedom of choice, which can be used by social players in many ways, only some of which are collaborative. Yet, to guard against centrifugal forces, social players also need to cooperate in order to achieve the best political outcomes. Therefore, *cooperation* (Tang, 2005; Thomas, 2003) reflects a mutual effort by all players based on the assumption that there are similar political interests that can be realized through collective action.

The sociocultural view is depicted on the extreme right of Figure 3.2. It illuminates how the bureaucratic-democratic conflict is implemented in the social arena. Social power and stratification, as well as traditional and less liberal views of race and ethnicity, are at the heart of our communities' old style structure. These are also core concepts used by sociologists to explain social structure and mobilization (Yanow, 2003), and they play a major role in policymaking and implementation. As new dynamics and types of interactions emerge in our societies, pre-modern social power and stratification are thus confronted with ideas of pluralism or liberalism (Etzioni, 1994, 1995). Modern societies generally seek increased pluralism and input from a broad range of citizens and ethnic groups. Social leaders also point to the key role played by the involvement of individuals, voluntarism, and social responsibility in the development of healthy communities (Box, 1998; Rimmerman, 1997). However, modern societies simultaneously need to struggle against conservative, old style forms of stratification, traditional norms, and rigid social clusters. Frequently, the power of economic, cultural, and political elites inhibits pluralistic processes and preserves old structures of governance and mobilization. The term *association* thus reflects a need for compromises among various social players and the search for mutual interests or alliances that can work on behalf of citizens and communities even in the face of old style conservative structures.

Finally, when we look at the situation from a business organization-management perspective, we see a more complex picture. The conflict between democracy and bureaucracy is close in type and in nature to the conflict between social power and stratification on the one hand, and pluralism and communitarianism on the other (Dominelli, 1999). The striving for (political) cooperation and (social) association echoes other terms from the organization-management world, such as (organizational) *coordination*, (work) *integration*, and (business) *partnership*. Whereas centralization is an old style structure aimed at safeguarding authority and governments' ability to rule, decentralization in bureaucracies ultimately means delegating power to other stakeholders and limiting the power of public agencies (Kincaid & Cole, 2002). Organizational management theory usually denotes such processes as participation in decision making (Irvin & Stansbury, 2004), or better, empowerment (Sanderson, 1999). In fact, this sharing of power is another critical obstacle to increased collaboration in government. As bureaucratic theory suggests, rulers and public administrators do not graciously yield power and authority to others due to the fear of losing control and weakening the government's ability to rule. Thus, the managerial task of coordination (i.e., Nicol, 1998) must balance the forces of centralization and decentralization. It may therefore be considered a managerial tool for intraorganizational collaboration. From the point of view of the labor market and labor studies, the same challenge exists when trying to balance the old style's notion of the cohesion of work with the need for the division of labor, specialization, and expertise in complex organizations. Collaboration in the labor market is based on the craft of bringing together the need for both the segregation and integration of tasks. Reconciling these contradictory forces is essential in every successful organization and is thus an indispensable phase of collaboration at the organizational/managerial level (i.e., Li & Hambrik, 2005). Last, in terms of business and financial management, the old style structure of organizations was based, for many years, on private money and ownership. The state and the interests of the public have become relevant in the modern economy only with the evolution of the welfare state (Peter, 1997). Thus, the new dynamics and interaction between states and the people has depended on the growing investment of public money and a greater involvement in and ownership by the state of projects designed for the public welfare. The type of collaboration that arises in this context may be termed a partnership (i.e., Bassett, 1996; Cloke et al., 2000), as it is based on the shared business interests of the private sector, the public sector, and their interactions as partners. Hence, the ideas of coordination, integration, and partnership, together with the political idea of cooperation and the social idea of association, may build a more inclusive interdisciplinary vocabulary of collaboration for public administration.

PLAYERS IN THE COLLABORATIVE GAME:
CROSS-SECTORAL TRADEOFFS

The interdisciplinary approach of sharing knowledge and the clarification of the concept of collaboration lead to the next step of this chapter. Here we followed Thomas (2003) and Shui-Yan (2005) who recently advocated the idea of cross-sectoral governance based on the recognition that most public problems are solved through the cooperation or collaboration of organizations from multiple sectors—public, nonprofit, and business. Thus, we try to identify some of the key stakeholders who take part in any collaborative process, be it on the local community, state, national, or even international level, and define their role in the collaborative process. According to the framework suggested thus far, and based on Thomas (2003), we have identified three major players in the cross-sectoral collaborative process: (1) governments and public administration; (2) businesses and the private sector; (3) citizens, communities, and the third sector.

1. Government and Public Administration (G&PA): G&PA is the major player in the public sector arena. This category refers to all formal agencies at the local, state, or federal levels with constitutive public standing and authority. These agencies are fully or partly governmental or government owned and include all government ministries, government authorities, public companies that are government owned, or other institutions where the government holds a major share in the budget or in the management. G&PA also includes local authorities and agencies that work under the supervision and control of these bodies (Nalbandian, 1999). In addition, the category covers the management boards of national projects created ad hoc for local-level or state-level tasks (e.g., in the fields of transportation, energy, infrastructures, welfare, etc.). G&PA also represents all individuals who work for these bodies and are paid by them directly.

2. Businesses and the Private Sector: The next category of social players that deserves special attention when studying collaboration is the powerful business/private sector. This is perhaps the largest and most influential sector in every open democracy and free-market society. It accounts for most of the economic activity and growth on the national and federal level and serves as a laboratory for many organizational and managerial experiments and reforms later applied in other organizations and in the public sector. Included in this sector are all firms, companies, and businesses that are primarily privately owned, privately sponsored, and privately managed and transact business based on the profit motive. Furthermore, it refers to individuals who work in such bodies. This sector, like the public one, is also highly structured and formal, but it is much less centralized and thus is more open to innovative entrepreneurial approaches.

3. Citizens, Communities, and the "Third Sector": The public and the third sector represent a third important player in this mix. In many respects, this group is more complex than the group of governments and public administration due to its lack of formal structure and its mass orientation. Three sections or subgroups should be distinguished in this context: (1) citizens as individuals; (2) citizens in small and unorganized groups; and (3) citizens who are part of larger groups or communities that are usually more formal, long lasting, and may be defined as third sector bodies or the civic society (Gidron, Kramer, & Salamon, 1992). While the civic society has some characteristics of a formal, organized group, the other two subgroups represent short term, ad hoc actions by individuals or small, informal groups of individuals that are more difficult to study and examine.

KNOWLEDGE COLLABORATION IN PUBLIC ADMINISTRATION: AN INTEGRATIVE APPROACH

Thus far, our discussion suggests an interdisciplinary approach to collaboration, an extension of relevant concepts, and an identification of key players in the collaborative game. Using these analytic tools, we can move forward toward an integrative approach to collaboration in public administration.

We argue that each disciplinary approach highlights the role of a different player in the mutual collaborative effort. Figure 3.3 presents this idea graphically. According to this design, three types of analysis exist that enhance our understanding of collaboration management in public administration. (1) Political, national and international-level analysis; (2) Community-level analysis; and (3) Managerial-level analysis. Our progress as societies is based on moving from a conservative format to a modern format on the evolutionary continuum of collaboration.

Political, National, and International-Level Analysis of Collaboration

The most conservative approach to collaboration is evident in the political ethos of putting the state and the bureaucracy at the center (Guy, 2003; Rosenbloom, 1998). The political-level analysis of collaboration will stress the G&PA branches as the prime initiators and leaders of collaborative ventures. The focus here is on what the state wants to do, can do, and

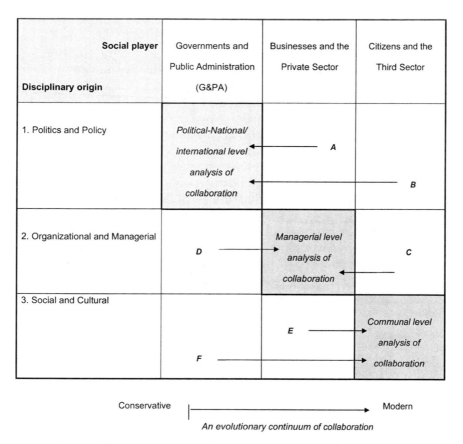

Social player Disciplinary origin	Governments and Public Administration (G&PA)	Businesses and the Private Sector	Citizens and the Third Sector
1. Politics and Policy	*Political-National/* *international level* *analysis of* *collaboration*	A	B
2. Organizational and Managerial	D	*Managerial level* *analysis of* *collaboration*	C
3. Social and Cultural	F	E	*Communal level* *analysis of* *collaboration*

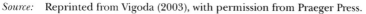

Conservative |————————————————→ Modern

An evolutionary continuum of collaboration

Source: Reprinted from Vigoda (2003), with permission from Praeger Press.

Figure 3.3.   An interdisciplinary spectrum of collaboration perspectives.

does do in practice to advance the idea of collaboration among various players. Naturally, each of these questions deserves separate consideration. Leading national legislators and senior public officials to the conclusion that collaboration is needed is a first stage. It should be followed by the actual recognition that these institutions have the power to change. Finally, it is in the hands of public administration officials to allocate resources and make them available for the process. According to this analysis, governments and their executive branches coordinate the actions of other social players such as businesses and the private sector (line A) and citizens and the third sector (line B). In fact, this is today's most typical method of collaboration among sectors, where G&PA lead the collaborative ventures and are the "conductors of the orchestra."

Business-Level Analysis of Collaboration

According to our view, a more modern approach to collaboration would transfer some power of "conducting" to the private sector. Here, collaborative ventures of partnership, integration, and coordination are controlled and directed by business-oriented bodies. The management level of analysis makes use of current organizational theory and business experience to discuss issues of conflict management, allocating business potential for growth and innovation, and wisely handling human resources in both the private and the public sectors. While the private sector serves as a benchmark for public organizations, there are still mutual benefits for both parties. The idea of a public-private partnership (PPP) (Kanter, 1989; Kennedy & Rosentraub, 1999) imparts practical meaning to the symbolic slogans of collaboration. These models of alliance allow the transfer of resources from one sector to the other and improve both parties' flexibility and responsiveness to customers and citizens. However, the philosophy of PPPs is mostly economic in nature. An alternative pattern of collaboration has emerged in the last few years with the creation of businesses for the community (BFC) projects (Khoury, 1993; Vigoda-Gadot, 2003). This alternative is a more authentic one that correlates best with the social movement of communitarianism and voluntarism. It is based on a spontaneous display of good citizenship that partly derives from economic considerations, but is mostly community rooted. Obviously, this pattern is advocated by the NPM approach, and by ideas such as running governments like a business and improving responsiveness to citizens. Thus, they are very typical of some of today's collaborative projects in many fields of service to the public. According to the organizational and managerial level of analysis, businesses and the private sector are the central engines for collaboration, supported by citizens and the third sector (line C) and by governments and public administration (line D) as secondary players.

Communal-Level Analysis of Collaboration

This is probably the most liberal and decentralized pattern of collaboration. In this approach, much of the power of "conducting" is transferred to citizens and to communities with the expectation that they will lead collaborative ventures (Fredrickson, 1982). Community level collaboration incorporates a less rigidly organized structure of activity built on loose contacts among most of the players. While contacts between individual citizens may be close, unless they assume a formal structure of VNPO (voluntary and nonprofit organization) they remain informal and should be considered ad-hoc voluntary activities. The community-level analysis of collaboration needs to classify the various patterns of citizenry involvement (Rimmerman, 1997). Such activities can take place at the federal or national level, but their most influential impact can be realized at the local level (i.e., neighborhoods and cities). These altruistic orientations (Monroe, 1994) and good citizenship behaviors (Vigoda & Golembiewski, 2001) may flourish only in a collaborative and supportive social environment. The community-level analysis of collaboration implies that business and the private sector (line E) and governments and public administration (line F) support and reenforce grassroots activities that are initiated and monitored by citizens as individuals or groups. This is definitely the most decentralized and modern pattern of collaboration that transfers power and responsibility to the community and to the citizens with the support of public administration on one hand, and the private sector on the other hand (Gidron et al., 1992).

MOVING BEYOND RESPONSIVENESS: SOME EMPIRICAL EVIDENCE ABOUT COLLABORATION

As suggested elsewhere (Vigoda, 2002a), a model of knowledge collaboration may express a step forward that goes beyond responsiveness in public administration. While responsiveness to citizens reflects a core concept in the current NPM approach to reforms in public administration (Crook, 1996; Hood, 1991; Pollitt & Bouckaert, 2000), collaboration, particularly those efforts led by citizens and communities, may point the way to future reforms in this arena. Thus, if collaboration as a whole, and more specifically collaboration of knowledge, is here to stay, it deserves more than merely theoretical justification and practical illustrations. It will progress only when bolstered by empirical studies conducted among those involved in the daily routine of serving the people. These individuals have already experienced the promises and barriers of collaboration in daily public work. Hence, they are ideal participants in empirical efforts that can enhance knowledge as well as explore some of the hidden domains of collaboration as a possible change agent in public administration doctrine (Box, 1998; Ott, 1998).

Based on the arguments developed thus far, an empirical approach to the study of collaboration must rely on current knowledge from various disciplines in the social sciences. Most important, it may benefit from the experience in organizational studies, management, politics, sociology, and psychology and from advanced tools that have been developed in these domains. Populations may comprise members of public-, private-, and third-sector organizations that interact with plans or programs of collaboration and can testify to their potential. Hence, managers in both the for-profit (PRS) and the nonprofit sector (PBS) have the advantage of initiating, participating in, and evaluating collaborative ventures. To empirically assess how collaboration works in reality, I conducted a survey of Israeli mangers from the private/for-profit sector and from the public/ nonprofit sector. I have tried to obtain information on collaboration by assessing senior managers' views and beliefs from various angles. Managers were asked to share their opinions on the current state of the field and on its potential advancement in the future.

The Managers' Survey

Participants in the survey were managers in various private- and public-sector organizations in Israel. Questionnaires were distributed directly to graduate students of executive programs in a large Israeli university. Of the 244 managers who participated in this survey, 144 were from the public and nonprofit sector (PBS) and 100 from the private sector (PRS). Response rate was 85%. Of the PBS managers, 48.5% were women and 51.5% were men. Their average age was 42.2 ($SD = 8.7$), and their average tenure with the organization was 14.5 years ($SD = 8.3$). The PBS managers were highly educated, with 95.2% of the total sample having an academic degree of some kind—54.4% had a bachelor's degree, and 40.8% had a graduate degree or higher. Jews accounted for 86.5% of the respondents, while 13.5% were non-Jews (Muslims, Christians, and Druze). By type of organization, 31.4% were in local government, 26.3% in education organizations, 11.9% in the security services (army, police, and other services), 8.5% in healthcare organizations, 6.8% in the Ministry of Finance and other economic-oriented authorities, 5.1% in government companies and authorities (aviation, transport, ports), and 10.0% were in welfare services, the Labor Ministry, and environmental agencies. Of the PRS managers, 41.9% were women and 58.1% were men. Their average age was 33.4 ($SD = 6.1$), and their average tenure with the organization was 4.9 years ($SD = 3.8$). The PRS managers were also highly educated, with 95.6% of the total sample having an academic degree of some kind—57.8% had a bachelor's degree and 37.8% had a graduate degree or higher. Of the PRS respondents, 94.8% were Jews and 5.2% non-Jews (Muslims, Christians, and Druze). By type of organization, 61.7% were in industrial and marketing firms, 24.6% in high technology firms, 8.2% in private law offices, and 5.5% were in privately owned firms.

Evidence about the state of current collaboration in and around the Israeli public sector was obtained through several questions targeted at distinguishing collaboration in numerous fields. I was primarily interested in managers' perceptions regarding the level of collaboration in these arenas: (1) education, (2) health, (3) welfare, (4) culture and sports, (5) employment, (6) other arenas (e.g., transportation, environment, communication).[1] Managers were asked to report separately on the level of collaboration between public administration and (a) private organizations and business firms, and (b) voluntary and nonprofit organizations, and citizens as individuals or groups in each of the above arenas. Next, evidence about the future vision of collaboration between the public-, private-, and third-sector organizations was obtained. Participants were asked to express their feelings about and attitudes toward various statements. Each statement presented a different view measured on a 5-point scale (1 = *not at all true*; 5 = *very true*). A sample of 14 core statements is presented in Table 3.1.

First, we found that managers were aware of collaborative ventures in their organizations and their surroundings. Most of the participants indicated that collaboration occurred more intensively in the fields of culture and sports, welfare, and education. However, almost all participants believed that the level of collaboration was not satisfactory and needed to be improved dramatically. Averages across fields ranged from 2.33 (attitudes of PRS managers toward collaboration in environment, transportation, and communication) to 3.18 (attitudes of PBS managers toward collaboration in cultural services). Thus, while there is some indication that the public sector does currently collaborate with private firms and with citizens and the third sector in various fields, managers expressed a desire for more activism in this direction.

In addition, a comparison of views on the current state of cross-sectoral collaboration between PRS managers and PBS managers revealed the existence of some meaningful differences. PRS mangers were more skeptical about the current state of collaboration than PBS managers, who expressed a higher level of optimism. A comprehensive statistical analysis based on *t* tests supported the conjecture that these differences were significant. For example, and according to Table 3.1, PBS managers were much more optimistic than PRS managers about statement #7 suggesting that "the public sector is looking for better ways to collaborate with private and third-sector organizations to improve services for citizens." Therefore, an interesting question that will need to be discussed in the future is the reason for such differences. A possible explanation is a social desirability bias (i.e., greater sensitivity among PBS managers to the presence of collaboration and the need to implement it more effectively). However, the relatively small sample size and the unicultural orientation of this study limits generalizations. Further studies need to replicate this one and test the differences among populations more closely.

**Table 3.1.   Managers' Perceptions of Collaboration With
Public Administration: Exploration and Comparison of the
Perceptions of PRS and PBS Managers**

	PRS (N = 100) Mean (SD)	PBS (N = 143) Mean (SD)	t test (t)
1. Today, more than ever before, government agencies collaborate with each other to improve services for citizens.	2.53 (1.03)	2.78 (1.03)	1.91
2. Collaboration among public organizations, private firms, and the voluntary sector needs to be improved.	4.08 (.85)	4.18 (.64)	.97
3. Senior managers in the public sector understand the advantages of collaboration with private and voluntary organizations and promote it accordingly.	2.79 (.84)	3.16 (.94)	3.15**
4. Many national ills would be solved if public organizations learned to collaborate with private and voluntary organizations and with citizens.	4.04 (.76)	4.06 (.77)	.23
5. The private sector is interested in collaborating with the public sector.	3.49 (.93)	3.71 (1.02)	1.73
6. Citizens and the third sector are interested in collaboration with the public sector.	3.87 (.96)	4.09 (.72)	2.06*
7. Today, more than ever before, the public sector is looking for better ways to collaborate with private and voluntary organizations to improve services for citizens.	2.77 (.81)	3.47 (.84)	6.36***
8. Personally, I am willing to become actively involved in public-sector initiatives aimed at improving the quality of life in our nation.	3.65 (.88)	4.24 (.70)	5.78***
9. I am willing to spend time on such activities (i.e., join citizens' committees).	3.36 (1.09)	3.93 (.87)	4.51***
10. I am willing to bring in knowledge and ideas (i.e., suggest new ways to improve quality of life).	3.78 (.93)	4.10 (.71)	3.01**
11. I am willing to bring other people into the collaborative process.	3.52 (1.05)	4.04 (.75)	4.45***
12. Advanced nations encourage collaboration among public-sector agencies and other private and voluntary organizations.	4.06 (.83)	4.27 (.65)	2.20*
13. In the future, the public sector will have to increase collaboration with private and voluntary organizations in order to achieve its goals.	3.73 (.82)	4.12 (.74)	3.80***
14. Collaboration between public and private organizations is more important than collaboration between public and voluntary organizations.	3.22 (.99)	3.05 (.99)	−1.32

Note: $*p \leq .05$. $**p \leq .01$. $*p \leq .001$.

It was interesting to find that PBS managers and PRS managers also differed substantially in other perceptions. For example, 83.5% of the PRS managers, but only 44% of the PBS managers, reported that the non-public organization is usually the initiator of collaborative projects. Thus, we concluded that PRS managers believed that the public sector was not doing enough to push collaboration forward and that most of the initiatives for collaboration come from the private or third sectors. PBS managers, however, perceived the current state differently, assuming that the public sector enjoyed just a small advantage over the private sector in the field of innovative collaboration projects. Still, 83% of the PBS managers and 68.6% of the PRS managers generally agreed that collaborative activities benefited the public as a whole, as well as the communities and the organizations involved. Thus, my interpretation is that managers view collaboration in a generally favorable manner. The alternative option of working alone or independently in the competitive world of the free market is balanced by a strong desire to share knowledge and resources to realize valuable social goals. In support of this contention, 80.6% of the PBS managers, but only 54.4% of the PRS managers, described their general understanding of and experiences with collaboration as successful and fruitful.

A further examination of the findings revealed mixed attitudes toward collaboration. Respondents generally believed that government agencies collaborate among themselves, but improvements are needed in cross-sectorial collaboration, and public managers need to enhance their understanding of the advantages of collaboration. Respondents also generally agreed that many national problems would be solved if the public sector could infuse a better culture of collaboration and use it as a strategic tool for policy implementation. Managers thought that the private sector as well as citizens and the third sector were really interested in such a move toward collaboration with public organizations. However, they were also quite critical about the effort invested by public officials in order to achieve a satisfactory level of collaboration. Moreover, PBS managers as well as PRS managers expressed their personal willingness to become involved in collaborative ventures and invest time, knowledge, and effort to promote them. Note, however, that PBS managers expressed a somewhat greater predilection towards such collaborative trends, perhaps due to the potential benefits that such ventures can bring to the public sector and to its leadership. Finally, despite some differences between PRS and PBS managers, all agreed that advanced nations are characterized by higher levels of collaboration among public-, private-, and third-sector bodies. According to their views, which closely conform to my general perception in this chapter, the future necessitates more activism in this direction. Managers across the board see no real difference as to where this collaboration should take place. In their opinion, it needs to increase in all possible directions and by all possible means.

SUMMARY

During the last century, modern societies made remarkable achievements in different fields, many of them thanks to an advanced public sector. Yet at the dawn of the new millennium, various new social problems still await the consideration and attention of the state and its administrative system. To overcome these problems and create effective remedies for the new challenges we now confront, more collaboration must be infused into the managerial processes of the public sector. The major emphasis of this collaboration leans on sharing knowledge. Models of competition do not deliver all of the necessary solutions, and more serious attention should be given to win-win models such as those reflected in the idea of collaboration. Moreover, various threats such as terror, diseases, and natural disasters have prompted an urgent call for cross-sectoral collaboration in and around modern public administration. The network society is striving for greater collaboration among nations, state agencies, private organizations, and third sector organizations, as well as individual citizens.

This chapter tried to develop a systematic discussion of the theory of collaboration based on integrative and interdisciplinary views. We believe that well structured and comprehensive thinking on collaboration, combined with empirical evidence on its chances of enduring, is a powerful tool for policymakers and for public administrators and managers in developed as well as less developed democracies. Our core assumption is that independent activity by public administration, governments, and other social players is no longer sufficient for our complex and demanding societies. Instead, we propose an integrative model of collaboration designed to stimulate debate among academics and practitioners in this arena and perhaps point to possible "collaborative reform" in public administration in the years to come. While current collaborative projects are dominated by G&PA or by private initiatives such as PPP or BFC, collaboration models of tomorrow are more grassroots oriented. They rely on citizens' empowerment and involvement in a growing civic culture. The call for and control of future collaborations among sectors in the public sphere is likely to shift, at least to some extent, from G&PA and businesses to the hands of citizens, communities, and especially the more organized form of the third sector and the civic culture. Thus, the third sector will probably remain third in size, but not necessarily in the impact it has on our lives.

Without a doubt, we live in an era of great challenges for public administration and management. As suggested by Peters (1996a) and Rhodes (1996), the twenty-first century will necessitate enormous changes in our conventional perceptions of governmental activities and responsibilities. It will require a similar reformation of the meaning of citizenship and a redefinition of the role of citizens, businesses, and private-sector firms, the third sector, the media, and academia in collaborative ventures. All of these actors, and others, will need to collaborate. Hence, higher level of civic engagement in a modern network society is a necessity. Citizens, as well as other players and sectors will need to collaborate with public administration as its tasks expand, in order to provide people with better services and high quality goods and knowledge. They will have to collaborate, mostly in knowledge and information, because the economic, social, and human potential of working together offers greater rewards than the option of "going it alone."

NOTE

1.   Full details on the scales and the items can be found in Vigoda (2003).

REFERENCES

Axelrod, R. (1984). *The evolution of cooperation*. New York: Basic Books.

Bardach, E. (1998). *Getting agencies to work together: The practice and theory of managerial craftsmanship*. Washington, DC: Brookings Institution Press.

Bassett, K. (1996). Partnership, business elites in urban politics: New forms of governance in an English city? *Urban Studies, 33*, 539-555.

Berman, E. M. (1995). Empowering employees in state agencies: A survey of recent progress. *International Journal of Public Administration, 18*, 833-850.

Box, R. C. (1998). *Citizen governance: Leading American communities into the 21st century*. Thousand Oaks, CA: Sage.

Box, R. C., Marshall, G. S., Reed, B. J., & Reed, C. M. (2001). New public management and substantive democracy. *Public Administration Review, 61*, 608-619.

Cloke, P., Milbourne, P., & Widdowfield, R. (2000). Partnership and policy networks in rural local governance: Homelessness in Taunton. *Public Administration, 78*, 111-133.

Crook, R. (1996). Democracy, participation and responsiveness: A case study of relations between the Ivorian communes and their citizens. *Public Administration, 74*, 695-720.

Dominelli, L. (1999). Community, citizenship and empowerment. *Sociology: The Journal of the British Sociological Association, 33*, 441-446.

Etzioni, A. (1994). *The spirit of community*. New York: Touchstone.

Etzioni, A. (1995). *New communitarian thinking: Persons, virtues, institutions, and communities.* Charlottesville: Virginia University Press.

Farnham, D., & Horton, S. (1995). The political economy of public sector change. In D. Farnham & S. Horton (Eds.), *Managing the new public services* (pp. 3-26). Basingstoke, United Kingdom: Macmillan.

Fredrickson, G. H. (1982). The recovery of civism in public administration. *Public Administration Review, 42,* 501-509.

Fredrickson, G. H. (1997). *The spirit of public administration.* San Francisco: Jossey-Bass.

Gawthorp, L. C. (1996). Democracy, bureaucracy, and hypocrisy redux: A search for the sympathy and compassion. *Public Administration Review, 57,* 205-210.

Gidron, B., Kramer, R. M., & Salamon, L. M. (1992). *Governments and the third sector: Emerging relationships in welfare states.* San Francisco: Jossey-Bass.

Goodwin, M. (1998). The governance of rural areas: Some emerging research issues and agendas. *Journal of Rural Studies, 14,* 5-12.

Guy, M. E. (2003). Ties that bind: The link between public administration and political science. *The Journal of Politics, 65,* 641-55.

Hood, C. (1991). A public management for all seasons? *Public Administration, 69,* 3-19.

Irvin, R. A., & Stansbury, J. (2004). Citizen participation in decision making: Is it worth the effort? *Public Administration Review, 64,* 55-65.

Kanter, R. M. (1989). *When giants learn to dance: Mastering the challenge of strategy, management, and careers in the 1990s.* New York: Simon & Schuster.

Kennedy, S. S., & Rosentraub, M. S. (1999). Public-private partnership, professional sports teams, and the protection of the public's interests. *American Review of Public Administration, 30,* 436-459.

Kettl, D. F., & Milward, H. B. (Eds.). (1996). *The state of public management.* Baltimore: Johns Hopkins University Press.

Khoury, G. (1993). From patrons to partners: Strategies for the 90s. *Canadian Business Review, 20,* 26-28.

Kincaid, J., & Cole, R.L. (2002). Issues of federalism in response to terrorism. *Public Administration Review, 62,* 181-192.

Li, J., & Hambrick, D. C. (2005). Fractional groups: A new vantage on demographic faultiness, conflict, and disintegration in work teams. *Academy of Management Journal, 48,* 794-813.

Lynn, L. E. (1996). *Public management as art, science, and profession.* Chatham, NJ: Chatham House.

Monroe, K. R. (1994). A fat lady in a corset: Altruism and social theory. *American Journal of Political Science, 38,* 861-893.

Nalbandian, J. (1999). Facilitating community, enabling democracy: New roles for local government managers. *Public Administration Review, 59,* 187-197.

Nash, J. F. (1953). Two person cooperative games. *Econometrica, 21,* 128-140.

Nicol, C. (1998). Collaboration and co-ordination in local government. *Local Government Studies, 24,* 51-66.

Nye, J. S., Zelikow, P. D., & King, D. C. (Eds.). (1997). *Why people don't trust government.* Cambridge, MA; Harvard University Press.

O'Toole, L. (1995). Rational choice and policy implementation: Implications for interorganizational network management. *American Review of Public Administration*, *25*, 43-57.

Ott, S., (1998). Government reform or alternatives to bureaucracy? Thickening, tides and the future of governing. *Public Administration Review*, *58*, 540-545.

Peter, T. (1997). Cash or kind? Partnership schemes and the welfare state. *Public Money and Management*, *17*, 4-6.

Peters, G. B. (1996A). Models of governance for the 1990s. In D. F. Kettl & H. B. Milward (Eds.), *The state of public management* (pp. 15-44). Baltimore: Johns Hopkins University Press.

Peters, G. B. (1996B). *The future of governing: Four emerging models*. Kansas City: University Press of Kansas.

Pfeffer, J. (1992). *Managing with power*. Boston: Harvard Business School Press.

Pollitt, C., & Bouckaert, G. (2000). *Public management reform*. Oxford, England: Oxford University Press.

Putnam, R. (1993). *Making democracy work: Civic traditions in modern Italy*. Princeton, NJ: Princeton University Press.

Rainey, H. (1990). Public management: Recent development and current prospects. In N.B. Lynn & A. Wildavsky (Eds.), *Public administration: The state of the discipline* (pp. 157-184). Chatam, NJ: Chatham House.

Rhodes, R. (1996). The new governance: Governing without government. *Political Studies*, *44*, 652-657.

Rimmerman, C. A. (1997). *The new citizenship: Unconventional politics, activism, and service*. Boulder, CO: Westview Press.

Rosenbloom, D. H. (1998). *Public administration: Understanding management, politics, and law*. Boston: McGraw-Hill.

Rourke, F. E. (1992). Responsiveness and neutral competence in American bureaucracy. *Public Administration Review*, *52*, 539-546.

Sanderson, I. (1999). Participation and democratic renewal in the U.K.: From "instrumental" to "community rationality." *Policy and Politics*, *27*, 325-341.

Shui-Yan, T. (2005). Individual-level motivation for interagency cooperation. *Public Administration Review*, *65*, 377-378.

Tang, S. Y. (2005). Individual-Level motivations for interagency cooperation. *Public Administration Review*, *65*, 377-378.

Thomas, C. W. (2003). *Bureaucratic landscapes: Interagency cooperation and the preservation of biodiversity*. Cambridge, MA: MIT Press.

Thompson, D. (1983). Bureaucracy and democracy. In G. Duncan (Ed.), *Democratic theory and practice* (pp. 235-250). Cambridge, England: Cambridge University Press.

Vigoda, E. (2000). Are you being served? The responsiveness of public administration to citizens' demands: An empirical examination in Israel. *Public Administration*, *78*, 165-191.

Vigoda, E., (2002a). From responsiveness to collaboration: Governance, citizens, and the next generation of public administration. *Public Administration Review*, *62*, 515-528.

Vigoda, E. (Ed.) (2002b). *Public administration: An interdisciplinary critical analysis*. New York: Marcel Decker.

Vigoda-Gadot, E., (2003). *Managing collaboration in public administration: Governance, businesses, and citizens in the service of modern society.* Westport, CT: Praeger

Vigoda, E., & Golembiewski, R. T. (2001). Citizenship behavior and the spirit of new managerialism: A theoretical framework and challenge for governance. *American Review of Public Administration, 3,* 273-295.

Weber, E., & Khademian, M. A. (1997). From agitation to collaboration: Clearing the air through negotiation. *Public Administration Review, 57,* 396-410.

Weimer, D. L. (2005). Institutionalizing neutrally competent policy analysis: resources for promoting objectivity and balance in consolidating democracies. *The Policy Studies Journal, 33,* 131-146.

Yanow, D. (2003). *Constructing "race" and "ethnicity" in America: Category-making in public policy and administration.* Armonk, NY: M.E. Sharpe.

CHAPTER 4

NEW WAYS OF WORKING

Civic Engagement Through Networks

Myrna Mandell

INTRODUCTION

Confronted by the growing reality of finite resources and the realization that many social, economic, and environmental problems do not respond to conventional linear thinking or single agency/sector responses, increasingly agencies and sectors have looked to work with and draw from the capacities and resources of other organizations and sectors. As a result of this shift from single/individual to multiactor focus, terms and concepts such as governance, networks, collaboration, and partnerships have become key terms in public policy and practice discourse.

While all sectors are confronted with the need to explore and experiment with interorganizational relationships, the government, or public sector, is particularly challenged by decreasing budgets, growing demands for more citizen involvement and the realization that they no longer hold all expertise and knowledge (if indeed they ever did). As a result, over the past 20 years the relationships between government and the community and voluntary sector have become increasingly important in the develop-

Civic Engagement in a Network Society
pp. 65–84
Copyright © 2008 by Information Age Publishing
All rights of reproduction in any form reserved.

ment of public policy and the implementation of services. Relations with community members and voluntary-sector organizations have shifted from the periphery to the center of government policy and practice, particularly in respect to community based and local government policy development and service delivery (Agranoff, 2003; Brinkerhoff, 2002; Cordero-Guzman, 2001; Goodwin, 2004; Huxham, 2005; Huxham & Vangen, 1996, 2005; Keast & Brown, 2002; Keast, Mandell, Brown, & Woolcock, 2004; Koppenjan & Klijn, 2004; Mandell, 2001a, 2001b; Osborne & McLaughlin, 2002, 2004; Provan & Milward, 1995).

This shift is reflected in the literature in a number of ways. These include the shift from government to governance, working through networks and the growing movement toward greater citizen engagement.

FROM GOVERNMENT TO GOVERNANCE

The field of interorganizational relations was based on the need for government agencies to work more closely with each other. More recently, the complex problems facing governments have led to the inclusion of not only other government agencies but also the nonprofit and private sectors as well as community groups. This broader change in how government operates has led to a change in how we perceive of the creation, execution, and implementation of public policy. This change is a reflection of an emphasis away from looking at government, per se, as being the focus in public policymaking, to looking at the concept of governance.

Governance refers to a new way of governing, one in which government is only one actor among a number of other actors involved in policymaking (Bingham, Nabatchi, & O'Leary, 2005; Cooper, Bryer, & Meek, 2006; Kickert, Klijn, & Koppenjan, 1997; Rhodes, 1996). Government refers to a legal and formal authority with powers to execute and implement public activities. Governance refers to the incorporation of many different organizations, groups, and/or individuals sharing this power even though they may not have the legal authority to do so. In addition, other authors have cited the critical importance of this shift to governance in terms of the need for public managers to now understand their role not only in a hierarchical bureaucratic mode, but also in a network of actors representing all sectors (Agranoff & McGuire, 2003; Frederickson, 1999; Kettl, 2002; Kickert et al., 1997; Mandell, 2001a). Rhodes referred to this as "self-organizing interorganizational networks" (1997, p. xi). This change in emphasis on what it means to work in government has led to an emphasis on the importance of networks.

THE SHIFT TO WORKING THROUGH NETWORKS

Working through networks is not new. Berry et al. (2004) indicate that scholars recognized networking as a public management mode of operation as early as the 1980s. The field of intergovernmental management grew out of this recognition (Agranoff, 1986; Gage & Mandell, 1990; Mandell, 1988). The field has grown until now networks have become an accepted part of our understanding of how public programs and policies can be achieved through not only hierarchical relationships, but through horizontal relationships as well (Agranoff & McGuire, 1998, 2003; Kickert et al, 1997; Mandell, 2001b; O'Toole, 1997; Provan & Milward, 1995).

Since O'Toole (1997, p. 45) defined networks as "structures of interdependence involving multiple organizations or parts thereof, where one unit is not merely the formal subordinate of the others in some larger hierarchical arrangement," there have been many other definitions given by a wide variety of authors (Koppenjan & Klijn, 2004; Mandell, 1994, 2001; Mandell & Steelman, 2003). In spite of this, there are a number of factors that are part of any definition of a network. These include the interdependence of the actors, the blurring of sector lines, and the need to include many different actors in order to handle complex or wicked problems.

In the literature and our discussions of networks we often refer to them as collaborations (Agranoff, 2003; Agranoff & McGuire, 2003; Alter & Hage, 1993; Kamensky & Burlin, 2004; Kickert et al., 1997; Koppenjan & Klijn, 2004; Lowndes & Skelcher, 1998; Mandell, 1994). Although networks are ways of different organizations, groups and individuals to work together, to refer to all of them as collaborations muddies the water (Mandell & Steelman, 2003). Instead, a distinction has been made among three different types of networks (Keast, Mandell, & Brown, in press). They are cooperative, coordinative, and collaborative.

Cooperative networks occur in a variety of settings and only involve a sharing of information and/or expertise. There is very little, if any, risk involved in the transactions. Each participant remains independent and only interacts with the others when necessary. This is the case, for instance, with professional social workers that routinely exchange information about best practices and methods for dealing with their clients.

Coordinative networks occur when organizations feel the delivery of services is not as efficient as possible, and it is in their best interests to find ways to integrate existing services among all organizations involved in their delivery. In a coordinative network, organizations, groups and/or individuals go one step beyond merely exchanging information and/or knowledge. They interact with each other in order to better coordinate their individual efforts. They still remain independent entities, but are willing to make changes at the margins in the way they deliver their services. Most of the literature on networks is based on these types of interactions (Agranoff, 1990; Alter & Hage, 1993; Bardach, 1999; Goes & Park, 1997; Gray, 1989; Mandell, 2001a; Provan, Sebastian, & Milward, 1996; Radin et al., 1996). Most prevalent is the work of Provan and Milward, and their associates on networks in the mental health arena.

Collaborative networks are only appropriate if there is a need for participants to come together to solve a complex problem or problems that they recognize they cannot solve on their own. In a collaborative network the participants are interdependent. This means they know they are dependent on each other in such a way that for the actions of one to be effective they must rely on the actions of another. This means that they can no longer only make changes at the margins in how they operate. The risks are very high. Participants must be willing to develop new ways of thinking, form new types of relationships and be willing to make changes in existing systems.

The emphasis on networks is a reaction by government not only to the complexity of the problems they are now facing, but also to the demand for more citizen involvement in public issues. This shift is also reflected in the growing literature on citizen participation and citizen engagement.

RECONNECTING CITIZENS:
FROM CITIZEN PARTICIPATION TO CITIZEN ENGAGEMENT

Cooper et al. (2006) indicate that the idea of civic engagement in the United States is not new. It goes back to the early Puritan communities and the Mayflower Compact that served as antecedents of the New England town hall. In addition there is a long tradition based on the ideas of Jefferson, as well as an emphasis on associations in America that served as the training ground for citizenship and civic competence. According to Cooper et al. (2006) the watershed was the Progressive Era that established referendums, recalls, and initiatives in many states.

In spite of this, there were many barriers to citizen participation in the administration of government. In the 1960s there were new and more demands by citizens. In the beginning these approaches were adversarial or filled with conflict. This led to the beginning of advocacy efforts to secure the demands of citizens. In the 1970s there was an even more aggressive push for meeting citizen demands. This led to the institution of legal mandates to include citizen participation, but these were weak, without adequate resources, and generally paid lip service to involving citizens in the administration of government. Not much changed until the

1980s when there was a shift in thinking from government to governance. It was at this point that new forms of civic engagement came about.

One of the big areas of concern is whether this new emphasis on civic engagement is actually a new way of operating public programs or merely a way for government to get its own objectives more broadly accepted by the public (Boxelaar, Paine, & Beilin, 2006). In actuality both can be the case. The critical difference is on how well the different methosds of citizen participation are implemented and used to engage a diverse number of stakeholders. (See America Speaks, 2007 for a comprehensive listing of these different methods. Also see Bingham et al., 2005; Friedman, 2006; Lukensmeyer & Torres, 2006).

Lukensmeyer and Torres (2006) discuss the difference between information exchange models (inform and consult) and information processing models (engagement and empowerment). This difference also relates to the difference between citizen participation and civic engagement. Lukensmeyer and Torres (2006, p. 7) indicate that citizen participation processes have been described as a "'spectrum' composed of four goals: to inform, consult, engage, and collaborate with citizens." For them the citizen participation processes of "inform" and "consult," by themselves, do little to give citizens a role in the decision-making process nor to change their perceptions of government and/or their trust in government. Instead, they emphasize the need to add "an active, intentional partnership between the general public and decision makers" (p. 7). This involves the goals of citizen participation to engage and collaborate, but also adds the goal to empower citizens. This idea is echoed by Bingham et al. (2005) who refer to the difference between the citizen as a client, that is a passive role, and an enhanced role for citizens. For them this difference refers to the issue of power and the difference between "power with" and "power over" (p. 540).

PUTTING IT TOGETHER

What is interesting is that although the literature on networks and citizen engagement actually compliment each other, and in many cases are mirror images of each other, there are few articles that actually discuss both at the same time (see Brown & Keast, 2003, for a notable exception). This is not to say that there are not many articles that discuss citizen engagement and refer to these interactions as occurring in networks (Bingham et al., 2005; Boyle, 2005; Kim, Halligan, Cho, Oh, & Eikenberry, 2005). Indeed, the various types of citizen engagement efforts are underpinned by a complex set of interorganizational and multiactor relationships through

Table 4.1.   Meshing Citizen Involvement and Types of Networks

Mode of citizen involvement	Inform-consult	Engage-collaborate-empower
Model of involvement	Information exchange	Information processing
Type of network	Cooperative	Collaborative
Techniques used	Public hearings Citizen advisory councils Citizen juries Local issues forums	Town hall meetings Multistakeholder negotiations Policy consensus process Neighborhood councils

networks. It is that there is no deliberate attempt to mesh the literature on these two concepts into one whole.

To begin with, the differences between citizen participation and civic engagement mesh with the differences between cooperative networks and collaborative networks. Cooperative networks are vehicles for sharing information and expertise just as citizen participation processes are meant to do. Collaborative networks, on the other hand, are vehicles for changing systems through changing attitudes, values, and perceptions, just as civic engagement is meant to do. Table 4.1 shows how these concepts work together.

In addition, the characteristics of civic engagement processes dovetail very nicely with the characteristics of collaborative networks. These characteristics include equality of all participants in the process, an overriding commitment to the whole, rather than to single solutions, an emphasis on meshing different values, using results to impact public policy, and the issue of trust. Table 4.2 shows these similarities.

In both the literature on networks and the literature on citizen engagement, the issue is raised as to which type of structural arrangement should be chosen. The choice of arrangement will make the difference between whether there is just input by citizens or whether they are actively involved in the decision-making process. The key is for all participants to better understand which type of arrangement will work best for them in their different types of activities and roles. According to Lukensmeyer and Torres (2006), managers need to think about the level of involvement that is most appropriate for them, and the role they want to play. This is echoed in the literature on networks and the choices public managers will have in terms of operating through cooperative, coordinative or collaborative networks (Brown & Keast, 2003; Keast et al., in press).

The difference between the two sets of literature is that, by and large, the literature on networks emphasizes the role of the public manager and the literature on citizen engagement emphasizes the role of the citizen.

**Table 4.2.   Comparison of the Characteristics of
Civic Engagement and Collaborative Networks**

Characteristic	Civic Engagement Processes	Network Processes
Equality	• No individual holds the best answer to a public problem • Free and equal sharing of information	• All stakeholders are equal • No one is in charge
Commitment	• Emphasis on examining solutions in terms of a common best interest	• Overriding mission • View of the whole
Values	• Use of values-clarification exercises	• Developing a "program rationale"
Using results	• Incorporate results of deliberation into policy	• Emphasis on systems changes
Trust	• Raising trust of the parties involved • Building new relationships	• Developing trust among all stakeholders • Building new relationships

This is not to say that the literature on networks completely ignores the role of the citizen or that the literature on citizen engagement ignores the impact of networks. For instance, the works in the field of community development (Crowley, 2004; Edwards & Stern, 1998; Harris, Cairns, & Hutchinson, 2004; Larner & Butler, 2004; Mandell, 2001a; Mandell & Harrington, 1999) all deal with the problems facing citizens in networks. Likewise, the work of Bingham et al. (2005) on citizen engagement refers to these activities as occurring in networks.

According to Cooper et al. (2006) there are six variables that need to be maximized in order to achieve a well functioning, citizen-centered collaborative public management. These include: "government trust in citizens, citizen efficacy, citizen trust in government, citizen competence, government responsiveness, and government legitimacy" (p. 79). This dovetails with the literature on networks that calls for new management roles and skills on the part of government and community groups alike (Agranoff & McGuire, 2003; Keast et al., 2004).

NEW ROLES AND RESPONSIBILITIES

The new types of relationships and efforts between government agencies, voluntary community agencies and citizens have the potential to allow for more targeted service delivery programs as well as to affect broader societal change by redefining what state-citizen relations mean. This can be seen in the literature on both networks and citizen engagement (Agranoff, 2003; Agranoff & McGuire, 2003; Brinkerhoff, 2002; Cooper et al., 2006; Keast & Brown, 2002; Keast, Mandell, & Brown, 2005; Lukensmeyer & Torres, 2006).

While such issues confront all participants, government organizations, because they exist in a legal/political environment with strong needs for transparency, accountability and effectiveness (Keast & Brown 2002; Klijn & Koppenjan 2000), are often confronted by competing service and operational goals including their own electoral survival. They are therefore particularly apt to renege or fail to fully meet the new terms of engagement. Indeed, as a number of authors have demonstrated when under pressure government tends to "revert" to known and comfortable authoritative relationships (Keast & Brown, 2002; Klijn & Koppenjan, 2000).

In addition, government agencies are faced with a Catch-22 situation. They establish collaborative networks and civic engagement efforts because they need a new way to handle their most complex and difficult problems and to better respond to the demands of citizens. Once established, however, they perceive that these networks take on a life of their own. As a result the very networks they created threaten them. As Keast and Brown (2002) note this is because by giving over decision-making ability to external players the networks created become a threat to their status quo. As a result they often revert back to their more comfortable position of a centralized authority telling others what to do. By doing so they destroy the very networks they set up to assist them.

Another difficulty for government agencies involved in these new types of relations is that they are still based in centralized, hierarchical structures (Goodwin, 2004; Keast et al., 2004). These new relations, however, are based on horizontal, not vertical, management techniques. This means that in the future, government agencies will have to be willing to give up some or all of their traditional control mechanisms.

Instead, what is needed

> is a mechanism or set of supplemental mechanisms that respects the role of communities in identifying issues which require attention, establishing the priority which should be accorded to each, and designing effective service responses. These mechanisms must also respect the different structures and processes in place in government agencies and the need to engage these agencies early in the process and at the appropriate level. In other words, mechanisms that provide for horizontal and vertical engagement for want of better terms. (Goodwin, 2004, pp. 25-26)

In addition the problem is that participants in civic engagement efforts come in with multiple roles (Innes & Booher, 1999). This is also cited in the literature on networks (Agranoff & McGuire, 2003; Keast et al., 2004;

Mandell, 1994). In this literature the emphasis is on the need for representatives in networks not only to be committed to the processes within the network, but also to their own (parent) organization that they represent. Innes and Booher (1999) discuss different methods to allow participants in civic engagement efforts to better understand each other's roles and positions. According to these authors, these processes "allow all participants to be heard and be informed, and [encourage] discussion that is respectful and open-ended" (p. 11). The literature on networks also addresses the need to "step into each other's shoes" (Agranoff & McGuire, 2001; Mandell, 2001b) in order to better understand and deal with each other.

Finally, another difficulty is that participants are expected to play the role of equal partners. This is complicated, however. The reality is more in keeping with George Orwell's insight in the book *Animal Farm* (1946, p. 92) that "all animals are created equal, but some are more equal than others." Nevertheless, if participants try to act as if they have more authority or power than the other participants, the network will not be effective. The same is echoed in the literature on civic engagement. The emphasis is on the difference between efforts that merely give lip service to the inputs of citizens and those in which citizens are part of the decision-making process (Boxelaar et al., 2006; Cooper et al., 2006; Lukensmeyer & Torres, 2006).

In the literature on civic engagement, Cooper (1984) discusses the need for the public sector to establish relationships with the public that allow for "power with" rather then "power over" (p. 143). But community organizations and citizens must also understand how to exert their newfound power without also abusing it. The reality is that although community organizations and citizens are now in a power-sharing position, government agencies still maintain a greater power base. They must therefore learn how to use their newfound power in a way that allows room for both government agencies and voluntary community organizations to maneuver. If voluntary community organizations and/or citizens abuse their power, they can easily lose it.

This has been referred to as the "enabling component" of networks, which is characterized as "power to" bring about cooperation of others, rather than "power over" others (Agranoff & McGuire, 2001). This requires the ability "to marshal resources, build coalitions and forge agreements, and [develop] a view of the whole to achieve a set of common objectives based on the whole" (Mandell & Steelman, 2003, p. 215). In this regard, the emphasis is on the need to build new skills and ways of working.

NEW SKILLS AND WAYS OF WORKING

These new forms of relationships are becoming more prevalent. They represent alternative ways of harnessing the capacities of various partners, bringing about strategic renewal and innovative responses and maximizing resources. However, they also represent a challenge to those engaged in them. Of particular importance is the need for those in the public sector to learn new management skills and ways of behaving (Agranoff & McGuire, 2001, 2003). Agranoff and McGuire (2001, p. 15), for instance, develop a framework that highlights the network management behaviors that are most appropriate in collaborations. These include: activation (identifying the participants and stakeholders that need to be involved and tapping into their skills); framing (establishing and influencing the operating rules of the network); and synthesizing (creating a favorable environment for productive interaction). Others in the field have also identified similar key variables (Kamensky & Burlin, 2004; Keast et al., 2004; Kickert et al., 1997; Koppenjan & Klijn, 2004; O'Toole, 1997). In addition, however, the literature specifically on civic engagement, community partnerships, regional development, community development and joined up governance also highlights the need for different types of management strategies (Codero-Guzman, 2001; Goodwin, 2004; Huxham, 2005; Innes & Booher, 1999; Kathi & Cooper, 2005; Larner & Butler, 2004; Mandell & Harrington, 1999; Ross & Osborne, 2004). These include the need to establish flexible and adaptable structures, nonhierarchical and participatory decision-making, building relationships through developing mutual respect, understanding and trust, capacity building, defining an overriding mission, building consensus, and managing conflict.

But of course, this is not without its difficulties. For government, the culture and hierarchical ways of behaving serve to keep old patterns of behavior intact. There is a need for new tools and skills that focus on "negotiation, persuasion, collaboration, and enablement, which includes activation, orchestration, and modulation skills" (Bingham et al., 2005, p. 519). Others in the field echo this (Boxelaar et al., 2006; Cooper et al., 2006; Innes & Booher, 1999). One promising new method is facilitated consensus building (Innes & Booher, 1999). The focus is "on processes in which individuals representing different interests engage in long-term, face-to-face discussions, seeking agreement on strategy, plans, policies, or actions" (p. 11).

The need to develop new skills and ways of behaving is perhaps even more important for citizens. This is because one of the critical problems cited particularly in the literature on civic engagement is the mistrust of citizens and their ability to engage on an equal footing with experts found in both government and voluntary community organizations (Bingham et al., 2005; Boxelaar et al., 2006; Cooper et al., 2006; Lukensmeyer & Torres, 2006). Part of the problem is fear of administrators to embrace a decision outside of administrators' self-interest (Cooper et al., 2006).

According to Boxelaar et al. (2006), the problem in one case was the difficulty stemming from the use of only scientific experts to solve problems, but a need to understand the social and organizational aspects of problems. In this case, the main actors in the collaborative arrangement remained the experts, and managers and nongovernmental actors were marginalized. This gave legitimacy to the project within the parent organization, but at the expense of the collaborative process involving nongovernmental actors and reinforced the status quo instead of being able to come up with more innovative ways of doing things.

To overcome this type of behavior, the literature on both civic engagement and networks indicates the need to focus on training programs and building capacity for nongovernmental actors (Agranoff, 1991; The Annie E. Casey Foundation, 1995; Cooper et al., 2006; Huxham & Vangen, 1996; Innes & Booher, 1999; Kathi & Cooper, 2005; Keast et al., 2004; Mandell & Harrington, 1999). Collaborations are based on supposed equal partnerships with all members. The reality, however, is that not all members have the ability to be equal partners. What is needed is training programs, ongoing mentoring and other types of capacity building programs (Innes & Booher, 1999; Kathi & Cooper, 2005).

Coupled with this is the underlying fear of including citizens in a public policy making process. The literature refers to the difficulty of determining whether the citizens in a civic engagement effort actually represent the population or are merely elites and/or interest groups (Cooper et al., 2006; Friedman, 2006; Kathi & Cooper, 2005; Levine et al, 2005). Friedman (2006, p. 2), for instance, raises the question of whether "it will be the most powerful, the angriest and most extroverted that are heard." There is a need to make civic engagement efforts more inclusive and to show that citizens can deliberate effectively. Citizens often feel intimidated by the formal language used and the expertise of the other participants. According to findings by The Joseph Rowntree Foundation (www.jrf.org.uk/knowledge/findings/government):

> This implies that in order for governance structures to become more widely accessible, not only do communities need to learn how to access them, professionals also need to learn to work in an accessible way. This means developing processes and language suitable for the full range of potential participants.

This highlights another area in which professionals, working in nonprofit and voluntary community organizations, need to learn new skills

(Mandell, 2001; Mandell & Harrington, 1999). The difficulty is that these professionals are trained to take care of their clients. This is actually counter to what their role is in civic engagement and citizen participation processes. Their role in this environment is to allow citizens (many of whom may also be their clients) to act independently. This is a problem, because as Mandell and Harrington (1999, p. 10) point out, professionals in nonprofit agencies and voluntary community organizations have become "prescribers." Professionals look for "prescriptions or answers of how to achieve change that will be beneficial to communities." The key is to recognize that when involved in civic engagement or citizen participation endeavors, professionals will need to understand that they must step back, have patience and let the process work at its own pace. In essence, they need to move from being prescribers to being learners to being participants and adding value to the process (Mandell & Harrington, 1999.)

FUTURE CHALLENGES

Both the literature on networks and civic engagement question whether these new ways of working will be a passing fad or evolve into established ways of working. In addition, the question is raised as to whether these new ways of working really will make a difference. There are a number of challenges that participants will have to face in order to determine if indeed these efforts will be worth the effort. Two of these are of particular importance. They are changing expectations of participants and accountability issues.

Changing Expectations of Participants

One of the critical questions in this regard is the extent to which the participants in these efforts can change their expectations as to what these new ways of working really mean (Keast et al., 2004). In this regard, the emphasis in both the literature on networks and civic engagement is that at the core of these efforts is the need to build new types of relationships (Agranoff, 2003; The Annie E. Casey Foundation, 1995; Cooper et al., 2006; Innes & Booher, 1999; Keast et al., 2004; Koppenjan & Klijn, 2004; Mandell, 2001). This presents two critical challenges for those in these types of efforts. One relates to the time it will take to achieve results. The other relates to accepting intangible rather than only tangible results.

The building of relationships has been identified as "the single most valuable outcome ... between service providers and the communities they serve, widening 'policy networks'" (Joseph Rowntree Foundation, 2006,

p. 2). The key, according to this foundation was moving from "Why don't you" and "It's not our fault" to "How can we." This critical element is echoed in the writings of many in both the fields of networks and civic engagement. In spite of this, however, there needs to be an understanding and appreciation on the part of the participants that this will not be an easy process and will take a long time to develop. In some cases the process of building relationships has taken as long as 3 to 5 years to occur (The Annie E. Casey Foundation, 1995; Innes & Booher, 1999). The difficulty is that there will be pressures on the participants, both from their parent organizations and/or other external stakeholders to show results quickly. In most cases consideration will not be given to the need to take the time to establish new relationships. When it is, however, the results can be dramatically different (Keast et al., 2004).

Second, the emphasis on building relationships (that are intangible outcomes) is contrary to the traditional emphasis on achieving tasks (that are tangible outcomes) in the short term. Government agencies involved in civic engagement efforts through networks are used to a focus on how to be as efficient as possible in the delivery of services. Instead, these agencies now have to deal with the realities of focusing, not on task accomplishment in the short term, but rather on changing attitudes, perceptions and building new relationships in the long term.

Both of these challenges relate to the degree of risk that participants must face when trying to achieve civic engagement through networks. Since participants in a network are representing their parent organizations, they cannot just agree to new ways of working without first knowing that they will have the support of their parent organization. The difficulty is that expectations and consequences need to be dealt with up front, before the effort is begun, but most often this does not occur (Keast et al., 2004).

Accountability Issues

The fact that administrators in the public sector are fearful of giving up power to nonexperts (citizen groups) is not only based on the culture of bureaucratic agencies. It is rooted in our belief that it is government's job is to be sure the public is served. One of the key aspects of working in any setting is making sure that participants both understand and live up to their responsibilities. In public agencies these center on the most efficient means of delivering services. Public agencies are held accountable for not only what services are delivered, but also the manner in which they are delivered. This includes the emphasis on making sure all contracts are awarded fairly (open bidding), all clients are treated equally (with an emphasis on being impersonal with everyone) and that services are delivered in a timely manner.

The issue is one of accountability. In civic engagement efforts where the public sector is just one of many actors, the question arises as to whom we can hold accountable for the final outcomes. The established belief is that "decision making proceeds according to the primacy of politics doctrine, holding that politicians in political bodies outline the objectives and civil servants faithfully execute policy which conforms to these political parameters" (Koppenjan & Klijn, 2004, p. 91). This is in spite of the existing knowledge of the complexity of decision making on public issues and the value of including non civil servants into the equation. The bottom line is: If no single organization is responsible for the operation of the network, then who can be held accountable for its actions? Chisholm (1998, p. 11) points out "horizontal member-controlled design" raises the question of "who's in charge." All members in collaborations need to discover that all of them are actually in charge. This means that government, voluntary community organizations and citizens must be ready to take on new responsibilities in terms of accountability. This type of problem requires the active participation of all members to "assist in resolving parallel and emerging confusion about the roles of decision-making responsibilities of [the collaboration], where it derives its authority" (Goodwin, 2004, p. 23) and how the members should respond to the various calls for accountability.

Another aspect of the accountability issue has to do with the fact that members of collaborations are also members of their own organizations (Huxham & Vangen, 1996; Mandell, 2000). This results in two problems. The first problem is the extent to which representatives in collaborations are actually representative (Huxham & Vangen, 1996). Members of collaborations often express views that go beyond the parameters of the community group that they might represent. As Huxham and Vangen (1996, p. 13) points out, "Given that such representatives are not accountable to anyone for these views, it can be difficult for other collaborators to judge how representative of community views they actually are."

The second is the constraints placed on members by their organization as to what they can and cannot agree to (Huxham & Vangen, 1996). This reduces the degree to which the collaboration can act as it sees fit. This also creates conflicts for the representatives themselves in terms of meeting the goals of the collaboration and meeting the goals of their individual organization (Mandell, 2000).

In essence then, accountability is a double-edged sword. Government agencies feel responsible to produce outcomes and thus feel voluntary community organizations should be accountable to them. In addition, however, voluntary community organizations are also held accountable for their support of specific community goals and priorities. As a result voluntary community organizations and government agencies alike are moving to more innovative ways to assess collaborations including "social audits in which the quality of relationships are assessed, and advocating for 'process' and 'formative' evaluations [to] play a mentoring rather than a monitoring role" (Larner & Butler, 2004, p. 19). The end result will be that both voluntary community organizations and government agencies will still be held accountable, but the emphasis will be not only on the tangible outputs (tasks achieved) but also for the intangible processes (relationship building) that are essential in order for collaborations to be effective.

CONCLUSIONS

Today, it is no longer a question of whether citizen participation is desirable, but the form it should take. For most authors in this field, the choice is actually between paying lip service to citizens through citizen participation efforts or to help citizens make real meaning of policy decisions and to be able to share in the decision-making process through civic engagement (Friedman, 2006; Kathi & Cooper, 2005; Lukensmeyer & Torres, 2006). In this regard, there are a number of new and promising ways to engage citizens in a meaningful dialog. These include consensus building models (Innes & Booher, 1999); deliberative approaches (Friedman, 2006); and neighborhood councils (Kathi & Cooper, 2005) (for a comprehensive listing of many other models, see the America Speaks Web site, www.americaspeaks.org/resources).

Despite the optimism and evidence of a broad process of experimentation with new ways of working between the government and community sectors, however, genuine and successful collaborative endeavors have been hard to achieve and even harder to sustain (Brown & Keast, 2003; Huxham & Vangen 1996). These new types of arrangements require a greater level of trust, communication, reciprocity and commitment than has previously been in place between the two sectors (Boxelaar et al., 2006; Brinkerhoff, 2002; Lyons, 2003). A primary reason for the apparent failure of the emergent collaboration endeavors is the inability of participating organizations, government and community alike, to make and sustain the necessary adjustments in the strength of relationships and changes in behavior required (Keast et al., 2004), including as Brinkerhoff (2002) notes, the need to share power and assume a joint identity.

Governments, voluntary community organizations as well as citizens must now learn new roles and ways of behaving (Agranoff & McGuire, 2003; Innes & Booher, 1999; Keast et al., 2004; Mandell, 1994). This is especially difficult for organizations used to dealing with each other through hierarchical organizations. Government agencies are no longer able to maintain the tight control over others in the collaboration that they are used to in hierarchical relations. Equally important, voluntary community organizations now have a greater amount of responsibilities, not only toward their own organization and to government agencies, but to community members as well. For citizens, they are now seen, not just as clients, but also as active participants, alongside government and community organizations.

Finally, both government agencies and voluntary community organizations will find themselves in greater risk-taking positions. These new types of relationships, for instance, are very time consuming and do not lead to immediate tangible outcomes (tasks accomplished). This means that they will need to make a decision as to whether these new types of relationships are worth the risks. This decision will need to be based on the complexity of the problem, their ability to continue to deal with the problem on their own and their assessment of whether the way they are currently working continues to be an option.

In the long term the benefits of these new types of relationships can result in building political and social capital and lead to more innovative solutions to the most complex problems facing the public sector. The question is whether those involved in these efforts can deal with the inherent difficulties they will encounter in the short term before they can realize these results. The choice is a difficult one, but at least, in the twenty-first century, these choices do exist.

REFERENCES

America Speaks. (2007). *Special report on engaging citizens on the tough issues.* Retrieved January 18, 2007, from www.americaspeaks.org/resources

The Annie E. Casey Foundation. (1995). *The path of most resistance.* Baltimore: Author.

Agranoff, R. (1986). *Intergovernmental management.* Albany: State University of New York Press.

Agranoff, R. (1990). Managing federalism through metropolitan human services intergovernmental bodies. *Publius, 20*(1), 1-22.

Agranoff, R. (1991). Human services integration: Past and present challenges in public administration. *Public Administration Review, 51*(6), 533-42.

Agranoff, R. (2003). *Leveraging networks: A guide for public managers working across organizations.* Arlington, VA: IBM Endowment for The Business of Government.

Agranoff, R., & McGuire, M. (1998). The intergovernmental context of local economic development. *State and Local Government Review, 30*(1), 150-164.

Agranoff, R., & McGuire, M. (2001). After the network is formed: Processes, power and performance. In M. P. Mandell (Ed.), *Getting results through collaboration: Networks and network structures for public policy and management* (pp. 11-29). Westport, CT: Quorum Books.

Agranoff, R., & McGuire, M. (2003). *Collaborative public management: New strategies for local governments*. Washington, DC: Georgetown University Press.

Alter, C., & Hage, J. (1993). *Organizations working together*. Newbury Park, CA: Sage.

Bardach, E. (1999). *Getting agencies to work together*. Washington, DC: The Brookings Institute.

Berry, F. S., Brower, R. S., Choi, S. O., Goa, W. X., Jang, H., Kwan, M., & Word, J. (2004). Three traditions of network research: What the public management research agenda can learn from other research communities. *Public Administration Review, 64*(5), 539-552.

Bingham, L. B., Nabatchi, T., and O'Leary, R. (2005). The new governance: practices and processes for stakeholder and citizen participation in the work of government. *Public Administration Review, 65*(5), 547-558.

Boxelaar, L., Paine, M., & Beilin, R. (2006). Community engagement and public administration: Of silos, overlays and technologies of government. *Australian Journal of Public Administration, 65*(1), 113-126.

Boyle, H. C. (2005). Reframing democracy: Governance, civic agency, and politics. *Public Administration Review, 65*(5), 536-546.

Brinkerhoff, J. M. (2002). Government-nonprofit relations in comparative perspective: Evolution, themes, and new directions. *Public Administration and Development, 22*(1), 3-18.

Brown, K., & Keast, R. (2003). Citizen-government Engagement: Community connection through networked arrangements. *Asian Journal of Public Administration, 25*(1), 107-131.

Chisholm, R. (1998). *Developing interorganizational networks: Learnings from three applications*. Paper presented at the 59th American Society for Public Administration Conference, Seattle, WA.

Cooper, T. L. (1984). Citizenship and Professionalism in public administration. *Public Administration Review, 44*(2), 143-149.

Cooper, T. L., Bryer, T. A., & Meek, J. W. (2006). Citizen-centered collaborative public management [Special issue]. *Public Administration Review, 66*(1), 76-88.

Cordero-Guzman, H. R. (2001). *Interorganizational networks among community-based organizations*. Unpublished manuscript, Community Development Research Center, Robert J. Milano Graduate School of Management and Urban Policy, New School University.

Crowley, K. (2004, December-February). Joined up governance: Pushing the youth policy boundaries?" *Today, 2*, 47-53.

Edwards, S. L., & Stern, R. F. (1998). *Building and sustaining community partnerships for teen pregnancy prevention* (Working paper). Washington, DC: Cornerstone Consulting Group.

Frederickson, H. G. (1991). Toward a theory of the public for public administration. *Administration and Society, 22*(4), 395-417.

Friedman, W. (2006). Deliberative democracy and the problem of scope. *Journal of Public Deliberation, 2*(1), 1-29.

Gage, R. W., & Mandell, M. P. (Eds.). (1990). *Strategies for managing intergovernmental policies and networks.* Westport, CT: Praeger.

Goodwin, A. (2004, December-February). Quality of life: A case study in community engagement at the regional level. *Today, 2,* 21-26.

Goes, J. B., & Park, S. H. (1997). Interorganizational links and innovation: The case of hospital services. *Academy of Management Journal, 40*(3), 673-696.

Gray, B. (1989). *Collaborating: Finding common ground for multi-party problems.* San Francisco: Jossey-Bass.

Harris, M., Cairns, B., & Hutchinson, R. (20042004). "So many tiers, so many agendas, so many pots of money": The challenge of English regionalization for voluntary and community organizations. *Social Policy and Administration, 38*(5), 525-540.

Huxham, C. (2005). The challenge of collaborative governance. *Public Management, 2*(3), 337-357.

Huxham, C., & Vangen, S. (1996). Working together: Key themes in the management of relationships between public and non-profit organizations. *International Journal of Public Sector Management, 9*(7), 5-17.

Huxham, C., & Vangen, S. (2005). *Managing to collaborate: The theory and practice of collaborative advantage.* London: Routledge.

Innes, J. E., & Booher, D. E. (1999). Consensus building as role playing and bricolage. *Journal of the American Planning Association, 65*(1), 9-26.

Joseph Rowntree Foundation. (2006). *Governance and public services.* Retrieved January 18, 2007, from www.jrf.org.uk/knowledge/findings/government

Kamensky, J. M., & Burlin, T. J. (2004). *Collaboration: Using networks and partnerships.* New York: Rowman & Littlefield.

Kathi, P. C., & Cooper, T. L. (2005). Democratizing the administrative state: Connecting neighborhood councils and city agencies. *Public Administration Review, 65*(5), 559-567.

Keast, R., & Brown, K. (2002). The government service delivery project: A case of the push and pull of central government coordination. *Public Management Review, 4*(4), 439-459.

Keast, R., Mandell, M. P., & Brown, K. (in press). Getting the right mixz: Unpacking integration meanings and strategies. *International Journal of Public Management.*

Keast, R., Mandell, M. P., & Brown, K. (2005, April). *Governance arrangements and network management: The impact on hybrid networks.* Paper presented at the International Research Symposium on Public Administration, Milan, Italy.

Keast, R., Mandell, M. P., Brown, K., & Woolcock, G. (2004). Network structures: Working differently and changing expectations. *Public Administration Review, 64*(3), 363-371.

Kettl, D. F. (2002). *The transformation of governance: Public administration for twenty-first century America.* Baltimore: Johns Hopkins University Press.

Kickert, W. J., Klijn, E. -H., and Koppenjan, J. (1997). *Managing complex networks: Strategies for the public sector.* London: Sage Publications.

Kim, P. S., Halligan, J., Cho, N., Oh, C. H., & Eikenberry, A. M. (2005). Toward particpatory and transparent governance: Report on the sixth global forum on reinventing government. *Public Administration Review, 65*(6), 646-654.

Klijn, E. -H., & Koppenjan, J. (2000). Public management and policy networks: Foundations of a network approach to governance. *Public Management Review, 2*(2), 135-158.

Koppenjan, J., & Klijn, E. -H. (2004). *Managing uncertainties.* London: Routledge.

Larner, W., & Butler, M. (2004). *Governmentalities of local partnerships, research paper number 12.* Auckland: University of Auckland, New Zealand, Strengthening Communities through Local Partnerships and Governance Research Group.

Levine, P., Fung, A., & Gastil, J. (2005). Future directions for public deliberation. *Journal of Public Deliberation, 1*(1), 1-13.

Lowndes, V., & Skelcher, C. (1998). The dynamics of multi-organizational partnerships: An analysis of change modes in government. *Public Administration, 76*(2), 313-333.

Lukensmeyer, C. J., & Torres, L. H. (2006). Public deliberation: A manager's guide to citizen engagement. *IBM Center for the Business of Government.* Retrieved January 18, 2007, from www.businessofgovernment.org

Lyons, M. (2003). Improving government-community sector relations. *Journal of Contemporary Issues in Business and Government, 9*(1), 7-20.

Mandell, M. P. (1988). Intergovernmental management in interorganizational networks: A revised perspective. *International Journal Of Public Administration, 11*(4), 393-416.

Mandell, M. P. (1994). Managing interdependencies through program structures: A revised paradigm. *American Review of Public Administration, 25*(1), 99-121.

Mandell, M. P. (2000). 'A revised look at management in network structures. *International Journal of Organization Theory and Behavior, 3*(1-2), 185-210.

Mandell, M. P. (Ed.) (2001a). *Getting results through collaboration: Networks and network structures for public policy and management.* Westport, Ct: Quorum Books.

Mandell, M. P. (Ed.). (August, 2001b). The impact of network structures on community-building efforts: The Los Angeles Roundtable for Children Studies. In *Getting results through collaboration: Networks and network structures for public policy and management.* Westport, CT: Quorum Books.

Mandell, M., & Harrington, M. (April 1999). *When collaboration is not enough: Learning From Our CITIES (Community Initiatives That Increase Everyone's Strengths).* Los Angeles: The Los Angeles Roundtable For Children.

Mandell M. P., & Steelman, T. (2003). Understanding what can be accomplished through interorganizational innovations: Importance of typologies, context and management strategies" *Public Management Review, 5*(2), 197-224.

Orwell, G. (1946). *Animal farm.* New York: Harcourt Brace Janovich.

Osborne, S. P., & McLaughlin, K. (2002, January-March). Trends and issues in the implementation of local "voluntary sector compacts." *England, Public Money and Management,* 55-63.

Osborne, S. P., & McLaughlin, K. (2004). The cross-cutting review of the voluntary sector: Where next for local government-voluntary sector relationships?" *Regional Studies, 38*(5), 573-582.

O'Toole, L. J. (1997). Treating networks seriously: Practical and research based agendas in public administration. *Public Administration Review, 57*(1), 45-51.

Provan, K. G., & Milward, H. B. (1991). Institutional norms and organizational involvement in a service-implementation network. *Journal of Public Administration Research and Theory, 1*(4), 391-417.

Provan, K. G., & Milward, H. B. (1995). A preliminary theory of interorganizational network effectiveness: A comparative study of four community health systems. *Administrative Science Quarterly, 40*(1), 1-33.

Provan, K. G., Sebastian, J. G., & Milward, H. B. (1996). Interorganizational cooperation in community mental health: A resource-based explanation of referrals and case coordination. *Medical Care Research and Review, 53*(1), 94-119.

Radin, B., Agranoff, R., Bowman, A., Buntz, O., Ott, G. C., Romzek, B. S., et al. (1996). *New governance for rural America: Creating intergovernmental partnerships*. Lawrence: University Press of Kansas.

Rhodes, R. A. W. (1996). The new governance: Governing without government. *Political Studies, 44*(4), 652-667.

Rhodes, R. A. W. (1997). Foreword. In W. J. M. Kickert, E. K. Klijn, & J. F. M. Koppenjan (Eds.), *Managing complex networks*. London: Sage Publications.

Ross, K., & Osborne, S. (2004). *Making a reality of community governance: Structuring government-voluntary sector relationships at the local level*. Retreived October 25, 2004, from http://www.york.ac.uk/depts/poli/pac/papers/ross.htm

CHAPTER 5

CONDUCTIVE PUBLIC ORGANIZATIONS IN NETWORKS

Collaborative Management and Civic Engagement

Robert Agranoff

Where do public organizations fit in a networked society? In what ways do public agencies promote and participate in civic engagement through its networks and partnerships? These are important questions as public organizations now exist in the era of collaboration. In fact, a myriad of lateral contacts, through regulations, grants, contracts, partnerships, networks and many informal informational and decisional interactions (Agranoff, 1998, 2001; Agranoff & McGuire, 2003) are part of the core of public work.

Today's public organizations nevertheless remain hierarchies that perform many of the same functions as those of the previous century (planning, organizing, staffing, etc.) but also face the overlay of "engaging" outside forces in a working fashion. Public managers thus need to involve people from disparate venues to participate with them in policy and

Civic Engagement in a Network Society
pp. 85–108
Copyright © 2008 by Information Age Publishing
All rights of reproduction in any form reserved.

entrepreneurial leadership. They must promote networking and related collaborative activity and participate in partnerships. The process of interactive participation also must contain automatic feedback mechanisms, listening to clientele needs and promoting coinvestment in programs. Finally, the public manager needs to use external engagement to help create organized learning entities where people working together can expand their capacities and be creative (Agranoff, 2005, pp. 34-39), and to promote external roles in decision making, management, and services delivery (Yang & Callahan 2005). As this chapter makes clear, such externalities of engagement can be achieved through the conductive public organization, that is an agency that enhances its performance through knowledge created by energetic external interactions.

Civic engagement has important role connections to the new public organizations. As Cooper, Breyer, and Meek (2006) trace the history of civic engagement in the United States, they identify several different approaches: adversarial, electoral, information exchange, through civic groups, and deliberative approaches. The latter, of major focus in this chapter, include those "efforts that seek joint action across sectors of society, classes of people, and types of individuals." Moreover, they are the types of engagement that seek consensus in action through lengthy, deliberative processes, extensive dialogue, joint action and shared responsibility for outcomes (p. 82). The quest for deliberative engagement involves governments, communities, organized interests and citizens, and it is caught up with the economic and geographic stability of communities, "the question of how to reinvigorate local-level participation in the process of democratic governance cannot be abstracted from the question of how to stabilize geographic communities economically. In the most dramatic cases economic dislocation entails the wholesale destruction of civic networks" (Williamson, Imbruscio, & Alperovitz 2005, p. 312). In other words, development and democracy are linked to communities and face-to-face interactions. "As in the New England town meetings, through much of the world democracy seems inseparable from the process of face-to-face conversations among people and their leaders who know each other and work together to govern their own communities" (Derber, 2002, p. 185). These efforts are geared to engage governments' conductive organizations with external interests to forge "a new collaborative civil society" that builds government-external bridges "by helping people work together on specific projects to improve their economy and community—reforming education systems, streamlining permitting processes, fostering business connections, revitalizing urban centers, and leveraging the information infrastructure" (Henton, Melville, & Walesh, 1997, p. xviii). Deliberative engagement therefore rests heavily on the openness, connectivity, and boundary spanning activity of key government agencies.

The conductive public organization and collaborative engagement is taken up here by primary focus on the agencies themselves. Although clearly an interactive process, the focus of discussion here is on how public bureaucracies must become deliberative. The illustrative context will be on development functions at federal, state, and local levels. The next section identifies and details the conductive public organization. That is followed by illustrations of what conductive organizations look like. The characteristics of the conductive organization are next examined through analysis of its noncore (external) processes along with the keys to public agency conductivity. Then the keys to linking in civic engagement with the public agency are identified. This is followed by an analysis of how to approach the public agency. A concluding section then talks about the future challenges to public agencies in an era of deliberative civic engagement.

THE CONDUCTIVE PUBLIC ORGANIZATION

Hierarchy today no doubt looks less like organizations in the days of the emerging bureaucratic organization, what was once known as Weberian, Taylorist, or Fordist. Organizational structures themselves have become more flexible and permeable over the twentieth century (Clegg 1990, p. 181). This has two important implications for public management. First, is that those public administrators and program specialists who work in bureaucracies are now more attuned to internal organizational experiences that are less rigid, cross the divisional boundaries of their own structures, reach out to other agencies of their government, and involve an increasing number of cross sector and intergovernmental experiences. Second, this exposure and experience with a changing bureaucratic paradigm has brought on a host of cross-boundary transactions. Boundary-spanning approaches—grants, contracts, regulatory interaction, cooperative agreements, joint ventures, networks, and the like—are familiar and now are regular bureaucratic transactions beyond the walls of the agency.

The emergent organization that faces the challenge of knowledge and resource management within also regularly collaborates externally. Any number of the newer management books in the past decade or so stress these themes, particularly how collaboration is changing the operation of the traditional organization (e.g., Campbell & Gould 1999; Davenport & Prusak 2000; Drucker 2001; Pasternack & Viscio 1998). Among the most thorough and thoughtful of this genre is the *Conductive Organization* by Saint-Onge and Armstrong (2004). They define the conductive organization as: "An organization that continuously generates and renews the capabilities to achieve breakthrough performance by enhancing the quality and flow of knowledge and by calibrating its strategy, culture, structure and systems to the needs of its customers and the marketplace" (p. 213). Obviously addressed primarily to business organizations, Saint-Onge and Armstrong address numerous organizational processes, including the importance of creating partnerships through internal-external interaction, building alliances and coalitions, forming and reforming teams across functions and organization boundaries, and collaborating to actively manage interdependencies (p. 191):

> The capability to effectively manage complex partnerships is growing in importance as organizations are reconfigured. Organizations are becoming more and more involved in complex value-creation networks, where the boundaries between one organization and another become blurred and functions become integrated. It's becoming a critical organizational and leadership capability to be able to create and leverage participation in network-designed and—delivered solutions.

In such organizations, it is usual for the professional and managerial staff to collaborate, learn, share, and then execute their responsibilities (p. 191).

Today's organizations, Groff and Jones (2003) maintain, contain more and more people who share knowledge. "Collaboration groups consist of formal and informal, often self-organized, groups of employees who possess complimentary knowledge and share interest in particular problems, processes or projects in their organization" (p. 20). Moreover, they suggest that sharing knowledge is not a zero-sum game. "Unlike conventional assets, knowledge grows when it is shared. The main limitation to infinite knowledge growth is the currency of the information economy-attention" (p. 20). They also underscore the importance of Metcalf's Law (utility = $[nodes]^2$), that is the usefulness of a network equals the square of the number of users (Metcalfe, 1996).

Today's public administrators particularly experience connectivity in dealing with the operations and practices of nonprofit and for profit organizations external to their structure. Over the past half century the phenomenon of an expanding network of alliances between governments and a host of public and private bodies—other levels of government, private business, banks, insurance companies, and, increasingly nonprofit agencies (Salamon, 1995, p. 2). These nongovernmental organizations are part of the core of the "third sector" among government and business comprised of structured organizations located outside of government. Some are not designed to distribute profits to owners/investors, self-governing, and involving substantial voluntary effort (Salamon, 1995, p. 249) whereas others are. In particular, nonprofit organization personnel and processes—boards, planning and technical staff, community-based task-forces, strategic planning—normally represent citizens as they engage government, particularly through deliberation. In turn, government interaction has affected nonprofit organizations as they have "become more broadly representative of community interests, as the organizations they serve have to deal more actively with their environments" (Smith & Lipsky, 1993, p. 41). In general, nonprofit organizations are known for their flexibility in operation and the application of such traditional managerial techniques as budgeting, governance, information management, and human resources to widely varying situations (Wolf, 1999, p. 20). The growth of government nongovernment interaction brings another important set of organizational experiences to the network experience, as these organizations also become more conductive.

It is within these increasingly connective contexts that public administrators, association executives, and program managers/specialists work today. To be sure, within agencies and organizations conventional processes such as legal powers and duties, rules and procedures, and hierarchical authority remain and form a continuing context of organizational concerns. These continuing procedures put important boundaries on what can be done, particularly for public agencies. But the overlays of external contacts in a variety of deliberative and nondeliberative contexts makes public organizations highly conductive.

THE LOOK OF THE CONDUCTIVE ORGANIZATION

A more detailed look at conductive organizations is presented by three hypothetical illustrations in the development arena. First, is a typical United States Department of Agriculture/Rural Development (USDA/RD) program located in one of the states. The second is a "typical" state economic development agency. Third, is a look at city government's development functions, including its mechanisms for deliberative public engagement. Together they illustrate that public administration today is more than planning, organizing, staffing, directing, coordinating, reporting and budgeting.

Surface observation might indicate that the 50 plus state USDA/RD agencies could not be more bureaucratic (or banking, some would say) with its 20 or so programs. But Figure 5.1 demonstrates what these programs entail. In many ways USDA/RD is the equivalent to Housing and Urban Development (HUD) for very small towns and rural areas. Most of its programs go to low-income citizens and small communities, and to small organizations. Its core rules and procedures are designed to deal with a host of external grant and contract clients. In addition, reading clockwise, it usually works on a series of joint projects with other federal

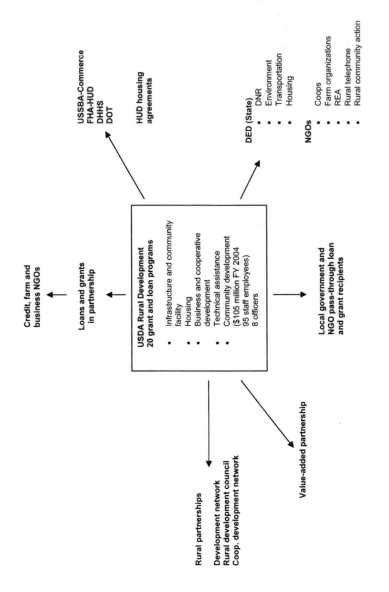

Credit, farm and business NGOs

Loans and grants in partnership

USDA Rural Development
20 grant and loan programs

- Infrastructure and community facility
- Housing
- Business and cooperative development
- Technical assistance
- Community development
($105 million FY 2004
95 staff employees)
8 officers

USSBA-Commerce
FHA-HUD
DHHS
DOT

HUD housing agreements

DED (State)
- DNR
- Environment
- Transportation
- Housing

NGOs
- Coops
- Farm organizations
- REA
- Rural telephone
- Rural community action

Local government and NGO pass-through loan and grant recipients

Rural partnerships

Development network
Rural development council
Coop. development network

Value-added partnership

USDA/RD — Core and Collaborative Operations

Figure 5.1.   USDA/RA as a conductive public organization.

agencies in the field, particularly HUD housing agreements. Each USDA/ RD engages with their counterpart state agencies and associations, particularly with the department of economic development (or its equivalent), and statewide cooperative and farm organizations. The agency provides grant and loan money for infrastructure/community development/civic improvement to small local governments and their nongovernmental organization pass-throughs. Most state agencies are in one or more partnerships with universities, agribusiness, and farm organizations to promote value-adding in agriculture, plus a series of engagements with networks like a rural partnership, with planning and development agencies, and a USDA promoted state rural development council where one exists. Finally, the agency provides loans and grants through partnerships and joint ventures with a host of statewide credit, commodity and business organizations. Of course, many of the NGOs operate through boards and membership bodies, the networks through which nonprofit-like boards, and the local governments engage local citizens. In sum, USDA/RD in most states is now a combination of the inside work of providing information, processing loans and reviewing grants and the myriad of external connections that are interactive with its core mission and internal functions (Agranoff 2007, ch. 9).

The same would be true only more complex with the typical state economic/community development department (ECD). Figure 5.2 demonstrates in perhaps a nonexhaustive but extensive fashion the range of connections such an ECD might have. The core agency is often small, depending on the size and scope of its mission, with as few as 20 persons of a professional nature, administering a limited number of state development programs: loans, grants, leadership development, information, planning, and promotion. The core work is even more outside than the federal agency illustrated. Working clockwise again, one would start with other state agency contacts, particularly transportation and environment. There are also numerous federal government contacts, such as, with USDA/RD, Commerce (Small Business Administration, Economic Development Administration), HUD (small cities Community Development Block Grant, housing) and special programs like Main Street. Next would be ECD contacts with city and county governments over state and federal pass-through programs, and interactively over various economic development tools, for example tax credits or loans. The same type of contacts would be made with local economic development bodies. Further contacts are made with substate planning and development agencies and/or councils of government on matters of planning and program development for small communities. Since development involves leadership and skilled workforces, higher education interaction is regular. Some departments are also in contact with higher education for basic research and technol-

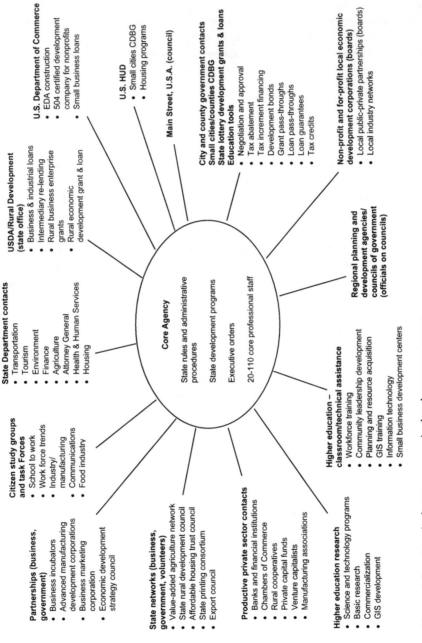

Figure 5.2. A typical state economic development agency.

Partnerships (business, government)
- Business incubators
- Advanced manufacturing development corporations
- Business marketing corporation
- Economic development strategy council

State networks (business, government, volunteers)
- Value-added agriculture network
- State rural development council
- Affordable housing trust council
- State printing consortium
- Export council

Productive private sector contacts
- Banks and financial institutions
- Chambers of Commerce
- Rural cooperatives
- Private capital funds
- Venture capitalists
- Manufacturing associations

Higher education research
- Science and technology programs
- Basic research
- Commercialization
- GIS development

Citizen study groups and task Forces
- School to work
- Work force trends
- Industry/manufacturing
- Communications
- Food industry

Higher education – classroom/technical assistance
- Workforce training
- Community leadership development
- Planning and resource acquisition
- GIS training
- Information technology
- Small business development centers

State Department contacts
- Transportation
- Tourism
- Environment
- Finance
- Agriculture
- Attorney General
- Health & Human Services
- Housing

Core Agency

State rules and administrative procedures

State development programs

Executive orders

20–110 core professional staff

Regional planning and development agencies/ councils of government (officials on councils)

USDA/Rural Development (state office)
- Business & industrial loans
- Intermediary re-lending
- Rural business enterprise grants
- Rural economic development grant & loan

U.S. Department of Commerce
- EDA construction
- 504 certified development company for nonprofits
- Small business loans

U.S. HUD
- Small cities CDBG
- Housing programs

Main Street, U.S.A. (council)

City and county government contacts
Small cities/counties CDBG
State lottery development grants & loans
Education tools
- Negotiation and approval
- Tax abatement
- Tax increment financing
- Development bonds
- Grant pass-throughs
- Loan pass-throughs
- Loan guarantees
- Tax credits

Non-profit and for-profit local economic development corporations (boards)
- Local public-private partnerships (boards)
- Local industry networks

ogy applications. The next set of key contacts would be with representatives of the state's productive sector: banking and financial institutions, chambers of commerce, rural cooperatives, venture capitalists and manufacturing associations. Most states engage a series of networks in various areas, ranging from an export council to affordable housing. Along with networks are a series of partnerships, normally for business promotion. Finally, many departments have citizen boards or study groups that examine intractable policy problems, for example school to work, and make recommendations through the agency. There are no doubt many more such contacts not illustrated in the highly external ECD. Unlike USDA/RD, it really has a few small programs of its own. Most of its work is mobilizing and engaging the work of others (Agranoff & McGuire, 2000).

The development approach can be illustrated at the local level by looking at a city's economic and community development collaborative connections. Figure 5.3 extrapolates these functions from the rest of city government for demonstration purposes. In the core city government, the planning and community development department is the lead development agency, but finance, public works, social services, and neighborhoods also play key conductive roles of a facilitative and operational nature. Again, looking clockwise the council has instituted a number of important engagement-oriented committees (nine are illustrated) ranging from communications technology to the more standard library board. Next are citywide mixed citizen/association/council member task forces devoted to planning, promoting and orchestrating important community/economic development programs such as downtown and civic events. There are state government (and infrequently federal) grant and loan contacts. The neighborhoods department works with city's nine ward/neighborhood planning associations and citizen councils. Meanwhile, social services works with the independent park and school districts as well as with social and health associations. Public works is in regular contact with the water and sewer district and private utility companies while legal engages numerous state regulatory inquiries and negotiations. The most regular and extended contacts are made with the city's Economic Development Corporation, a partnership with county government, chamber of commerce and other important entities. This body carries the economic development load for the city government through the planning department. Finally, are contacts with the substate regional development agency, mostly through city council representation and for occasional assistance. Looking at the economic and community development function, this illustrative city is not only connective through its boards, task forces, and intergovernmental contacts, but operates its economic development operation through a joint venture or public-private partnership. While not every city would have such a development corporation, all of

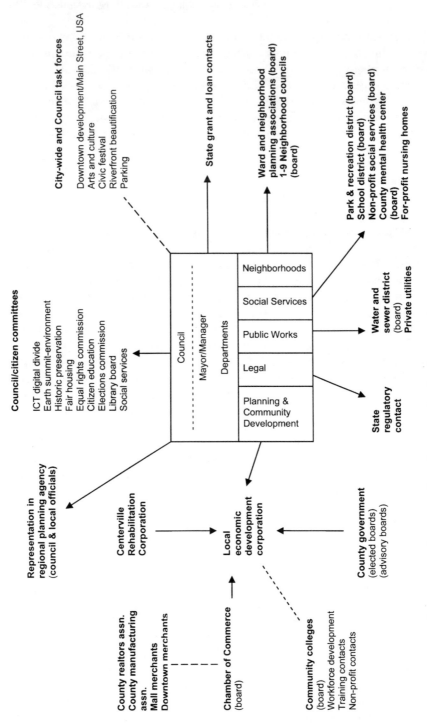

Figure 5.3. Local government in economic and community development.

those engaged in development would have to regularly interact with the same local interests as the corporation (Agranoff & McGuire 2003).

The three conductive organizations illustrate the public bureaucracy of the twenty-first century more than that of earlier times. In addition to internal operations, they use the variety of inter and intra governmental instruments illustrated (Salamon, 2002). The conductive agency neither controls the entities that it deals with nor are they controlled by these agencies. Each party has its legally or contractually chartered mission, roles, and rules. Their joint efforts come at the margins not the core of each party, although both sides must be willing to work with one another to smooth transactional flow. These are public agencies that are dependent on their external clientele and by the same token, their external clientele are dependent on them. They have core operations and are legally chartered, and the connectivity is an overlay, not an operational substitute.

This interdependence is fostered by interactive engagement in a world where exchange opens the door to success through a myriad of linkages. USDA/RD cannot advance the cause of improving the lives of rural citizens without local leaders and communities reaching out and successfully working with them through winning projects. A state ECD cannot successfully advance its economy to contemporary expectations without engaging the business, financial, educational, and associational communities. No city can attract new businesses or make their community a better place to live without lots of citizen involvement, organized partners, and joint ventures. They all leverage their public investments through other organizations. That is why the conductivity burden is so heavy. As Saint-Onge and Armstrong (2004, p. 34) conclude, "High performing organizations know how to build and maintain the relationships that are conduits for knowledge flow, leveraging capabilities, and strategy-making processes."

RULES OF CONDUCTIVE ENGAGEMENT

The emergent interest in deliberative democracy has identified a number of government-to-citizen or citizen-to-government face-to-face techniques: choice-work dialogues, citizens' juries, consensus conferences, deliberative polling, issue forums, study circles, twenty-first century town meetings and citizens' assemblies (Lukensmeyer & Torres 2006). To the deliberative public agency these may be interesting and useful sidelights to receive input on how to manage but they pale in comparison to the regular formal and informal transactions that are needed to execute contracts, monitor grants, and gather information on compliance, not to speak of their participation *with* nongovernmental representatives over questions of policy and services delivery. Many of these are routine and of the most mundane of organization-to-organization questions (Agranoff, 1986) and they involve a myriad of contacts with a series of partners. This type of transactional work involves *both* the interactive transmission of information and deliberative negotiations related to program adjustments (Agranoff & McGuire, 2003).

As a result, to the manager in a conductive public agency a new and different set of "clientele relationships" would appear to be important. The external publics are not only potential service recipients but potential partners in some type of joint or collaborative effort. This brings on a different set of external rules:

1. Recognize incredible variety of potential lateral concepts. They include interest associations, nonprofit organizations, substate planning agencies, public-private ventures, statewide networks, government-to-government linkages, intergovernmental contacts, and many others, along with elected and appointed advisory boards. By the same token, the interactive advisory board that deliberates and recommends policy is not the only vehicle. Grants, contracts, interagency agreements, joint services and resources exchanges and many more potential deliberative vehicles exist. Many parties become involved in the policy/implementation process. Administrators must see that many of these vehicles go beyond the traditional advice-giving to involve the type of "cogoverning partnerships" (Fung, 2006, p. 69) illustrated in Figures 5.1-5.3. In this type of process more than consultation is involved, as persons that were once thought of as advocates become partners. The public administrator operates in a broad field of potential deliberative mechanisms to a myriad of "external agents."

2. Deliberative work under these circumstances involves a different kind of process than consultation or reacting to proposals. It involves growing and learning together. As Forester (1999, p. 62) suggests, in deliberative work citizens integrate the worlds of "is" and "ought" as well as "science" and "ethics" as they learn how to get something done and what ought to be done in application to new and unique situations. "Connecting governance and dispute resolution, politics and ethics, deliberative practice involves the most intellectually intriguing issues ... how can we learn not only about technique but about value; how can we change our minds about what is important, change our appreciation of what matters, and, more, change our practical sense about what we can do together too." The administrator in the conductive agency cannot sit back and react but must become a part of this process of looking for and helping respond to concern and need by forging the new and possible. Partner creators rather then bureaucratic responders are needed.

3. Calibrate the organization to be able to work with external groups, needs, and interests. This goes well beyond the normal tenets of organiza-

tional design, including the standard building of teams. Indeed, the three public conductive agencies illustrated here have quite standard divisions and departments based on functional program needs. They engage many teams to launch their collaborative work. The key is not divisional realignment or more and more teams but to open these functions to organized agency clientele through constant processes that informs the agency's thinking, actions and relationships through constant knowledge flow, that is intimate understanding of its external working interlocutors. This can invoke a number of mutual actions, such as continuing work with stakeholders, codeveloped solutions, accepting input on shaping rules, cross functional integration (e.g. joint production), integration with external agency/organization operating systems, developing solutions based on externally perceived value, and strategic partnerships (Saint-Onge & Armstrong 2004, p. 57). In effect, these practices have become part of the new organizational design, a set of lateral overlays on the enduring hierarchical structure.

4. Capture the information based nature of the conductive agency. Deliberation works better when the parties engaged in joint undertakings are better informed. Many of the programs of a state economic and community development agency, for example those illustrated in Figure 5.2, provide many nontangible goods and services, for example developing community leadership, helping cities understand their local economies, helping them conduct institutional and environmental evaluations, and assisting in strategic development. Indeed, one of the most essential tasks that state agency administrators can perform in rural development is to gather information about rural communities and to assess the capacities of the institutions and people in these communities. Through community assessment, often conducted locally by citizen groups with state agency or university assistance, the uncertainty felt by communities can be reduced and locals can raise the level of policy/program possibility, fitting the array of programs with the community (Agranoff & McGuire, 2000, p. 394). These types of information strategies definitely make the quality of deliberation easier and that is why conductive administrators invest increasing resources in programs of technical assistance, planning and skill-building, community leadership, needs analysis, action planning, education and training, as well as impact studies.

5. Knowledge employees wanted. The conductive organization needs a knowledge-oriented administrator base. As information is converted into knowledge that is transacted and modified through deliberation the agency needs to capture those invisible assets that reside largely in the minds of humans, requiring less strict supervision and with "worker" and manager working side by side. The rules of supervision for knowledge workers are different. According to Davenport (2005, pp. 192-201) they

entail: (1) participation by managers in the work instead of overseeing work; (2) from organizing hierarchies to organizing communities; (3) retaining workers rather than hiring and firing them; (4) building knowledge skills rather than manual skills; (5) assessing invisible knowledge achievements instead of evaluating visible job performance; (6) building knowledge-friendly cultures instead of ignoring culture; (7) fending-off bureaucracy rather than supporting it; (8) relying on a variety of human resources, wherever they may be located, instead of reliance on internal personnel. These principles of human resource management clearly apply to those public agency employees who are working out of the organization with others on joint resolution of issues and problems.

6. Building high-quality relationships through communities. It is common practice for conductive agencies to deliberate through the building of communities of practice and taking advantage of epistemic communities. Many of the joint ventures, networks, consultative bodies, partnerships and the like operate as communities of practice, that is self-organizing systems that share the capacity to create and use knowledge through informal learning and mutual engagement (Wenger, 2000). Most communities are self-organized and bring in new knowledge bearers when needed, from wherever they can be found. Maintenance of communities of practice requires effort to keep different types of knowledge bearers in, by challenging busy people with solving important public problems and by calling on their experience and know how in an interdisciplinary manner. This is an emergent challenge for the conductive agency administrator.

Community can be facilitated by mobilizing a multiagency group of professionals from different disciplines who share common outlooks and similar solution orientations. Haas (1992, p. 3) suggests that these persons can represent a variety of disciplines and share normative and principled beliefs which provide a value-based rationale for social action. They also tend to share causal beliefs, notions of validity, and a common policy enterprise. An epistemic community normally produces consensual knowledge. Even in the face of anomalous data the community may suspend judgment in order to maintain their scientific legitimacy, maintaining for the moment its power resource (Hass, 1990, p. 55). Epistemic communities can be important knowledge sustainers, as they can have a disproportionate effect on organized learning and behavior, and even though epistemic community members may not constitute the most powerful decision makers, they "are well situated to provide a driving logic for cooperation" (Thomas, 2003, p. 41). Bringing together these communities for enhanced deliberation is among the tasks of the collaborative administrator.

7. Create an agency knowledge strategy. It has been suggested that the conductive organization enhances value by interacting with organized external clientele in collaboration, particularly through communities. A conductive organization can then capture intangible assets through the exchange of knowledge. According to Saint-Onge and Armstrong (2004, p. 38) value creation involves the managed interaction between: (1) the human capital of the agency, (2) the structural or organizational capabilities, and, (3) interacting external agents and partners. All three need to be developed in a knowledge strategy on an integrated basis. Many activities are involved in the process of knowledge management (Davenport & Prusak, 2000), a process that entails identification, extraction, and capturing fluid mixes of framed experiences, values, contextual information and expert insight that constitutes the assets of any undertaking. In the case of public conductive organizations knowledge is derived on a highly interactive basis and is geared to adding some form of public value (Agranoff, 2007, chs. 7, 8).

There are many knowledge management activities that the conductive agency might pursue. Working with its organized clientele they can begin by surveying the universe of data and information among those involved in a project or program. They can also search for external data bases of potential internal use. Extant data can then be used to develop "own source" explicit (codified) knowledge, through such means as libraries, map inventories, strategic plans, fact sheets and policy guides, focused studies, surveys, conferences and workshops, electronic bulletin boards, process reviews, long range plans, models and simulations, and market studies. Although tacit (noncodified) knowledge is harder to deal with it can be approached through stakeholder consultations, best practices or benchmark exchanges, workgroups as "communities of practice," study project report panels, expert presentations, specialized workshops, SWOT workshops, hands-on technical assistance, community leadership development sessions, forums on "what works," direct agency outreach, "help desks," and public hearings. Fourth, the agency can work at the explicit/tacit interface through informal feedback on the myriad of activities they engage, usually through some informal postproject assessment. Finally, some of the knowledge needs of partner agencies the agency works with can be served through formal reports, responses for data requests, supplying modeling and planning data, circulating policy reports, sponsoring in-agency forums and report sessions, providing technical expert linkages, and in possibly providing agency-requested studies.

8. Establish support through electronic communication. It will come as no surprise that all of these knowledge activities are now supported by the use of different types of information and communications technology (ICT): E-mail, teleconferencing, Web-based geographic information sys-

tems, decision-support software, and the like. These are essential tools since partners are situated in disparate organizational locations. However, because of the collaborative nature of their tasks, they are not a substitute for face to face, but a parallel mode of collaborative work. In the same way that organizations seek structured predictability, organized collaborative actions require the use of open-ended processes of coordinating purposeful individuals who can apply their unique skills and experiences to particular problems confronting the collaborative undertaking at hand. They are part of the distributed knowledge systems that are created across boundaries, possessing somewhat fewer constraints or rule-bounded actions. Often at the center of such relationships, the conductive agency needs to foster ICT links along with the more direct community-building mentioned above.

9. Calibrate, assess, and account for values added. Agency managers should not, as Bardach suggests, be impressed by the idea of collaboration per se, but only if it produces better organizational performance or lower costs than its alternatives (1998, p. 17). The rationale for investment in collaboration normally entails more than collective public purpose, vaguely understood, but also those advantages collaboration can bring to each partner's mission and operations and to the specialists and managers as professionals. Thus, value adding can be accounted for from the perspective of the (a) administrator/specialist, (b) participating organization, (c) network process, and (d) network outcomes. This value adding helps to bridge the gap of difficult-to-measure outcomes by shifting the ground to intermediate ones (Wye, 2002, p. 27).

Most important with regard to the conductive agency the processes of joint engagement can provide the potential value in both process and tangible ways. From a process standpoint, collective rather than authority-based organizing, decision making, and programming prevail but follow group dynamics similar to these of single organizations (Agranoff, 2003; McGuire, 2002). Managing a collaborative enterprise involves formal or informal benchmarking of joint "steering" of interaction processes (Kickert & Koppenjam, 1997, p. 47) that sequence: activation, framing, mobilizing, and synthesizing adjustment (Agranoff & McGuire 2001). These actions contribute to productive collaborative products. Tangible outcomes vary considerably by joint undertaking but specific products can include Web sites, service agreements, mutual referrals, joint investment projects, incidents of business assistance, loans arranged, grants facilitated, investments leveraged, and so on. Another set of tangible results includes end states of collaborative processes: adapted policies, joint or collaborative databases, exchanged resources, new program interfaces, mutually adapted technologies, and enhanced interagency knowledge infrastructures (Agranoff & McGuire 2001; Kickert & Koppenjan 1997;

O'Toole 1997). These are examples of the type of values that conductive agency managers must focus their output assessments toward when they monitor, measure, and otherwise account for performance.

CIVIC ENGAGEMENT AND THE CONDUCTIVE AGENCY

Since the focus of this chapter is on the agency itself, the so-called rules of engagement for citizen and other organized groups will necessarily be briefly identified. That work has been carefully addressed by others (Bryson, Crosby, & Stone 1966; Cooper et al., 1996; Fung 2004; Smith & Ingram, 2002).

1. Public agencies are not necessarily a barrier to civic engagement. Skocpol (1998, pp. 39-40) suggests that contrary to those who view federal social policies as harmful to voluntary groups, popularly rooted voluntary associations have often grown up in a mutually beneficial relationship with federal policies, even tax and spend programs. They have not choked off voluntary efforts, but have increased them. Moreover, "most local voluntary groups are directly or indirectly linked to parallel efforts across many communities, states, regions, and (often) the entire nation. People in local groups take heart or example from what others linked to them are doing at the same time elsewhere." It has allowed for local participation and democracy to be combined with state and national collective decisions. This is one way that conductive public agencies are engaged.

2. Civic engagement in collaborative management with the public agency. Bottom-up local efforts, citizen boards, and joint administrator private agency executive/citizen efforts, and multi-organization alliances, partnerships and networks help to breakdown the "towering bureaucracies of elites and experts" in government and nonprofits who have vested interests in nationalization of community (Schambra, 1988, p. 48). In hundreds of communities small groups and organizations are battling problems like inadequate housing, fighting teen gangs, dealing with substance abuse, educating children and developing neighborhood economies. It appears imperative that these interests advance their causes by engaging the conductive agency.

3. Consensus is essential. In engaging the conductive public agency the mission and legal requirements of the agency need to be blended with those organized self-interest. As Wolfe (1998) has pointed out, despite high level political divisiveness in public life a vibrant civil society flourishes as people focus on mutual problem solving. It means finding that line between self-interest and those of others. "That is what civil society means: it is the place where people, neighborhoods, and communities

define, mediate, and argue as they work to forge consensus. The common theme in all of these struggles is empowerment, both for the individual and the community as a whole" (Solo & Pressberg, 1998, p. 83). Problem-solving cannot be left to government alone, because enhanced policies emerge from collaborative efforts between conductive agencies and the interests of citizens and communities.

4. Privatization of government raises additional burdens on engagement. For example, third party organizations such as managed care firms that contract with government or garbage collection firms have little incentive to involve citizen and community interests. Many are part of large for-profit chains making the relationship between government and citizens more indirect (Smith & Ingram 2007). As a result, engagement and decision influence is difficult and puts extra burdens on citizens organizations despite the fact that such contracting makes the public agency more conductive.

5. Nonprofit contracting, voucher programs, and other means of government-to-community organization linkages enlist new constituencies in public service delivery. Many nonprofits and community organizations have developed a "keen stake in government funding and regulatory policy" (Smith & Ingram 2002, p. 57). This in turn has led to trade associations of service providers who organize politically on individual and collective bases, some of whom have a stake and role in policy development. This is the case, for example, with state associations of agencies that serve the developmentally disabled. Conductive agencies are now used to dealing with this type of advocacy/coparticipation.

6. Recognition of the learning component of engagement with government. Identified as the New Citizenship by Rimmerman (2005, 5), it is based on the idea that people are not born citizens but require education and training and experience through regular community participation, grass roots mobilization, service learning and the use of the internet as a participatory vehicle. "The New Citizenship is also an important means for bridging the ever increasing gap between the public sphere (the area of the intersection between an individual's interests and those of the larger community) and the private sphere (the locus of the individual's own interests."

7. Participation in public dialogue. To engage in deliberation involves joint learning and multiple flows of communication, involving "the degree to which they include the general public, occur in a public space, foster genuine deliberation, privilege different forms of discourse, are empowered by government, and focus on policy-specific outcomes" (Booher, 2005, p. 65). Public dialogue is critical in forming policy, argues Matthews (1994) because people need time to reflect, listen, digest, and be exposed to many sides of a question. "A public dialogue is a natural home

for democratic politics. It is a home that people feel forced out of and want back into" (p. 42).

8. Empowerment along with dialogue. "The new vigour of civil, society reflects a large increase in the capacity and will of people to take control of their own lives and to improve or transform them" (Commission on Global Governance, 1995, p. 35). Empowerment entails taking action beyond voting, controlling peoples' destinies in their neighborhoods, cities, states, and more. It may include various self-help programs/homeowners' associations and cooperatives), control over local enterprises (community development corporations), neighborhood improvement and business associations, power over credit or retail transactions and practices, self-protection from fraudulent and abusive practices, and building of leadership skills (advocacy, group process, speaking). Empowerment enhances one's ability to engage in the dialogue, exert leadership and deal with important policy issues (Booker, 2005).

9. Leadership and connectivity with the conductive public agency. There are clearly no magic formulas for organized interests to deal with the new public sector. It clearly involves the best of collaborative methods, of which there are many important and venerable books and manuals on public organizing (e.g. Bacow, 1995; Brody, 1992; Ross 1973). One of the most experience based is the process formulation by Chrislip and Larson (1994, pp. 52-54), where they found nine keys to successful collaboration: (1) good timing and clear need, (2) broad-based involvement, (3) credibility and openness of process, (4) commitment of high-level and visible leaders, (5) support or acquiescence of established governmental bodies, (6) overcoming mistrust and skepticism, (7) strong leadership of the process, (8) initially creating smaller or interim successes, and (9) a shift to broader concerns as the effort evolves.

10. Understand that despite a public agency's conductivity it remains an administrative unit of government. The government is the authoritative repository of values. Its decisions, regulations, codes, while potentially malleable, represent current legitimization. As Michael Walzer (1998, p. 138) reminds us, "I want to warn against the antipolitical tendencies that commonly accompany the celebration of civil society. The network of associations incorporates, but it cannot dispense with, the agencies of state power." This then, is what he calls the paradox of civil society. "Citizenship is one of the many roles that members play, but the state itself is unlike all other associations. It both frames civil society and occupies space within it, fixing the boundary conditions and the basic rules of associational activity, compelling association members to think about the common good." As Himmelfarb (1998, p. 121) once concluded, "The appeal to civil society is a salutary corrective to big government but should not be taken as an invitation to demean government itself."

These points of interest appear to be important for those involved in joint engagement with the conductive public agency. They represent not so much how to approach the conductive agency or how to advocate before it, but how to work with public managers and program specialists. In these ways government must be understood and respected as partners or cointerlocutors at the same time that those bureaucrats that engage external interest must shed earlier conceptions of the hierarchical, rule-bound or even command and control agency.

CONCLUSIONS

The public agencies illustrated here as conductive are not unique in any way. Thousands of city and county governments not only engage in similar development activities, but work externally with services-oriented citizen boards, contracts for services, and partner with other governments and nongovernmental entities. At the state level, most highway construction is by contracting by state transportation agencies and highway planning is shared with networks of metropolitan organizations. Many state human services agencies operate by vouchers, purchase care, contract for services or grants. State environmental management agencies administer federal legislation through its local governments and regulated industries and organizations. At the federal level, more and more agencies, such as, HUD, Community Development Block Grants, Economic Development Administration, Commerce-Small Business Administration, Health and Human Services, Medicaid and Older Americans Act all operate intergovernmentally, as contract and grant intermediaries, making them equally conductive. In various ways they all have to connectively engage, and to most, with forms of deliberative engagement.

Such engagement involves citizens and their organized interests working with government in a different kind of public agency to interactively develop knowledge-based decision and action. These new possibilities are captured by Boyte (1989, p. 5) in his influential book *Common Wealth*:

It is the central thesis of *Common Wealth* that new possibilities for a wider, more active democracy are beginning to emerge in the modern "information age." Effective citizen action in our times is possible if—and only if—citizens develop the abilities to gain access to information of all kinds (from the roads and sewers to educational, environmental, and economic patterns) and the skills to put such information to effective use. Moreover, the possibilities for a reinvigorated popular sovereignty are dependent not only on information and knowledge but also on what might best be called "wisdom": the ability to *guide* and frame action with integrative concepts and a clear, if flexible and evolving, set of public values and purposes. Thus, "commonwealth" in our times points especially to the importance of knowledge itself as a resource that needs to be shared, shaped, and governed by the political community of citizens.

It is, as Boyte concludes, an argument for the importance of public life, community and active citizenship.

For the administrator in the conductive agency it means more than listening at hearings, engaging in information exchanges, dealing with advocates and adversaries, or taking cues from voting returns. It involves working together to create public dialogue over problems of mutual concern. This is the emergent role for the public administrator/program professional in the public agency. Calibration of external information, concerns and needs are now part of a regularized connectivity through interactive joint problem resolution processes. Conductive public agencies work with clients, from calibration to knowledge to strategy to implementation—all collaborative processes. Nonconductive, mostly hierarchic public agencies follow the older textbooks and merely calibrate.

REFERENCES

Agranoff, R. (1986). *Intergovernmental management: Human services problem-solving in six metropolitan areas*. Albany: State University of New York Press.

Agranoff, R. (1998). Partnerships in public management: Rural enterprise alliances. *International Journal of Public Administration, 21*(11), 1533-1575.

Agranoff, R. (2001). Managing within the matrix: Does collaborative federalism exist?" *Publius: The Journal of Federalism, 31*(Summer), 31-56.

Agranoff, R. (2003). *Leveraging networks: A guide for public managers working across organizations*. Arlington, VA: IBM Endowment for the Business of Government.

Agranoff, R. (2005). Managing collaborative performance: Changing the boundaries of the state?" *Public Performance and Management Review, 29*(1), 18-45.

Agranoff, R. (2007). *Managing within networks: Adding value to public organizations*. Washington, DC: Georgetown University Press.

Agranoff, R., & McGuire, M. (2001). Big questions in public network management research." *Journal of Public Administration Research and Theory, 11*(3), 295-326.

Agranoff, R., & McGuire, M. (2003). *Collaborative public management: New strategies for local governments*. Washington, DC: Georgetown University Press.

Agranoff, R., & McGuire, M. (2000). Administration of state government rural development policy. In J. J. Gargan (Ed.), *Handbook of state government administration* (pp. 385-420). New York: Marcel Dekker.

Bacow, A. F. (1995). *Designing the city: A guide for advocates and public officials*. Washington, DC: Island Press.

Bardach, E. (1998). *Getting agencies to work together*. Washington, DC: Brookings Institution Press.

Booker, D. E. (2005). A call to scholars from the collaborative democracy network. *National Civic Review, 94*(3), 64-67.

Boyte, H. C. (1989). *Common wealth: A return to citizen politics*. New York: The Free Press.

Brody, R. (1992). *Problem solving: Concepts and methods for community organizations* (2nd ed.). New York: Human Sciences Press.

Bryson, J. M., Crosby, B. C., & Stone, M. M. (2006). The design and implementation of cross-sector collaborations. *Public Administration Review, 66*(6): 44-55.

Campbell, A., & Gould, M. (1999). *The collaborative enterprise*. Reading, MA: Perseus Books.

Chrislip, D. D., & Larson, C. E. (1994). *Collaborative leadership*. San Francisco: Jossey-Bass.

Clegg, S. R. (1990). *Modern organizations: Organization studies in the postmodern world*. London: Sage.

Commission on Global Governance. (1995). *Our global neighborhood*. Oxford, England: Oxford University Press.

Cooper, T. L., Bryer, T. A., & Meek, J. W. (2006). Citizen-centered collaborative public management. *Public Administration Review, 66*(6): 76-88.

Davenport, T. H. (2005). *Thinking for a living: How to get better performance and results from knowledge workers*. Boston: Harvard Business School Press.

Davenport, T. H., & Prusak, L. (2000). *Working knowledge: How organizations manage what they know*. Boston: Harvard Business School Press.

Derber, C. (2002). *People before profits*. New York: Picador/St. Martin's.

Drucker, P. F. (2001). *The essential drucker: Selections from the management works of Peter F. Drucker*. New York: Harper Collins.

Forester, J. (1999). *The deliberative practitioner: Encouraging participatory planning processes*. Cambridge, MA: MIT Press.

Fung, A. (2004). *Empowered participation: Reinventing urban democracy*. Princeton: Princeton University Press.

Fung, A. (2006). Varieties of participation in complex governance. *Public Administration Review, 66*(6), 66-75.

Groff, T. R., & Jones, T. P. (2003). *Introduction to knowledge management*. Amsterdam: Butterworth-Heinemann.

Haas, P. M. (1990). *Saving the Mediterranean: The politics of international environmental cooperation*. New York: Columbia University Press.

Haas, P. M. (1992). Introduction: Epistemic Communities and International Policy Coordination. *International Organization, 46*(1), 1-35.

Henton, D., Melville, J., & Walesh, K. (1977). *Grassroots leaders for a new economy: How civic entrepreneurs are building prosperous communities*. San Francisco: Jossey-Bass.

Himmelfarb, G. (1998). Second thoughts on civil society. In E. J. Dionne, Jr. (Ed.), *Community works: The revival of civil society in America*. Washington, DC: Brookings Institution Press.

Kickert, W. J. M., & Koppenjan, J. F. M. (1997). Public management and network management: An overview. In W. J. M. Kickert, E. -H. Klijn, & J. F. M. Koppenjan (Eds.), *Managing complex networks* (pp. 000-000). London: Sage Publications.

Lukensmeyer, C. J., & Torres, L. H. (2006). *Public deliberation: A manager's guide to citizen engagement*. Washington, DC: IBM Center for The Business of Government.

Matthews, D. (1994). *Politics for people*. Urbana: University of Illinois Press.

McGuire, M. (2002). Managing networks: Propositions on what managers do and why they do it. *Public Administration Review, 62*(5), 426-433.

Metcalfe, R. (1996). *The Internet after the fad*. Retrieved December 15, 2003, from http://americanhistory.si.edu/csr/comphist/montic/

O'Toole, L. J. (1997). Treating networks seriously: Practical and research-based agendas in public administration. *Public Administration Review, 57*(1), 45-52.

Pasternack, B. A., & Viscio, A. (1998). *The centerless corporation*. New York: Simon & Schuster.

Rimmerman, C. A. (2005). *The new citizenship: Unconventional politics, activism, and service* (3rd ed.). Boulder, CO: Westview.

Ross, D. K. (1973). *A public citizens action manual*. New York: Grossman.

Saint-Onge, H., & Armstrong, C. (2004). *The conductive organization*. Amsterdam: Elsevier.

Salamon, L. M. (1995). *Partners in public service*. Baltimore: Johns Hopkins University Press.

Salamon, L. M. (Ed.). (2002). The new governance and the tools of public action. In *The tools of government* (pp. 1-47). New York: Oxford.

Schambra, W. A. (1998). All community is local: The key to America's civic renewal. In E. J. Dionne, Jr. (Ed.), *Community works: The revival of civil society in America*. Washington, DC: Brookings Institution Press.

Skocpol, T. (1998). Don't blame big government: America's voluntary groups thrive in a national network. In E. J. Dionne, Jr. (Ed.), *Community works: The revival of civil society in America* (pp. 37-43). Washington, DC: Brookings Institution Press.

Smith, S. R., & Ingram, H. (2002). Policy tools and democracy. In L. M. Salamon (Ed.), *The tools of government* (pp. 565-584). New York: Oxford.

Smith, S. R., & Lipsky, M. (1993). *Nonprofits for hire: The welfare state in the age of contracting*. Cambridge, MA: Harvard University Press.

Solo, P., & Pressberg, G. (1998). Beyond theory: Civil society in action." In E. J. Dionne, Jr. (Ed.), *Community works: The revival of civil society in America* (pp. 81-87). Washington, DC: Brookings Institution Press.

Thomas, C. W. (2003). *Bureaucratic landscapes: Interagency cooperation and the preservation of biodiversity*. Cambridge, MA: MIT Press.

Walzer, M. (1998). The idea of civil society: The path to social reconstruction. In E. J. Dionne, Jr. (Ed.), *Community works: The revival of civil society in America* (pp. 123-144). Washington, DC: Brookings Institution Press.

Wenger, E. (2000). Communities of practice: The key to knowledge strategy. In E. L. Lesser, M. A. Fontaine, & J. A. Slusher (Eds.), *Knowledge and communities* (pp. 3-20). Boston: Butterworth-Heinemann.

Williamson, T., Imbroscio, D., & Alperovitz, G. (2005). *Making a place for community: Local democracy in a global era*. New York: Routledge.

Wolf, T. (1999). *Managing a nonprofit organization in the twenty-first century*. New York: Simon & Schuster.

Wolfe, A. (1989). *One nation, after all*. New York: Viking Press.

Wye, C. (2002). *Performance management: A "start where you are use what you have" guide*. Arlington, VA: IBM Endowment for the Business of Government.

Yang, K., & Callahan, K. (2005). Assessing citizen involvement efforts by local governments. *Public Performance and Management Review, 29*(2), 191-216.

PART II

CASE-BASED PERSPECTIVES ON
CIVIC ENGAGEMENT AND NETWORK SOCIETY

CHAPTER 6

CIVIC ENGAGEMENT AS COLLABORATIVE COMPLEX ADAPTIVE NETWORKS

David E. Booher

Our economy, society, and culture are built on interests, values, institutions, and systems of representation that, by and large, limit collective creativity, confiscate the harvest of information technology, and deviate our energy into self-destructive confrontation. This state of affairs must not be. There is no eternal evil in human nature. There is nothing that cannot be changed by conscious, purposive social action, provided with information, and supported by legitimacy. (Castells, 1998, pp. 359-360)

INTRODUCTION

Thus Castells concludes his seminal three volume investigation of the network society with a pessimistic diagnosis and hopeful prognosis. How can we collectively change this state of affairs? How can we collectively realize the conscious and purposive social action provided with information and supported by legitimacy? This chapter starts from the assumption that such a change requires thinking about civic engagement and democracy in new ways. I argue that emerging practices in collaborative planning

Civic Engagement in a Network Society
pp. 111–148
Copyright © 2008 by Information Age Publishing
All rights of reproduction in any form reserved.

and social mobilization and research in complex adaptive networks offers insights into how civic engagement and democracy may evolve so the social action Castells envisions can be realized.

But as Machiavelli observed centuries ago, "There is nothing so hard as to change the existing order of things" (1952, p. 9). Many scholars and practitioners have pointed out the dilemmas and strains of democracy, leading to what Castells calls the "crisis of democracy" (1997). Certainly addressing these strains and tensions is not an easy task. But I hope to show that thinking about civic engagement in democracy as collaborative complex adaptive networks (CCANs) can lead to new insights about how practices can be purposively changed to create a path to civic engagement in democracy. We can take advantage of the dynamics and structures of complex adaptive networks to speed us along the path. In this view, civic engagement is not solely about individual citizens voting and showing up at public hearings to voice their concerns. Nor is it solely about bringing all citizens together to reason jointly. Instead, it's also about emerging structures of networks of publics around common identities, consulting with each other and with administrative agencies that carry out the public's work. But taking advantage of these structures and their dynamics requires new ways of thinking and working together, for both public agencies and civic leaders, based on collaborative processes and heuristics.

My argument in this chapter will proceed along the following lines. In the next section I will briefly summarize some of the challenges for civic engagement in democracy as it is embodied in existing institutions. Democracy has largely become an inside game among politicians, the media, and special interests which has little meaning for much of the public except as entertainment value. Many deliberative democracy theorists have offered an alternative to aggregative and adversarial democracy, but this intellectual project is also troubled by critiques and contradictions that seem to create a shadow over its long-term prospects. The arguments of both proponents and critics will inform the model I will sketch out for the relevance of CCANs later in the chapter. Then in the following section I will briefly summarize the growing practice of collaborative planning. Collaborative processes in policy and planning have become an important dimension of these fields. These processes bring stakeholders together in structured deliberations where they are able to jointly craft innovative paths forward while learning from each other and transforming their relationships. I will use these processes to help inform the model by suggesting how they may help clarify the conditions and procedures for a theory of deliberative democracy that addresses many of the critiques of that theory.

Next I will briefly summarize some of the research in the structure and dynamics of complex adaptive networks as it may apply to thinking about civic engagement. Complex adaptive networks are networks of agents that interact dynamically and nonlinearly in an open system so as to generate novelty and emergent adaptive patterns. These patterns create a tension that maintains the system between falling into stasis and spinning off into chaos. Scientists use the phrase "at the edge of chaos" to describe this tension. Complexity science grew out of the work of physical and biological scientists (Holland, 1992, 1998; Kauffman, 1995; Waldrop, 1992). Increasingly their research is informing studies of social systems and organizations, and hopefully it will help inform the sketch in this chapter.

I will bring the argument together in section five by suggesting how CCANs are relevant for civic engagement in what Castells (1997) calls a "reconstructed democracy." But in keeping with the approach of this argument, I will use a different metaphor for the task: an *evolving democracy*. Metaphors are important because, as Lakoff and Johnson (1980) have pointed out, metaphors structure the concepts that guide our actions. For example, how we deal with conflict will be different if we view it as a "battle" than if we view it as a "dance." In my view, democratic change isn't so much about building something as it is about nurturing learning networks and communities of networks that are both robust and capable of adapting. They are robust in the sense that they can resist serious threats to their viability. They are adaptive in the sense that they can learn and innovate to evolve in the face of a changing world. I will suggest a sketch for CCANs that may be helpful in thinking about how to nurture such learning networks. Central to this sketch is the role that collaborative heuristics play in guiding interactions. For this reason I call such a network a "collaborative complex adaptive network" (CCAN). I will also offer specific suggestions for steps we can take to help enable the emergence of CCANs and a comparison of how civic engagement in these networks differs fundamentally from traditional views of the practices of institutions of democracy.

I will make the argument more tangible in section six by summarizing the case of CALFED, a complex adaptive network that evolved to address stalemate in California water policy. In this case the complex adaptive network evolved around heuristics and practices grounded in collaborative processes and informed by public involvement. The characterization of CALFED as evolved rather than as created is deliberate. CALFED was established as a rudimentary interagency agreement among state and federal agencies. But my summary will show that in fact it evolved from this form to a much more complex entity. Indeed it continues to evolve even today as it is buffeted by the dilemmas and strains of trying to operate in the context of aggregative and adversarial democratic practice. I will suggest that CALFED evolved into a network that demonstrated many of the features of a CCAN and that it provides insights about what such a network looks like in a policy management issue domain. In the conclusion I will note the existence of a key element for CCANs, the emergence of social mobilization, and speculate about the future of civic engagement in network society.

THE CRISIS IN DEMOCRACY

By many accounts democratic institutions leave much to be desired, especially as those institutions relate to engaging citizens. Partially in response to the critiques a new theory of democracy, deliberative democracy, is emerging. This theory posits that deliberative institutions should at least supplement, if not replace, the focus on adversarial processes and aggregative decision making relying on contemporary voting practices. However, many scholars have pointed out dilemmas for such deliberative institutions. My own view is that deliberative democracy offers much potential if it is informed with lessons from the field of collaborative planning and policy.

Based on his survey of the network society, Castells concludes about the state of representative democracy that "public opinion, and citizens' individual and collective expressions, display a growing and fundamental disaffection *vis a vis* [sic] parties, politicians, and professional politics" (1997, p. 343). Similarly the British political theorist Dunn, in his survey of the history of democracy, argues that democracy as it is currently practiced:

> cannot hope to render professional politics ingratiating to most of us anywhere for any length of time; and it duly fails to do so. It guarantees a disconcerting combination of shabbiness of motive and pretense to public spirit throughout most of the cohorts of practicing politicians. (2005, p. 183)

Indeed a myriad of scholars argue that the public is disengaging from democracy's political institutions, leaving these to be controlled by a small corps of inside players (Burnham, 1982; Cappella & Jamieson, 1997; Gitlin, 1995; Habermas, 1989; Hunter, 1991; Inglehart, 1997; Nye, Zelikow, & King, 1997; Phar & Putnam, 2000; Rahn, 1997; Wattenberg, 1994). Mutz (2006) found that citizens who engage in heterogeneous networks where they are exposed to opposing view points are less likely to participate in traditional political activities than those who do not. Little wonder that Hibbing and Theiss-Morse found in their research that the public doesn't even want to be involved in traditional politics (2002). Perhaps Patterson states it most succinctly:

Ordinary citizens have been buffeted by developments they do not control and only vaguely comprehend, and which have diminished their stake, interest, and confidence in elections. The great tools of democracy-its electoral institutions and media organizations-have increasingly been used for private agency. Personal ambition now drives campaigns, and profit and celebrity now drive journalism. Candidates, public officials, and journalists operate in a narrow world that is largely of their own making and that is remote from the world of the public they serve. (2002, p. 22)

Parallel or perhaps convergent with this assessment are those who argue that on the whole the public is not well enough informed to be involved in the political system. In this view an informed electorate is indispensable for democracy because lack of knowledge prevents government from reflecting their will. Lack of public knowledge also opens the door for manipulation of the public and serious policy errors caused by politicians' need to appeal to an uninformed public. The conclusion is "overwhelming evidence suggesting that the American electorate fails to meet even the most minimal criteria for adequate voter knowledge" (Somin, 1998, p. 414).

Surveying the current state of democratic theory, Shapiro builds on Schumpeter's view of democracy as a competition between teams of politicians for the public's vote and the power to govern that flows from that vote. He argues that this competitive view of political institutions was "intended to both embody and advance the idea that democracy should be geared to limiting domination" (2003, p. 146). At least this competitive form of democracy among elites offers the prospect of minimizing oppression. Of democracy he says "we should recognize its claim to our allegiance as the best alternative system for managing power relations among people who disagree about the nature of the common good, among many other things, but who nonetheless are bound to live together" (p. 148). Castells recognizes this minimalist view of the existing institutions of democracy, while acknowledging both its inadequacy for the network society and its impact on citizens:

But the new institutions have made obsolete the existing party system, and the current regime of competitive politics, as adequate mechanisms of political representation in the network society. People know it, and feel it, but they also know, in their collective memory, how important it is to prevent tyrants from occupying the vanishing space of democratic politics. Citizens are still citizens but they are uncertain of which city, and of whose city. (1997, p. 349)

Public agency performance is also implicated in this crisis of democracy. In his recent review of the state of public administration Kettl observed, "The challenge facing government administrators in the twenty-first century is that they can do their jobs by the book and still not get the job done" (2002, p. 22). Lack of civic engagement in agency decision making is one factor in this performance challenge. Without that engagement agencies are handicapped in developing policy choices that take into account the diversity of public concerns and respond to the uncertainty, fragmentation, and rapid change in society. Agencies play a key role in the CCAN model I will sketch. Of particular significance here is the state of public participation in public administration. Many laws and practices often discourage deliberative engagement by the public (Bohman, 1996; Boxer-Macomber, 2003), and reforms are often directed to gain public support, or at least acquiescence, to decisions agencies have made rather than to involve citizens in those decisions (Innes & Booher, 2004). Hence, with the current state of democratic institutions it seems improbable that the public will actively participate in politics.

While there are numerous tinkering prescriptions offered by scholars and practitioners to reform public agencies, many of these do not recognize the changed context of the network society. As one administrative law scholar has argued, such reforms do not respond to the most serious weaknesses of the present public agencies because they are based on an adversarial administrative decision-making process driven by interest representation. Instead she argues collaborative governance, joint problem solving, broad participation of the public, sharing of regulatory responsibility across the public-private divide, and flexible engaged agencies are required (Freeman, 1997). A change is needed in these institutions for civic engagement in policy to become a reality.

Since the 1990s many political theorists have been debating an alternative to existing democratic institutions and a prescription for the "crisis of democracy" that has come to be called deliberative democracy (Bohman, 1996; Bohman & Rehg, 1999; Cohen, 1999; Dryzek, 2000; Fishkin & Laslett, 2003; Gutman & Thompson, 1996; Richardson, 2002). These theorists differ on such matters as the goal and conditions for deliberative democracy to be democratic, the appropriate procedural requirements, the design of deliberative institutions, and the relations between reason and politics. (Even if existing democratic practices were perceived as fair and "democratic," they might not be deliberative.) They also differ on whether deliberative democracy is focused on deliberation among citizens or among elites. A common definition for deliberative democracy is suggested by Bohman and Rehg: "Broadly defined, *deliberative democracy* [emphasis in original] refers to the idea that legitimate lawmaking issues from the public deliberation of citizens … it presents an ideal of political autonomy based on the practical reasoning of citizens" (1997, p. ix). The suggestion is that deliberative processes are more likely to result in laws that are recognized as legitimate and are in fact more rational and just. They are also more likely to bridge differences between citizens. Finally, proponents argue deliberative democracy will be better at realizing the core normative values of autonomy, equality, and responsiveness to the public good.

Broadly speaking deliberative democracy as discussed by many theorists requires that four conditions must be met.

1. Action must be suspended to create the opportunity for cooperative engagement by the participants.
2. The process must be inclusive with all parties affected included or alternatively all points of view represented.
3. The deliberation must be public so that those who are affected but not involved can be informed and potentially respond to the content.
4. The results of the deliberation must be binding on all involved.

Generally four procedural requirements are advocated by many theorists for deliberations.

1. All participants must be free to speak and have their views heard respectfully.
2. Each participant must have equal opportunity to speak and present his/her case.
3. The outcomes must be consistent with the democratic principles of equality and autonomy.
4. The deliberation must consist primarily of communications to make each other's views heard and to understand the meaning and reasoning of others in their own terms.

Deliberative democracy has generated extensive critical assessment as well (Berkowitz, 2003; Macedo, 1999). Space does not permit a discussion of these critiques here. But two of them that are relevant to this discussion go to the practicality of deliberative democracy within the existing form of democratic institutions and the realism of meeting the conditions and/ or maintaining the procedures that deliberative democracy requires:

> But deliberative processes can be manipulated by people with ulterior motives, they can marginalize the inarticulate (who will also be those most vulnerable to domination), and they can result in stonewalling by the powerful in the face of needed change. (Shapiro, 2003, p. 148)

Shapiro goes on to suggest that he is not advising a rejection of deliberation. Rather, he "suggested that the right to insist on it is best placed in the hands of those whose basic interests are at stake in a given setting" (p. 148). I will revisit his suggestion in section five when I sketch out a model for the relevance of CCANs to civic engagement.

For now it is useful to point out that some theorists have taken up the challenge of the practicality of deliberative democracy in the present institutions of democracy. They have focused on the role of administrative agencies. Bohman proposes three principles for democratic legitimacy:

1. If they result from a fair and open participatory process in which all publicly available reasons have been respected;
2. If the outcome is such that citizens may continue to cooperate in deliberation rather than merely comply; and
3. If this process makes the public deliberation of the majority the source of sovereign power (1996, p. 187).

He then argues that the mechanisms of the interchange between elected representatives and the public are not sufficient for ensuring deliberation. Hence we must focus on bureaucratic agencies because "Only then do occasions for public input provide opportunities to resist the bureaucratic tendencies of taking more and more issues out of the public sphere and making them matters for administrative or economic efficiency rather than practical reason" (p. 187). Bohman goes on to argue that:

Indeed, the interchange between public and bureaucratic and administrative institutions constitutes the biggest challenge for public deliberation. Democracy itself has made such institutions necessary in order for laws and policies to be exercised and enacted. Without their own public spheres, such institutions are invested with too much unchecked power. At the very least, such political publics can make administrative institutions more reflexive and democratic, governed by public reason. (p. 188)

Bohman suggests that administrative processes should be provided to ensure such interchange. "In democratically structured administration, citizens should be regarded not as passive citizens but as sources of information and judgments, especially concerning the contextual features of applying laws and agreements to specific local situations" (p. 189).

In a similar vein Richardson argues that:

It is necessary to examine whether and how democratic input can be brought to bear on administrative rulemaking in such a way as simultaneously to take further account of citizens' voices and to keep agency decision within bounds set by the legislature, thereby fulfilling the demanding ideal of nondomination that arises from interpreting the concept of nonarbitrary power in a liberal-populist way. (2003, p. 219)

He dismisses traditional notice and comment as not providing sufficiently for public participation. Instead he writes:

> In order to participate more seriously in a process of continued deep compromise at the rulemaking stage, representatives of the public would need to be able to engage with one another and with agency representatives in a face-to-face process of debate and negotiation. (p. 220)

Richardson points to the U.S. Negotiated Rulemaking Act of 1990 as an illustration. This act provides for agencies and stakeholders to engage with each other in drafting of administrative rules.

In the second critique discussed here Rosenberg takes up the conditions and procedures for deliberative processes. While he is sympathetic to the cause of the deliberative democracy proponents, he believes the conditions and procedures assume certain capacities of individuals that empirical evidence does not support:

> I argue here that the foundational assumptions regarding individuals over estimate their cognitive abilities, incorrectly equate the abilities of all individuals, and fail to attend to the emotional dimension of interpersonal relations. Consequently the social dimension of cognition is underestimated and the relationship between cognition, communication and community is misunderstood." (in press)

He points to research from psychology that suggests individuals are not likely to think about policy issues in a logical, rational manner or engage in reasoned argument and consider the reasoned arguments of others. In addition this research indicates that some individuals reason in a structurally more developed way than others creating an inequality in "the ability to be logical, to be self-reflective, to take the perspective of the other, to construct arguments, to understand policy problems, and to comprehend issues of fairness" (in press). Finally Rosenberg argues that deliberative processes require a certain degree of positive emotional engagement not taken into consideration by most accounts of deliberative democracy.

Rosenberg's project is not intended to discredit deliberative democracy, but to revise it consistent with these facts. Hence deliberation can not be just about liberation and equality. "It must also be about transformation and constructive engagement.... Deliberative institutions must also be designed as pedagogical devices for fostering the capacity for personal autonomy and constructive interpersonal relations that the governance of the lives of real people requires" (in press). He offers several suggestions for how to accomplish this. Rosenberg's conception is a more activist approach to the deliberative process that converges with the growing practice of collaborative planning to which I will now turn.

COLLABORATIVE PLANNING PRACTICE

Collaborative planning is a broad term encompassing many types of cooperative efforts (Booher, 2004; Healey, 1997; Innes & Booher, 1999b). But this chapter focuses on processes in which individuals representing differing interests engage in long-term, face-to-face dialogue, seeking agreement on strategy, plans, policies, or actions. The processes are often ad hoc and self-organizing. They are sometimes established by government agencies to deal with what seem to be intractable problems, and sometimes put together by developers, environmentalists, and other private players frustrated by years of conflict and stalemate, or threatened with loss of a limited, common resource (Innes, Gruber, Neuman, & Thompson, 1994; Ostrom, 1990). Processes range in size from a handful of participants to hundreds organized into interlocking committees and task forces, each working on different aspects of complex questions.

Collaborative planning is summarized here at its purest form as a process that is truly facilitated, as opposed to merely chaired. A professional neutral facilitator or a chair acting as a neutral facilitator may help the group establish equality among the stakeholders and achieve the ability to have a free-wheeling dialogue. The processes use special meeting management techniques that allow all participants to be heard and be informed, support different ways of knowing, and encourage dialogue that is both respectful and open-ended. These processes go beyond the conditions and procedures typically offered by deliberative democracy theorists and suggest steps and details that are crucial for deliberative processes.

The processes also go beyond the assumption that seems to be implicit in theoretical discussions about deliberative procedures that participants can be brought together for rational dialogue without conscious attention to the dynamics of group processes generally (Johnson & Johnson, 1997) and a process design. They include the kind of techniques Rosenberg and others discuss to help grow affective connections, cognitive capacity, and connections across the boundaries of different ways of knowing (Feldman, Khademian, Ingram, & Schneider, 2006; Rosenberg, in press). For example they often include time for informal interactions such as shared meals; time set aside for personal story telling; field trips to jointly experience the real world dimensions of the issue being addressed; and the sharing of artifacts or objects such as pictures, models, graphs and reports. Notably research has shown that story telling, role playing, and group intellectual bricolage are more prevalent forms of discussion and joint reasoning than trade offs and logical argumentation (Innes & Booher, 1999b) The techniques discourage the taking of positions, instead following the interest-based model of bargaining (Fisher, Ury, & Patton, 1991). Assumptions and constraints are not taken for granted, but explored, often using a process of joint fact finding which recognizes different ways of knowing about the issues under discussion and helps create conditions for participants' joint learning about the issues they face (Corburn, 2005; McCreary, 1999).

The processes also are based on significant preparation and planning, often with guidance by a neutral facilitator, for a design that reflects both the dynamics among the stakeholders and the content of the issues under discussion (Booher, 2004; Straus, 2002; Susskind & Cruikshank, 1987). The process typically includes five phases: assessment, convening and organization, joint fact finding, deliberation and negotiation, and implementation. (Space allows only a summary of these phases. For more detail see Booher, 2007; Straus, 2002; Susskind & Cruikshank, 2006; Susskind, McKearnan, & Thomas-Larmer 1999.)

Assessment

The collaborative process design begins with an assessment—a research effort that involves interviewing potential stakeholders and persons knowledgeable about the topic. Potential stakeholders include both representatives of groups affected by the issue and representatives of public agencies responsible for the issue. Often public agencies serve as conveners of collaborative processes. Hence collaboration is consistent with the suggestion of some theorists about the importance of administrative agencies for deliberative democracy (Bohman, 1996; Richardson, 2002). The assessment provides data about the issues, the different perspectives and interests of stakeholders regarding the issues, the relationships and power dynamics among the stakeholders, the political context that may affect a collaborative process, and whether the stakeholders are willing to participate in a collaborative process. It also surfaces networks with which the stakeholders are engaged. The assessment has multiple purposes. First, it informs all parties of whether the conditions are present to potentially bring the stakeholders together. For example if a needed stakeholder is unwilling to participate, moving forward does not make much sense. In addition the assessment provides the facilitators and planners with information about the stakeholders, the issues, and the dynamics to inform the preparation of a process design. It also identifies stakeholders not previously recognized who need to be involved. Third, the assessment is a way to inform the stakeholders and other interested publics about each other's perspectives and engage them in the design of the process. The draft assessment is typically circulated among the stakeholders for their review and comment. These comments are then reflected in the final version, which is made available to the general public as well as the constituents of the stakeholders. Fourth, the assessment is a pedagogical technique that informs the stakeholders about the nature of the collaborative process. This includes a discussion about the collaborative process during the interviews and review of the assessment draft report by the stakeholders.

Organization and Convening

In the second phase, organization and convening, the facilitators work with the stakeholders to design the process that will be used for the remaining phases, starting from the draft suggested in the assessment. Four points related to organization and convening are useful for this discussion because they may augment the conditions and procedures for deliberative democracy. First, the process is inclusive and self organizing. The stakeholders participate and must agree to the final version for the process to go forward. Although the process is typically revised along the way, this is done with stakeholder consent. Any stakeholder is free to withdraw from the process at any time. Hence the process meets the suggestion of Shapiro that those most knowledgeable about the issues are responsible for convening and designing the process they will use (Shapiro, 2003), and the condition of theorists that deliberative processes must be inclusive. But it does not meet the precondition proposed by many theorists that decisions of the deliberation must be binding on all participants.

Second, this phase includes crafting ground rules that are agreed on by all stakeholders. In a sense the ground rules are the constitution of the deliberations. The ground rules include the procedures and standards of conduct that will be adhered to, as well as the consequences for violations. These include the procedural requirements for communication and speech advocated by theorists as noted above. They also include decision rules, how decisions will be made along the way. Typically while seeking consensus, they do not require unanimity, rather relying on some version of a super majority. Hence they are consistent with Bohman's suggestion for a deliberative process (Bohman, 1996). The ground rules also specify how stakeholders' constituents and other interested publics are to be kept informed and involved, thus addressing one of the typical conditions for deliberation set forth by theorists. Finally, they include provisions for how action on the issue will be held in abeyance, or if not, how the stakeholders will relate to each other in other arenas while the deliberations continue. This is a departure from the ideal for deliberations typically offered by theorists. Frequently action in other arenas cannot be delayed and stakeholders agree with each other on how they will manage between the deliberations and the other arenas for action. A phrase for this dynamic that is commonly used in the practice is "living in two worlds."

Third, the deliberative process that is designed in this phase typically includes the element of multiple groups and task forces working on various elements of the problem under deliberation, as well as times when the entire group will be brought together to consider the issues and make decisions. This departs from the treatment of many theorists who seem to assume that a deliberation always involves all of the stakeholders. This is not feasible within the context of group processes with large meetings because it is difficult to achieve the kind of interactions and sharing of information that is required for deep understanding and relationship transformations that evolve shared identities. Finally, planning for the deliberation in the organization phase is a pedagogical experience because the stakeholders learn more about collaboration and communication methods during the process.

Joint Fact Finding

In the third phase, joint fact finding, the group works together to develop a common understanding of the issues. This often requires significant resources, but it is essential to create a foundation for stakeholders to generate and experiment with possible options. Two points are central to help clarify deliberative processes. First, the group does not immediately launch into deliberations and negotiations about how to solve the problem. Instead they work together to gain a shared understanding about the important facts to help inform their decision making and help create new options. Deliberative democracy theorists do not typically provide for such a step. They seem to assume that the public can engage in deliberations without much preparation. Second, the joint fact finding is not limited to facts about the issue. It also importantly includes education by the stakeholders of each other's interests and concerns and their different ways of knowing about the issue. In joint fact finding the stakeholders also draw on the indigenous knowledge of their respective networks. This activity goes to the concern of Rosenberg about the inequality of cognition among stakeholders because it surfaces up differences that can be addressed in the deliberative process.

Deliberation and Negotiation

In the fourth phase, deliberation and negotiation, the stakeholders engage with each other about how to solve the problem before them. Two points are important about this phase for the discussion here because they also may augment theories of deliberative democracy. First, the process encourages stakeholders to invent approaches that respond to all the interests of the stakeholders, instead of debating the merits of their various positions. Only if they fail to find mutual-gain solutions that they can all agree to do they resort to traditional distributive bargaining and trade-offs. Hence collaborative processes include both deliberation and the bargaining which many theorists have been skeptical of. Second, the process is consensus seeking. Every effort is made to find solutions that all stakeholders can support. If this is not possible (and often it's not) then stakeholders search for a solution that they can live with and still allow future deliberations to be possible. Hence collaboration is consistent with Bohman's suggestion that a key condition for deliberation is that it results in an outcome in which participants can continue to deliberate together (1996). During deliberation and negotiation the stakeholders draw on their networks to test options for agreement, generate still more options, and build support for future agreement. The deliberation phase also includes how the decisions will be implemented, what actions each of the participants are responsible for, and assurances of accountability among the stakeholders. The stakeholders set the context for continued deliberation as needed during implementation.

Implementation

In the final phase, implementation, the stakeholders work together to carry out the agreement if one has been reached. A key point here is that in a world of uncertainty and rapid change the agreement is likely to require adaptation along the way to be successful. The implementation phase creates the space for the stakeholders to continue deliberating about the changed conditions and how they will jointly or individually respond, setting up the context for adaptive management of the resource, problem, or issue.

Collaborative planning owes a substantial debt to the practice and literature of negotiation, mediation, public dispute resolution, and consensus building which have produced techniques for meeting management that ensure a civil environment where all can express their interests and become informed, where constructive dialogue can occur despite conflict, and where consensus is the goal (Susskind et al., 1999). Such face-to-face communication allows the sincerity, legitimacy, comprehensibility, and accuracy of statements to be tested, and the inclusion of opposing stakeholders makes it highly likely that assumptions are questioned. Innes and I use the phrase "authentic dialogue" to name these communication procedures (Booher & Innes, 2002). Innes has equated this communicative ideal to communicative rationality as articulated by the social theorist Habermas (1984, Innes, 1998).

A number of conditions distinguish ideal collaborative planning from other forms of cooperation:

1. Inclusion of a full range of stakeholders.
2. A task that is meaningful to the participants.
3. Participants who set their own ground rules for behavior, agenda setting, making decisions, and many other topics.
4. A process that begins with mutual understanding of interests and avoids positional bargaining.
5. A dialogue, preferably aided by a neutral facilitator, where all are heard and respected and equally able to participate.
6. A self-organizing process unconstrained by conveners in its time or content and which permits the status quo and all assumptions to be questioned.
7. Information that is accessible and fully shared among participants.
8. An understanding that "consensus" is only reached when all interests have been explored and every effort has been made to satisfy these concerns.
9. Explicit and transparent steps to link the agreement to means of implementation.
10. Review of the draft agreement by the networks of stakeholders and the public (Innes, 2004).

Collaborative planning can lead to several results besides agreements and ending stalemates. It can enhance trust among stakeholders and generate political and social capital. It can lead to innovations that are more adaptive and context dependent than the existing practices for the policy issue. It can lead to agreed on information among stakeholders and shared understandings, as well as changes in beliefs, attitudes, and behaviors. These are often carried over into future cooperative activities among them (Innes & Booher, 1999a; Connick & Innes, 2003).

COMPLEX ADAPTIVE NETWORKS

Theory and research on complexity from the fields of physical and biological sciences are increasing being used to inform thinking about social systems and organizations (Allen, 2001; Axelrod & Cohen, 1999; Bar-Yam, 2004; Braha & Bar-Yam, 2006; Brown & Eisenhardt, 1997; McKelvey, 2001; Stacey, 1996, 2001; Uden, 2005). Insights from complex adaptive systems can help inform our effort to evolve democracy so that it is more meaningful in the context of the network society. My hope is also that these insights may help inform the research on networks in planning and policy by many scholars in the United States, Canada, and Europe (Agranoff, 2006; Healy, 2005; Howlett, 2002; Innes, 2005; Le Gales, 2001; Schneider, Focht, Lubell, Mindruta, & Edwardsen, 2003).

I start from a similar perspective as to that of Toffler who more than 20 years ago, in looking at the challenges for business, argued: "Instead of being routine and predictable, the corporate environment has grown increasingly unstable, accelerative, and revolutionary.... The adaptive corporation, therefore, needs a new kind of leadership. It needs managers of adaptation equipped with a whole set of new, nonlinear skills" (1984, p. 2). Since then many corporations have adopted insights from complexity science to their organization as can be seen from numerous case studies. For example some of these look at response to change (Brown & Eisenhardt, 1997), product design (Chiva-Gomez, 2004), innovation (Rose-Anderssen, Allen, Tsinopoulos, & McCarthy, 2005), organizational development (van Eijnatten & van Galen, 2005), and strategy (Allen, Boulton, Strathern, & Baldwin, 2005; Eisenhardt & Tabrizi, 1995).

My argument is based on two assumptions from complexity science, one epistemological and one purposive. First, democratic systems are not objective realities that researchers can stand outside of and observe so that they can be modeled, predicted, and, in some way, controlled. They are much too complex and too dependent on our individual experiences of them (Cilliers, 2005; Stacey, 2001; Tsoukas, 2005). Instead

> we have to give up the notion that we can understand the system by formulating hypotheses and then seeking to disconfirm them. Instead we have to reformulate what we are doing as trying to make more sense of our own and others' experience of organizational life. (Stacey, 1996, p. 262)

Second, my purpose is not to propose an institutional design for an evolved democracy that better integrates civic engagement. Instead my purpose is to better understand how an evolved democracy could emerge. "The purpose of theory and research is then to undertake how conditions might be established within which spontaneous self-organization might occur to produce emergent outcomes." (Stacey, 1996, p. 264)

I summarize five key features of complex adaptive systems from the literature relevant to the discussion because they are helpful in making sense of the structure and dynamics of CCANs (Cilliers, 2005; Stacey, 2001; Tsoukas, 2005).

1. **Agents:** The system comprises large numbers of individual agents connected through multiple networks.

2. **Interactions**: The agents interact dynamically, exchanging information and energy based on heuristics that organize the interactions locally. Even if specific agents only interact with a few others the effects propagate through the system networks. As a result the system has a memory that is not located at a specific place, but is distributed throughout the system.

3. **Nonlinearity:** The interactions are nonlinear, iterative, recursive, and self-referential. There are many direct and nondirect feedback loops.

4. **System behavior:** The system is open, the behavior of the system is determined by the interactions, not the components, and the behavior of the system cannot be predicted by examination of the components. The behavior cannot be understood by looking at the system as whole. It can only be understood by looking at the interactions (Schelling, 1978; Stacey, 2001). Coherent and novel patterns of order emerge.

5. **Robustness and adaptation:** The system displays both the capacity to maintain its viability and the capacity to evolve. With sufficient diversity the heuristics will evolve, the agents will adapt to each other, and the system can reorganize its internal structure without the intervention of an outside agent.

The agents of a CCAN, such as stakeholders, are linked together in a network structure, either directly or through hubs, and to other networks through switching nodes and hubs, creating clusters or community structures. Several types of "roles" related to these linkages in the network are played by the different nodes (Guimera & Amaral, 2006). One aspect of network structure that comes out of sociological research is relevant to this discussion. Granovetter argues that one's acquaintances (what he calls weak ties) are less likely to be socially engaged with one another than are our close friends (strong ties). Weak ties are a low-density network and strong ties are a dense network. Individuals with few weak ties will be deprived of information from distant parts of the social system compared to those with many weak ties. The effect of this is that:

> social systems lacking in weak ties will be fragmented and incoherent. New ideas will spread slowly, scientific endeavors will be handicapped, and sub-groups separated by race, ethnicity, geography, or other characteristics will have difficulty reaching a *modus vivendi*. (Granovetter, 1983, p. 202)

He uses the phrase the "strength of weak ties" (SWT) to capture this phenomenon. Significant empirical research seems to support his argument (Granovetter, 1983). Weak ties are similar to "bridging" connections that Putnam describes (Putnam & Feldman, 2003); for a detailed discussion of network structures see Barabasi, 2003.)

There are several dynamics of the interactions of the agents that are relevant because they help us make sense of the way agents interact in a CCAN over time (Allen, 2001; Braha & Bar-Yam, 2006; Guimera, Uzzi, Spiro, & Amaral, 2005; Mitchell, 2006). First, network structures are not static. Instead the roles of nodes (agents) in the network change over time, often on a frequent basis. (Consider a stakeholder who is a link to another related network who takes on new responsibility in his organization and thereby ceases to be such a link.) The existence of a link between two agents at one time does not make it much more likely that a link will appear between them at some later time. In addition the nodes that are prominent in terms of being highly connected with other nodes are not necessarily important in daily networks. (For example a high level official who is an important hub in the aggregate network may not be very active in daily interactions.) New networks of teams are continually self-organizing and disbanding. Experience from earlier networks may inform the agents in creating new networks of teams.

Second, system information is encoded as data and dynamics of patterns over the system's components, not in one place. The information is accessed by sampling data acquired by the network's component agents locally from other agents they encounter, or the environment. It is also the agents who interpret the information and take action based on that interpretation. (For example in ant colonies a nest-maintenance ant switches to foraging only if it encounters enough of other successful foragers.)

Third, randomness and probability of the agents' interactions with each other and with data are key aspects of the dynamics. This creates multiple possible responses where diverse possible actions can be explored and potentially amplified. "An important point is that much exploration will be entirely accidental, resulting from ignorance, and the inherent impossibility of transmitting information perfectly" (Allen, 2001, p. 153).

> It appears that such intrinsic random and probabilistic elements are needed in order for a comparatively small population of simple components...to explore an enormously larger space of possibilities, particularly when the information to be gained is statistical in nature and there is little a priori knowledge about what will be encountered. (Mitchell, 2006, p. 1200)

However randomness is balanced with intention. The network system continually adjusts probabilities for actions and how deeply to explore particular options.

> What will also matter over time, however, is how the rest of the system acts on the results of these explorations, rewarding the more successful explorations with high pay-off and amplifying them, while suppressing the others. Indeed, it is the rest of the system that defines 'success' for an exploratory behavior and either amplifies or suppresses it. (Allen, 2001, p. 153)

Fourth, the network system carries out a fine-grained, parallel search for possible options. Because the network is composed of many members of relatively simple agents that work together in a parallel fashion, there can be a simultaneous exploration of many possible actions and options. However, not all possibilities are explored at the same speeds or to the same depth. Information is used as it is gained to continually reassess what is important to explore.

Finally, the network system exhibits a constant interplay of bottom-up and top-down processes. Maintaining the balance between these is crucial for success, and the balance may shift over time. As information is obtained by the early bottom up explorations and acted on, exploration gradually becomes more intentional, focused, and top down, in response to what has been perceived by the network system. Holland (1992) has argued that exhibiting such a shift in exploration mode is a general property of adaptive and intelligent systems.

One additional point is helpful to our understanding of the composition of complex adaptive networks because it indicates the importance of diversity in a CCAN. The world is characterized by profound uncertainty and the impossibility of knowing how many different things can change. If a network system is to respond successfully to this in the future, than it must have within itself more diversity than is necessary for its functioning at present. As a consequence, Allen has proposed the "law of excess diversity": "For a system to survive as a coherent entity over the medium and long term, it must have a number of internal states *greater* than those considered requisite to deal with the outside world" (2001, p. 175; See also

Morgan's concept of "requisite variety" [1986]). This means that either there is deep diversity within the network system or it has the means to generate diversity when it's required. It also implies that some overhead of maintaining an underlying diversity or the means to generate it must be carried before it is shown to be necessary. This brings into focus an underlying instrumental need for inclusion of the full range of diverse stakeholders in a deliberative process to complement the normative one offered by theorists.

EVOLVING DEMOCRACY

My task in this section is to sketch out a model for the relevance of collaborative complex adaptive networks (CCANs) for civic engagement in democracy. As I stated earlier my purpose is not to propose a design for democratic institutions integrating civic engagement. My purpose is to suggest conditions by which democratic institutions may evolve to integrate civic engagement and provide more meaningful and sustainable governance for the network society. Two caveats are appropriate to this model. First, I do not argue that the model is fully existent today. Rather I suggest that the elements of the model exist and that these elements could evolve so that the model could emerge. I also suggest that there are practical steps that we can take to facilitate this emergence. Second, this is an ideal type model and is incomplete. The world is much too complex for any model to show all the necessary components and relationships. And the model needs much iteration to bring it closer to the real world.

The core concept of this model is that civic engagement in democracy can occur through participation of citizens in policy deliberations through many interconnected networks of interest and geography. These networks link citizens together with each other and with their administrative agencies. As Le Gales (2001) notes, the hope is that "the integration of different policy networks paves the way to reintroducing politics, legitimacy, public sphere, collective choice" (p. 170). The heuristics of collaborative planning guide the interactions among the citizens in this posited system of networks.

This model departs from both the competitive view of democracy as described by Shapiro and the deliberative theory of democracy described by its proponents. Rather it includes features of each. From competitive theory it includes the concept that individuals pursue their own interests in the best way that they can, and that they do this through interactions with each other and with public agencies. It departs from the concept that these interactions are largely aggregative and adversarial. Instead it posits that they are also collaborative, guided by specific heuristics and norms. From deliberative democracy theory it includes the concept that citizens must deliberate together and that these deliberations must be guided by conditions and procedures. It departs from the nature of some of these, such as the emphasis on reasoning, and augments the deliberation procedures with more specific details. For now the model does not take up the normative concern of theorists that the outcomes should be consistent with the democratic values of autonomy and equality. This is a task of theory building and empirical research for a later time. Leach (2006) has made an excellent start on the task of addressing normative issues.

In this sketch of a CCAN, citizens engage with each other in networks and clusters of networks about issues they care about. In addition to the networks which include those of similar concerns, cultures, and interests (strong ties), they are also connected to other networks that have different concerns, cultures, and interests (weak ties). These networks may be composed of interest groups, non profits, civic groups, and public agencies for example. They are periodically connected through stakeholder hubs in clusters with administrative agencies working on various policy issues that are "wicked problems" (Rittel & Webber, 1973). These are stakeholder processes with many subnetworks. In a sense these issue driven policy networks are a "hub" in a "network of networks." The policy network and the cluster of networks around it are characterized by diversity and interdependence. The full range of parties affected, all points of view, and all relevant sources of knowledge are represented. These parties are interdependent because they recognize their success depends upon others in the network. The system of networks is in constant motion and transition. Links are continuously being added and lost. Roles of nodes are constantly changing.

The policy network agents evolve procedures and norms of collaborative planning. These become the heuristics for local interactions. These heuristics propagate through the system of clustered networks and gradually become the interaction heuristics for the system as a whole. Energy and information flow between the policy network and organizations and individuals in the network of networks. Hundreds or even thousands of individuals may be connected. Energy and information also flow from these agents to the policy network.

The system of networks carries out a "bottom up," fine-grained parallel search for possible options relevant to the issues, exploring a large space of possibilities. Because many possibilities are being explored by many agents, imperfect information and miscommunication are tolerated and compensated for. Results from these explorations of options feedback through the network system and agents adjust their explorations to take account of this feedback. Some options are explored faster and more deeply. The policy network focuses on the most promising of the options. As it modifies and amplifies its attention to specific options this information feeds back through the network system in a "top down" way that focuses more attention of the agents on those options. The policy network and administrative agencies act on some of those options. The results of these actions are observed and explored by the network system and the process starts over, informed by the exploration. As a result of the diversity of the agents in the system and the flow of information through the system, it is capable of generating the diversity of internal states necessary to deal with the changes and uncertainty of the outside world. Novelty and variety are created for actions that were previously not envisioned.

More broad based civic engagement may be encouraged. Agents in the policy network may use the structure and dynamics which has evolved to address other community problems. They now may have more common identities, for example relating to their community or their common concerns, and shared meaning about the nature of the problems they face. They also have new heuristics about how to work together despite their differences. Clusters of networks within the policy network may use their connections and interaction heuristics to explore jointly other mutual problems they confront. They may grow to create a new system network, bringing in other agents that are affected by the new problem or implicated in the problem. These networks also may be capable of influencing political institutions. For example, when legislation is needed the agents can focus the energy and information of the network system on achieving influence within the political power dynamics of the legislature. How many politicians are willing to ignore environmental, business, civic, agricultural, and local government groups when they all agree on needed action regarding an environmental issue?

Figure 6.1 is a simplified rendering for the foundation of this model (DIAD) displaying its crucial conditions (diversity, interdependence), and process (authentic dialogue), the results of the conditions and process, and the expected adaptations of the system. (Booher & Innes, 2002). (The word "heuristics" in this figure refers both to new interaction heuristics and to new heuristics for solving problems.)

There are six practical steps that can be taken to facilitate the emergence of this model.

1. Agency leaders can convene stakeholder processes for the wicked problems (Rittel & Webber, 1973) they confront, using collaborative planning procedures and heuristics, and encouraging the network structure and dynamics summarized above. I agree with Bohman, Putnam, and Richardson that administrative agencies are crucial to the future of civic engagement in democracy (Bohman, 1996; Putnam & Feldman, 2003; Richardson, 2003).

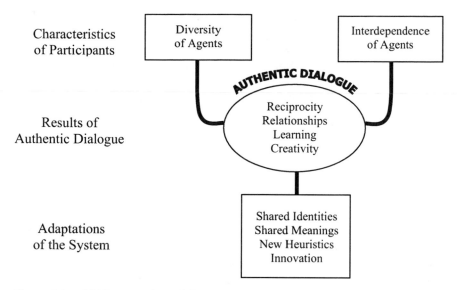

Figure 6.1.   DIAD network model.

2. Leaders of stakeholder groups, such as interest groups, nonprofits, businesses, civic groups, and local governments, can focus on developing "bridging" connections with other dissimilar groups. Funding agencies can provide resources to help these groups overcome the significant challenges of developing and sustaining these nascent weak ties (Putnam & Feldman, 2003).

3. Administrative agencies, interest groups, nonprofits, civic groups, and foundations can provide education on collaborative planning and working in complex adaptive networks for leaders and potential leaders.

4. Scholars can develop theory and carry out empirical research on questions that need to be addressed in order to better understand CCANs. Some of these include when and how these networks emerge and evolve; the policy outcomes; the extent to which they realize the democratic values of autonomy and equity, the strategies and methods that enhance their effectiveness; and the role of technologies in communication, decision analysis (Bankes, 2002) and group process (Schrage, 1990) in furthering civic engagement through the networks.

5. We can all think more deeply about the metaphors we use for democracy and policy that help us structure our concepts and the actions that flow from those concepts (Lakoff & Johnson, 1980).

For example, we often think of policy as being a "machine" and problems as being evidence the machine is "broken." This leads us to think we need to deconstruct the machine, find the broken part, and "fix" it. If we think of policy as an organism we are led to different concepts and actions. We may recognize that the organism is much too complex, change much too volatile, and our knowledge much too limited to deconstruct and fix anything. Instead we may think of problems as signals that the organism's sustainability is at risk, of actions as what interventions we can make to improve its robustness and adaptability, and of monitoring the results of our intervention to guide further interventions.

6. We can all rethink and modify some of our ideas about the work of planning and management. Traditionally planning is understood as a linear stepwise process flowing from goals through analysis, formulation, and implementation. This model infers that a different nonlinear idea may be needed for planning, similar to that shown in Figure 6.2. In this figure the boxes indicate the activities of the process and the lines show the flow of energy and information among the activities. This model also infers that different activities and roles may be required for management and leadership (Roberts, 1997). Table 6.1 displays several of these compared to some traditional ideas about management.

AN EXAMPLE FROM CALIFORNIA WATER POLICY

In this section I will offer an example of the kind of structure and dynamics that may occur in a policy domain from the case of California's CALFED program. CALFED may be seen as a complex adaptive network that evolved to address stalemate in California water policy. This complex adaptive network evolved around heuristics and practices grounded in collaborative processes and informed by public involvement. The characterization of CALFED as evolved rather than as created is deliberate. CALFED was established as a rudimentary interagency agreement among state and federal agencies which itself emerged out of a number of water related networks that preceded it.

Two caveats are needed. First, space does not permit a complete inquiry into this example here. Instead I will only sketch some of the essential features of the case to help make sense of how a CCAN may self-organize and evolve in the context of a policy issue. Second, my objective is not to show that CALFED is an ideal type CCAN. Rather I hope to bring out some of the real-world manifestations of the structure and dynamics of a CCAN in a policy context. Moreover it is a relatively young

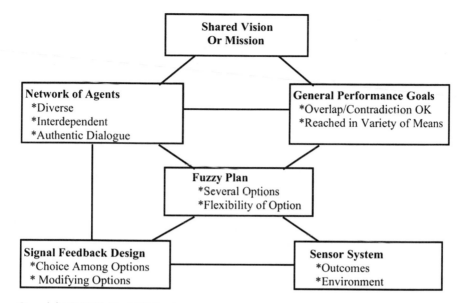

Copyright © 2000, David E. Booher.

Figure 6.2.   Network planning model.

Table 6.1.   Comparison of Ideas About Traditional and CCAN Management

Management Dimension	Traditional Management	CCAN Management
Structure	Hierarchical	Distributed networks
Source of direction	Top down	Bottom up and top down
Goals	Clear with defined problems	Various and changing goals and problems
Origin of system behavior	Determined by roles of participants	Determined by relational interactions of participants
Role of manager	Organization controller	Mediator, process manager
Managerial tasks	Planning and guiding organization process	Guiding interactions, providing opportunities
Managerial activities	Planning, designing, and leading	Engaging participants and resources, influencing conditions
Leadership style	Directive	Generative
Criteria for success	Attainment of the goals of formal policy	Realization of collective action
Organizational context	Single authority	Multiple authorities
Source of democratic legitimacy	Representative democracy	Deliberative democracy

program that is still undergoing change. It was and continues to be buffeted with forces generated by the traditional aggregative and adversarial
democratic institutions. How CALFED will evolve remains to be seen.
Indeed the dynamic over time between the traditional institutions and
CALFED is an interesting topic for further inquiry. (For a more complete
discussion of CALFED see Booher & Innes, 2006.)

The CALFED Bay-Delta Program emerged in December 1994 when
state and federal agencies signed a memorandum of understanding in
which they committed to jointly address four major (and sometimes conflicting) goals in the management of California water policy: water quality; ecosystem quality; water supply reliability; and levee system integrity.
This agreement became known as the Bay-Delta Accord (Rieke, 1996). It
became a collaborative effort to manage the state's far-flung water system
and ultimately it involved 25 state and federal agencies and more than 35
major stakeholder groups. The immediate apparent stimulus was the economic, environmental, and political strains on the state brought about by
the stalemated decision making up to that time. The political system of
pluralist pressure on legislatures, hierarchical public agencies with narrow
and conflicting mandates, and adversarial legalism through the courts
offered no opportunity for collective problem solving–only a promise of
continuing policy stalemate, deteriorating environmental conditions, and
dwindling or erratic water supply for users (Freeman, 1997). No one was
happy.

The 1994 agreement was possible because many of the agencies and
stakeholder groups had been engaged with each other in several other
collaborative networks. Stakeholder groups and public agencies had
accrued significant social, political and intellectual capital in the years
before through a series of processes, including the San Francisco Estuary
Project (Innes & Connick, 1999), a policy council set up by the governor,
and years of dialogue among three of the major stakeholder groups. This
context created a favorable interest group configuration, in which interests from the north and south, as well as from agriculture and urban water
purveyors, had already created coalitions as they had come to understand
that they could not get their needs met working on their own (Rieke,
1996). Environmentalists were well organized and able to participate in a
knowledgeable way. The business community was mobilized. Ultimately
these players came not only to see their interests as interdependent, but
also to agree that ecosystem restoration was essential. Hence, in a sense
CALFED was not a new network. It was the evolution of several networks
that had preceded it.

One of its extraordinary features was that it operated informally, without enabling legislative authority, for more than a decade while at the
same time making major changes in the way water was managed and

investing billions in ecosystem restoration projects (Innes, Connick, & Booher, 2007) Rather than a distinct governance form, CALFED created "transversal linkages that cut across the formal structures, practices, and boundaries of established organizations, creating linkages in the interstices between them" (Healey, 2005, p. 311). Hence, CALFED operated within the "shadow" of the existing institutions, that is, within the existing legal framework of environmental protection, water rights, and agency mandates, but not as an agency with its own mandate, procedures or rules. It can be understood as a shadow system at work amidst the traditional system (Stacey, 1996). "The key notion here is that of a space for creativity at the operational level, which consists of a psychological state in the shadow system that puts it in tension with the legitimate system" (p. 265). As Stacy has pointed out this has major implications for management. One of these "is the tremendous importance of the shadow system as the generator of the mess and disorder that are vital if a learning, evolving system is not to be trapped on a local fitness peak" (p. 264).

Since CALFED was a new space created in the shadow of the traditional system, the agents participating in CALFED were faced with how to sustain such a new practice within the limitations of the traditional governmental and political context. CALFED did things for which there was no official authorization, in ways that were not business as usual. It created collaborative ways of addressing crucial problems of the Bay-Delta which could not have emerged from agencies making decisions independently of one another. Moreover CALFED deeply engaged stakeholders, not just in advisory or review and comment modes, but also in teams which actually did the work of designing programs and participated directly in water management decisions. This is one of the central features of a CCAN that differentiates it from more traditional democratic institutions. Agency heads participated, contributed resources, and even adapted their agencies' activities.

CALFED was led by a Policy Group made up of heads of state agencies and high level officials from federal agencies. It was directly accountable to the governor and the U.S. Secretary of the Interior. A management team of agency deputy directors turned policy group decisions into action. The CALFED agencies had diverse and conflicting mandates. They came together, motivated in part by internal organizational needs, such as ensuring the agency's ability to put its appropriations to good use and securing the support of their constituencies and the legislature. The interdependence of their missions, their varied interests, resources, and power created a negotiating space. It provided the opportunity to move forward on agendas that had long been stalled.

CALFED included a shifting set of ad hoc task groups, engaging hundreds of agents over time and typically building trust and joint learning as well as finding creative solutions to issues or setting direction. These work groups offered forums for ideas to be aired, developed, tested, and improved. The groups created many of the processes and ideas that were carried forward. These small work groups also played key roles in what became CALFED's system of distributed intelligence and adaptive policy making, as the stakeholders linked to agents across the state and brought in up-to-date information from their direct knowledge about conditions and political issues. It exemplified the notion of a "networked water space" (Medd & Marvin, 2005).

Beyond the work of the ad hoc task forces, four interlinked groups played a central role by collectively providing advice about changes in operations of the water projects, advice which the policy group typically followed. These groups were made up of stakeholder representatives and agency staff from around the state. The operations group (Ops) coordinated operations of the water projects; another evaluated water supply alternatives; a third looked at the effects of water diversions on fisheries; and a fourth was a coordinating team made up of members of the other groups. Participants provided indicators about fish or water levels, which they monitored in their areas. They met by conference call when conditions required and worked together to analyze the implications of the data. They thus operated on a real-time basis, reacting quickly to changing conditions. This is in contrast to traditional management, where formal decisions must await formal analysis, rule-making, and public comment. Yet the process had a remarkable degree of legitimacy among stakeholders because they were engaged in it themselves and the effort was so transparent.

Although there were 25 agencies and 35 stakeholder groups participating in CALFED, all of these agencies and groups had numerous agents actually participating, including agents working at local and regional levels. An accurate account of the total number of agents is probably impossible because of the fluidity and open nature of the system. However, there were at least hundreds of direct agents and probably thousands of indirect agents in its civic engagement reach. As the above description illustrates the structure was characterized by the "patching" hierarchy that Kauffman (1995) has articulated. Patching is the concept that networks are structured in clusters instead of all directly with each other. As Stacey has argued, "patching reduces the number of connections across the whole system and so tends to stabilize it enough to avoid the destructiveness of highly unstable dynamics" (2001, p. 177).

CALFED provided for additional public involvement, to augment the civic engagement generated through the networks of stakeholder groups, through its Bay-Delta Advisory Council (BDAC). BDAC was made up of nongovernmental stakeholder representatives drawn from agriculture, environmental justice, business, tribal, and other interests. BDAC became a forum for stakeholders to air concerns. Agencies looked to BDAC, in the words of one participant, as a group where they could "gauge the likely zone of agreement" and "vet proposals [to] find out if you're in the range of a deal." BDAC meetings in different parts of the state also served as a "moving road show" for CALFED to present its ideas to the public, obtain information, and try to win support.

Subcommittees to BDAC did the real work that became part of what CALFED did, and they operated in a more informal way, relying more on collaborative dialogue. These groups focused on a range of tasks including ecosystem restoration, assurances, finance, water use efficiency, water transfers, drinking water, and watersheds. Subcommittee composition depended on the topic, but each committee included a diverse set of knowledgeable stakeholders, experts, and agency personnel. One group created the process for reviewing funding proposals and developed much of CALFED's watershed program. Some broke down in conflict. Meetings were not professionally facilitated nor were participants trained in collaborative dialogue, so much depended on the skills and social capital members already had acquired.

Finally, CALFED also provided technical and fiscal support to regional efforts, conducted statewide grant programs that required regional review, appointed regional coordinators and teams, conducted regional workshops, and integrated regionally developed goals and objectives into CALFED planning as part of its public involvement efforts.

Several innovations and adaptations emerged from CALFED. Two of the most interesting for purposes of this discussion illustrate both the new heuristics that evolved and a different non-linear planning approach that better fit the nature of a CCAN. The agents in CALFED evolved new collaborative heuristics for their interactions. As these emerged the participants recognized them, discussed them at meetings, and gave the new heuristics a name—"the CALFED way." Basically these heuristics included collaborative norms, emphasis on public involvement, multi agency and multi project reviews with a comprehensive framework, inclusion of local and regional decision making, joint independent science reviews, and process transparency and accountability. In their work they also emphasized flexible and adaptive management and learning.

The CALFED nonlinear planning approach as it evolved looked more like that in Figure 6.2 and less like the traditional approach to planning. It can be understood as emerging from a tension between the need to comply with the procedural mandates for agency decision making and the desire to have a collaborative long range planning process for an extremely complex resource system using extensive stakeholder and public involvement. Agencies were constrained by federal and state "sunshine" laws which, while trying to assure public involvement, ironically interfered both with open-ended, evolving, collaborative interactions of the agents and the ability to incorporate stakeholders directly (Boxer-Macomber, 2003). In addition the National Environmental Policy Act (NEPA) and California's equivalent (CEQA) called for linear, stepwise processes, which are at odds with the dynamic of collaborative interactions, which go back and forth between such things as idea generating and considering implementation issues.

To comply with procedural mandates CALFED followed standard early steps in the first phase: defining issues and problems; identifying possible actions; and refining them into alternatives for evaluation. In collaborative practice, however, defining issues and problems takes time and only occurs once agreement begins to emerge on solutions. Much happens simultaneously as participants become aware of the complexities and uncertainties. For the process to succeed the stakeholders realized there would have to be a package of actions with linkages among them and assurances to all the parties that their needs would be met. This could not be done in a linear way. Stepwise decision making would not assure the balanced outcomes necessary to resolve conflicts over the course of the program. Accordingly stakeholders moved away from the traditional planning approach in subsequent planning as they worked on the options and began taking agreed on actions. They developed six solution performance principles in the planning process that provided useful heuristics for further exploration of options. These criteria for choosing actions included that solutions should be affordable, equitable, implementable, and durable and they should reduce conflict and not redirect negative impacts. Establishing such criteria early on in a collaborative process follows best negotiation practice (Fisher et al., 1991). Critical to the degree of success that CALFED had in its planning was the fact that the agencies began with an agreed-on framework for working together on an agreed-on set of issues. No one had to precommit to anything. Moreover they did not set up detailed procedures. They could develop their interactions in their own way, relying on trial and error learning.

CALFED demonstrated two conditions of the DIAD network model. It was diverse, involving all the water policy stakeholders, and these stakeholders recognized and acted on their interdependence. Although the stakeholders' interaction heuristics evolved toward authentic dialogue, it was imperfect in many ways. Sometimes formal meeting laws interfered with the kind of free-wheeling and open atmosphere that is helpful for sincere and candid interchange (Bohman, 1996). The groups did not have professional facilitation and so had to rely on the chance that one of their members had acquired the skills to provide facilitation. In some cases this occurred and in some cases it did not. However, as a whole the process was collaborative and the stakeholders themselves recognized this as a transformation.

Despite this limitation the example is instructive of how the sketch of a CCAN suggested in the previous section is manifested in a policy issue context. CALFED was composed of many strong- and weak-tie networks connected to the various stakeholder task forces and subcommittees working with state and federal agencies. This structure of networks involved perhaps thousands of citizens through the stakeholder organizations' constituents and the regional level outreach to other interested citizens. The stakeholder organizations did not just review and comment on proposals by agencies, but also were involved in the search for options and making decisions about which options to pursue. Energy and information flowed up and down in the system of networks, despite changes of participants.

As options were identified by the hub of groups at CALFED, they became the focus of the system. It manifested the principle of both top down and bottom up control, the distributed search for option solutions, and the agent collection and interpretation of data. It also exhibited the ability to develop innovative approaches, even in the face of imperfect information and miscommunications. Most importantly it demonstrated the capacity to engage a large and diverse citizenry through its complex structure of task forces and subcommittees that were connected to local and regional constituencies and, through them, the interested public. Finally the stakeholders were able to obtain the support of the legislature and citizens to approve general obligation bond measures amounting to billions of dollars.

THE FUTURE OF DEMOCRACY IN NETWORK SOCIETY

In his survey of the Network Society Castells found three trends that he suggests are important for "potential paths of democratic reconstruction": the flourishing of local democracy in many places, the opportunity offered by electronic communication, and political mobilization around causes (Castells, 1997, p. 350). Each of these is important for the story of this chapter. Both local democracy and electronic technology play a crucial role in civic engagement through CCANs. The third trend however is particularly interesting because of the key role that political mobilization plays in this view of civic engagement. Here at some length is what he says:

> Most of the time these mobilizations are in between social movements and political actions, since they address themselves to citizens, asking people to put pressure on public institutions or private firms that can make a differ-

ence on the particular matter targeted by the mobilization.... Ultimately, their horizon is to act on the political process; that is, to influence the management of society by the representatives of society. But they do not necessarily, and in fact not frequently, use the channels of political representation and decision-making, for instance by electing their candidates to office. These forms of political mobilization, which could be defined as issue-oriented, non-partisan politics, seem to win increasing legitimacy in all societies, and to condition the rules and outcomes of formal political competition. They re-legitimize the concern with public affairs in people's minds and lives, thus furthering the crisis of classic liberal democracy while fostering the emergence of the yet to be discovered, informational democracy. (pp. 352-353)

It is in these entities that he sees the "embryos of a new society" (p. 362).

"A *networking decentered form of organization and intervention, characteristic of the new social movements,* mirroring, and counteracting, the networking logic of domination in the informational society" (emphasis in original). Likewise Bennett argues:

Replacing traditional civil society is a less conformist social world of the sort that Pool (1990) envisioned in which individuals were liberated from the grasp of governments: a society characterized by the rise of networks, issue associations, and lifestyle coalitions facilitated by the revolution in personalized, point-to-point communications. (1998, p. 745)

This is possible because the dynamics of power have changed in the network society. As Castells notes power is no longer concentrated in traditional political institutions. "*The new power lies in the codes of information and in the images of representation around which societies organize their institutions, and people build their lives, and decide their behavior. The sites of this power are people's minds*" (1997, p. 359, emphasis in original).

Putnam and Feldman chronicled 12 such successful "harbingers of a broader revival of social capital in this country" (2003, p. 5). Many other harbingers around the globe are being documented by scholars (Booher, 2004; Chrislip, 2002; Coenen, Huitema, & O'Toole 1998; Fung & Wright, 2003; Gastil & Levine, 2005; Innes & Rongerude, 2005; Office of the Deputy Prime Minister, 2003).

This evidence is the final strand in my argument because it demonstrates that the final element is present today for the evolution of CCANs as structures for civic engagement. These entities of political mobilization and social capital, together with administrative agencies, are the nodes that can be connected through collaborative complex adaptive networks to deliberate together about our future. As Mutz (2006) argues: "Only when such skills are equitably distributed—the ability to build and maintain diverse networks, and to evaluate and promote ideas through them—

will the metaphor of a marketplace of political ideas ring true for American political culture" (p. 150). By better understanding these nodes and the structure and dynamics of these networks and nurturing norms of collaborative interaction, we can help create conditions and take steps to evolve a democracy with civic engagement that better reflects the historic central value of the ideal of democracy—that the people rule themselves.

REFERENCES

Agranoff, R. (2006). Inside collaborative networks: Ten lessons for public managers. *Public Administration Review, 66*(6), 56-65.

Allen, P. M. (2001). A complex systems approach to learning in adaptive networks. *International Journal of Innovation Management, 5*(2), 149-180.

Allen, P. M., Boulton, J., Strathern, M., & Baldwin, J. (2005). The implications of complexity for business process and strategy. In K. A. Richardson (Ed.), *Managing organizational complexity: Philosophy, theory, applications* (pp. 397-418). Greenwich, CT: Information Age.

Axelrod, R., & Cohen, M. D. (1999). *Harnessing complexity: Organizational implications of a scientific frontier.* New York City: Free Press.

Bankes, S. C. (2002). Tools and techniques for developing policies for complex and uncertain systems. *PNAS, 99*(3), 7263-7266.

Barabasi, A. -L. (2003). *Linked: How everything is connected to everything else and what it means for business, science, and everyday life.* New York: Perseus.

Bar-Yam, Y. (2004). *Making things work: Solving complex problems in a complex world.* Newton, MA: NESCI.

Bennett, W. L. (1998). The uncivic culture: Communication, identity, and the rise of lifestyle politics. *Political Science and Politics, 31*(4), 741-64.

Berkowitz, P. (2003). The demagoguery of democratic theory. *Critical Review, 15*(1-2), 123-146.

Bohman, J. (1996). *Public deliberation: Pluralism, complexity, and democracy.* Cambridge, MA: MIT Press.

Bohman, J., & Rehg, W. (Eds.). (1999). *Deliberative democracy: Essays on reason and politics.* Cambridge, MA: MIT Press.

Booher, D. E. (2004). Collaborative governance practices and democracy. *National Civic Review, 93*(4), 32-46.

Booher, D. E. (2007). Collaborative governance. *Encyclopedia of public administration and public policy.* New York: Taylor & Francis.

Booher, D. E., & Innes, J. E. (2002). Network power in collaborative planning. *Journal of Planning Education and Research, 21*(3), 221-236.

Booher, D. E., & Innes, J. E. (2006). Complexity and adaptive policy systems: CALFED as an emergent form of governance for sustainable management of contested resources. *Proceedings of the 50th Annual Conference of the International Society of Systems Sciences.* Retrieved November 26, 2007, from www.csus.edu/ccp/publications

Boxer-Macomber, L. D. (2003). *To much sun?: Emerging challenges presented by California and federal open meeting legislation to public policy consensus building processes.* Sacramento, CA: Center for Collaborative Policy.

Braha, D., & Bar-Yam, Y. (2006). From centrality to temporary fame: Dynamic centrality in complex networks. *Complexity, 12*(2), 59-63.

Brown, S. L., & Eisenhardt, K. M. (1997). The art of continuous change: Linking complexity theory and time-paced evolution in relentlessly shifting organizations. *Administrative Science Quarterly, 42*(1), 1-34.

Burnham, W. D. (1982). *The current crisis in American politics.* New York: Oxford University Press.

Cappella, J. N., & Jamieson, K. H. (1997). *Spiral of criticism: The press and the public good.* New York: Oxford University Press.

Castells, M. (1997). *The power of identity.* Malden, MA: Blackwell.

Castells, M. (1998). *The end of millenium.* Malden, MA: Blackwell.

Chiva-Gomez, R. (2004). Repercussions of complex adaptive systems on product design management. *Technovation, 24*(10), 707-711.

Chrislip, D. D. (2002). *The collaborative leadership fieldbook: A guide for citizens and civic leaders.* San Francisco: Jossey-Bass.

Cilliers, P. (2005). Knowing complex systems. In K. A. Richardson (Ed.), *Managing organizational complexity: Philosophy, theory, applications* (pp. 7-20). Greenwich, CT: Information Age.

Coenen, F. H. J. M, Huitema, D., & O'Toole, L. J. (Eds.). (1998). *Participation and quality of environmental decision making.* Dordrecht, Netherlands: Kluwer Academic.

Cohen, J. (1999). Deliberation and democratic legitimacy. In J. Bohman & W. Regh (Eds.), *Deliberative democracy: Essays on reason and politics* (pp. 67-92). Cambridge, MA: MIT Press.

Connick, S., & Innes, J. (2003). Outcomes of collaborative water policy making: Applying complexity thinking to evaluation. *Journal of Environmental Planning and Management, 46*(2), 177-197.

Corburn, J. (2005). *Street science: Community knowledge and environmental health justice.* Cambridge, MA.: MIT Press.

Dryzek, J. S. (2000). *Deliberative democracy and beyond: Liberals, critics, and contestations.* Oxford, England: Oxford University Press.

Dunn, J. (2005). *Democracy: A history.* New York: Atlantic Monthly Press.

Eijnatten, F. van, & Galen, M. van. (2005). Provoking charordic change in a Dutch manufacturing firm. In K. A. Richardson (Ed.), *Managing organizational complexity: Philosophy, theory, applications* (pp. 521-556). Greenwich, CT: Information Age.

Eisenhardt, K., & Tabrizi, B. (1995). Accelerating adaptive processes: Product innovation in the global computer industry. *Administrative Science Quarterly, 40*(1), 84-110.

Feldman, M. S., Khademian, A. M., Ingram, H., & Schneider, A. S. (2006). Ways of knowing and inclusive management practices. *Public Administration Review 66*(6), 89-99.

Fisher, R., Ury, W., & Patton, B. (1991). *Getting to yes: Negotiating agreement without giving in* (2nd ed.). New York: Penguin Books.

Fishkin, J. S., & Laslett, P. (Eds.). (2003). *Debating deliberative democracy.* Oxford, England: Blackwell.

Freeman, J. (1997). Collaborative governance in the administrative state. *UCLA Law Review, 45,* 1-98.

Fung, A., & Wright, E. O. (2003). *Deepening democracy: Institutional innovations in empowered participatory democracy.* London: Verso.

Gastil, J., & Levine, P. (Eds.). (2005). *The deliberative democracy handbook: Strategies for effective civic engagement in the 21st century.* San Francisco: Jossey-Bass.

Gitlin, T. (1995). *The twilight of common dreams: Why America is wracked by cultural wars.* New York: Henry Holt.

Granovetter, M. (1983). The strength of weak ties: A network theory revisited". *Sociological Theory, 1*(1), 201-233

Guimera, R., & Amaral, L. A. N. (2006). Functional cartography of complex metabolic networks. *Nature, 159*(3), 895-900.

Guimera, R., Uzzi, B., Spiro, J., & Amaral, L. A. N. (2005). Team assembly mechanisms determine collaborative network structure and team performance. *Science, 308,* 697-702.

Gutman, A., & Thompson, D. (1996). *Democracy and disagreement.* Cambridge, MA: Harvard University Press.

Habermas, J. (1984). *The theory of communicative action.* Boston: Beacon Press.

Habermas, J. (1989). *Structural transformations of the public sphere: An inquiry into a category of bourgeois society.* Cambridge, MA: MIT Press.

Healey, P. (1997). *Collaborative planning: Shaping places in fragmented societies.* London: MacMillan.

Healey, P. (2005). Governance capacity, policy networks, and territorial specificities. In L. Albrechts & S. J. Mandelbaum (Eds.), *The network society: A new context for planning?* (pp. 307-311). London: Routledge.

Hibbing, J. R., & Theiss-Morse, E. (2002). *Stealth democracy: American's belief about how government should work.* Cambridge, England: Cambridge University Press.

Hollard, J. H. (1992). *Adaptation in natural and artificial systems.* Cambridge, MA: MIT Press.

Hollard, J. H. (1998). *Emergence: From chaos to order.* Reading, MA: Addison-Wesley.

Howlett, M. (2002). Do networks matter? Linking policy network structure to policy outcomes: Evidence from four Canadian policy sectors. *Canadian Journal of Political Science, 35*(2), 235-267.

Hunter, J. D. (1991). *Culture wars: The struggle to define America.* New York: Basic Books.

Ingelhart, R. (1997). *Modernization and postmodernization: Cultural, economic, and political change in 43 societies.* New York: Basic Books.

Innes, J. E. (1998). Information in communicative planning. *Journal of the American Planning Association, 64*(1), 52-63.

Innes, J. E. (2004). Consensus building: Clarifications for the critics. *Planning Theory, 3*(1), 5-21.

Innes, J. E. (2005). Networks and planning thought. In L. Albrechts & S. J. Mandelbaum (Eds.), *The network society: A new context for planning?* (pp. 57-61). London: Routledge.

Innes, J. E., & Booher, D. E. (1999a). Consensus building and complex adaptive systems: A framework for evaluating collaborative planning. *Journal of the American Planning Association, 65*(4), 412-423.

Innes, J. E., & Booher, D. E. (1999b). Consensus building as role playing and bricolage: Toward a theory of collaborative planning. *Journal of the American Planning Association, 65*(1), 9-26.

Innes, J. E., & Booher, D. E. (2004). Reframing public participation: Strategies for the 21st Century. *Planning Theory and Practice, 5*(4), 429-436.

Innes, J. E., & Connick, S. (1999). San Francisco estuary project. In L. Susskind, S. McKearnon, & J. Thomas-Larmer (Eds.), *The consensus building handbook: A comprehensive guide to reaching agreement*. Thousand Oaks CA: Sage Publications.

Innes, J. E., Connick, S., & Booher, D. E. (2007). Informality as a strategy of planning: Collaborative water management in the CALFED Bay-Delta program. *Journal of the American Planning Association, 73*(2), 195-210.

Innes, J. E., Gruber, J., Neuman, M., & Thompson, R. (1994). *Coordinating growth and environmental management through consensus building* (Policy Research Report). Berkeley: University of California.

Innes, J. E., & Rongerude, J. (2005). *Regional initiatives: Civic entrepreneurs work to fill the governance gap*. San Francisco: The Irvine Foundation.

Johnson, D. W., & Johnson, F. P. (1997). *Joining together: Group theory and group skills*. Needham Heights, MA: Allyn & Bacon.

Kauffman, S. A. (1995). *At home in the universe: The search for laws of self-organization and complexity*. London: Viking.

Kettl, D. (2002). *The transformation of governance: Public administration for the 21st century*. Baltimore: Johns Hopkins University Press.

Lakoff, G., & Johnson, M. (1980). *Metaphors we live by*. Chicago: University of Chicago Press.

Leach, W. D. (2006). Collaborative public management and democracy: Evidence from the field. *Public Administration Review, 66*(6), 100-110.

Le Gales, P. (2001). Urban governance and policy networks: On the urban political boundaries of policy networks: A French case study. *Public Administration, 79*(1), 167-84.

Macedo, S. (Ed.). (1999). *Deliberative politics: Essays on democracy and disagreement*. New York: Oxford University Press.

Machiavelli, N. (1952). *The prince* (W. K. Marriott, Trans.). Chicago: Great Books of the Western World, Encyclopaedia Britannica.

McCreary, S. (1999). Resolving science-intensive public policy disputes: Reflections on the New York bight initiative. In L. Susskind, S. McKearnon, & J. Thomas-Larmer (Eds.), *The consensus building handbook: A comprehensive guide to reaching agreement* (pp. 829-858). Thousand Oaks CA: Sage Publications.

McKelvey, B. (2001). Energising order-creating networks of distributed intelligence: Improving the corporate brain. *International Journal of Innovation Management, 5*(2), 181-212.

Medd, W. P., & Marvin, S. (2005). Complexity and spatiality: Regions, networks, and fluids in sustainable water management. In K. A. Richardson (Ed.), *Man-*

aging organizational complexity: Philosophy, theory, applications (pp. 493-504). Greenwich, CT: Information Age.

Mitchell, M. (2006). Complex systems: Network thinking. *Artificial Intelligence, 170*(18), 1194-1212.

Morgan, G. (1986). *Images of organization.* Beverly Hills, CA: Sage.

Mutz, D. (2006). *Hearing the other side: Deliberative versus participatory democracy.* New York: Cambridge University Press.

Office of the Deputy Prime Minister. (2003). *Participatory planning for sustainable communities: International experience in mediation, negotiation and engagement in making plans.* London: Author.

Ostrom, E. (1990). *Governing the commons: The evolution of institutions for collective action.* Cambridge, England: Cambridge University Press.

Nye, J. S., Zelikow, P. D., & King, D. C. (1997). *Why people don't trust government.* Cambridge, MA: Harvard University Press.

Patterson, T. E. (2002). *The vanishing voter: Public involvement in an age of uncertainty.* New York: Alfred A. Knopf.

Putnam, R. D., & Feldman, L. M. (2003). *Better together: Restoring the American community.* New York: Simon A. Schuster.

Pool, I. D. S. (1990). *Technologies without boundaries: On communication in a global age.* Cambridge, MA.: Harvard University Press.

Phar, S. J., & Putnam, R. (Eds.). (2000). *Disaffected democracies: What's troubling the trilateral countries.* Princeton, NJ: Princeton University Press.

Rahn, W. M. (1997). *Media messages, political culture, and national identity: Communication in the future of democracy.* Paper presented at the Annenberg Policy Center Workshop on Mediated Politics, Washington, DC.

Richardson, H. S. (2002). *Democratic autonomy: Public reasoning about the ends of policy.* Oxford, England: Oxford University Press.

Rieke, E. A. (1996). The Bay-Delta accord: A stride toward sustainability. *University of Colorado Law Review, 67,* 341-369.

Rittel, H., & Webber, M. (1973). Dilemmas in a general theory of planning. *Policy Sciences, 4,* 155-169.

Roberts, N. (1997). Public deliberation: An alternative approach to crafting policy. *Public Administration Review, 57*(2), 124-32.

Rose-Anderssen, C., Allen, P. M., Tsinopoulos, C., & McCarthy, I. (2005). Innovation in manufacturing as an evolutionary complex system. *Technovation, 25*(10), 1093-1105.

Rosenberg, S. W. (in press). Rethinking democratic deliberation: The limits and potential of citizen participation. *Polity, 39*(3).

Schneider, M., Focht, W., Lubell, M., Mindruta, D., & Edwardsen, M. (2003). Building consensual institutions: Networks and the National Estuary Program. *American Journal of Political Science, 47*(1), 143-158.

Schrage, M. (1990). *Shared minds: The new technologies of collaboration.* New York: Random House.

Shapiro, I. (2003). *The state of democratic theory.* Princeton, NJ: Princeton University Press.

Schelling, T. C. (1978). *Micromotive and macrobehavior.* New York: Norton.

Somin, I. (1998). Voter Ignorance and Democracy. *Critical Review, 12*(4), 413-458.

Stacey, R.D. (1996). *Complexity and creativity in organizations.* San Francisco: Berrett-Koehler.

Stacey, R. D. (2001). *Complex responsive processes in organizations: Learning and knowledge creation.* London: Routlege.

Straus, D. (2002). *How to make collaboration work.* San Francisco: Berrett-Koehler.

Susskind, L., & Cruikshank, J. (1987). *Breaking the impasse: Consensual approaches to resolving public disputes.* New York: Basic Books.

Susskind, L., & Cruikshank, J. (2006). *Breaking Robert's rules.* New York: Oxford University Press.

Susskind, L., McKearnan, S., & Thomas-Larmer, J. (Eds.). (1999). *The consensus building handbook: A comprehensive guide to reaching agreement.* Thousand Oaks, CA: Sage Publications.

Toffler, A. (1984). *The adaptive corporation.* New York: McGraw Hill.

Tsoukas, H. (2005). *Complex knowledge: Studies in organizational epistemology.* Oxford, England: Oxford University Press.

Uden, J. (2005). Using complexity science in organization studies: A case for loose application. *Emergence, 7*(1), 60-66.

Waldrop, M. M. (1992). *Complexity: The emerging science at the edge of chaos.* New York: Simon & Schuster.

Wattenberg, M. (1994). *The decline of American political parties: 1952-1992.* Cambridge, MA: Harvard University Press.

CHAPTER 7

TRACING THE DISORDERLY REAL

Performing Civic Engagement in a Complex World

Jean Hillier and Joris Van Wezemael

The birth of a new [plan] is never a linear process.
It is knotty, a mangle-prone emergence across a threshold of surprise.

—Massumi (2002, p. 215)

INTRODUCTION

We open with the poststructuralist recognition that policy, at least that which effects change, is not simply imposed from above, but emerges or evolves "on the ground" within and as part of a context of "communities, contingencies and dynamic processes" (Lejano, 2006, p. 199). Theorizations and practices of strategic spatial planning policymaking and implementation have increasingly emphasized the agency of civil society in an engagement of (but not always "with") people as "active consumer-partic-

Civic Engagement in a Network Society
pp. 149–185
Copyright © 2008 by Information Age Publishing
All rights of reproduction in any form reserved.

149

ipant[s] in knowledge production" (Leadbeater & Miller, 2004, cited in Hinchliffe, Kearnes, Degen, & Whatmore, 2005, p. 2).

While deliberation by citizens has a long history (from ancient Greek *agora* through Parisian *salons* to the global ether of Internet chatrooms), it is only in the last decade or so that citizen groups and neighborhood organizations have become essential partners in governance activities, contributing resources, competencies and capacities to policymaking and delivery far beyond traditional activities of voting, attending public meetings, and lobbying. Civic or citizen engagement and participatory deliberation, if appropriately empathetic, egalitarian, open-minded, and reason centered (delli Carpini, Cook, & Jacobs, 2004), theoretically produce a range of positive democratic outcomes, including increasingly more active citizens (Barber, 1984), increased tolerance and empathy with the "other" (Gutmann & Thompson, 1996), increased understanding of citizens' own needs and preferences (Chambers, 1996) and resolution of deep conflicts in democratic decisions which are "informed, enlightened and authentic" (Gastil, 2000, p. 25).

Citizen engagement is now a statutory duty in England for many agencies of governance who are forced to rethink their roles, their responsibilities and their values. Officers are having to develop new skills of networking, facilitation, collaboration, and negotiation in order to act with confidence and authority in a postbureaucratic world; a world in which "old stabilities, certainties and lines of progress and responsibility appear to be gradually displaced by more fluid and dynamic kinds of participation and negotiation" (Iedema, 2003, p. 101). Postbureaucratic governance is multimodal, bringing an increasing number of frequently unpredictable, heterogeneous voices into dynamic, contingent play. Policy making is multidisciplinary and participatory, informed by stakeholders and negotiated with actants including politicians (plus their advisors and lobbyists), private-sector businesspersons, and lay citizens (Hillier, 2007). It insists on the open-endedness of social contexts and "the precarious institutionalization" of arenas of debate and decision making which allow "both for rational deliberation and for the agonistic, sometimes antagonistic, struggles to dominate public space and the policy agenda" (Devenney, 2002, p. 192).

Lejano (2006) highlights the importance of such policies being coherent not only with governance structures, but with places and with actants' everyday lives. This would suggest that policies should be fashioned and instituted in a place, using resources of that place. The policymaker becomes an "improviser who fashions a program out of the materials at hand and finds ways to make those pieces fit" (Lejano, 2006, p. 201). Alternatively, Lejano suggests that sometimes the policy "landscape" has to be reworked or manipulated to make the new policy work. Citizen engagement in such instances may be more akin to Arnstein's (1969) rungs of manipulation, therapy, and informing (nonparticipation and tokenism) at the bottom of her ladder of citizen participation.

The "turns" to civic engagement in public policymaking have been documented and analyzed at length in the literature (see, for example, Chess & Purcell, 1999; Hillier, 2002; Innes & Booher, 1999a, 1999b, 2004; McGuirk, 2000; Lowndes, Pratchett, & Stoker, 2001a, 2001b; Webler, Tuler, & Krueger, 2001), while manuals, handbooks, and guidelines for best practice abound (including Moffitt and Bordone, 2005; Straus, 2002; Susskind, McKearnan, & Thomas-Larmer, 1999). Several specialized journals exist (such as the *International Journal of Public Participation*) and public deliberation models are supported by institutions such as Carnegie-Mellon, the International Association for Public Participation, the Collaborative Democracy Network, the Consensus Building Institute, and the Association for Conflict Resolution. There are now literally thousands of local and national deliberative fora for civic engagement on issues ranging from crime to economic development (delli Carpini et al., 2004).

Despite theorists' and practitioners' enthusiasm for processes of civic/ citizen engagement, much of the literature is concerned solely with process, or links between process and output. Few authors in the planning field, with the notable exception of Patsy Healey (2002, 2004, 2006a, 2006b), have explored the importance of place meaning and place attachment for citizens. Such analysis has tended to be undertaken by community psychologists, including McMillan and Chavis (1986), Chavis and Wandersman (1990) and Perkins and Long (2002). Theory and analysis are thus often located within the confines of disciplinary "silos" in which certain readings and interpretations are hegemonic.

We seek to resist the hegemonic readings of citizen engagement found in spatial planning and community participation texts. We propose a reading based on baroque complexity, "looking down" (Law, 2004a) and Deleuzoguattarian geophilosophy to suggest how we might work more effectively with the disorderly real rather than ordered networks through an awareness of rhizomic connections, of multiplicities and how they might interconnect, and of potential becomings or actualizations, and what the pragmatics of dealing with all these might be (see Wise, 2006, p. 177).

We critically analyze an empirical case of civic engagement in the development of a local strategic area action plan from Newcastle-upon-Tyne in North-East England. We pose questions including:

- Do collaborative processes of civic engagement produce different outputs than noncollaborative processes? (after Koontz & Thomas, 2006)

- How does this particular network for civic engagement perform?
- How has it evolved? What underlying mentalities, perceptions and assumptions exist and develop, with what impacts on performance?
- What challenges and opportunities can be discerned both theoretically and practically?

We bring both insider and outsider perspectives to our analysis. Following many years of involvement in both practice and theoretical analysis of participation strategies in Western Australia, Jean Hillier's relocation to Newcastle gives an outsider perspective, while Joris Van Wezemael has been working with the regeneration team for several months, mainly reviewing their practices of community involvement. In what follows we briefly outline the policy context for strategic spatial planning in England. We then present our Deleuzoguattarian theoretical frame before turning to describe and critically analyze the Newcastle case in depth. We conclude by suggesting that Deleuzoguattarian processes of fabulation might offer a form of civic engagement which mobilizes complex, heterogeneous understandings and desires to stimulate creative action in a leap toward actualizing the virtual futures of our cities.

A FLEXIBLE, "FRONTLOADED" PLANNING SYSTEM?

Since implementation of the Planning and Compulsory Purchase Act 2004 in England and Wales, local authorities are required to "frontload" their development of strategic plans by involving communities from the very beginning of the plan-preparation process. In fact, "the community," not led by planning officers, should prepare its community strategy for the area before the spatial planning process commences. The community strategy should then drive local plans, with stakeholders being consulted constantly throughout the plan's preparation in a "continuing, accessible and transparent process" (Office of the Deputy Prime Minister, 2005). The intention is to deal with as many potential objections upfront so that the plan should receive few objections when submitted for inspection by the planning inspectorate.

As the government itself acknowledges, this means changing the culture of planning. The creation of a more "relevant, creative and dynamic" planning system (Planning Officers Society, 2004), according far more weight than previously to expressed community needs and desires from the start of plan preparation processes, exemplifies Fung and Wright's (2003) concept of "empowered participatory governance":

Our guiding principle is that people must come first. (Department of the Environment, Transport and the Regions, 2000, p. 2)

Sustainable development needs the community to be involved with developing the vision for their areas. Communities should be able to contribute ideas about how that vision can be achieved and have the opportunity to participate in the process for drawing up specific plans and policies and to be involved in development proposals. (Office of the Deputy Prime Minister, 2004a, p. 15)

Community involvement should ... enable the local community to say what sort of place they want to live in at a stage when this can make a difference. (Office of the Deputy Prime Minister, 2004b, p.4).

Stakeholders will need to unlearn the practices and habits of the previous system as much as they need to learn and adapt to the new emphasis on flexibility and creativity as they attempt to come to terms with recognition of multiple horizontal and vertical networks interrelating; of trajectories which are multiple, nonlinear and continually emerging; and where emphasis is less on fixed structures than on fluidity and change.

In Newcastle we encounter an example of development of a local plan for strategic urban regeneration in which major process and policy directions are set centrally (via acts, guidance notes and statements), regionally (via regional strategies) and by the municipal authority. Local cultural practices of policymaking and implementation are often multiple, dynamic and contingent, often with little shared ideological ground with broader policy frames. Such a situation offers an opportunity for Deleuzoguattarian-inspired mapping and analysis.

BETWEEN THE VIRTUAL AND THE ACTUAL: A DELEUZOGUATTARIAN THEORETICAL FRAMEWORK

In this section we outline a theoretical framework which conceptualizes the relational complexities and multiplicities, nonlinearities, nonfixities and contingencies embodied in civic engagement processes. Based on key elements of Deleuze and Guattari's "geophilosophy," we regard space as a multiplicity which brings together characteristics of externality, simultaneity, contiguity or juxtaposition and qualitative and quantitative differentiations (Bergson, 1932/1988, p. 206; Grosz, 2001, p. 113). This connects to a relational (rather than a Euclidean) concept of the production of place. As Amin notes "cities and regions possess a distinctive spatiality as agglomerations of heterogeneity locked into a multitude of relational networks of varying geographical reach" (Amin, 2004, p. 43).

Urban areas are viewed no longer as objectively identifiable, integrated economic and social systems, but rather as spaces of complex multiple social relations; each having their own space-time dynamics and scalar reach.

In this view a place is not a given, rather, what is at stake is the manner in which it is produced and maintained by the connection of physical and mental, relational networks. Therefore, a place can no longer be seen as a distinct, unitary physical entity. It is materially experienced as a significant but fluxing conjunction of multiple networks. The connections of those networks can be mapped in order to grasp not just their momentary fixity (represented, for instance, in a local area plan), but also the intensive processes of their becoming. These networks produce different systems of values; truths are multiple. There are often several dimensions at play simultaneously in network multiplicities of rich and diverse layers and flows of entities and practices. Spatial planning can be regarded as the art (or science) of spatial manipulation—the manipulation of the actualization of difference. Planning is a mediator between multiple representations of the "good" in the continuous process of space-becoming or spacing. Thus the phenomena with which planning struggles have become "less about territorial boundaries and states and more about connection and flow" (Law & Urry, 2003, p. 10). People and places are "flexible constellations of identities-on-the-move" (Sheller, 2004, p. 49) rather than stationary nodes in a network. Such conception implies fluidity, slipperiness, instability, movement, and transformation in form which, nevertheless, has the capacity for momentary stabilization.

We offer, below, a topological tracing of relations in a civic engagement process in Newcastle-upon-Tyne. A topology may be described as "a multiplex and integrated whole that exists as the coming together of diverse and multiple dimensions of action and being" (Lejano, 2006, p. 231) in which it is the relationships, associations, and encounters between entities which are important. Relations, however, are not simple "units of dimension," but rather forces or "directions in motion" (Deleuze & Guattari, 1987, p. 21). Relations, therefore, cannot be fixed and determined with any degree of finality. Any tracing must necessarily be tentative, recognizing its contingency. Nevertheless, we believe that tracing topologies allows us to focus more closely on new and important aspects of civic engagement in systems of governance which are increasingly reliant less on authoritarian bureaucratic structures and more on "transactive systems ... where policy actors are inextricably bound together in rich relations" (Lejano, 2006, p. 235) of mutual concern.

Relations as practices inevitably involve plays of power and politics. Deleuze suggests that power works on and through subjects via the relations produced within various contexts. In this chapter we trace the interrelations between the networks of actors/actants in our case example, highlighting different forms of power, such as instrumental legislative power. We then begin to deconstruct the complex interactions we have traced, affording greater understanding of what is happening and of potential impacts. Referring to Deleuze and Guattari's (1987, p. 106) distinction between power as *pouvoir*, power of domination, and power as *puissance*, power as capacity or force, we examine how the processes of citizen engagement in place-making as organized by the local state serve to reify the asymmetries in the abilities of individuals and social groups to define and realize their needs.

Power operates through Deleuzoguattarian stratification in which social strata (often regarded by planning actants as "us" and "them") are created by processes of subjectification and signification, underlain by a process of organization. As Thanem and Linstead (2006, p. 46) explain, subjectification positions the subject through grammar, "through the way in which it orders and positions its speakers and sets out their choices for them—they may enter into these forced, conjugated choices or be silent." Chains of signification invoke normative interpretations of subjectivity. The use of "plannerspeak"—such as jargon-replete reference to statutory process—serves to order activities and command compliance. Organization performs through segmentation; the "compartmentalization of human existence, and by extension of space … rigidified in the modern State" (Bonta & Protevi, 2004, p. 139). Segmentation is binary (an either/or of us/them, is/is not, has/has not), circular (in concentric rings of "myness" [Bonta & Protevi, 2004, p. 140] from home to neighborhood to city and so on) and linear (in time and space). It is achieved through creating functions for spaces and times; coding land uses in performances of molar[1] segmentation which process molecular energies (including local residents' desires), ordering them and draining them of power of variation. Organization, moreover, imposes chronological timescales: "the time of the creation of possibles must be curtailed and fenced in with rigorous established procedures and deadlines" (Lazzarato, 2006, p. 176). As Thanem and Linstead (2006, p. 48) write, "for Deleuze, organization is about order, order is about power."

We are cognizant, moreover, that any enactment of presence in spatial planning processes is co-constituted with absence. Whilst some elements in the case example stories are foregrounded and rendered visible, other "relations, processes and contexts that are necessary to presence" (Law, 2004b, p. 54) are excluded and disappear. Absences can be deliberate "to make the narrative work" (Law, 2002, p. 121) or to secure ease of manipulation. Statistical data, such as data gathered by questionnaire survey, for instance, are notorious for their absent underlying assumptions and low response rates. Law (2004b, p. 157) distinguishes two forms of absence:

manifest absence, "that which is absent, but recognized as relevant to, or represented in presence," and absence as Otherness, "that which is absent because it is enacted by presence as irrelevant, impossible or repressed." Otherness is necessary to presence, but is repressed, excluded and forced into absence (Law, 2004b, p. 162). Absence does not necessarily mean "not present" and recorded presence will not be an objective representation (Hillier, in press). Any decision, or writing, is but a temporary fixity or punctualization (Callon, 1991; Law, 2003) in an ongoing oscillation (Hillier, 2007).

We also refer to the Deleuzoguattarian conceptualization of striated space. Striated spaces are regulated, ordered and closed; spaces "inhabited by subjects with supposed free will, but bound together by a compromise with power" (Bonta, 2001, p. 2). Striated spaces are classified, regulated and managed in networks which perform realignment of economic, political and socio-cultural elements (Hillier, 2007). Striated space tends to be associated with the state: "one of the fundamental tasks of the State is to striate the space" (Deleuze & Guattari, 1987, p. 479). Striating space attempts to inscribe some form of stability or fixity into flux, to draw lines and situate "locales," such as the Newcastle regeneration area, within universal coordinate systems such as central government policy frames and planning legislation. Uncertainties, unpredictabilities and possibilities of variation must be codified and neutralized. As Deleuze and Guattari (1987, p. 494) explain, striated space is dominated by "the requirements of long-distance vision: constancy of orientation" and "constitution of a central perspective." The result is a space of sites rather than of places.

Deleuze and Guattari use the term "territory" in a metaphorical sense to depict sites of political engagement, their lines of power, practices and institutions (O'Neill & McGuirk, 2005, p. 285). Territorialization is a form of action on, or capture of, individual or social forces which seeks to limit or constrain their possibilities for action. It involves "the creation of meaning in social space through the forging of coded connections and distinctions" (Brown & Lunt, 2002, p. 17) into some form of uniformity or consistency, such as regulations, land use development plans and so on; Deleuzoguattarian striations.

Our view of the world is rhizomic (Deleuze & Guattari, 1987), tracing and mapping connections between organizations of power, semiotic or discourse chains and circumstances. The fabric of the rhizome is conjunction: "and." Planning officers *and* local residents *and* politicians *and* planning inspectors, "and, and, and" (Deleuze & Parnet, 2002, p. 9). We regard practices of governance and strategic spatial planning as rhizomic. Practices evolve, function and adapt somewhat chaotically, always pragmatically, concerned with what can be done. They are driven as much by situation and event as by their particular concerns (Thoburn, 2003).

Deleuze and Guattari (1987, p. 21) characterize a rhizome as connecting points to other points, bringing into play different and heterogeneous regimes of signs, composed of directions in motion, with neither a beginning nor an end, but always a middle: "always incomplete, always in the midst of being formed" (Deleuze, 1997, p. 1). A rhizome is constructed by the interplay of the multiple relations which constitute its complex entity.

In order to trace and map rhizomes associated with our case example, we do not ask what a thing *is* (its essence), but *what it can do* (Deleuze & Guattari, 1987, p. 40) and *how it changes* (Patton, 2006, p. 27). What an entity can do refers to how it can connect/relate both materially and expressively (for instance, through language). How it changes refers to the way connections are maintained, cut, (re)established. This means that no "network" as an entity is given for analysis; rather its becoming must be "mapped" (Deleuze & Guattari, 1987, pp. 12-16). The production of actual individuals and places thus moves into the focus of attention, drawing out the connection between the actual world of things and the processes of individuation (the production of subjectivity) or morphogenesis (the generation of form). The ontological tool for this research perspective is the conceptualization of reality as virtual-actual.

The virtual is the Deleuzoguattarian ontological element of potentiality; a "pressing crowd" (Massumi, 2002) of multiplicities from which some "thing" will emerge, take on sociolinguistic meaning and become part of actants' lives: "a concrete presence" (Goodchild, 1996, p. 4). Any such actualization of potentiality, however, never coincides with the virtual. Actualization performs stratification; the burying of the virtual under the congealing or temporary fixing of fluidity enabling the emergence of functional structures or striations.

The concept of virtual-actual presents a radical break with traditional philosophies (such as of spatial planning and governance) which have tended to think only in terms of "the real" and "the possible." As Thanem and Linstead (2006, p. 51) summarize, "the possible is always determined by the real in such a way that what can exist always depends on what already exists." Deleuzoguattarian thinking, as we have indicated, moves in the opposite direction: the actualization of the virtual. Each place is an actualization of virtual spatiality. So, if we think strategic spatial planning, we should think processes of morphogenesis (Delanda, 2006).

TRACING AND MAPPING: PUTTING THE TRACING ON THE MAP

Casey (1997, p. 307) suggests that space should be experienced "at close range" by "legwork" (walking and hearing) and, we would add, by tracing and mapping. We follow, in particular, John Law's (1997/2003, 2004a) notion of baroque complexity. Baroque complexity sees individual actants in turbulent, unstable motion. Individuals act in multiple networks simultaneously, contingent on context. Representations are similarly contingent on the hinterland "baggage" of those representing and perceiving: "contextualized through and through" (Cilliers, 2002, p. 80).

Law's conceptualization of baroque complexity is founded in Deleuze's (1993) work on Leibniz. Baroque complexity looks "down" to discover complex detail, rather than "up" in quest of a coherent big picture based on homogenization of difference and an increase in abstraction.

Deleuze and Guattari (1987, p. 12) remind us to "make a map, not a tracing." Too often, what we regard as "mapping" is actually "tracing"; reproducing in "tabulated, graphic, and geographic representations what is present in the real" (Wise, 2006, p. 186) and forming the basis of analysis which compares one tracing (such as an opinion poll) with another (a policy document), overcoding the real with particular, subjective interpretations.[2] Tracing thus translates a map into an image: "[i]t has organized, stabilized, neutralized the multiplicities according to the axes of significance and subjectification belonging to it ... and when it thinks it is reproducing something else it is in fact only reproducing itself" (Deleuze & Guattari, 1987, p. 13).

What distinguishes a map from a tracing is that a map is oriented toward experimentation. As Deleuze and Guattari (1987, pp. 12-13) describe, "it is itself part of the rhizome. The map is open and connectable in all of its dimensions"; it is detachable, reversible, susceptible to constant modification.... A map has multiple entryways.... The map has to do with performance, whereas the tracing always involves an alleged 'competence.'" Tracing and mapping rhizomes unpacks not only spatial dimensions, but also the beliefs, allegiances and habits which express actants" desires (Fuglsang & Sørensen, 2006). Deleuzoguattarian maps are concerned with creative potential rather than with tracing exact copies of predetermined overcoded categorizations.

Maps and tracings are intrinsically related, however. In terms of methodology, "the tracing should always be put back on the map" (Deleuze & Guattari, 1987, pp. 99-100). This means that we trace networks, actants, encounters, power plays, subjectifications, categorizations, discourses, significations, and so on, and notice where any blockages, categories, oppositions, or resistances affect policy decisions and implementation. These tracings become part of the map, together with "the complexities of the social" (Wise, 2006, p. 187); the ideological mentalities, assumptions, and so forth, underlying actants' knowledges and performativities. If performativities are "traced" on a geometry of horizontals and verticals, mapping complexities involves locating diagonals or transversals (Rajchman, 2000, p. 99) and the possibilities they open up in Deleuzean diagrams.[3]

A diagram is thus a map of the relations of force; the "distribution of the power to affect and the power to be affected" (Deleuze, 1986/1986, p. 73, cited in McCormack, 2005, p. 124). Rather than being merely a graphic representation of relations, a diagram for Deleuze is creative; an operative set of lines and zones which opens onto moments of affective and connective potential (Hillier, 2007). Diagrams can be defined by the degrees of freedom in the intensive processes of individuation and by the uneven distribution of what is deemed important and unimportant, relevant and irrelevant.

The diagram as a map establishes a relationship between the discursive and nondiscursive. As Semetsky (2004a, p. 334) explains, a diagram functions to "establish a mediatory space between the visible and the articulable, between sensible and intelligible, between mental and physical, and between a form of content and a form of expression." It performs a creative synthesis; "a differential, a breakthrough, and an operational closure" (Semetsky, 2004a, p. 334).

Rather than tracing civic engagement as numbers of votes cast for "option A versus option B," we trace relations between the ideologies and processes which lie behind the production or actualization of the options. These processes refer to elements (who and what) which are absent in the options as actualized, but without which they cannot be fully understood. We, therefore, address the "why" and "how" rather than merely the "what" by tracing the "semantic, syntactic and figurative steps" (Titlestad, 2001, p. 32) through which civic engagement processes are turned into the text of the plan. We therefore describe the "migration" of strategies across maneuvers which produce the text. We recognize that we can only offer "a limited arc of meaning, a small story of the inextricable practices and representations" (Titlestad, 2001, p. 32) which comprise the area action plan processes. We must inevitably select certain texts, events and stories for description from a multiplicity of complex and chaotic elements, imposing a subjectivity which we cannot avoid. As Titlestad (2001, p. 32) comments, however, "the alternative, though, silence in the face of the multiple and provisional, leads nowhere."

Through tracing we illustrate how various actant discourses and trajectories attempted to make realities using varieties of "truths" or discursive representations. We describe how policy officers in the Newcastle regeneration area attempted to address the multiplicities, flexibilities, imaginations and capacities of other actants. Were they "in tune" with other actants or did they simply "qualculate" (Callon & Law, 2005); a process in which "entities are detached from other contexts, reworked, displayed, related, manipulated, transformed and summed in a single space" (Callon & Law, 2005, p. 730)? Qualculation involves re-presenting tracings of information in a normalized, striated form in which it can be manipulated and utilized to set or justify objectives for plans and policies.

The methods we used in this study comprise critical reviews of both formal and "gray" documents, interviews and focus groups with major stakeholders, including members of the regeneration team, their preferred private-sector regeneration partners, and representatives from the regeneration area. One author also undertook participatory research within the regeneration team for several months during the main phase of civic engagement. In accordance with ethical conventions of anonymity, all quotations from the focus group held with regeneration team members are attributed as "FG" and documents cited are generically, rather than specifically, referenced.

ORGANIZING FIELDS OF RELEVANCE
AND WINDOWS OF OPPORTUNITY

In this section we trace the practices and strategies of citizen engagement in what will be one of the first area action plans (AAP) produced under the 2004 planning legislation. This plan aims at bringing about major changes in a former heavy industrial riverside area of Newcastle. The AAP will have the status of the city council's statutory plan for future planning decisions in the area.

Strategic planning processes were initiated due to official perceptions that the riverside area was suffering from socioeconomic problems that required a drastic initiative to break vicious cycles of (population, social, economic, and infrastructural) decline. The key objectives of plans produced since 1999 have been to stem population decline and attract new people to the area, thus sustaining the community: "a challenge for this master plan, and those who will implement it, to break this cycle of decline, to put [the area] back on the map, and to raise the profile of the place to one of real choice where people want to live, work and spend their leisure time" (LD, 2004b, p. 17).[4] Plan goals include a reduction in low-demand property, increased community cohesion, and better use of green spaces (Newcastle City Council, 2002, p. 9)

The population of the area is described as "respectable working class" (LD, 2004c, p. 51), although it is increasingly losing its sources of income and much of its pride. This formerly thriving part of the city is one of those places where 'losers' of economic globalization are concentrated. Low in-migration rates, however, do not simply reflect the area's degeneration. Rather they mirror the long-term settled nature and "closed-ness" of the fairly homogeneous population: "a sense of solidarity developed through working and living together for a long time" (LD, 2004c, p. 51).

In recent years piecemeal demolition of residential and other properties has taken place, but this has failed to significantly reduce the number of void units. It demonstrates, however, that a piecemeal approach is unable to "turn around" (LD, 2004c) the area and break the circle of decline. The so called evidence-based analysis (LD, 2004c), the first step in the well-defined formal planning procedure, states that "the housing, population and services in the area are now in a state that is fundamentally unstable: and unsustainable beyond the short term" (LD, 2004c, p. 137). Trend extrapolation and evidence from this analysis make it clear that regeneration must stretch well beyond just "patching-up" the existing situation (LD, 2004c). The report states that without radical action, the population will continue to fall; more and more dwellings on more and more estates will fail to let; yet more demolitions will take out blocks and units, leaving increasing gaps in the fabric; community services will dwindle and close; and dereliction will worsen the image and stigma of the area even further (LD, 2004c).

The regeneration of this riverside area is thus a tough and challenging task. The official process of regeneration commenced in 1999 and is still ongoing in 2007. The process comprises distinct phases of civic engagement which differ in terms of their major goals and "degrees of freedom" offered:

1. An initial phase of capacity building during the citywide Going for Growth regeneration initiative (1999-2002)
2. A phase of master planning, producing a set of visions for the area (January 2002-November 2004)
3. A phase of compulsory consultation on the 'options' (September/ October 2005)
4. A phase which aims at working with the community in implementation of the chosen strategy.

We focus discussion on phases 2 and 3, since they aimed at more extensive civic engagement.

Two basic conditions for community involvement assumed that:

*   the process must aim at participation of a heterogeneous community in the development of draft plans in a "community approach," and
*   it must develop a number of visions for the development of the whole area (drawn from LD and NCC texts).

Table 7.1.   Overview of Selected Civic Engagement Events

Timeframe	Project	Stated Goal/Achievement in Planning Process	Outcome
1999–January 2002	Going for Growth	Capacity building	The "network" was formed in a process of capacity building in order to support and bring together community groups who would be most effected by the Going for Growth plans. They have been involved in the procurement process to select a development partner for the area and engaged in work to develop an initial master plan and community consultation process.
June 2002	Residential weekend	Establish strong working relation between the preferred partner and the network.	Strong working relation.
September 2002	Round I community events	Open event. Community asked to give comment on "What is good about X that they wouldn't want to lose" and "What needs to be improved in X to make it a better place to live."	Low attendance: 115 people in 5 meetings.
November 2002	Round II community events	Discuss emerging ideas and the development framework plan.	Very low attendance.
November 2002	Discussions in specific areas	Discussion of impacts of local development plan prior to the development of options.	Strengthening local concerns about demolition of housing.
March 2003	Round III community involvement	Discuss emerging thinking for initial master plan. Exhibition material shows material for initial master plan, particularly outline of early action areas.	Very mixed feedback. Attitude of community hard to tell. Hardly a view on the vision for the AAP-area. Commitment to establish working groups which concentrate on early action areas.
September-October 2005	Consultation on preferred options report	Wider range of consultation techniques used. Includes, outreach sessions' and the focus groups.	Option 3, "major impact" chosen.

As we have stated, strategic objectives for the plan were predetermined, but the "solution" to those given objectives needed to be developed in conjunction with local communities (Newcastle City Council, 2002, p. 9). Thus, although the target is given, the actualization of a limited set of "solutions" from the multiplicity of potential options should be developed jointly in a process of frontloaded regeneration planning. As we shall demonstrate, however, in our example frontloading tended to become the rhetorical/discursive representation of "top-loading." Although discursively signified as front-loaded, engaged participants, local citizens were organized into particular segmented, linear, time-slots for "consultation" and into circular segments of residence. The dominant molar power (*pouvoir*) of the regeneration team to organize a heavily-striated plan-making process prevented molecular variation and the emergence of local capacities (*puissance*).

Fields of Relevance: "The Community" or Multiple "Communities"?

As our theoretical approach makes clear, place is a nodal point of multiple networks. People with postal addresses within a particular geographical area do not automatically constitute one or the "community." Furthermore, since the multiple networks often exceed the physical area of the place, relevant voices may not be found exclusively within the area. Since the regeneration process aims at transforming the area—that is, it interferes with the actualization or individuation processes of relations that produce people and place—it is crucial to understand how "civic society" is both subjectified and signified in this instance.

We trace the purpose of community involvement as being to:

- help build crucial relationships between different community groups in order to produce an inclusive development plan;
- involve the community in decision-making and in reviewing the content of development plans and to produce transparency so that everybody involved knows when he/she is engaged in the project;
- report on the involvement and how engagement has influenced the decisions made (LD, 2004a).

The major regeneration partner made a commitment to "close working with local communities" (LD, 2004a, p. 4) in the master planning process and beyond. This should ensure that the plan is "robust and has the broad support of the community and reflects the community's hopes and aspirations for the future" (LD, 2004a, p. 4). Interestingly the major goal of master planning—developing a vision for the area—is not explicitly mentioned.

Despite discursive reference to producing an "inclusive" plan by "involv[ing] the community in decision making," planners had little intention of performing such inclusivity. They explained that they do not believe in a "holy grail of community involvement" (FG). As experts, they territorialised the process, since "we know what is realistically deliverable, we give people a window to work within" (FG). As another team member commented, "we steer them to our predetermined choice" (FG). Residents are subjectified as people to whom both process and outcome needed to be "sold" (FG).

Throughout reports of the master planning process "the community" is mostly addressed in the singular. This enacts a mentality of a homogeneous population with a given, fixed and stable identity. Although there was a series of typical community-participation events, such as public meetings, drop-in sessions and displays, no analysis of participants (by age, gender, ethnicity or neighborhood) was made. Where different groups are mentioned, the planners connect or merge them in order to produce an "inclusive plan"; a very different interpretation of "inclusive" to that which we believe was intended. Without exception master planning makes present groups who are already present. They are conceptualized as given entities rather than as results of dynamic relations. There is no concept of a multiple community as being more-than-one coherent entity, but less-than-many separate entities. A concept of the connection of heterogeneous relational networks would have opened up a more dynamic perspective on the absent; especially the area's people-to-come (Deleuze, 1997).

The relational topology between the planners' attitudes and assumptions toward the inhabitants of the regeneration area thus cannot accommodate the opportunity to nudge the process away from stable states and pregiven issues to a space where alternative potential states can be actualized, where the degrees of freedom are higher, and where community identities and subjectivities are unstable and not yet defined. The likelihood of routine or habitual organization, as opposed to problematization, is increased. For instance, since the regeneration project aims at attracting new people to the area, the question should be problematized of how potentially agonistic relations between the hopes and aspirations of the present community/ies and the potential new residents will be approached.

The planners' approach illustrates the mentality of space as a container: the community is constructed not as a rhizome with multiple connections, but as a closed network of people living within predesignated boundaries. What are the reasons for this conceptualization of community, and what are its effects in terms of individuation/actualization in the course of the plan development process? In reply, we trace engagement of the community network.

From the start of the master planning process in early 2002 the council's preferred regeneration partners established close collaboration with the "community network." This increasingly formalized group of people, which is not only uncritically signified as a network, but also referred to as "the Network" (singular), is the product of the antecedent capacity building process (phase 1, in the aftermath of a citywide regeneration initiative, Going for Growth).

The Network consists of members of locally active resident associations and community groups, who are signified and subjectified as "representatives." There had been common concern about the extensive demolition plans of the Going for Growth initiative which brought resident groups together in order to have a stronger, united voice around a shared interest: the protection of people's homes from demolition.[5] Although the planners aimed at building capacity, no new connections were initiated and the process served merely to amplify already-present voices. The community was subjectified into hitherto fixed identities and allegiances signified exclusively by the Network. This produces repressed absence of all actants not gathered around the network's particular (residential) focus.

In planners' reports the network is stratified as an entity with no internal differentiation. Furthermore, assumptions are made that feedback from the representatives (the "nodes" of the alleged communitywide network) to the residents whom they represent, as well as support from the community to the representatives, is taking place. The nodes of the Network are clearly defined, but there is no effort or awareness about what is produced along the lines of their relations. It is "easier" for the planners to deal with a small group of representatives rather than with the Network or the multiplicity of networks and connections that actually exist. The majority of the local population are thus repressed into absence by being addressed via the Network.

Network representatives tend to be elderly, long-term residents. Most are women. They exemplify what planners assume as the "core population" (LD, 2004b). Most representatives have been involved since the earliest Going for Growth initiative, which caused panic and anger amongst the area's residents. The representatives are elected by formal assemblies. They theoretically speak for the people and represent them. However, attendance at meetings comprises generally only between 10 and 20 active people. This is obviously a minute and self-selected subset of the area's estimated 13,000 residents. Representatives thus represent the views of a tiny minority rather than the varied opinions which may exist amongst residents. The majority of the residents are never present, but are always absent.

These poorly attended meetings are the only forum for internal discussion of information passed down from the Network and the planners. The Network can by no means be considered as an inclusive instrument for engagement of the people of the AAP area. It rather reflects a closed group of long-standing residents who tend to represent one "identity" and allegiance out of a multiplicity of potential identities and allegiances of the place. The relations which initially created a strong estate-focus in the area are thus stabilized. The population is homogenized due to the chosen procedures of civic engagement which organize the process, its significations and subjectifications. There are too many absences for citizen engagement to be truly inclusive. This makes the development of a vision highly unlikely which would reinvent the place, reconnect physical places and social relations and move beyond the narrow scope of Network representatives' views of individual estates.

The review of feedback rates and attendance at community events (LD, 2004a, 2004b) suggests that about 90% of the population should be considered as "highly apathetic" in terms of engagement with the regeneration process. We argue, however, that this so-called "apathetic" mentality has been fueled and amplified significantly by the design of the civic engagement process. In terms of both the territorialization of the Network as "the community" with a signified capacity which builds solely on the basis of the concern about the future of particular estates, and the selection of particular resident-based groups as the only entry point to the community, the limitations of civic engagement are apparent.

The planners and residents involved in the citizen engagement processes possess different hinterlands, significations and subjectifications when visioning the area's future. The process produces many, what are regarded as, "irrelevant truths" on all sides. This gives rise to defensive reactions and frustration: "trust goes out the window" (FG). The process sharpens the binary segmentation of "us" and "them" (such as, residents versus planners, community versus council, lay people versus expert professionals), which further subjectifies and normalizes a community, whose heterogeneities, multiplicities and rhizomic connectivities ought to be addressed if creative energies of individuation and morphogenesis are to be triggered.

Framing Processes, Limiting Windows of Opportunity

As mentioned above, the regeneration process involved a succession of phases of civic engagement with differing objectives, reflecting both different territorializations of the issues and different subjectifications of the residents by those with power to set the objectives. Throughout, however, residents were absent from processes of objective setting. The planners, as expert professionals, used their organizing power (*pouvoir*) to frame the civic engagement process largely according to habit and to suit their own desires. They perceived themselves as approaching plan making "differently" to the area's residents. Local residents, perceived as "not singing from the same hymn sheet" (FG), were othered; rendered irrelevant, impossible, repressed. The multiple communities of the Newcastle regeneration area were "consulted" in a heavily striated space, rather than permitted to develop capacities and become fully-engaged in the plan-making network.

The master planning process focused on a "shared vision" (LD, 2004b) for the area to be developed jointly by the planners and the communities. The predetermined objectives include a reduction in low demand property, increased community cohesion and better use of green space. The area should accordingly become attractive to in-migrants, transgress strong estate-focused identifications and develop green recreational spaces. All three objectives demand a vision which addresses the whole of the area. However, in late 2002, the planners organized three local workshops concerned with specific areas in reaction to residents' demands to find out what might happen to their homes. Attendance at the workshops was low (a total of 120 people "dropped in"). We argue that different visions for the area cannot emerge from such downscaling of the scope of civic engagement. Yet, if viewed from the objectives of the master planning process, such different, or multiple, visions become "irrelevant" to the planners' search for one shared vision. Signification became institutionalized not only by the subjectification of the people as mere "residents" by the planners, but also by the organization of the workshops as a stage for this subjectification and signification. The lock-in or reification of signification and subjectification produced at the end of 2002 closes down alternative becomings. It stabilises physical and mental borders and loci of power, homogenizes groups, and reduces the dynamic for any emergent becoming of an experimental or innovative plan.

One regeneration team member referred to the process as "going in with the alphabet"—an "anything-goes approach" of traditional consultation techniques which produce a large amount of information which the planners regard as "irrelevant." In discussion, the planners admitted that they perceived the outcomes rather than the process as relevant. Referring to the statutory legislation, several stated that they were interested in following "correct procedure rather than right process" (FG): "we do this headache of engagement ... because the process says so" (FG). Communication would be preferably one-way, *from* planning officers who regarded their task as being to get "this person on that street [to] understand what we're trying to communicate to them" (FG). However, since "some people won't engage" and have "entrenched views" which are "out of touch with reality" (FG), the planners saw the "need to sell them the wider product" (FG).

There was one "minor" opinion stated, however, by a regeneration team member with a background in community development rather than in planning. Hers was the only voice to raise the issue of process legitimacy and to distinguish between what she termed "auditable legitimacy," as undertaken in our case example, and "moral legitimacy."

With the topological relations traced above between planners and local residents, and without an inclusive participatory strategy by which visions for the area could be produced, the mandatory "preferred options report," not surprisingly, is not related to the communities" desires. The options were technically produced in the planning office and include alternatives which are out of scope with regard to the established objectives for regeneration of the wider area. Thus the "options" were not "preferred" since they could not be linked to alternative "visions" for the area derived from citizen involvement exercises.

We trace the three options identified in Table 7.2 as differing less in kind than in the amount of demolition and construction promised—they differ in extensity rather than in intensity. They reflect more or less of the same. The area's "problems" have been framed in such a way that only certain solutions or actions are likely to occur (Shields, 1996). However, the wording of the options is clearly not neutral. Under the heading "What you are unlikely to get," options 1 and 2 listed "the best-quality streets and housing" (Newcastle City Council, 2005), while option 3 stated that people were "likely to get" "much better public transport, open spaces and parks" (NCC, 2005) and the "unlikely to get" column was empty. Option 3 – "Major Impact," with its promise of "having it all," in terms of new homes, new schools, a new Community Resource Center and so on, is likely to be more attractive to local residents. Respondents voted overwhelmingly for Option 3, the highest impact of demolition and new construction. Given the high level of territorial framing undertaken by the planning officers, any other result would have been extremely surprising.

Overall, the feedback rate was low with only 560 individuals responding to local proposals. With respect to individual areas response rates range from 2.2% to 9.6% of households in the different subareas. In terms of a wider vision, only 370 responses were received. This reflects only 2.8% of the regeneration area's population. Whilst planners undertook detailed analysis of the feedback, we suggest that the low number of

Table 7.2. Outline of Options From the Preferred Options Report

	Option 1	*Option 2*	*Option 3*
Number of new houses	• up to 700 new homes.	• 900 new homes and some environmental improvements.	• 1,600 to 2,200 new homes, a new shopping center, leisure facilities, and improved public transport.
The community is likely to get …	• Around £2million investment in parks and open space. • New homes built that are more energy efficient, i.e. cheaper to run.	• Around £2-3 million investment with priority in parks and open space • New homes built that are more energy efficient, i.e., cheaper to run. • Green corridors and riverside improvements • A new primary school/ schools in the east of the area.	• Over £6 million investment in parks and open spaces. • New homes built that are more energy efficient, i.e., cheaper to run. • Community resource center. • New primary schools in the east and west of the area. • Improved leisure facilities. • Improved shopping center. • Green corridors and riverside improvements. • Wider environmental improvements along Walker Road/Station Road.
The community is unlikely to get	• Planting, pavement improvements, and better lighting along Walker Road and Station Road • Improved bus service/ transport • New primary schools • Improved leisure facilities • Improved shopping center • Green corridors and riverfront improvements	• Wider environmental improvements along Walker Road/Station Road • Improved shopping center • Improved bus service/ transport • Community resource center • Improved leisure facilities	
Public investment	£65 Million	£85 Million	£185 Million
Private investment	£105 Million	£160 million	£340 Million

Source: Newcastle City Council (2005).

responses raises severe doubts about the legitimacy of any decision made "in the name of the community" on such a basis.

Some residents complained about apparent bias in the preferred options report, making submissions to the planning inspector that:

> "The percentages of support for option 3 was presented in a biased manner" (no. 1);

> "The consultation was flawed.... This means that the claim that option 3 was the preferred choice of the community is false" (no. 43);

> "The consultation was flawed. The AAP does not have regard to the community strategy" (no. 44);

> "The draft AAP does not demonstrate that partners have been consulted in order to consider the relevant alternatives" (no. 46);

> "The plan is not based on credible evidence" (no. 52) (Newcastle City Council, 2006).

Faced with an apparently biased set of options not developed through participatory engagement, these residents were obliged to return to the legal institutional rights afforded by the statutory planning system. As such, "disagreements, such as objections ... have to be solved outside of the sphere of public communication" (Pløger, 2001, p. 235).

The above submissions indicate that some, more vocal, local residents did not "buy" into organization of the civic engagement processes nor into the significations of the draft AAP even though the planners claimed that "Major change was sold to the people pre consultation" (FG). The regeneration team planners, however, were unrepentant about what Habermas (1970) would term their systematic distortion of communication. In our attempt to trace underlying rationales and mentalities behind such actions, focus group participants discussed the questions "how honest should we be? Should we have explained to people what the major option entailed?" (FG) and agreed that honesty would not have been the best policy in this instance for reasons including a belief that:

> "the Minor impacts won't do the job, so it was unacceptable, even if it had been chosen";

> "the Minor option wasn't an option";

> "If the Minor option had been chosen, there would be no program" (FG).

It is only in the privacy of the office that team members would admit what they honestly felt about the process and the participants. Jokes and ironic comments were used in order to deal with issues which were deemed to be "forbidden" in official meetings, representations and texts when planners were subjectified by the grammar of "plannerspeak." Cultural differences and contrasting lifestyles between people from the regeneration team and from the AAP area became part of humorous office-talk, a "release" (Forester, 2004) from feelings of frustration with the seemingly endless processes of community involvement, particularly when the planners already knew what the "solution" should be. The planners and local residents inhabited different allegiances and social strata of "us" and "them," between which there flowed little, if any, Habermasian reciprocity. The molecular energies of local residents" desires were made ironic, stratified, ordered and drained of power.

The regeneration team used its professional expertise to determine the technically-best outcome for the AAP area. They then used their statutory power to organize the options in favor of this particular outcome. They used techniques of qualculation to represent and justify the options, retaining tight control over territorialization of the spaces involved. Only one world is allowed to pass for actualization. This is a "technical-bureaucratic rationality,... advocated in order to solve problems" (Pløger, 2001, p. 237). Our case example clearly supports Fung's (2006, p. 69) claim that "many (perhaps most) public policies and decisions are determined not through aggregation or deliberation but rather through the *technical expertise* of officials whose training and professional specialization suits them to solving particular problems" (emphasis in original).

When asked about the negative submissions, one regeneration team member replied that objections are actually good: "what you really want is conflict and people shouting at you. Because then you know you're really tackling the issue" (FG). However, given the planners" perception that "the community don't understand the statutory planning process" (FG) and that "people have entrenched views" (FG), it becomes an issue of "steer[ing] the community towards certain outcomes and individuals away from what they want" (FG).

Finding Communities Without Exploring Them

The qualitative approach of the outreach sessions and focus groups provides more interesting and deeper insights into the views of local citizens. We suggest that this aspect of the consultation process would have been of immense value if carried out at the start of community involvement at least 3 years earlier.

The outreach sessions were concerned with manifest absence. Until this phase, so-called "hard-to-reach" groups had not been engaged satisfactorily. Ninety-nine people participated in twelve outreach sessions. Four sessions, run by planning consultants, were held with young people, three with older people, two with young parents, two with asylum seekers and one with community center users. These sessions introduced a different approach to civic engagement than that taken by the city council regeneration team. The consultants performed a different social construction of "community" and created a different individuation of community relations by means of rupturing the hitherto purely geographical and residential focus represented by the limited Network.

The difference between tracing and mapping in our analysis becomes particularly evident. Reporting the mere succession of actual events (tracing) produces an image but it does not indicate what is relevant or contains creative potential. Unfortunately, little happened after the outreach sessions as the planners did not pay particular attention to information gathered. However, if we try to think the map or diagram rather than trace the mere actualized line of events, it appears that the outreach sessions generated the highest degree of potentialities or "intensity" in the process so far. There is little focus on residential issues and "doorstep problems." Instead, the process spans a field of multiple becomings. The outreach sessions demonstrate that civic engagement can be a creative process rather than a mere linguistic method to "rubber-stamp" or obtain agreement for predetermined representations.

The outreach groups referred to many issues relating to specific local areas, but also to the regeneration area as a whole and beyond to the wider city. Thus the connectivities of people (such as around age-related issues) create a relational entity other than the geographical residential allegiance as imposed by the planners. Outreach approaches trigger multiplicities of communities and go beyond the alleged unity of "the community" or the "core population." The groups in the outreach sessions demonstrate an ability to address issues from multiple angles and to move well beyond the (often self-centered) interest in how exactly a neighborhood would be changed. They embraced issues that went "far beyond the needs of their particular group, reflecting a concern about all aspects of the area and all sections of the community" (Consultants, 2005, p. 36). They recognized and accepted that different and often agonizing visions and virtualities can and do exist simultaneously. The outreach sessions illustrate that the planners" decision, in 2002, to work primarily with resident groups organised the entire civic engagement process around specific and pregiven subareas instead of along networks of interests, problems and issues. The future morphogenesis of the area as a multiplicity of places to become was never problematized.

The outreach program also contained telephone interviews. These interviews represent the only attempt to give voice to those who will supposedly break the cycle of decline; potential new residents. No other attempt was made to reach beyond the geographically defined area and to follow a potential relational link which, if actualized, would realize a very different place. Young professionals, for instance, would be likely to connect to different relational networks and to build other interactions with the area than the existing population. Such an input would never be ascertained from the Network or from localized events, since it stems from different physical and mental networks not geographically congruent with the regeneration area.

It would appear from our mapping that collaborative processes of civic engagement, such as the outreach sessions, can generate capacity to produce different visions (virtuals) and to lead to actualization of potentially different outcomes to those produced through consultation processes as in our regeneration case. Based on noncircular segmentarities and different subjectification of actants, there is a potential for civic engagement to become diagrammatic; for network relations to release affective and connective potential and to generate opportunities for the empowerment (*puissance*) of local people that is so-often promised.

In terms of the theoretical framework, the outreach action made visible a diagram of the multiplicity of concerns and opened up the process of imagining a different future for the area. However, since the outreach sessions were largely ignored by the regeneration team, the manifest absence of these groups was turned into repressed absence. "What was felt, undergone, sensed and suffered from had no place in official discussions and discourses" (Lohmann & Steyaert, 2006, p. 88).

CONCLUSIONS: FABULATING THE POSSIBLES

Citizen engagement in strategic spatial planning through associations such as neighborhoods, interest groups, community panels, and so on performs in agonistic (if not antagonistic) tension between nationally territorialized, (post)bureaucratic programs and rationalized projects (such as frontloading), central and local political direction and the desires of the subjects of government (local residents) themselves. We would like planning practice to pay attention to the connectivity of human and nonhuman networks and especially to the ways in which different realities of time and space interrelate or clash. Planning is the art of "bringing into line the significance of the irretrievable, indeterminate, and excessive qualities of everyday life with an immanent, creative and pragmatic project for future social explication" (Thrift & Dewsbury, 2000, p. 428). Planning practice is a performative (Dewsbury, 2000) shaping of time-space: "every move ... is an untimely moment redistributing what has gone before while opening up what may yet come" (Deleuze, 1960/1991, p. 96).

Strategic spatial planning attempts (but generally fails) to articulate contingencies, described by Massumi (2002, p. 240) as "potential relational modulations of contexts that are not yet contained in their ordering as possibilities that have been recognized and can be practically regulated." Strategic spatial planning is thus practically impossible; it invokes the positive, indeterminate potential of possibilities (the Deleuzoguattarian virtual). Potential, however, as we have demonstrated in the Newcastle case, may be "actually captured" (Massumi, 2002) by the vicissitudes of habit (both in terms of participation techniques used and level of control assumed) and normalized into strategy or policy content which is discursively, economically, socially and politically largely predetermined. As Massumi (2002, p. 88) comments, "control is modulation made a power factor.... It is the powering up—or powering away—of potential." Policy outcomes are thus likely to reveal more about their own frames, assumptions and ideologies than about the actual places and people they are intended to affect.

In this chapter we have attempted to trace the diagonals or transversals of civic engagement strategies in the production of a Newcastle area action plan. Regeneration team planners have traced geographical boundaries, statistical data, and information from previous consultation exercises in the area and provided by the Network. They have thereby "organized, stabilized, neutralized the multiplicities according to the axes of signifiance and subjectification belonging to it" (Deleuze & Guattari, 1980/1987, p. 13). As Deleuze and Guattari continue, "this is why the tracing is so dangerous. It injects redundancies and propagates them." Tracings reproduce blockages and points of structuration, thus denying the "endlessly proliferating lines of force, the accelerations and ruptures, the slippages and viscosities which are experienced and created in the course of practitioners" innumerable turns, detours, operations, actualizations and avoidances" (Titlestad, 2001, p. 31).

We have traced discourses, organization, subjectification, and signification in plan-preparation processes and documents and situated our tracings in the topological relationalities of actants' ideological mentalities, assumptions, and beliefs locating the potential for performativities. We thus trace the relations of force between actants; between presence and absence, between that deemed relevant and irrelevant, in demonstration of the operational closures effected by the regeneration team and the blocking of creative potential. Such closures subordinate "problems" to, in our case, habitual practices and predetermined "solutions." Rather than fashioning a plan out of materials at hand (Lejano, 2006), or "flushing a form out of a seemingly infinite plethora of possibilities" (Frichot, 2006,

p. 112), the planners framed the process, and informed and manipulated people to select a particular option. As one team member suggested, the design of the civic engagement strategy was a choice between "skewed consultation or no consultation or Iraqi-style democracy" (FG).

Organization of citizen involvement was performed through segmentation; compartmentalisation of actants, places and times. Residents were subjectified, homogenized and normalized according to where they lived, assuming no other interest and ignoring Deleuze and Guattari's (1980/ 1987, p. 311) comment that "home does not preexist," but is a "limited space," an "uncertain and fragile center" among forces of chaos. Being "somewhere" should not be restricted to being in a single location and belonging to an exclusive network of geographically based housing-focused residents. The regeneration team desired power-full, striated territorialization of the area, rendering it increasingly homogeneous (Deleuze & Guattari, 1980/1987, p. 488) and thus capable of measurement, order and control. Residents were "caught between governance and empowerment" (Pløger, 2004, p. 79).

The power (*pouvoir*) of the planners operated through signification and subjectification to "sell" a particular concept (the major option) to stakeholders whose desires resulted from "a highly developed, engineered set-up ... a whole supple segmentarity that processes molecular energies" (Deleuze & Guattari, 1980/1987, p. 215) and seeks to immobilize them, denying multiplicity, repressing absence and domesticating potential generation of *puissance* which might lead to de- and re-territorialization along any different lines. Having framed the outcome for local people, the planners then faced a new issue; "the problem is now we have to prove that we've done what they told us" (FG) for the planning inspectorate.

Our tracing located the transversal of the consultants' outreach program. As the sessions demonstrated, "locality is not delimited; the absolute, then, does not appear at a particular place but becomes a nonlimited locality; the coupling of the place and the absolute is achieved not in a centered, oriented globalization or universalization but in an infinite succession of local operations" (Deleuze & Guattari, 1980/1987, p. 383). Participants in the sessions rhizomically "went far beyond" (Consultants, 2005, p. 36) the needs and wants of their own groups. They recognised simultaneous connectivities, juxtapositions and instabilities and envisioned very different virtuals or potentialities for the area to the stratified visions of those with allegiance to the Network. However, the virtuals diagrammed by the outreach groups have little, if any, chance of "planned" actualization. The regeneration team employed techniques of qualculation to present and/or absent information gathered from the citizen engagement processes. Information from the outreach sessions seems to have played little, if any, part in influencing decision makers. The planners thus closed off actualization (individuation or morphogenesis) of a multiplicity of other visions or virtuals. While we concur that planning "is perpetually involved in processes of actualization" (Frichot, 2006, p. 14), in our case example the virtuals of many actants, including the people-to-come, were repressed and rendered absent. The shutters at these windows of opportunity remained firmly closed.

The final question which we posed in the Introduction concerned challenges and opportunities for the future. Whilst any challenges and opportunities are inevitably virtual, we argue that the roles and unreflexive habits of planners and other actants involved in processes of civic engagement related to plan-making should be radically rethought in order to value the multiplicity of differences, rather than the reductionism of people, places and opinions to a unitary "this is." Planners operate in complex open systems of interconnecting social, cultural, economic, environmental and political networks. It follows that plan contents are no longer questions of form or land use, but of interrelationships between different actants (including land uses). Planners, therefore, in Deleuzoguattarian terms, have to "map out a range of circumstances" (Deleuze, 1990/1995, p. 26), situations and relations or lines: "lines are the basic components of things and events. So everything has its geography, its cartography, its diagram. What's interesting, even in a person, are the lines that make them up, or they make up, or take, or create" (Deleuze, 1990/ 1995, p. 33). Mapping lines and diagrams of relations of power or forces enables construction of trajectories representing desired virtualities of future development of the place or territory. Deleuzoguattarian pragmatic epistemology may facilitate creative opportunities for the development of concepts both for those "who are missing" (Deleuze, 1993/1997) or those people and places "yet to come" (Deleuze & Guattari, 1980/1987, p. 5).

While we do not advocate developing a Deleuzoguattarian "template" for civic engagement in strategic spatial planning, we do suggest that several Deleuzoguattarian concepts might usefully be introduced "into the vicinity of policy making" (Wise, 2006, p. 190) as an alternative form of identifying, mapping and understanding particular relationships and the possibility of rethinking them. Wise suggests that we should think in terms of procedurally driven frameworks for policymaking and planning. No single rule of *knowing that* will suffice, but perhaps procedural *knowing how* might help (Semetsky, 2004b). If policies are to accommodate a multiplicity of complex, often conflictual, processes and practices in an effective framework, then policy itself "should invite rhizomic relationships with its constituencies" (Wise, 2006, p. 190). Policy makers should recognize their own ideological "baggage," clichés and habits and move beyond them to work with the inclusive disjunctions of actants" contradictions and challenges, lines of flight, fractures and realignments, de- and reterritorializations: "one never sees from a distance in a space of this kind, nor does one see it from a distance" (Deleuze & Guattari, 1980/ 1987, p. 493).

Policymakers need to notice the "diagonals" which suggest new desires and new spaces. In order to notice diagonals, one should "look down" in a baroque manner, to trace detailed data (such as that gained from young people in the outreach exercise) onto a map which, in turn, will affect complex multiplicities and generate zones of indistinction which can suggest sites or locations of potential policy experiments "already … in the making" (Rajchman, 2000, p. 100). This would be a pragmatic approach in which "policy plugs into production, and production into policy" (Wise, 2006, p. 191; 2002, p. 230). It would be bureaucratically and politically unsettling and "risky," for, as Wise (2006, p. 191) explains, "it will not only apprehend the probability of 'opportunities that are unforeseen,' but simultaneously anticipate the movements of the city and accept that policy outcomes are experimental and unpredictable."

We argue the need for such "risks," however. We imply the significance of a trajectory or direction (perhaps toward sustainable regeneration as in our case example) while simultaneously affirming the complex multiplicity of potential paths which might be followed. We do not offer a normative, prescriptive methodology, but suggest Bruno Latour's (2004a, 2004b) process of "learning to be affected." Learning to be affected involves an openness to "listening for things that matter, a willingness to be confronted with matters whose mattering is not yet determined, things already exteriorized by a previous learning, things outside but which have never been left for dead" (Hinchliffe, 2004, p. 14). Rather than predetermining things that matter as in the Newcastle case, learning to be affected involves a recognition that such qualculation is inevitably reductionist. Consideration would be given to the constitutive outside, the Deleuzean (1993/1997) "people who are missing," as to who and what they are, with what implications for their exclusion. The "people who are missing" require an enabling image that can summon them at least into imagined existence. As such, Boundas (2006, p. 24) suggests that "the becoming-democratic of the missing people requires the art of fabulation."

Deleuze (1990/1995, p. 174) refers to Henri Bergson's (1932) notion of fabulation and "give[s] it a political meaning." Fabulation (Deleuze, 1983/ 1986, 1989) is comprised of creation and prognosis.[6] As Lambert (2002, p. 137) describes, it is "the art of invention as well as a conceptual avatar of a 'problem-solving' instinct that remedies an unbearable situation"— particularly with regard to the situation of "the people who are missing." The aim of fabulation as a "genuinely creative process" (Bogue, 2006, p. 209), is "where the writer and the people go toward one another"

(Deleuze, 1985/1989, in Lambert, 2002, p. 137) in attempts to make new possibilities visible.

Fabulation concerns telling "stories." In the original French, Deleuze uses the word *récits*, which infers "an oral or written relating of real or imaginary acts" (Rodowick, 1997, p. 5). Fabulation is thus a performative process of documentation which oscillates between the oral and the written, the factual and the nonfactual, the true and the nontrue. As such, we argue that processes of civic engagement engage in fabulation; narrating and documenting stories verbally and in written form. While stories enable the past (of people and place) to enter the present, fabulations "prioritize the future in the present" (Lohmann & Steyaert, 2006, p. 88) and express a virtual multiplicity. Further, civic engagement in policy making plays out patterns of conflict and resolution, the latter often performed, as in Newcastle, by planning officers (Deleuzean intercessors) from a transcendent perspective who reserve for themselves "all the authority of an unrestricted narration" (Rodowick, 1997, p. 6).

Fabulations go beyond description and narration. In fabulation the subject (geographical area or people) is constructed as a site of oscillation between reality and the virtual, which intersect in a state of transformation or passage: a becoming. Deleuze (1985/1989) suggests that becoming should be expressed as a collective will; "a collaborative process of invention" (Bogue, 2006, p. 212). Becoming and its fabulation belong "to a people, to a community, to a minority whose expression they practice and set free" (Deleuze, 1989, p. 153). Fabulation, then, is the discourse of minorities: a collective but nonunifying discourse of a multiplicity of people who struggle to define themselves through the forces of domination and exclusion. By bringing the absent into the present, fabulation can facilitate "undoing power relations in the very structures of one's subject position" (Braidotti, 2000, cited in Gough, 2004, p. 256).

Strategic spatial plans are inevitably political fictions or "visions" (Deleuze, 1997) which "speak the possibles" (after Boundas, 2006, p. 24), created "from both directions" (Lambert, 2002, p. 138) by actants with planning officers and politicians acting as intercessors between the voices and desires of citizens, interest groups and the final planning text. All-too-often, as our case example illustrates, fabulation opens a space of conflict and struggle between representations in which the power of bureaucratic intercessors dominates. We would prefer situations in which planners and (emergent) communities serve as mutual intercessors, "each aiding the other in a process of metamorphic departure from received categories and simultaneous approach toward only partially specified possibilities" (Bogue, 2006, p. 221).[7]

Planning is a virtual practice. Rajchman (1998, p. 117) regards the virtual city as the city that holds together the most, and most complicated, "different possible worlds," allowing them to exist together along a constructed plane with no need of a pre-established harmony. A virtual city, like a virtual plan, is agonistic; it allows insurgencies and encounters. As Foucault (1991, p. 121) wrote, "we must produce something that doesn't yet exist and about which we cannot know how and what it will be."

Planning policymaking could become a performative process which mobilizes complex, heterogeneous understandings, such as performed through outreach programs, to temporarily fix the meanings of dynamic entities: "a strategy for mapping-becoming without immobilizing it" (Rodowick, 1997, p. 5). It could seek out in particular, understandings from the interstices, those "cracks" and liminal spaces in which lines of flight or new fabulations appear.

Fabulation creates visions of "yet to be explored possibilities" (Bogue, 2006, p. 220) which break historical continuities and disrupt conventional narratives. As Bogue continues, they are "untimely visions, becomings and powers that are dynamic but unspecified in their narrative possibilities, and hence temporal forces that may generate stories." Fabulation offers the vision of a world radically different from that which planning practitioners "know," but which returns to confront that known in a cognitive manner (Scholes, 1976). Fabulation should thus stimulate creative action ("une puissance métamorphique," Rancière, 1998, p. 188), especially in situations of crisis, where something has to be done.[8] It is both a reaction to a disorienting event and a leap forward toward the future (Bogue, 2006, p. 22) in which new possibilities emerge.

We conclude, therefore, by suggesting that if citizens are to really engage with processes of strategic spatial planning, public officials need to think differently, to "step outside what's been thought before, ... [to] venture outside what's familiar and reassuring, ... to invent new concepts for unknown lands" (Deleuze, 1995, p. 103) and to allow possibilities for something new to emerge. In the words of Thomas Bay, they "must learn to believe and to invent" (2006, p. 98).

NOTES

1. Molar lines depict a hierarchical system of well-defined structures often affiliated with government. The molecular relates to more individual or microlevel entities and their behavior.
2. Examples of tracings include tabulated data, such as unemployment statistics, GIS representations of census data and data from opinion polls which offer seemingly "objective facts," but which are underpinned by a multiplicity of subjective (and often political) decisions and assumptions with regard to data definition, collection and interpretation. (For illustration,

see Hillier's (2007) discussion of evidence-based policymaking in the
United Kingdom.)

3. However, in empirical research we can only trace the actual. In order to
map the potential we must think processes of morphogenesis as well as
their topological relations and thereby put the tracing back on the map.

4. See also Vigar, Graham, and Healey, (2005) for analysis of a similar strategy employed in another area of Newcastle.

5. Personal communication with representatives of resident groups.

6. The term "fabulation" has been derived more recently from Robert
Scholes' work, *The Fabulators* (1967) to describe a literary style which experiments with subject matter and style, fusing the everyday with the fantastic
and blurring distinctions between the serious and the trivial, the practical
and impractical.

7. We have no space to explain the Foucauldian (1979) play on words between
l'infâme (that which is not to be told) and *l'infâme* (that which deserves to be
told) to which Deleuze (1995, p. 108) refers. For further detail, see Valentin
(2006a, 2006b).

8. See Bogue (2006) for further explanation.

REFERENCES

Amin, A. (2004). Region unbound: Towards a new politics of place. *Gegrafisker
Annaler, 86*(B), 33-44.

Arnstein, S. (1969). The ladder of citizen participation. *Journal of the Institute of
American Planners, 35*(4), 216-224.

Barber, B. (1984). *Strong democracy.* Berkeley: University of California Press.

Bay, T. (2006). I knew there were kisses in the air. In M. Fuglsang & B. Sørensen
(Eds.), *Deleuze connections* (pp. 96-111). Edinburgh, Scotland: Edinburgh University Press.

Bergson, H. (1932) *Les deux sources de la morale at de la religion* [The two sources of
morality and religion]. Paris: PUF.

Bergson, H. (1988). *Matter and memory* (N. Paul & W. Palmer, Trans.) New York:
Zone Books. (Original work published 1896)

Bogue, R. (2006). Fabulation, narration and the people to come. In C. Boundas
(Ed). *Deleuze and philosophy* (pp. 202-223). Edinburgh, Scotland: Edinburgh
University Press.

Bonta, M. (2001). *Toward a cultural geography of complex spaces.* Paper presented at
SE Division AAG meeting, Lexington, KY. Retrieved August 8, 2004, from
http://ntweb.deltastate.edu/mbonta/Deleuze.html

Bonta M., & Protevi, J. (2004). *Deleuze and geophilosophy: A guide and glossary.* Edinburgh, Scotland: Edinburgh University Press.

Boundas, C. (Ed.). (2006). What difference does Deleuze's difference make? In
Deleuze and philosophy (pp. 3-28). Edinburgh, Scotland: Edinburgh University
Press.

Braidotti, R. (2000). Teratologies. In I. Buchanan & C. Colebrook (Eds.), *Deleuze and feminist theory* (pp. 156-172). Edinburgh, Scotland: Edinburgh University Press.

Brown, S., & Lunt, P. (2002). A genealogy of the social identity tradition: Deleuze and Guattari and social psychology. *British Journal of Social Psychology*, 41, 1-23.

Callon, M. (1991). Techno-economic networks and irreversibility. In J. Law (Ed.), *A sociology of monsters? Essays on power, technology and domination* (pp. 132-161). Routledge, London.

Callon, M., & Law, J. (2005). On qualculation, agency, and otherness. *Environment and Planning D, Society and Space, 23*, 717-733.

Casey, E. (1997). *The fate of place*. Berkeley: University of California Press.

Chambers, S. (1996). *Reasonable democracy*. Ithaca, NY: Cornell University Press.

Chavis, D., & Wandersman, A. (1990). Sense of community in the urban environment: A catalyst for participation and community development. *American Journal of Community Psychology, 18*, 55-81.

Chess, C., & Purcell, K. (1999). Public participation and the environment: Do we know what works? *Environmental Science and Technology, 33*(16), 2685-2692.

Cilliers, P. (2002). Why we cannot know complex things completely. *Emergence, 4*(1/2), 77-84.

Consultants. (2005). *Consultation Feedback Report*. Retrieved February 2, 2007, from http://www.newcastle.gov.uk/

DeLanda, M. (2006). Deleuzian social ontology and assemblage theory. In M. Fuglsang & B. Sørensen (Eds.), *Deleuze connections* (pp. 250-266). Edinburgh, Scotland: Edinburgh University Press.

Deleuze, G. (1986). *Cinema 1: The movement-image* (H. Tomlinson, Trans.). Minneapolis: University of Minnesota Press. (Original work published 1983)

Deleuze, G. (1989). *Cinema 2: The time-image* (H. Tomlinson & R. Galeta). Minneapolis: University of Minnesota Press. (Original work published 1985)

Deleuze, G. (1991). *Bergsonism* (H. Tomlinson & B. Habberjam, Trans.). New York: Zone Books. (Original work published 1960)

Deleuze, G. (1993). *The fold: Leibniz and the baroque* (T. Conley, Trans.). London: Athlone Press. (Original work published 1988)

Deleuze, G. (1995). *Negotiations 1972-1990* (M. Joughin, Trans.). New York: Columbia University Press. (Original work published 1990)

Deleuze, G. (1997). *Essays critical and clinical* (D. W. Smith & M. Greco, Trans.) Minneapolis: University of Minnesota Press. (Original work published 1993)

Deleuze, G., & Guattari, F. (1987). *A thousand plateaus: Capitalism and schizophrenia* (B. Massumi, Trans.) London: Athlone Press. (Original work published 1980)

Deleuze, G., & Parnet, C. (2002). *Dialogues II* (H. Tomlinson & B. Habberjam, Trans.). London: Athlone Press. (Original work published 1977)

delli Carpini, M., Cook, F., & Jacobs, L. (2004). Public deliberation, discursive participation and citizen engagement: A review of the empirical literature. *Annual Review of Political Science, 7*, 315-344.

Department of the Environment, Transport and the Regions. (2000). *Our towns and cities: The future—Delivering an urban renaissance*. London: Stationery Office.

Dewsbury, J. D. (2000). Performativity and the event: Enacting a philosophy of difference. *Environment & Planning D, Society & Space, 18,* 473-496.

Devenney M. (2002). Critical theory and democracy. In A. Finlayson & J. Valentine (Eds.), *Politics and post-structuralism* (pp. 176-192). Edinburgh, Scotland: Edinburgh University Press.

Forester, J. (2004). Responding to critical momemts with humor, recognition and hope. *Negotiation Journal, 20*(2), 221-237.

Foucault, M. (1991). *Remarks on Marx: Conversations with Duccio Trombadori* (J. Goldstein & J. Cascaito). New York: Semiotext(e).

Frichot, H. (2006). Showing vital signs: The work of gilles deleuze and félix guattari's creative philosophy in architecture. *Angelaki, 11*(1), 109-116.

Fuglsang, M., & Sørensen, B. (2006). Deleuze and the social: Is there a d-function? In M. Fuglsang & B. Sørensen (Eds.), *Deleuze connections* (pp. 1-17). Edinburgh, Scotland: Edinburgh University Press.

Fung, A. (2006). Varieties of participation in complex governance [Special issue]. *Public Administration Review, 66*-75.

Fung, A., & Wright, E. O. (Eds.). (2003). Thinking about empowered participatory governance. In *Deepening democracy: Institutional innovations in empowered participatory governance* (pp. 3-42). London: Verso.

Gastil, J. (2000). *By popular demand.* Berkeley: University of California Press.

Goodchild, P. (1996). *Deleuze and Guattari: An introduction to the politics of desire.* London: Sage.

Gough, N. (2004). RhizomANTically becoming-cyborg: Performing posthuman pedagogies. *Educational Philosophy and Theory, 36*(3), 253-265.

Grosz, E. (2001). *Architecture from the outside.* Cambridge, MA: MIT Press.

Gutmann, A., & Thompson, D. (1996). *Democracy and disagreement.* Cambridge, MA: Harvard University Press.

Habermas, J. (1970). On systematically distorted communication. *Inquiry, 13,* 205-218.

Healey, P. (2002). Place, identity and governance: Transforming discourses and practices. In J. Hillier & E. Rooksby (Eds.), *Habitus: A sense of place* (pp. 173-201). Aldershot, England: Ashgate.

Healey, P. (2004). The treatment of space and place in the new strategic spatial planning in Europe. *International Journal of Urban and Regional Research, 28*(1), 45-67.

Healey, P. (2006a). *Collaborative planning* (2nd ed.). Basingstoke, England: Palgrave Macmillan.

Healey, P. (2006b). *Urban complexity and spatial strategies: A relational planning for our times.* London: Routledge.

Hillier, J. (2002). *Shadows of power.* London: Routledge.

Hillier, J. (2007). *Stretching beyond the horizon: Towards a multiplanar theory of spatial planning and governance,* Aldershot, England: Ashgate.

Hillier, J. (in press). On justice between absence and presence: The "ghost ships" of Graythorp. *International Journal of Urban and Regional Research.*

Hinchliffe, S. (2004). *Towards a careful political ecology.* Retrieved August 8, 2006, from http://www.open.ac.uk/socialsciences/habitable_cities/habitable_citiessubset/habitable_citiesinfopops/political_ecology.pdf

Hinchliffe, S., Kearnes, M., Degen, M., & Whatmore, S. (2005). *Ecologies and economics of action—Sustainability, calculations and other things.* Retrieved August 12, 2006, from http://www.open.ac.uk/socialsciences/habitable_cities/ habitable_ citiessubset/habitable_citiesinfopops/ecologies.pdf

Iedema, R. (2003). *Discourses of post-bureaucratic organisation.*Amsterdam: John Benjamins.

Innes, J., & Booher, D. (1999a). Consensus building and complex adaptive systems: A framework for evaluating collaborative planning. *Journal of the American Planning Association, 65*(4), 412-423.

Innes, J., & Booher, D. (1999b). Consensus building as role playing and bricolage: toward a theory of collaborative planning. *Journal of the American Planning Association, 66*(1), 9-26.

Innes, J., & Booher, D. (2004). Reframing public participation: strategies for the 21st century. *Planning Theory and Practice, 5*(4), 419-436.

Koontz, T., & Thomas, C. (2006). What do we know and need to know about the environmental outcomes of collaborative management? *Public Administration Review, 66*(Supplement 1), 111-121.

Lambert, G. (2002). *The non-philosophy of Gilles Deleuze.* New York: Continuum.

Latour, B. (2004a). *Politics of nature.* Cambridge, MA: Harvard University Press.

Latour, B. (2004b). How to talk about the body? The normative dimension of science studies. *Body and Society, 19*(2-3), 205-229.

Law, J. (2002). On hidden heterogeneities: Complexity, formalism, and aircraft design. In J. Law & A. Mol (Eds.), *Complexities* (pp. 116-141). Durham, NC: Duke University Press.

Law, J. (2003). *Topology and the naming of complexity.* Retrieved May 31, 2004 from the Centre for Science Studies, Lancaster University Web site: http:// www.comp.lancs.ac.uk/sociology/papers/Law-Topology-and-Complexity.pdf

Law, J. (2004a). And if the global were small and noncoherent? Method, complexity and the baroque. *Environment & Planning D, Society & Space,* 22, 13-26.

Law, J. (2004b). *After method.* London: Routledge.

Law, J., & Urry, J. (2003). *Enacting the social.* Retrieved May 31, 2004 from the Centre for Science Studies, Lancaster University Web site: http://www.comp .lancs.ac.uk/sociology/papers/Law-Urry-Enacting-the-Social.pdf

Lazzarato, M. (2006). The concepts of life and living in the societies of control. In M. Fuglsang & B. Sørensen (Eds.), *Deleuze connections* (pp. 171-190). Edinburgh, Scotland: Edinburgh University Press.

LD. (2004a). *Statement of community involvement.* Retrieved February 10, 2007, from http://www.newcastle.gov.uk/

LD. (2004b). *Master plan.* Retrieved February 10, 2007, from http://www.newcastle .gov.uk/

LD. (2004c). *Change.* Retrieved February 10, 2007, from http://www.newcastle.gov .uk/

Leadbeater, C., & Miller, P. (2004). *The pro-am revolution—How enthusiasts are changing our economy and society.* London: Demos.

Lejano, R. (2006). *Frameworks for policy analysis: Merging text and context.* London: Routledge.

Lohmann, P., & Steyaert, C. (2006). In the mean time: vitalism, affects and meta-morphosis in organisational change. In M. Fuglsang & B. Sørensen (Eds.), *Deleuze connections* (pp. 11-95). Edinburgh, Scotland: Edinburgh University Press.

Lowndes, V., Pratchett, L., & Stoker, G. (2001a). Trends in public participation, Part 1—Local government perspectives. *Public Administration, 79*(1), 205-222.

Lowndes, V., Pratchett, L., & Stoker, G. (2001b). Trends in public participation, Part 2—Citizens' perspectives. *Public Administration, 79*(2), 445-455.

Massumi, B. (2002) *Parables for the Virtual*, Duke University Press, Durham, NC.

McCormack, D. (2005). Diagramming practice and performance. *Environment and Planning D, Society and Space, 23*, 119-147.

McGuirk, P. (2000). Power and policy networks in urban governance: local government and property regeneration in Dublin. *Urban Studies, 37*(4), 651-672.

McMillan, D., & Chavis, D. (1986). Sense of community: A definition and theory. *Journal of Community Psychology, 14*, 6-23.

Moffitt, M., & Bordone, R. (Eds). (2005). *The handbook of dispute resolution.* San Francisco: Jossey-Bass.

Newcastle City Council. (2000). *Going for growth.* Retrieved February 8, 2007, from http://www.newcastle.gov.uk

Newcastle City Council. (2002). *City sub-regional plan.* Retrieved February 8, 2007, from http://www.newcastle.gov.uk

Newcastle City Council. (2005). *Preferred options report.* Retrieved February 8, 2007, from http://www.newcastle.gov.uk

Newcastle City Council. (2006). *Submission responses.* Retrieved February 8, 2007, from http://www.newcastle.gov.uk

Office of the Deputy Prime Minister. (2004a). *Planning policy statement 1: Creating sustainable communities, consultation paper.* London: Author.

Office of the Deputy Prime Minister. (2004b). *Community involvement in planning: the government's objectives.* London: Author.

Office of the Deputy Prime Minister. (2005). *Planning policy statement 1: Delivering sustainable development.* London: HMSO.

O'Neill, P., & McGuirk, P. (2005). Reterritorialisation of economies and institutions: the rise of the Sydney Basin economy. *Space and Polity, 9*(3), 283-305.

Patton, P. (2006). Order, exteriority and flat multiplicities in the social. In M. Fuglsang & B. Sørensen (Eds.), *Deleuze connections* (pp. 21-38). Edinburgh, Scotland: Edinburgh University Press.

Perkins, D., & Long, D. (2002). Neighbourhood sense of community and social capital. In A. Fisher, C. Sonn, & B. Bishop (Eds.), *Psychological sense of community* (pp. 291-318). New York: Plenum.

Planning Officers Society. (2004). A more relevant system. In Office of the Deputy Prime Minister in association with *Planning, Delievering Planning Reform: Meeting the challenge of culture change* (p. 6). London: ODPM/Haymarket.

Pløger, J. (2001). Public participation and the art of governance. *Environment and Planning B: Planning and Design, 28*(2): 219-41.

Pløger, J. (2004). Strife: urban planning and agonism. *Planning Theory, 3*(1), 71-92.

Rajchman, J. (1998). *Constructions.* Cambridge, MA: MIT Press.

Rajchman, J. (2000). *The Deleuze connections.* Cambridge, MA: MIT Press.

Rancière, J. (1998). *La chair des mots* [The flesh of words]. Galilée, Paris: Politiques de l'écriture,

Rodowick, D. (1997). Fabulation: Towards a minor cinema. Retrieved January 15, 2007, from http://www.thing.at/immedia/sehen.ds03rod.htm

Scholes, R. (1967). *The fabulators.* New York: Oxford University Press.

Scholes, R. (1976). The roots of science fiction. In M. Rose (Ed.), *Science fiction: A collection of critical essays* (pp. 46-56). Englewood Cliffs, NJ: Prentice-Hall.

Semetsky, I. (2004a). The complexity of individuation. *International Journal of Applied Psychoanalytic Studies, 1*(4), 324-346.

Semetsky, I. (2004b). The role of intuition in thinking and learning: Deleuze and the pragmatic legacy. *Educational Philosophy and Theory, 36*(4), 446-454.

Sheller M. (2004). Mobile publics: Beyond the network perspective. *Environment & Planning D, Society & Space, 22,* 39-52.

Shields R. (1996). A guide to urban representation and what to do about it: Alternative traditions of urban theory. In A. King (Ed.), *Re-presenting the city* (pp. 227-252). New York: New York University Press.

Straus, D. (2002) *How to make collaboration work.* San Francisco: Berrett-Koehler.

Susskind, L., McKearnan, S., & Thomas-Larmer, J. (Eds.). (1999). *The consensus building handbook.* Thousand Oaks, CA: Sage.

Thanem, T., & Linstead, S. (2006). The trembling organisation: Order, change and the philosophy of the virtual. In M. Fuglsang & B. Sørensen (Eds.), *Deleuze connections* (pp. 39-57). Edinburgh, Scotland: Edinburgh University Press.

Thoburn, N. (2003). *Deleuze, Marx and politics. Chapter two: Minor politics: The style of cramped creation.* Retrieved November 6, 2006, from http://libcom.org/library/deleuze-marx-politics-nicholas-thoburn-intro

Thrift, N., & Dewsbury, J. D. (2000). Dead geographies—And how to make them live. *Environment & Planning D, Society & Space, 18,* 411-432.

Titlestad, M. (2001). Contesting maps; Musical improvisation and narrative. *Pretexts: Literary and Cultural Studies, 10*(1), 21-36.

Valentin, J. (2006a). Gilles Deleuze's political posture. In C. Boundas (Ed.), *Deleuze and philosophy* (pp. 185-201). Edinburgh, Scotland: Edinburgh University Press.

Valentin, J. (2006b). La fabulation chez Gilles Deleuze ou la force du *rien* politique [The fabulation with Gilles Deleuze and the strength of *nothing* policy]. *Symposium, 10*(1), 305-325.

Vigar, G., Graham, S., & Healey, P. (2005). In search of the city in spatial strategies: past legacies, future imaginings. *Urban Studies, 42*(8), 1391-1410.

Webler, T., Tuler, S., & Krueger, R. (2001). What is a good public participation process? Five perspectives from the public. *Environmental Management, 27*(3), 435-450.

Wise, P. (2002). Cultural policy and multiplicities. *International Journal of Cultural Policy, 8*(2), 221-231.

Wise, P. (2006). Australia's Gold Coast: A city producing itself. In C. Lindner (Ed.), *Urban space and cityscapes* (pp. 177-191). London: Routledge.

CHAPTER 8

A COMPARATIVE STUDY OF CITIZEN ENGAGEMENT IN INFRASTRUCTURE PLANNING IN JAPAN AND THE UNITED STATES

A Look at Legal Frameworks and Two Successful Cases

Shunsaku Komatsuzaki and Hindy Lauer Schachter

INTRODUCTION:
CITIZEN PARTICIPATION IN INFRASTRUCTURE ISSUES

This chapter analyzes and compares the growth of citizen engagement in infrastructure planning in the United States and Japan in an era of networked societies. For much of the twentieth century, governments tended to consider infrastructure development an area requiring technical expertise and hence, not amenable to citizen involvement. During this period,

Civic Engagement in a Network Society
pp. 187–205
Copyright © 2008 by Information Age Publishing
All rights of reproduction in any form reserved.

governments in the United States, Europe, and East Asia built large-scale developments including highways, railroads, international airports, ports, dams, and power plants without soliciting citizen opinions. As MacDougall (2001, p. 3) noted, residents near constructions "benefited or suffered, as the case might be, without much, if any, opportunity to influence the siting and details of the project."

By the 1960s-1970s, however, infrastructure development suddenly faced public criticism at least partly because of its adverse effects on pollution. Citizens in many countries began demanding a role in issues affecting environmental protection (Society for the Study of Consensus Building Methodology, 2001; Vig & Kraft, 2003). Inglehart (1977) has theorized that economic growth precipitated a postmaterialist value shift in the mass publics of industrialized democracies. Clark and Rempel (1997) have documented the growth of this ethos in the United States and other Western countries. Umemori and Rempel (1997) used survey evidence to show its spread in Japan as well although with less emphasis there on political activism. Tanaguschi (2006) also documented the shift in Japan through content analysis of newspaper editorials.

Since industrialized societies have extensive infrastructures (transportation networks, airports, etc.) in place, a part of their population give greater importance to quality-of-life issues such as sustainability rather than concentrating solely on continued development (Box, 1998; Harashina, 2006; Randolph, 2004; Torgerson, 1995). Economic benefit was no longer the only decisive value for evaluating infrastructure projects. In Japan, environmental concerns led to sit-in protests against constructing Narita International Airport outside Tokyo and a freeze on building the Outer Tokyo Belt Highway (which presently remains unfinished). In the United States, extensive protests against a 1969 Boston, Massachusetts long-range infrastructure plan led the state's governor to declare a moratorium on building highways in the area.

Contemporary, globalized society diffuses political ideas rapidly among polities with innovations generally originating in the United States or Europe and then moving to other areas (Schachter 2004). In the second half of the twentieth century, the United States and Japan both faced similar demands for citizen participation in infrastructure planning despite their different cultural, social, and historical contexts. Both polities were part of a global trend toward a rapidly expanded public-policy role for networks p. of nongovernmental organizations (e.g., Shin'ichi 1999). Boyte (2005, 237) described this shift "as a move from seeing citizens as voters, volunteers, clients, or consumers to viewing citizens as problem solvers and cocreators of public goods."

In both countries, bringing citizen groups into the planning process required new rules and procedures. To deal with the issue, the Japanese government used an amalgam of foreign (principally American) models and their own home-grown experiences (MacDougall 2001). Today, American and Japanese proponents of greater engagement make similar arguments that scientific and economic rationality are not the only important planning values in infrastructure development but rather that governmental accountability is also a key value.

Randolph (2004) has noted that in the United States the traditional system of expertise bred pervasive mistrust, a declining sense of responsibility, and high costs of impasse and conflict. As a remedy, he proposed stakeholder involvement through collaborative environmental planning.

In Japan, Harashina (2006) argued that a democratic government has representativeness and responsiveness obligations and must be accountable to the public. In order to augment accountability, governments must provide citizens with (1) access to information, (2) procedures to participate in decision making, and (3) support from the legal system.

As Easton (1965) posited, extensive public demands to participate led governments to enact new outputs in the form of laws and regulations. To involve stakeholders in infrastructure planning, governments had to write legislation and guidelines inaugurating participation forums. While civil engineering had developed procedures and regulations for channeling technical expertise, few methods to encourage citizen participation in technical areas existed. In the second half of the twentieth and the opening decade of the twenty-first centuries, many governments started to adopt structures, rules, procedures, and processes to facilitate citizen participation (Society for the Study of Consensus Building Methodology, 2001; Yai & Maekawa, 2004).

Since countries vary in culture and history, each nation is likely to benefit from channels designed to take into account its unique circumstances. A country's historical pattern of deference to expertise will influence the respective roles it assigns to citizen involvement and technical rationality. Innovations designed for one polity may not work well in others.

The organizational-behavior literature has contrasted the United States and Japan in terms of their respective privileging of individual and communal values—particularly in areas pitting individual rights against conformity (e.g., George & Jones, 2005). Such differences suggest that the United States and Japan might approach citizen engagement in different ways. In fact, since the Meiji era (1868-1912), when Japan started to adopt Western policy innovations on a large scale, it has altered them to fit its unique circumstances (Yamamoto, 2006).

A relatively unexplored question is whether citizen participation techniques that are useful in the United States would also generate involvement in Japan. The American literature on citizen engagement suggests that certain tactics facilitate involvement in a wide range of circumstances. In the United States, Baker, Addams, and Davis (2005) have noted, for example, the importance of administrators carefully planning participation processes; agency personnel need to design a set of procedures and use them to interact with citizens from the problem definition stage through decision making and follow-up. Cole and Caputo (1984) recommended establishing multiple participation forums. Halvorsen (2003) found a correlation between high quality participation which was deliberative, open and respectful, and an increase in citizen perceptions that agencies were responsive. Holzer, Melitski, Rho, and Schwester (2004) found that agencies using information and communication technologies (ICTs) experienced greater levels of citizen participation in a number of Western polities.

Comparing how American and Japanese administrators have approached demands for citizen forums can give some evidence as to whether the American literature's advice on which channels to use is also viable in an Asian context. Examining comparative case studies serves to highlight issues in cross-polity diffusion of political ideas, spotlighting where similar approaches work across cultural divides and where solutions from the United States may not be effective in Japan because of different cultural, political, or social settings. The chapter helps to explain how and when to engage the public in different polities. The study adds to our understanding of which forums work across national boundaries.

A comparative case-study overview of emerging processes in the United States and Japan shows the influence of social/cultural setting on citizen participation in a technical area traditionally governed by considerations of economic rationality; it adds to our understanding of how citizen engagement policies have different outcomes in different societies, what differences occur and why. It helps identify factors that influence effectiveness of specific techniques and policy reforms in various polities. More controlled, large-scale studies can then further examine the import of these factors.

This comparative citizen-engagement study has two dimensions. The first two sections identify the major American and Japanese legislation and guidelines that give citizens an infrastructure planning role. The next section analyzes two cases—one from America and one from Japan—that show how citizen groups used governmentally-established processes to influence specific projects through a variety of channels including ICTs. We consider these cases examples of successful involvement as in both instances citizen participation affected decision making. Since both the United States and Japan delegate extensive infrastructure-planning authority to states and/or localities, the focus is on processes at the subsidiary level. A final section offers conclusions.

LAWS AND REGULATIONS: THE UNITED STATES

The importance of participation as a way of responding to citizen demands in transportation was recognized in U.S. law before the law of Japan. In transportation planning, the Federal-Aid Highway Act of 1950 was the initial piece of legislation to require public hearings in cases where federal highways traversed a municipality (Miura, 2000; U.S. Department of Transportation, Federal Highway Administration, 1996). In 1964, the Urban Mass Transportation Act established further citizen participation channels including public hearings on the location and design of specific projects (Yai, 2004).

As public hearings came under fire for allowing involvement after key decisions were already made (Adams, 2004), the FHWA responded with a dual hearing process in 1969. The first hearing was held before the U.S. Department of Transportation picked a location; discussion was to center on whether a need existed for a highway. A subsequent, second hearing allowed members of the public to speak about specific placement and design issues.

Additional outlets for citizen comments emerged from the 1969 National Environmental Policy Act in relation to environmental impact statements which the law required for new construction projects. The 1991 Intermodal Surface Transportation Efficiency Act (ISTEA) required public involvement in all federally subsidized transportation planning; it mandated that each state's metropolitan planning organizations introduce hearings. Both of ISTEA's successor acts—the 1998 Transportation Equity Act for the 21st Century (TEA-21) and the 2005 Safe, Accountable, Flexible and Efficient Transportation Equity Act: A Legacy for Users (SAFETE-LU) continued to include participation mandates.

State laws afforded additional citizen-engagement opportunities. For example, in California the Bagley-Keene Open Meeting Act required state boards and commissions to open meetings to the public and allow time for citizen input. The Ralph M. Brown Act did the same for local forums (Council of Local Authorities for International Relations, 2005; Okabe, 2003). Other states initiated their own legal frameworks to introduce a citizen voice.

In 1996, the U.S. Department of Transportation produced a guideline identifying which methods its affiliates should use to encourage public involvement (U.S. Department of Transportation, Federal Highway Act, 1996).

As Table 8.1 shows, the agency divided the methods into four categories: ways for the agency to route information to citizen groups, forums for citizens to speak before agency members, methods of getting information

**Table 8.1.   Public Involvement Techniques for
Transportation Decision-Making**

Public Information and Publicity	Information Exchange	Getting Feedbacks From the public	Other Techniques
• Civic advisory committees • Mailing lists • Public information materials • Key person interviews • Video techniques, telephone techniques, media strategies • Speakers' bureaus and public involvement volunteers	• Public meetings/ hearings • Open houses/open forum hearings • Conferences and workshops	• On-line services • Hot lines • Drop-in centers • Public opinion surveys • Facilitation, negotiation and mediation	• Game and contests • Role playing • Interactive TV/ video displays • Computer presentations and simulations • Teleconferencing

Source: U.S. Department of Transportation, Federal Highway Administration (1996.)

from individuals, and a miscellaneous category of "other" techniques. Many of the methods envisioned "top-down" communication efforts. Staff members were more concerned with distributing agency information or surveys than having citizen groups deliberate with each other. Another limitation was that the guideline did not relate how the transportation agency would use the perspectives it received from citizen groups nor did it mandate that any of these perspectives had to actually affect outcomes. Nevertheless, the guideline did show an interest in disclosing information to outside groups and hearing opinions in return. The agency defended bringing the public into the planning process by stating

> People have a key role in the decisions shaping what transportation systems and services will be part of their communities.... Consulting with the public—the transportation consumer—is a crucial way to identify public values and needs, to gather information, and to build consensus on transportation programs. Finally, and most importantly, public participation makes for better transportation decisions. (U.S. DOT FHWA, 1996, A Note From The Administrators: FHWA and FTA)

LAWS AND REGULATIONS: JAPAN

Unlike the United States, Japan enacted no laws or regulations prescribing citizen participation in infrastructure development at the national level until 2003. A 1969 revision of the City Planning Law made nominal provision for consultation at the municipal level (MacDougall 2001). Some individual municipalities, regional bureaus of the Ministry of Land, Infrastructure, and Transport (MLIT) and public corporations (e.g., the Japan Highway Public Corporation) voluntarily introduced some relatively top-down oriented citizen-participation channels in the 1960s and 1970s (Hitachi Research Institute, 2004). The city of Yokohama developed legally mandated consultation windows, neighborhood city halls and a citizen assembly consisting of 10,000 randomly selected individuals who met in small groups to discuss public concerns (MacDougall 2001). In Tokushima Prefecture, representatives of the regional bureau of the Ministry of Land, Infrastructure, and Transport and the prefecture government met with citizens who opposed the construction of a weir across the Yoshino River and built a compromise consensus that enabled construction to continue. However, many environmental nongovernmental organizations (NGOs) decried the lack of mandated procedures for these interactions which they believed placed them at a disadvantage vis-à-vis the bureaucrats. At a World Lake Conference NGO Workshop in 2001 discussing the weir, a network of NGOs insisted that greater governmental efforts were needed to solve environmental problems and posted an online complaint to elected officials stating, "We demand from them better understanding and cooperation in our activities on a level playing field" (World Lake Conference NGO Workshop 2001).

In June 2003, the national Ministry of Land, Infrastructure, and Transport finally established a standard framework for citizen participation in Japan called the "Public Involvement Guideline in the Design Phase of Infrastructure Development" (Ministry of Land, Infrastructure, and Transport, 2003). This guideline prescribed a process of citizen participation in infrastructure development including an agency obligation to disclose its planning procedures and techniques in order to let citizens participate. The government expected the establishment of a participation framework to standardize citizen involvement practices across regions and stimulate local governments to more efforts toward citizen engagement.

Figure 8.1 adumbrates the process of citizen participation in the infrastructure design phase. Agencies have an obligation to frame and disclose alternative plans including a choice that no project be constructed. Agencies have obligations to ascertain citizens' opinions through various methods including use of the Internet, explanatory meetings, and public hearings. Agencies should establish a committee or a third-party organization to mediate, negotiate, build consensus and reconsider plans in light of participation processes with committee members being learned people with experience in the infrastructure field as well as representatives from residents' groups, and construction and public-sector organizations. Committees must keep and disclose a log of meeting discussions. When agencies determine a development plan, they must disclose the whole decision-making process. Public organizations should set a time limit for participation activities.

The Japanese and American guidelines have certain similarities. Both documents mandated agencies to disseminate information. Both proposed agency-initiated and controlled efforts to ascertain public opinion, and both required forums for public speech. But the Japanese guidelines were more government- or expert-oriented than their American counterpart. Although the Japanese mediating committee or third-party organization included representatives of citizen groups, most members were expected to be experts, politicians and bureaucrats. Forming the committee was a governmental choice with details of the formation process left to the discretion of local governments or regional bureaus. Implementation was thus heavily dependent on local government mindsets. Not all administrators relished the risks to their routines attendant on genuine citizen involvement. Some bureaus initiated development plans in a relatively top-down manner and did not really reflect citizens' opinions. In other areas, citizens could effectively participate in development.

We turn now to examine two cases of authentic participation. Although one case focuses on long-range planning and the other case on building a single road, the narratives help us identify certain procedural similarities that seem important for having a participation process that influences policy in different political and sociocultural systems.

TWO SUCCESSFUL PARTICIPATION CASES

Florida Makes a Long-Range Plan

In 1994, the Florida Department of Transportation (FDOT) developed a 25-year statewide transportation plan—the 2020 Florida Transportation Plan (2020 FTP)—whose goal was to form a policy framework to strengthen the economy, provide mobility choices for all people and support the environment and communities (FDOT, 2000). Beachy (1999) has noted that in earlier state transportation planning efforts, public involvement occurred only at a few formal hearings which drew few citizens and produced even fewer useful public comments. This time, however, FDOT introduced an energetic citizen participation process. The Florida Transportation Commission announced that as the new ISTEA regulations mandated participation channels, FDOT would therefore recognize the need to actively engage the public (Patrenos, 2000).

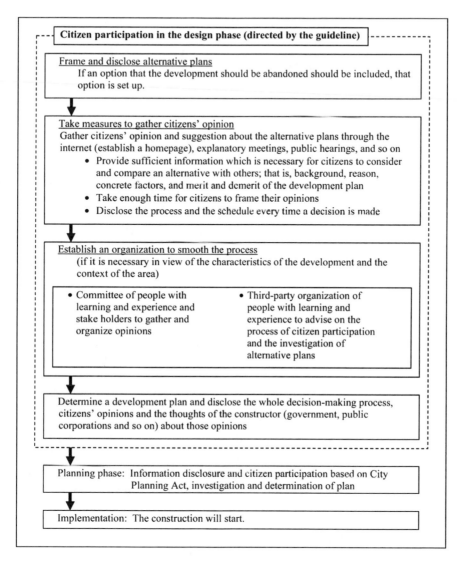

Source: Ministry of Land, Infrastructure, and Transport (2003).

Figure 8.1.   Citizen participation guideline in Japan.

In the summer of 1994, FDOT held more than 50 public meetings and other events in 33 towns and cities to gather and exchange information between citizens and the local government. The meetings consisted of 24 public workshops, 14 focus groups, 9 technical brainstorming sessions, 4 transportation fair exhibits and a 3-day area orientation. Those meetings were held at various locations including airport terminals, FDOT offices, and shopping centers and more than 3,000 people participated. According to Beachy (1999), each of the seven FDOT districts held at least five events. The efforts yielded more than 500 pages of comments which covered a wide range of topics, from a call for an exclusive expressway limited to truck traffic to a proposal to eliminate noxious weeds and plants along roadsides.

In August 1994, FDOT held a Statewide Consensus Building Workshop with over 200 participants. Representatives of state and local governments met with a diverse group from nonprofit and neighborhood organizations including metropolitan planning organizations, regional planning councils, environmental interest groups, and private-sector interests. Their purpose was to review public comments and related materials and reach consensus on strategic actions to respond to public concerns. Computers logged all participants' comments at the sessions and assigned a tracking number to make sure they did not get lost. FDOT made an effort to publicize the workshop through newsletters, public information materials and various outside media. The agency's website featured a short movie and video on the consensus-building process (FDOT, 2000). Workshop participants decided that among the most important strategic actions that the agency should pursue were increasing coordination of land use and transportation, public involvement in transportation decisions at all stages of the process, and coordination between the Florida Department of Transportation, metropolitan planning organizations and local governments.

In fall 1994, the agency compiled a draft plan and held another public hearing, mandated by state law, to get additional comments; FDOT adopted the plan in January 1995. Beachy (1999) noted that Florida's process had five innovative features which other agencies might want to emulate.

The agency asked citizens to give their initial input before it compiled a draft rather than as a response to agency documents. This timing gave citizen groups leeway to direct the discussion into paths unforeseen by FDOT.

A small-group format was used for gathering much of the workshop input rather than requiring people to speak only at formal public hearings. This format allowed greater interaction and deliberation among participants.

The agency recorded comments as each citizen spoke and entered them into a database using typists and laptop computers. Each comment was categorized by location, session, and general area of interest, such as, air quality, bicycles as alternate transportations, and so forth. Each FDOT advisory committee on a specific substantive area reviewed the relevant comments to its issues when revising reports to the steering committee. The tracking procedure protected against selective retention of off-beat or initially unpopular ideas.

A team of professional facilitators designed the process and facilitated all public sessions. This procedure helped ensure that the individuals supervising interactions did not have an overwhelming interest in seeing any particular outcome ensue.

Input was gathered in a uniform format, across the state over a very short time frame (3 weeks). This procedure ensured that all participants were involved under reasonably similar environmental circumstances.

All these tactics, especially recording comments, motivated people. Many participant groups believed that their efforts paid off in effecting changes. The nonprofit, growth-management watchdog group, 1000 Friends of Florida (n.d.) claimed on its Web site that it helped to get inclusion of the final document's language promoting citizen participation and flexible design. FDOT's Public Transit Office (n.d.) acknowledged relationships between citizen comments and the final state document by placing representative comments next to each of the plan's objectives and strategies on its Web site. Under the objective to increase transit service, for example, the office placed several focus group complaints where people reported having to leave events early because of sporadic bus service.

Moreover, even participants at the meetings whose ideas did not influence change, reported that they were satisfied with the process because the agency recorded their comments (Yai & Terabe, 1996). They felt that they had an important role as players in the governmental project. The ability of the forum itself to influence satisfaction echoes a finding in Yanow's interpretive study of the Israel Corporation of Community Centers where she noted that residents expressed satisfaction with getting community centers even if these centers did not bring substantive benefits since "the presence of a community center in a neighborhood became itself a symbol of a certain status" (Yanow, 1993, 53). Simply having the government record citizen comments made some people see the process as open and democratic—and view themselves as important, respected participants. (Summaries of comments from participants are available at http://www.dot.state.fl.us/planning/2025ftp/)

After the revised 2020 Florida Transportation Plan incorporating citizen comments was adopted, the succeeding plan, called Florida Transportation Plan 2025, inherited the public meeting procedures developed for the 2020 FTP process. Thus, this case of citizen participation had an impact both on policy and subsequent decision making, and can be considered a success.

Yokohama Builds a Road

Before the introduction of Japan's national guideline on involvement, Yokohama city introduced citizen participation in planning for a city road, the "Onda-Motoishikawa Line." Residents disputed how to handle 4 out of the total length of 7 kilometers (City Planning Bureau of Yokohama, 2003), preferring a two- rather than a four-lane configuration. The public's assumption was that a four-lane road would have more traffic, and that, therefore, a two-lane road would be better for environmental protection (Kurosawa, 2000).

As in the Florida case, the government initiated participation forums at a relatively early stage before the authorities committed to one plan. Indeed, at this early stage an advisory committee identified four alternative route plans including one to abandon the project (Harashina, 2006, pp. 240-241; Korenaga, Mataki, & Watanabe, 2000; Suzuki, 1998).

Yokohama's citizen-participation process can be divided into three periods (Watanabe, 2001). Table 8.2 identifies the activities that occurred in each.

The city opened the participation process by sending a questionnaire to the 40,000 households it deemed construction would affect and fol-

Table 8.2.   The Process of Citizen Participation in Yokohama City

1992-1995 (From questionnaire to determination of route plan)

- Questionnaire about citizen participation and its process
- Public meetings/round-table conferences (about 100 people participated from three areas in the district)
- Tours of planned construction sites which were demanded by residents
- Explanatory meetings and symposiums in each area concerned
- Route plan based on the residents' demand and establishing an advisory committee.
- Questionnaire about the advisory committee

1996-1997 (Investigation of alternative plans)

- Committee to discuss alternative plans (including not to carry out the construction)
- Open learning meetings, round-table conferences, workshops

1998-1999 (Proposal of alternative plans to the determination of a development draft)

- City disclosure of three alternative plans along with the results of each one's environmental evaluation
- Explanatory meetings of the plans in each area of the city
- Polls conducted about the alternative plans (10,000 out of 100,000 households in the district, response rate: 27%)
- Meeting to the planning process which presented a report to the city
- Draft of development proposal
- Material on the plan distributed to every house in the district and explanatory meetings held

lowed the survey with neighborhood forums. In the public meetings in the first period between 1992 and 1995, few people got involved and some decried the city's tokenism. But learning from this deficit, the city improved the process by relying more on making connections with non-profit and neighborhood organizations that cared about the project.

This new concern with group networks led the government to structure the second-period advisory committee to emphasize participants chosen by NGOs and self-selection. This committee consisted of seven citizens recommended by community groups (one from each neighborhood affected by the road), 12 citizens who responded to an advertisement requesting participants (26 people applied), two people with experience in road landscape engineering and environmental planning who lived in the affected area, and three city administrators (Korenaga, Mataki, & Watanabe, 2000). The committee developed four alternatives. Based on the results of citizen participation throughout the three periods, the government accepted resident requests to have a two-lane road that was 22 meters wide, even though Japanese roads 22 meters in width generally have four lanes.

As in the Florida case, the government made efforts to publicize the planning process and the plan itself through newsletters, independent media, and exhibitions. It released information necessary for informed public deliberation, such as, traffic volumes and pollution levels. The government kept hard-copy logs of meetings at city hall and also placed the material on its Web site. It let citizens know about the plan and how to participate through distributing material to every house in the district, developed drafts of alternative plans made by a citizen-based committee helped by experts, and reached consensus through the participatory process despite the original citizen dissatisfaction.

Special emphasis should be placed on the makeup of the citizen-dominated advisory committee which was much more heterogeneous than most analogous Japanese bodies. One can compare, for example, the Yokohama committee's composition with that of a Tokyo committee established to give advice on the Outer Belt Highway conflict. The latter body had 18 citizens, but all were recommended by governments (rather than NGOs) and it had 11 administrators—rather than the three civil servants in the Yokohama group. With participation reserved for experts and politically chosen people, the Tokyo committee could not articulate a community vision as the Yokohama committee had (Ministry of Land, Infrastructure and Transport Kanto Regional Bureau, 2005; Yai, 2004; Yai & Maekawa, 2004, pp. 147-151). In fact no consensus was achieved in the Tokyo dispute and the government never completed sections of that highway (PI Gaikaku-Ensen Conference, 2004; Setagaya District, 2006).]

Although it was the Yokohama government that made the final decision for the Onda-Motoishikawa Line, citizens did effectively participate in the planning process; they had an impact on development. Yokohama's citizen participation process was, therefore, successful.

CONCLUSIONS

As early as 1978, Rosener noted that evaluating citizen participation required identifying the outcomes involvement should produce. Do planners expect policy changes or simply a more democratic process with greater citizen satisfaction? The Florida and Yokohama cases suggest that under certain circumstances citizen engagement can produce both outcomes in a variety of sociocultural systems.

Much literature comparing American and East Asian administration has stressed East/West differences, such as, Jun (2005), Pearson and Hui (2001), Rudolph (2005), and Welch and Wong (1998). Analyses based on difference would highlight the esteem many Japanese people have for the expertise and education of public officials who are graduates of a few well-regarded universities and have passed difficult examinations. An analysis of difference stresses the respect for expertise and authority instilled by the worldviews of Confucianism or Shinto. This respect leads some Japanese citizens to refrain from participating in public conferences or to speak at such events even if they do attend. An analysis focused on East/West differences helps to explain why Japan took much longer than the United States to prepare national guidelines on engagement in the infrastructure field. It also helps explain why the Japanese guideline puts more explicit emphasis on involving experts and educated people in advisory committees.

But concentrating solely on sociocultural difference obscures the case-study evidence that similar factors precipitated successful engagement experiences in Florida and Yokohoma. In both jurisdictions, agencies prepared forums where citizen organizations could participate in infrastructure planning, heard various citizen insights, and then to some degree incorporated citizen feedback into public plans. When polities experience the pressures of democratization and modernization, they may facilitate similar forms of citizen participation even though their populations come from different cultural traditions.

One factor that seems important in both cases is the involvement of a diverse group of people including representatives of organized interest groups and individuals. In both Florida and Yokohama, the government publicized the participation opportunities widely and gave each citizen who wanted to get involved an option to join the process. This bid for a representative engagement contrasts with the problematic case of Tokyo's Outer Belt Highway, mentioned earlier, where the participation process was closed to most members of the public who did not have administrative backers. Making the process open and securing citizen representativeness seem to be crucial factors if citizens are to have success in influencing policy.

Establishing frequent, varied forums also seems important. Cole and Caputo (1984) found that a greater number of public hearings seemed to stimulate greater public interest in local affairs in the United States. The Florida and Yokohama agencies both held many public meetings unlike some other local governments which elected to hold only one conference where the public could speak (e.g., Ministry of Land, Infrastructure and Transport Kanto Regional Bureau, 2005). Clearly, when a government holds only one forum it becomes difficult for many citizen-group representatives to attend. Such a forum may privilege well-organized associations over ad hoc groups or individuals. Multiple forums allow citizens to have the "deep and continuous involvement" that King, Feltey, and Susel (1998, p. 320) considered crucial for authentic participation.

The Florida and Yokohama agencies used advanced information technologies—principally the Internet—as one channel to distribute information while also paying attention to traditional hard-copy distribution modes. The multi-channel approach acknowledged that variant ways of accessing information appealed to different people. Many younger people gravitate to electronic media while older participants may be more comfortable with hard-copy materials. In both cases studied in this chapter, citizens had an opportunity to access information in multiple formats from early on until the end of the planning process. The Internet also served as a channel for distributing citizen comments to large audiences.

Both agencies used technology to link citizens to networks of organizations. Technology networks enabled two-way distribution of information. As Lawrence and Kamensky (2004, p. 3) have stated, "Technology has now created new tools for allowing citizens to ... participate in a dialogue with their fellow citizens and their government."

As noted earlier, Baker, Addams, and Davis (2005) have suggested that civil servants who plan public hearings need to design a set of procedures and use them from the problem definition stage through to decision making and follow-up. Administrators in both Yokohama and Florida spent time designing procedures for multiple forums. In most respects, they carried out their original scenarios. However, Yokohama did switch to making greater attempts to include citizen groups, a shift that helped propel greater involvement. Yokohama seems to have moved from a bilateral model conceptualizing participation as involving governments and individual citizens to a tripartite model that also acknowledged the increasingly important role of citizen groups. This switch accentuates the importance of conceptualizing the network aspect of modern societies.

Halverson (2003) stressed the importance of high quality participation which means involvement that includes deliberation opportunities. The Florida and Yokohama forums included space for respectful deliberation where participants could interact, learn from each other and work toward forming a consensus. The respect that administrators had for citizen perspectives is seen in the Florida case when FDOT's transit office placed citizen comments on its web site and related impending changes in service provision to specific citizen complaints.

Although caution must be taken in generalizing from two case studies, the Florida and Yokohama processes suggest that certain success factors transcend sociocultural fault lines. Further study of successful and unsuccessful cases in Japan and the United States can clarify the influence of cultural factors on citizen engagement in infrastructure planning. Such research can help ascertain where modifications will aid cross-polity diffusion and where a single set of factors undergird successful engagement in a wide range of societies. The chapter suggests that in a globalized networked society civic engagement techniques may be transferable.

REFERENCES

Adams, B. (2004). Public meetings and the democratic process. *Public administration review, 64*(1), 43-54.

Baker, W. H., Addams, H. L., & Davis, B. (2005). Critical factors for enhancing municipal public hearings. *Public administration review, 65*(4), 490-499.

Beachy, S. (1999). The 2020 Florida Transportation Plan: An innovative approach to the collection and analysis of public input. *1999 APA national planning conference proceedings*. Retrieved November 20, 2005, from http://www.asu.edu/caed/proceedings99/BEACHY/BEACHY.HTM

Box, R. C. (1998). *Citizen governance: Leading American communities into the 21st century.* Thousand Oaks, CA: Sage Publications.

Boyte, H. (2005). Reframing democracy: Governance, civic agency, and politics. *Public Administration Review, 65*(5), 536-546.

City Planning Bureau of Yokohama. (2003). *Citizen participation for the planning of Onda-Motoishikawa line.* Retrieved November 20, 2005, from http://www.city.yokohama.jp/me/aoba/onmoto/

Clark, T. N., & Rempel, M. (Eds.). (1997). *Citizen politics in post-industrial societies.* Boulder, CO: Westview Press.

Cole, R., & Caputo, D. (1984). The public hearing as an effective citizen participation mechanism. *American Political Science Review, 78*(2), 404-416.

Council of Local Authorities for International Relations. (2005). Citizen participation in the United States—Consensus building methods in transportation planning. *Clair Report, 265,* 15-16. Retrieved November 22, 2005, from http://www.clair.or.jp/j/forum/c_report/cr265m.html

Easton, D. (1965). *A systems analysis of political life*. New York: Wiley.

Florida Department of Transportation. (2000). *2020 Florida Transportation Plan*. Retrieved November 20, 2005 from http://www.dot.state.fl.us/planning/ftp2020/default.htm

Florida Department of Transportation, Public Transit Office. (n.d.). *2020 plan*. Retrieved October 24, 2006, from http://www/dot.state.fl.us/transit/Pages/transit2020plan.htm

George, J., & Jones, G. (2005). *Understanding and managing organizational behavior*. (4th ed.). Upper Saddle River, NJ: Pearson.

Halvorsen, K. (2003). Assessing the effects of public participation. *Public Administration Review, 63*(5), 535-543.

Harashina, S. (2006). *Citizen participation and consensus building: The development of urban and environmental plan*. Kyoto, Japan: Gakugeishuppansha.

Hitachi Research Institute. (2004). *Public involvement*. Retrieved November 19, 2005, from http://itpro.nikkeibp.co.jp/free/NGT/govtech/20050414/159238/

Holzer, M., Melitski, J., Rho, S., & Schwester, R. 2004. *Restoring trust in government: The potential of digital citizen participation*. Washington, DC: IBM Center for the Business of Government.

Inglehart, R. (1977). *The silent revolution: Changing values and political styles*. Princeton: Princeton University Press.

Jun, J. (2005). The self in the social construction of organizational reality: Eastern and Western views. *Administrative Theory and Praxis, 27*(1), 86-110.

King, C. S., Feley, K., & Susel, B. (1998). The question of participation: Towards authentic public participation in public administration. *Public Administration Review, 58*(4), 317-326.

Korenaga, D., Mataki, T., & Watanabe, Y. (2000). *A report on Onda-Motoishikawa line in Yokohama city*. Retrieved November 20, 2005, from http://web.sfc.keio.ac.jp/~s97051yw/project/reports/yokohama.doc

Kurosawa, I. (2000). *Participatory road planning: The case which considered the abandonment of construction*. Retrieved September 19, 2006, from http://www.nui.or.jp/ZIGYOU/sem11-3.htm

Lawrence, P., & Kamensky, J. (2004). Foreword. In M. Holzer, J. Melitski, S. Rho, & R. Schwester, (Eds.), *Restoring trust in government: The potential of digital citizen participation* (p. 3). Washington DC: IBM Center for the Business of Government.

MacDougall, T. (2001). *Towards political inclusiveness: The changing role of local government in Japan*. Washington, DC: World Bank Institute.

Ministry of Land, Infrastructure and Transportation. (2003). *Public involvement guideline in the design phase of infrastructure development by Ministry of Land, Infrastructure and Transport*. Retrieved November 19, 2005, from http://www.mlit.go.jp/kisha/kisha03/01/010630_.html

Ministry of Land, Infrastructure and Transport Kanto Regional Bureau. (2005). *Outer Tokyo Belt Highway*. Retrieved November 20, 2005, from http://www.ktr.mlit.go.jp/gaikan/home/top.html

Miura, H. (2000). *Explanation of keywords—PI (public involvement)*. Retrieved November 22, 2005, from http://research.mki.co.jp/eco/keyword/pi.htm

Okabe, K. (2003). *City planning and citizen participation in the United States.* Retrieved November 20, 2005, from http://www.nagoya-toho.ac.jp/staff/okabe /ronbun/redev.html

1000 Friends of Florida. (n.d.). *An overview of 1000 Friends transportation reform initiative, 1994-1997.* Retrieved October 24, 2006 from http://www.1000fof.org/ Transportation Planning_for_People.asp

Patrenos, S. (2000). *Florida Department of Transportation—Tallahassee, Florida.* Retrieved November 20, 2005, from http://www.planning.dot.gov/ Documents/Rural/FLDOT.htm

Pearson, C., & Hui, L. (2001). A cross-cultural test of Vroom's expectancy motivation framework. *International journal of organizational theory and behavior, 4*(3 & 4), 307-327.

PI Gaikaku-Ensen Conference. (2004). *Summary of 2002-2004.* Retrieved October 5, 2006, from http://www.ktr.mlit.go.jp/gaikan/pi/matome/p1.pdf

Randolph, J. (2004). *Environmental land use planning and management.* Washington, DC: Island Press.

Rosener, J. (1978). Citizen participation: Can we measure its effectiveness? *Public administration review, 38*(5), 457-463.

Rudolph, S. (2005). The imperialism of categories: Situating knowledge in a globalizing world. *Perspectives on politics, 3*(1), 3-14.

Schachter, H. L. (2004). Citizen participation and development policy studies: The limits of concept transfer. In G. Mudacumura & M. S. Haque (Eds.), *Handbook of development policy studies* (pp. 595-606). New York: Marcel Dekker.

Setagaya District. (2006). *Outer Tokyo Belt Highway district PI meeting.* Retrieved October 5, 2006, from http://www.city.setagaya.tokyo.jp/030/d00004968.html

Shin'ichi, Y. (1999). Rethinking the public interest in Japan. In Y. Tadashi (Ed.), *Deciding the public good* (pp. 13-49). Tokyo: Japan Center for International Exchange.

Society for the Study of Consensus Building Methodology. (2001). *Road planning in Europe and America and public involvement.* Tokyo, Japan: Gyousei.

Suzuki, T. (1998). *A study on citizen participation in the decision-making process of city planning—A case study of Onda-Motoishikawa line in Yokohama city.* Retrieved November 20, 2005, from http://www.a.dendai.ac.jp/~w3nishi/soturon/1998/ suzuki1.htm

Tanaguchi, M. (2006). A time machine: New evidence of postmaterialist value change. *International Political Science Review, 27*(4), 405-426.

Torgerson, D. (1995). The uncertain quest for sustainability: public discourse and the politics of environmentalism. In F. Fischer & M. Black (Ed.), *Greening environmental policy: The politics of a sustainable future* (pp. 3-20). London: Paul Chapman.

Umemori, N., & Rempel, M. (1997). *The new political culture in Japan.* In T. N. Clark & M. Rempel (Eds.), *Citizen politics in post-industrial societies* (pp. 85-109). Boulder, CO: Westview Press.

Au: add chapter
page numbers.

U.S. Department of Transportation, Federal Highway Administration. (1996). *Public involvement techniques for transportation decision-making*. Retrieved November 5, 2005, from http://www.fhwa.dot.gov/reports/pittd/cover.htm

Vig, N. J., & Kraft, M. E. (2003). *Environmental policy: New directions for the twenty-first century* (5th ed.). Washington, DC: CQ Press.

Watanabe, M. (2001). *Method of consensus building by the government and the public*. Retrieved November 20, 2005, from http://www.japanpost.jp/pri/reserch/monthly/2001/155-h13.08/155-topics-3.pdf

Welch, E., & Wong, W. (1998). Public administration in a global context: Bridging the gaps of theory and practice between Western and non-Western nations. *Public Administration Review, 58*(1), 40-50.

World Lake Conference NGO Workshop. (2001). *Water century NGO declaration*. Retrieved October 18, 2006, from http://www.ses.usp.ac/jp

Yai, T. (2004). *Public involvement in regional planning*. Retrieved November 19, 2005, from http://www.tpi.or.jp/tpi/pi-sinpo/yai.pdf

Yai, T., & Maekawa, H. (2004). *Citizen-participatory road planning: Public involvement handbook*. Tokyo, Japan: Gyousei.

Yai, T., & Terabe, S. (1996). Public involvement process for transportation planning and project development in the U.S. *Journal of the City Planning Institute of Japan, 31*, 403-408.

Yamamoto, K. (2006). Performance of semi-autonomous public bodies: linkage between autonomy and performance in Japanese agencies. *Public Administration and Development, 26*(1), 35-44.

Yanow, D. (1993). The communication of policy meanings: Implementation as interpretation and text. *Policy Sciences, 26*(1), 41-61.

CHAPTER 9

CITIZENSOURCING

Citizen Participation in a Networked Nation

Carolyn J. Lukensmeyer and Lars Hasselblad Torres

Our community is an opportunity to take a look at the rules that govern society, and to the extent that we are able, rewrite them as best seems to fit us."

—Philip Linden (Second Life founder) to Lawrence Lessig in Wikinomics:
How Mass Collaboration Changes Everything

Second Life, a fast-growing virtual world-cum-game online, is a great place to get an idea of the passions that beat in the collective breast of citizens in a networked society. Take a paid tour of this online world entirely created and maintained by its users (who number more than 2.8 million today) and you'll find residents building and populating entire cities, entrepreneurs generating economic activity to the tune of $800,000 every 24 hours, activists organizing around real-world concerns like genocide and intellectual property rights, and universities finding new ways to create and share knowledge (Tristan, 2007). Second Life is a vibrant example of shared creativity: it is an open environment for innovation and collaboration governed by a few simple rules, empowered by a powerful set of tools.

Civic Engagement in a Network Society
pp. 207–233
Copyright © 2008 by Information Age Publishing
All rights of reproduction in any form reserved.

"Second Life," the authors Don Tapscott and Anthony D. Williams have written, "set the standard for customer innovation in all industries" (Tapscott & Williams, 2006, p. 126) By opening up the narrative and content of "the game" to its users, Second Life rewrote the rules of mass innovation. "The reigning orthodoxy in innovation has long been that it is best to create and commercialize ideas within the confines of closed entities" (p. 126) write Tapscott and Williams. Second Life reflects a radically different approach to innovation: it's not the "fringe" activity of a small group of amateurs and hobbyists but a core, expanding source of business value that drives the company's performance in the marketplace.

What we are describing is a revolution in *stewardship:* by making nearly everything in Second Life open to the influence of its residents, Second Life fosters something *better* than traditional corporate practice would deliver, something that its users value *more* and in which they share a deeper stake. This ownership society-cum-game hasn't been created by incremental tweaks at the edges of traditionally insular business practice—for example improving customer service and customer relations—instead it represents a shift in company organization driven by a fundamentally different understanding of innovation.

Second Life is reaping the rewards of breaking from the business-as-usual pack, experiencing healthy and completely unrivaled growth—it is on a path to becoming the largest massively multiplayer game (MMORG) ever—and it enjoys strong loyalty from its users. The residents who invest in Second Life reap real rewards from their continued involvement and contribution—whether social pleasure or income—completing a virtual cycle in which the consumer is also the producer, sharing with Second Life's owner Linden Labs the benefits of a thriving business environment. Second Life is such a powerful marketplace, real-world companies are starting to set up shop, hoping to sell products like cell phones and financial services to residents, fueling the rise of in-world innovation and design. It is not uncommon for these companies to hire experienced Second Life residents to build and brand their in-world presence.

THE NETWORKED SOCIETY

The innovation phenomena represented by a firm like Linden Labs doesn't revolve around a constellation of fringy companies run by twenty-something Internet enthusiasts. "Mature" companies like Proctor and Gamble, Lego, Converse, and many others are learning to push innovation out to their consumers and specialized communities. In today's environment of rapid innovation and a growing "do it yourself" (DIY) culture, companies are learning that the public is a source of business value: each time a customer contributes a new idea or develops a new product, the company increases its intellectual assets—an established measure of its market value. The emerging culture of creativity and collaboration within the Web 2.0 environment promises, many hope, to "engage, rejuvenate, and activate the public in new ways" (Institute for Politics, Democracy and the Internet, 2006, p. iii)

In government, significant public policy innovation is pretty rare; much of what constitutes legislative activity arises from reauthorizations and incremental changes to existing programs and policies. When public policy innovation does happen, it occurs within the thick apparatus of policy-advocacy organizations that have sprung up around Congress over the last several decades and is often driven by crisis. In rare cases innovation centers around the ideas of policy entrepreneurs who bring a fresh and unique perspective to the policy process.

Is it possible for governments to learn from the lessons of "crowdsourcing," to open the policymaking process to ordinary citizens? We think so, though not without caution. In this chapter we hope to share some of our enthusiasm for the possibilities of cultivating—and tapping—growing networks of citizens for policy advice. In fact, we think there is a critical role for citizens at four points along the policy development continuum: agenda setting, policy design, decision making and evaluation. There are other areas less specific to the policy process—for example land-use planning and budgeting—where we feel the public can add tremendous value as well.

NETWORKED DEMOCRATIC GOVERNANCE

Effective policymaking open to robust citizen participation is the hallmark of good governance in the twenty-first century. Advanced democracies are no longer judged solely on the basis of their constitution, independent judiciary, fair elections and free press; today, democratic governments are being asked to square their accounts of freedom and fairness against measures of transparency, accountability, and participation.

At AmericaSpeaks we have been working to improve public sector transparency, participation and accountability through the deployment of new governance mechanisms. We have developed a state-of-the-art forum in which thousands of citizens representing the diversity of a polity come together to solve public problems. These include large-scale planning projects—from the redevelopment of Ground Zero after 9/11 to recovery in New Orleans after Hurricane Katrina—as well as public budgeting and policy-agenda setting, including tough issues like social security and health care reform. We have managed these complex public engagement exercises at all levels of governance as well: municipal budgeting for the City of Washington, DC; regional economic planning in Northeast Ohio; targeted multistate initiatives tackling child and adolescent health; and national conversations on complex policy issues like social security. We have also had the privilege of working at the international level, with the Ministry of Health in the United Kingdom to advance health care reform[1] and bringing together citizens across the European Community to advise the future direction of brain science research for the European Commission.[2]

From our experience over the last decade, we have come to believe that important innovations in governance like ours coupled with exciting new ideas about networks and "mass collaboration" together point the way toward a new kind of governance: governance as sustained dialogue and interaction between citizens and the public officials who serve them. We call this dynamic "citizensourcing," borrowing and adapting a set of emerging practices from the private sector ("crowdsourcing") to explain a new relationship between government and its people. In fact, there are many ways the concept of networked collaboration can benefit governments—by changing the definition and scope of government research to transforming government accountability—but for the purposes of this discussion we will limit ourselves to the proposition that the concept of "citizensourcing" will enlarge and enhance policy-advisory processes, policymaking, and policy feedback.

There are also severe structural imbalances in our society—education and income disparities among them—that poison the wells of our civic culture. Without real attention to power imbalances in the United States and a real agenda to open the political process, the reforms we raise in this chapter will bear little fruit in the long term. In spite of our optimism for new modes of governance, we readily acknowledge that citizensourcing is not "quicksilver," and it is not a magic bullet. Citizensourcing should not replace scientific research, stakeholder collaboration, or legislative entrepreneurialism either. We believe that effective citizen participation can extend the body of evidence available to decision-makers, widen the range of views and experiences considered under policy impact, and harness the civic energies of citizens to solve public problems when networked innovation is applied to policy agenda setting, design, decision making and evaluation. To do this will require not insignificant transformation in government: from a predominant "authority" culture to collaborative, power-sharing organization structures within enabling policy frameworks.

The fundamental question we want to ask and open up for discussion in this chapter is whether networks of citizens in all of their diversity can better tackle—and solve—some of our most urgent public policy dilemmas, among them climate change, healthcare reform, natural resource management, and public education. From our experience engaging tens of thousands of citizens across the country in public policy conversations around issues they care deeply about, we believe they can. Idea marketplaces represent new sources of policy advice that extend the competencies and specialized functions of agencies, enabling policy makers to bring together divergent ideas that would not come from traditional sources of policy advice, which too often are invested in particular outcomes.

THE RISE OF CROWDSOURCING

At the close of 2006 *TIME Magazine* named "You" its Person of the Year. During the same year, "social networking" Web sites like MySpace.com—where members develop affinity groups and friendships online by sharing text, audio, and video information and rating one another's content—became the most popular destination on the Web. In a nod to the videosharing platform that gave "You" its standing, *TIME Magazine* put its finger on one of the biggest—and least studied—trends of the last 3 years: "crowdsourcing," the name given to private-sector efforts to tap "the wisdom of crowds," first explored in a meaningful way in *New Yorker Magazine* staff writer James Surowiecki's 2004 book of the same title.

Crowdsourcing is the informal name given to an Internet-driven business trend in which companies get amateurs and professionals outside traditional organization boundaries—sometimes from competitors or completely unrelated industries—to "design products, create content, and even tackle corporate R&D problems in their spare time" (Boutin, 2006). Though this trend of "outsourcing" to the public a role traditionally held within a corporation is a way of doing business that emerged in the late 1990s, it made its first big impact in the world of online advertising in 2004. Converse's legendary Chuck Taylor "All Stars Gallery" campaign—which invited consumers to produce their own Chuck Taylor's video ad for the popular shoe—reportedly boosted parent company Nike's sales by 25% during the quarter the campaign ran (Howe, 2006b).

Today crowdsourcing is a common way for companies to involve consumers and the interested public in brand make-overs and the launch of new products. It is even a business model: YouTube, a popular video-hosting and social networking site, is premised on the idea that people want to create and share multimedia content, and that the best content can be filtered "up" by users to attract wide audiences. Thus, crowdsourcing is business as a dialogue, an iterative, dynamic feedback process; creativity as a community-mediated process. The incentives to get "prosumers"—

consumers who act like producers—to participate in crowdsourcing endeavors are many, and not always the same: some love a creative challenge (problem solving). Others want to cultivate audiences and gain notoriety (attention). Others do it for the money (cash incentives).

Regardless, more and more companies are finding new ways to spur their customers to take charge of product development and marketing. In the best cases, like our Converse All Stars example, crowdsourcing campaigns boost product sales and drive business value. In the worst cases, crowdsourcing efforts can backfire, embarrassing a company whose product challenges consumer loyalties. In the case of a recent GM user-created video ad contest around its Chevy "Tahoe" SUV, the most popular ad produced (read, the most widely visible ad) both parodied traditional ad gimmickry by placing the four-wheel drive in impossible locations and skewered the muscular auto itself for guzzling gas in an age of human-accelerated climate change. Regardless of the substance of any individual ad, the campaign overall was considered enormously successful by its sponsors and creators. "By losing that control over the brand experience," one marketing expert has observed, "Chevy actually brought more people into it" (Li, 2007).

In their excellent work on innovation networks "Wikinomics," authors Don Tapscott and Anthony Williams describe crowdsourcing as it occurs in "ideagoras:" marketplaces for ideas, innovations and solutions. These ideagoras have helped to open up innovation within businesses to the public—to solve problems that improve business performance. Ideagoras are becoming spaces for product development, service creation, process innovation, and other forms of collaboration online. Two types of ideagoras exist, according to Tapscott and Williams: those centered on solutions looking for questions, and those with questions seeking solutions. The promise of ideagoras for solution-seekers, the authors suggest, is that a "large, diverse network of talent will solve well-defined problems faster and more efficiently than an internal R&D group" (Tapscott & Williams, 2006, p. 99) The promise for problem seekers and solvers is often financial—some ideagoras like InnoCentive (discussed later) offer cash prizes for applicable solutions—as well as the fun, status, and networking that is associated with membership in a problem-solving network.

Here are just a few examples that illustrate how crowdsourcing is being used across business sectors:

Visual and Performing Arts.   One of the earliest and most widely discussed examples of crowdsourcing as a business model was described by *Wired* magazine's Jeff Howe when he profiled the stock photography Web site iStockPhoto.com for the magazine in June 2006. iStockPhoto.com, founded in 2000, enables its members to upload photographs to the site in exchange for compensation each time the image is downloaded by another user. Fees to download iStockPhoto.com images range anywhere from $1 to $40. It was not a surprise to many that Getty Images, the largest professional stock photo company, acquired iStockPhoto.com for $50 million in 2005.

And it's not just aggregation-driven companies sourcing this kind of creativity: artists themselves are turning to their fans for creative material and support. In 2004 founding Beastie Boys band member Adam Yauch hatched the idea of handing out 61 handheld video cameras to fans at a Madison Square Garden concert, later editing the 7,600+ minutes of footage into a 90-minute documentary of their live performance. More recently, the indie band The Shins partnered with the online video portal Current.TV, inviting fans to use their cell phones and video recorders to shoot an Austin City Limits performance of their popular song, "Phantom Limb." 200 submissions were whittled into a 5-minute video that included bits from each submission. Interviewed by *Wired* magazine for its January 2007 edition, Shins keyboardist Marty Crandall observed, "With the Internet redefining a band's success, ideas like this are the future of how music will be perceived—and received.... Audience enthusiasm should be harvested" (Leckart, 2006).

Scientific Research.   InnoCentive is one of the earliest and best known examples of crowdsourcing in the scientific community. Developed by the pharmaceuticals company Eli Lilly in 2001, InnoCentive.com structures its Web site around the needs of problem "Seekers"—typically companies with an R&D challenge—and problem "Solvers."—scientists with the know-how and resources to tackle the challenge—offering cash rewards ranging from $10,000 to $1,000,000 to the scientist submitting a workable solution to the problem. But it's not just professional scientists solving problems in their free time: many of the solutions are coming from science and technology junkies, "hobbyists working from their proverbial garage," writes Jeff Howe in Wired.com. And it seems like they are doing a pretty good job, good enough for Jill Panetta, InnoCentive's chief scientific officer, who says "more than 30 percent of the problems posted on the site have been cracked" (Howe, 2006a).

The concept is taking off and spreading to new arenas. In late December, InnoCentive and the Rockefeller Foundation announced a partnership that would seek science- and technology-related solutions to some of the world's most urgent development problems (Philanthropy News Digest, 2006). The Rockefeller Foundation, which has a long history of addressing development challenges in the global south through philanthropy, is seeking to infuse traditional development practices with an entrepreneurial spirit. According to the foundation's president Judith Rodin, "Our agreement with InnoCentive will enable researchers and entrepreneurs addressing the needs of the developing world to access one

of the same, cutting-edge opportunities to innovate now enjoyed by For-
tune 500 companies." Breaking out of the mold of traditional philanthropy, the Foundation has pledged to support InnoCentive by putting up
the award monies and will also sponsor nonprofit organizations that need
assistance posting their problem to the InnoCentive site.

To understand the fundamental impact networked innovation is having in the world of corporate R&D, consider the case of Proctor and Gamble, a leading company in the consumer products industry. While the
company employs plenty of researchers and doesn't plan to downsize
them any time soon, it has made "Proudly made elsewhere" (read, developed) an internal mantra. Why? Because by 2010 the company intends to
source 50% of their new product and service ideas outside the company.
The idea, Tapscott and Williams write, "isn't to replace these nine thousand researchers, but to better leverage them to drive growth and innovation" 2006, p. 106). Proctor and Gamble has brought 137 products
developed through its "connect and develop" initiative to market over the
last three years.

Finance and Philanthropy.   Financial services are experimenting with
crowdsourcing-like activity. Web sites like prosper.com enable credit seekers to list their financial need along with their credit score and a proposed
loan payback timeline. Individual lenders compete with one another to
"buy" the loan in part or in whole, bidding against each other for causes
they care about or returns that look good. The competition for "good
loans" works in the borrower's favor, lowering their final interest rate as
more lenders bid for the loan. When the bidding period has closed, and if
the loan request has been filled, the lowest-bidding lenders are bundled
together in a loan package for the borrower and the funds transferred
electronically.

Other sites like Marketocracy.com track and analyze the stock-picking
activities of its 55,000-plus members—some of the top investors in the
world—across some 65,000 "model portfolios" to create its m100 Index:
the top 100 portfolios of its individual members. What is the goal of Mar-
ketocracy.com? To outperform the financial market itself: to "achieve
higher returns at lower risk" (Marketocracy, 2006). The m100 Index has
performed better than the S&P 500 Index—the financial services industry's most trusted indicator of the top-performing companies in the
United States—in 8 of the last 11 quarters.

Even the traditional practice of philanthropy is being reshaped by the
crowdsourcing   ethos.   Web   sites   like   DonorsChoose.org   enable
philanthropic-minded users to experience the satisfaction of direct
giving: contributions that go straight to small projects, not high overhead
fees often associated with larger nonprofits and glitzy giving campaigns.
DonorsChoose.org works by enabling resource-strapped teachers to post

classroom needs online, along with a brief description of the project, subject area, and students. Donor-members browse projects and can choose to fund them in part or in whole, as gifts for others or as an act of personal philanthropy. Other charitable Web sites like Kiva.org offer more than a social return on investment: they promise to pay back their users who invest in the "microbusiness" needs of small-scale entrepreneurs around the world.

Perhaps one of the most understated models is Omidyar.net, a social network that exists for a single purpose, "so that more and more people discover their own power to make good things happen" (Omidyar Network, 2007). There, the community's founders invite users themselves to make modest investment decisions in nonprofits through several trial and error (read, learning) rounds of community-driven philanthropy. Nearly $200,000 has been given away through user-defined processes since 2005 when the network was opened to the public. The same approach is being used by sites like NetSquared.org which recently asked its user-members to distribute $100,000 in three awards for technology innovation in the nonprofit sector. The social entrepreneurism portal Changemakers.net regularly engages its user base in "collaborative competitions" through which proposals are refined before they are submitted to a user-driven round of voting through which awardees are selected.

Journalism. "Any serious news organization today," Tapscott and Williams write, "should also allow its community of readers to join the editorial process" (2006, p. 146). Back to the idea of "business as a conversation," Rupert Murdoch, chairman of NewsCorp which owns MySpace.com, once told *The Economist*, "News providers had better get web-savvy, stop lecturing their audiences, become places for conversation and destinations where bloggers and podcasters congregate to engage our reporters and editors in more extended discussions" (*The Economist*, 2005). Perhaps no other industry is undergoing as profound a transformation to its core business model as journalism. Today, in the wake of an astonishing growth of news gathering and news dissemination channels through the Web, traditional news corporations must remake themselves into dynamic user-driven content portals to survive.

Besides well-known examples like Wikipedia, which allows users to create and add new content to articles that are often generated in response to real-world events as they unfold, Web sites like Slashdot.com have built their business model around user creation and interaction. Reputation systems enable users to rate content, ensuring that the best content is visible to others. NowPublic.com is an international news portal that makes it easy for users to post news from across the Internet (using a simple browser plug-in) as well as their own material in text, audio, and video formats. Users who have signed up for a free account can interact with the news in many ways: post comments to one another, rate one another's content, share it (using syndication and email tools) as well as meet one another by using the site's internal mail system and user profile pages. The site bakes in search and sorting features that draw on the usability and popularity of tags and folksonomies. Replacing to some degree the "filtering" role of journalism review journals, sites like NewsTrust.net enable users to post and rate articles from traditional sources across a range of topics, using specific rating criteria. These articles are then ranked to drive the most newsworthy and trusted items to the "front page" of the site.

Web 2.0 tools like syndication, tags (user-associated keywords) and folksonomies (the shared language of tags surrounding various subjects and content) power the "new" news sites by enabling users to share what they value with others. Crowdsourcing in the field of journalism is driving reporting back to "hyperlocal" content relevant to readers—and creating spaces for them to interact with that content. Through tagging sites like Digg.com and Del.icio.us users are able to easily tag content from anywhere on the Web, rate it and share it with others. According to some, this "socializing" of the news is turning it back into what it once was, a community activity.

And traditional news companies are catching on. During the last quarter of 2006, Gannet News Service, which owns *USA Today* and 90 papers across the country, announced a major shift in business strategy: its newsrooms were to be transformed into "Information Centers" by May 2007. "The Information Center," wrote Gannett CEO Craig Dubow in a November memo, "is a way to gather and disseminate news and information across all platforms, 24/7. The Information Center will let us gather the very local news and information that customers want, then distribute it when, where and how our customers seek it" (Gahran, 2006). According to findings from the company's pilot efforts at 11 of its newspapers, "Asking the community for help, gets it—and delivers the newspaper into the heart of community conversations once again. Rich and deep databases with local, local information gathered efficiently are central to the whole process" (Gahran, 2006).

A recent round of grant-making by the Knight Foundation, established by the founders of the Akron Beacon Journal in 1950, illustrates the enthusiasm for new modes of citizen-journalism interaction. The recent awards, which total $5 million, were distributed to more than a dozen teams and individual journalism entrepreneurs who are creating greater access to news gathering and reporting processes for their audiences. According to a press release from the foundation, "If the quality of entries warrant it, the foundation may spend as much as $25 million during the next five years in the search for bold community news experiments" (Knight Foundation, 2006).

Campaigns and Elections.   Howard Dean and his DeanforAmerica.com Web site demonstrated, like no other candidate before him, that the Internet—and the spirit of community that can be built within networks—is a powerful force in democratic politics. The former Vermont governor's people-powered campaign swept him from June 2003 to the Iowa caucuses in February 2004, raising more than $15 million from over 185,000 individual contributions. The governor's campaign, while it failed to translate into on-the-ground votes, nonetheless galvanized the passions of ten of thousands of volunteers across the country and signaled a new era in Internet politics.

Today, sites like DemocracyforAmerica.org (DFA) use an identical organizing platform to the one Governor Dean's staff and volunteers built during his bid for the Democratic nomination for President. The database driven platform enables users to maintain close contact with local and national organizers, bringing unprecedented levels of information and coordination to the craft of political campaigns. For example, in the 2006 general election, DFA was able to replace "robocalls" by inviting its users to sign up for phone-banking responsibilities. Once a user logged into the Web site, they were assigned telephone numbers of swing voters who were likely to sit out the election and encourage them to vote for particular candidates. Users would simply dial the number, follow a simple script and at the end of the call ask, "Can I count on your vote for Candidate Soandso?" The results of these informal discussions were recorded in a webform and the user would move on to the next call. By crowdsourcing its phone banking needs to members across the country, DFA was able to cut campaign costs while acquiring valued field intelligence and at the same time engage its members.

"The major parties have clearly been studying the explosion of social networking sites" says Micah Sifry, executive editor of Personal Democracy Forum Web site, "and both are also obviously interested in figuring out how to tap the energies of bloggers and other online activists" (Sifry, 2006). The Democrats, led by former Governor Dean, have launched PartyBuilder, which aims to give party-members a broad set of tools that empower them to shape the party platform, define their attachment to the party, influence the future of the party. For their part, the Republicans have developed MYGOP, a narrower platform that channels members' energies into local campaign activities. Both sites provide tools to create and maintain basic webpages, recruit friends as fellow volunteers, get in touch with fellow party members, manage events, and of course fundraise. In essence, any user of either campaign site can access powerful tools that enable the grassroots to play a significant role in campaigns once dominated by campaign staff and consultants.

Among the major democratic candidates in the 2008 contest, Senator Barack Obama (D-IL) has proven to be the most Web-enabled candidate in the most Internet-driven primary contest ever. Senator Obama has been able to enlist the support of Chris Hughes, cofounder of the popular social-networking site Facebook.com, who left a job in Silicon Valley and a "'serious' pay cut" to develop the Senator's campaign site, My.Barack-Obama.com (Schatz, 2007). Weeks later, the company announced that Facebook would release a major upgrade to its Facebook Platform, enabling developers to create their own applications and businesses to work with the networking site's "unique social context" (Facebook, 2007). Open innovations like the Facebook Platform will enable Web-savvy candidates, more than ever, to interact with the user-bases of today's most popular social networking sites, deepening the transformation of politics online.

CROWDSOURCING TO CITIZENSOURCING

No government is perfect. One of the chief virtues of a democracy, however, is that its defects are always visible and under democratic processes can be pointed out and corrected.

—President Harry S. Truman
(quoted in *Government 2.0* by William Eggers)

Crowdsourcing consumer creativity for advertising and product development might be one thing; but what about public problems and the political decision making necessary to solve them? Skeptical about how each of these examples relates to government, the improvement of governance, and solving public problems? We'll try to shed some light on these questions over the next several pages. There are good reasons to be cautious, if not skeptical, of applying lessons from crowdsourcing to citizensourcing. In the evolving ecology of the "social web," citizens seem to be more sensitive to government privacy concerns than corporate privacy concerns. Many governance problems are substantially different from the low-risk challenges of corporate advertising and product development. Enabling government-wide transformation is a challenge of a dramatically greater order than shifting practices within a single corporation. And last but not least, the present policy framework for citizen engagement creates a "chilling effect" on reform that all but guarantees innovation in citizen engagement will continue at a glacial pace.

At the same time, consider the risks of the current "go slow" approach afflicting the public sector: as civil society and political parties further develop their tools and capacities online, the gap between government practice and the culture at large will widen; government will find itself ill-prepared for the sustained press of citizen-driven policy activism. In other words, as the organizing capacity of citizens and interest groups deepens and widens, the risks of public skepticism, mistrust, and distance rise.

Consider the case of 2005's Hurricane Katrina. The failure of the United States government to respond effectively doesn't need to be recounted here. What hasn't been championed widely enough is the way ordinary citizens, working together in temporary, ad hoc networks—what author Howard Rheingold calls "smartmobs"—were able to deliver solutions to the human tragedy when government could not.

One example of many is Peoplefinder, a "mashup" of GoogleMaps—one of the Internet's most used mapping technologies—and a quickly cobbled together database of displaced hurricane survivors called Katrinalist (powered by the leading "customer relations management" platform Salesforce.com), went live 72 hours after Katrina wrecked the gulf coast across Louisiana, Mississippi, and Alabama. This site—developed, deployed, and refined by thousands of citizens across the country—enabled users to access a database of over 640,000 names of Katrina survivors, evacuees and those who remained in the devastated cities and towns along the gulf coast.[3] Through this simple yet powerful tool developed by citizens with no motive more powerful than to serve their fellow citizens, families were reunited and desperate friends were able to locate one another.

Crowdsourcing—whether creativity or its finance—is about placing problem-solving within the public's grasp—"democratizing innovation," as MIT professor Eric Von Hippel writes in his recent book of the same title (Von Hipple, 2005). "Cocreating with customers is like tapping the most uniquely qualified pool of intellectual capital ever assembled," write Tapscott and Williams (2006, p. 147). What is essential here is that, by encouraging open (transparent) and widespread (mass) participation, organizations enlarge and diversify the space in which talent and ideas interact. As evolving spaces like Second Life demonstrate, the right minimum structure can foster an environment for creativity and innovation within which information, ideas, products and services of real value are produced, exchanged and often rewarded. Well-managed ideagoras are proving more than capable of tapping our shared appetite for social connection and directing our experience, knowledge, ideas and energies toward problem-solving. By deftly harnessing the creativity that is unleashed when people come together informally and around shared interests and passions, crowdsourcing offers a dynamic, complex and emergent model of public problem-solving.

At AmericaSpeaks we believe the kinds of results that business are just beginning to achieve can be realized in the public sector through the design and application of new governance mechanisms to public policy processes. By widening the public space in which problem solving takes place, creating what Kennedy School of Government professor Archon Fung has called "mini-publics," governments deepen their role as a "convenor" (Fung, 2003). Fostering the emergence of both short-term and lasting "mini-publics" through citizensourcing, governments increase the opportunity for diverse groups of citizens to learn about policy issues, encounter one another's ideas, be challenged in their own thinking, and in turn to spark new, shared solutions to public problems. These processes may also yield additional benefits—what have been called "spill-over benefits"—civic learning, strengthen relationships between citizens and government, minimize conflict, and increase the prospects of successful policy implementation.

> *What's missing from our democracy is an engaging and participatory*
> *governance system that involves citizens....*
> *Democracy needs an online, interactive public commons."*
>
> —Steve Clift
> (Minnesota eDemocracy co-founder in *Government 2.0* by William Eggers)

A HYBRID MODEL OF CITIZENSOURCING

AmericaSpeaks taps the passion and creativity of citizens every time we convene a twenty-first century town meeting (21stCTM), our way of bringing together several thousand citizens at a time to address urgent matters of public policy. But this isn't just a sophisticated online process facilitated by the latest Web 2.0 mashup. At AmericaSpeaks we seek to leverage both the benefits of bringing people together where they live with unique capacities of network technologies. When governments embrace and deploy new governance mechanisms like the 21st Century Town Meeting, they access the knowledge, experience and wisdom of architects, mothers, lawyers, corporate executives, social welfare beneficiaries, teachers—in short, a cross section of the population as a whole, each of whom has a real stake in the communities in which they live. When these citizens are asked to discuss public problems with each other and develop solutions they can live with, unprecedented levels of knowledge-sharing, creativity and shared commitment to outcomes are achieved. We like to think of this as citizensourcing at its best.

More Than Just a Meeting

A 21stCTM is a sophisticated combination of face-to-face discussion and networked technology that enables very large groups—as many as

4,000 citizens in a room—to interact. A typical town meeting creates the experience of intimate discussion and the excitement of massively scaled instant reporting. It is the New England Town Meeting *mashed* with audience response technologies like those used on popular shows like *Who Wants to Be A Millionaire*, along with collaborative computing to create a highly charged, temporary public forum for public problem solving.

There are essentially seven indispensable components to this experience that make it a forum for effective mass collaboration:

Carefully Produced Script.   A town meeting is a finely tuned public process that turns on the organization and the substance of the day. The day's agenda is developed during several weeks of close collaboration among senior AmericaSpeaks staff, decision-makers, and stakeholders. The purpose of the script is to guide the communication of factual information related to the issues at hand, provide carefully framed discussion questions for public input, and help participants navigate trade-offs, prioritization, and decision making. A key feature of a 21stCTM script is its flexibility—clear openings where the content is generated real-time through public discussion. In a real sense, citizens play a key role in shaping the direction of discussion as they prioritize recommendations to decision makers.

Small Group Dialogue.   Citizens participate in roundtable discussions throughout the day, deliberaitng issues at tables with nine fellow citizens and a facilitator. Throughout the day, participants get to know each other, share their experiences, and come to agreement around shared recommendations. The role of the facilitator is to ensure that everyone has a chance to speak on any given issue, that the group remains focused on the topic at hand, and that participants refrain from personal attacks. We believe this format fosters a climate of openness, learning and joint problem-solving and generates a positive experience of civic engagement that can have lasting positive effects on participants' attitudes toward sustained involvement.

Table Reporting.   Each table is equipped with a laptop computer that is used as an electronic flipchart. Early in the day each table identifies someone who will serve as a "recorder" or note-taker for at least part of the day (the role can be passed among participants). Areas of shared agreement that emerge during discussion are entered by the recorder into the laptop running easy-to-use collaboration software. Participants are typically encouraged to discuss issues for at least 20-minutes before they begin to identify points of agreement and action to enter into the laptop.

Real-Time Data Theming.   The theme team is the brain or the central processor of the town meeting. Comprised of volunteers from the community recruited through stakeholder networks—journalists, graduate students, and others with a natural capacity for neutrality—the theme team consists of pairs of reviewers who scan the data coming in from table laptops. The team is looking for common themes across tables that emerge as possible priorities of the entire group. These priorities are used to build the agenda and drive voting.

Video Projection.   Large-scale video projection is used to communicate both background information on issues participants are asked to discuss as well as options for voting identified by the theme team. In preparation for the town meeting, decision-makers often produce short videos, maps, data graphs and other visual tools to communicate important factual information about key issues. Themes identified by the theme team are also displayed to the entire group for polling.

Keypad Polling.   Each participant has a wireless keypad with a unique identifier used for polling throughout the day. While participant registration data is not associated with the keypad, votes can be tracked across basic demographic data collected through a poll early in the day. The wireless keypad devices, in combination with the output of the theme team, allow the town meeting facilitators to transparently build the agenda in real-time as participants identify policy preferences during table discussion and prioritize them during polling. Keypads provide a critical opportunity for participants to express individual preferences with a context of shared understanding and collaboration.

Instant Reporting.   At the end of every 21stCTM, a preliminary report of who was in the room and a summary of the day's findings is produced for participants, decision makers and the media. This report—which pulls together the results of keypad votes and substance from the theme team in the order they were discussed—is essential to demonstrating that the public's input is recognized and valued, that there is a public record with which to hold decision-makers accountable at the end of the day, a document with which to build policy-momentum and a tangible "outcome" that the media can report.

FOUR PRINCIPLES OF CITIZENSOURCING

To be effective, every 21stCTM embodies four organizing principles which we feel should form the center of any citizensourcing effort. These are:

Involve Decision Makers.   No exercise in public involvement will be successful without buy-in from decision makers. From the moment planning begins, a 21stCTM embodies a commitment from decision makers to participate, listen to, and consider fully the recommendations of citizens. Without decision makers committed to the process and outcomes, public involvement efforts risk alienating the public by involving them in processes that generate little interaction with public officials and yield no tangible benefits.

In our experience, decision-makers are always rewarded—often surprised—by the level of public discourse they encounter during public forums that pay close attention to structure, content and process. Most come away with a renewed commitment to work more closely with the public. Some go as far as to "embed" such processes in governance going forward. Town meetings can renew political capital within a community, bring new actors into the process, strengthen the commitment to shared outcomes across interests, and provide decision-makers with new momentum behind often difficult policy decisions.

Representation. It is essential that every 21stCTM serve as a microcosm of the public. AmericaSpeaks invests substantial resources from every town meeting budget in the processes of outreach, recruitment and registration to ensure that on town meeting day the public is fairly represented. This means traditionally under-represented groups are in the room, that there is balance across age, race and gender, that youth have a voice, and that there are ways for sizable non-English-speaking populations to participate. Without guarantees of reasonable levels of demographic representation, it would be hard for anyone to describe the results of the meeting as representative of how the public at-large would feel about the same set of problems, yielding a very weak mandate for decision-makers.

Balanced Information. Often, 21stCTM tackle tough issues that not all participants will have thought about in equal turn. Therefore, balanced discussion guides are provided, ensuring that the major options are fairly represented. Furthermore, decision makers will often produce informative background videos, data graphs, and other educational materials to ensure that participants have some of the basic facts behind the issues on the table, the same information decision-makers themselves are working with. Together, the materials help to create a baseline of shared knowledge from which participants can enter discussions.

Transparency. Ensuring that the process is visible and open to influence is essential to fostering a climate free of coercion. From the beginning of the day when participants respond to demographic questions to the end, when participants receive a copy of the preliminary report that captures the day's proceedings, an environment of openness and responsiveness is created. This level of transparency, combined with the participation of key decision-makers, fosters a shared sense that citizens both own the process and that its outcomes are legitimate and not driven by any dominant interests.

The Big Leap: Reversing the Innovation Model

Right now, much—if not all—of the innovation within the crowd- and cit-izensourcing movements are taking place outside of government. In some cases federal agencies have contracted innovative consultation efforts to vendors like Information Renaissance, Neighborhood America, and the Public Forum Institute. And while there is growing attention to inter-agency collaboration, it is rare to find true innovation in public engage-ment within government. Regulations.gov—the interagency federal e-rulemaking initiative headed by the Environmental Protection Agency—is perhaps the notable exception. Through regulations.gov, the rule-writing function of regulatory agencies is made more accessible to the public and groups outside of Washington by bringing federal dockets and the review and comment process online. Thanks to regulations.gov citizens can now view rules open for comment across agencies using a single interface, and can post their comments on any rule. By law, these agencies must respond to any substantive comment received.

Most innovation in sourcing citizens for policy advice is taking place within private companies looking to capture a greater share of govern-ment contracts and advocacy groups looking to find new ways to tap and augment the power of their constituents. What we find is that the *supply* of consultation mechanisms outside of government outstrips the *demand* for consultation within government. This is a marked difference from many European governments where we see a range of authorities actively and routinely reaching out to the public at large for advice on key public pol-icy initiatives. As we have suggested earlier, this may put agencies in a pre-carious position: without transformations in the culture and practice of citizen engagement governments will find themselves *behind* thin barriers that won't serve a changing public culture and surges in citizen activity. A more prudent approach would be to develop the internal systems and human resource capacities that will enable these agencies to *invite* and *convene* the public on an ongoing basis.

So we call this "reversing" the innovation model: government itself must become a more active partner in the areas of both researching the public's appetite for engagement as well as experimentation with new modes of mass public involvement. Systems for storing and disseminating key lessons from practice will be vital to cultivating institutional memory and excitement around what works. Staffing and incentive structures must be developed to create communities of practice and reward success. New policies and guidelines for effective practices in citizensourcing must be developed to ensure that effective innovations are identified and institu-tionalized in agency practice.

SOME POTENTIAL BENEFITS OF CITIZENSOURCING

In addition to the normative claims for improving democratic governance—it's what governments that are transparent and accountable to their citizens *should* do—we believe that there are at least four key benefits of citizensourcing. These are: reducing the costs of developing and implementing policy and program innovations; increasing the speed at which innovations can be developed and implemented; increasing citizen competence; and improving government-citizen relations.

Reduce Cost. Talking to the public directly and getting their input on public policy at the front end of policy design and implementation can dramatically reduce costs. Large-scale citizen engagement reduces the necessity for salesmanship-like communication strategies—less of a need to convince the public it's the "right thing to do"—and it can reduce the likelihood of lengthy and costly litigation when opposition groups challenge government decisions.

Increase Responsiveness. Large-scale citizen engagement exercises quickly gather and process policy advice from the public, producing workable results that can be more quickly implemented. Government agencies are spared lengthy courtroom challenges when the public feels the policies and programs proposed reflect the informed judgments of citizens. At the same time, as policy development adapts to the new modes of citizen involvement, traditional feedback cycles must be retooled. First, governments must rethink public input timelines and synchronize face-to-face approaches with the realities of a dynamic Internet culture. A six-week public hearing timeframe will be a poor match for an Internet process that will command attention for significantly less time. Second, the time between the collection and reporting on public input must narrow: competition for citizens' attention has never been greater. Therefore governments don't have a lot of time to spend between the moment citizens provide input and the day the process loses credibility for lack of response.

Increase Competence. Consultations serve to collect the views of citizens on key issues various agencies and the legislature are grappling with, providing public officials with better information on which to base their decisions. At the same time, well-run consultations deepen the public's understanding of important dimensions surrounding various public problems—for example, the values that often underlie competing views and the tradeoffs associated with certain decisions. This kind of civic education deepens citizens' substantive knowledge of issues, broadens their understanding of key actors and the government's role, and hones citizens' skills in the use of governance tools in a networked society, skills that are improved with successive application.

Strengthen Confidence.   Democratic governments around the world face a common problem, namely that engagement and trust in government institutions has been falling steadily since the 1980s. By broadening and deepening opportunities for citizens to engage decision makers in matters that affect them directly, governments close the distance between citizens and the policy process. When citizens feel less alienated from policy makers and processes, their perceptions about government change: government is no longer seen as a distant adversary but a partner in the joint effort to improve the quality of life for all citizens.

Apart from the few noticeable exceptions, is the public sector at large ready to embrace a "culture" of citizensoucing? Probably not, and here are seven obstacles to citizensourcing in government we see:

Resistant Culture.   There is pretty good evidence that public officials carry sizable skepticism about the capacity of citizens to come to sound judgment on public policy matters. At AmericaSpeaks we believe that it is the process that defines the quality of citizen contributions to policy processes. Given the right structure, process and content, we have demonstrated over and over that the public will make outstanding contributions to policy processes. The dominant culture of agencies—and governments in general—encourages the use of a select, often inadequate, set of expert-driven tools: public hearings, public comment, and surveys of public opinion. Too often, citizens are set up to fail when they are thrust into adversarial public meetings, when they are asked a battery of questions around which they are poorly informed, or invited to participate in online "consultations" that provide no mechanisms to explore values and trade-offs.

Predominance of e-services.   The President's Management Agenda, which outlined a set of eGov initiatives, simultaneously opened a window on important agency reforms around bringing frontline services online while closing a window on broader e-participation and e-democracy reforms. By focusing almost exclusively on reducing costs, increasing efficiency, and improving customer service satisfaction across agencies that routinely deal with the public, the president's e-gov agenda left little room for vital upgrades to agencies' capacity to engage citizens in policy and program development and evaluation activities.

Top-Down Government.   "Companies that want to change the game with open innovation should be driving for a qualitative change in approach, not just incremental tinkering" (Tapscott & Williams, 2006, p. 113). Likewise, pushing for open collaboration between central governments and citizens is going to require entirely new, perhaps bold policy frameworks that deliver broad management reforms capable of changing hierarchal, often expert oriented models of policy advisory processes into flatter, more collaborative frameworks that encourage broad and direct citizen engagement.

Furthermore, organizing federal agencies into networks that capture, share and put to use public knowledge is an enormous administrative challenge, and a key source of the value in new governance mechanisms. Knowing where and when "sourcing" policymaking to citizens adds value to the policy process is central to the success of these reforms. Federal coordination and oversight agencies like the General Services Administration (GSA) and the President's Office of Management and Budget (OMB) will need to work closely with agencies and the public to develop appropriate staffing, incentive, coordination, and evaluation frameworks that enable citizensourcing to thrive.

Representation. Citizensourcing through mass participation offers challenges to fundamental notions of representation and legitimacy. While there is no particular reason a crowdsourcing company would want to exclude the views and ideas of contributors around the world—it's seeking customer engagement after all—citizensourcing governments must ensure that the "rights" of representation and participation are safeguarded. Governments must think carefully about whom they engage when they source their citizenry for policy innovation and advice and how they justify their decisions against a backdrop of large-scale, often privacy-protected public involvement.

Producing Reliable Results. Related to representation is the idea that the outcomes of a public engagement process can be said to be reproducible through repetition and verifiable through alternative documentation methods. Validity of a public input process is the degree to which the results or findings are reproducible. In other words, the *preferences* expressed by citizens who participate in a public input process should be stable and generalizable. In a citizensourcing environment, vulnerable as it is to variations of circumstance and the attitudes of participants, precautions must be made to ensure that participants are representative of the population at large, and that the findings can be tested against other valid means of public input in the event they are called into question.

Connecting Input to Outcomes. Many public agencies routinely seek citizen input on pending decisions. There is already great variation in the quality of methods used to gather public input, the transparency of the process, and certainly the level of accountability to which the agency will be held to demonstrate their use of the public's input. For citizensourcing to work long term, agencies must adopt clear guidelines for how they will receive public input and set expectations for how that information will be used. Different from the private sector, the incentive to participate on the part of citizens is almost never monetary, and it certainly is not prestige or acclaim. Instead, the motivations that agencies will likely tap when they source policymaking to citizens will be self-interest and civic, a shared sense that each of us is an owner and a steward of our democratic government and an interest in securing from it the very best decisions.

Surrendering Agendas.   Most times citizens come together to address a public problem significant control has already been wrested from their hands: the agenda has been set. Who decides what problems the public should solve is still a question left to public policy experts, advocates, and policy makers themselves. Nonetheless, this does not need to be the case: just as the "prosumer" movement deepens customer engagement in product innovation, citizensourcing pushes the boundaries of acceptable citizen work and includes agenda-setting within its influence. When citizens participate in an engagement exercise they bring many more ideas to the table than are included on the agenda. To be credible, new governance mechanisms must be responsive to the interests and agendas of citizens directly, when necessary capable of bypassing the apparatus of policy influence in Washington. It should be expected that once citizens become accustomed to dialogue with government, once platforms for direct involvement have been deployed, citizens will seek—and sometimes discover—more and more ways to exercise their voice and influence in policy.

RECOMMENDATIONS

Governments building Web sites is one thing. Creating the environment in which these sites—and the citizensourcing culture—can thrive is another. Clearly, change won't happen on its own, and it won't take place overnight. It is sobering to see how far behind much of government in the United States remains, both relative to where citizens and the market are headed and in relationship to many of the leading "wired" governments around the world. In the EU for example—demonstrative perhaps of member-nations' commitment to citizen participation—where no explicit eparticipation policy exists, the European Commission has granted Vice-President for Institutional Relations and Communication Strategy Margot Wallström a 49 million euro budget to improve communication with EU citizens through participation including online consultation and other means of debate and dialogue.[4]

To help get lagging governments back on track, we have come up with some recommendations that should be looked at much more closely and evaluated for their potential impact to both improve service delivery and bring citizens closer to decision making. First, there are two broad reforms that we think are necessary for citizensourcing to become a part of the way "the business of government" is carried out.

First, governments must expand notions of citizen participation from an outcomes orientation. For citizensourcing to take off, the focus of much policymaking must shift from the present preoccupation with the design and development of public policy products to the design and facilitation of the processes themselves that will enable citizens to make and shape policy. In business leaders face the challenge of shifting from a stance of enabling *mass customization*—the "swapping" of interchangeable parts—to one where customer innovation (design and development of new products and services) is enabled (Tapscott & Williams, 2006, p. 148). Similarly, the democracy scholars John Gaventa and Andrea Cornwall have observed that bureaucratic conceptions of citizens must shift from "users and choosers" to "makers and shapers" of public policy (Cornwall & Gaventa, 2001). Therefore, immediate questions should revolve less around concerns about *what kinds* of policy outcomes citizens will produce and more around *how* these outcomes will be produced.

Second, governments must invest more in the infrastructure of engagement. One of the lessons from the private sector's experience with crowdsourcing is that its success is built on a shared "infrastructure of rules, institutions, knowledge, standards, and technologies provided by a mixed public and private sector initiative" (Tapscott & Williams, 2006, p. 178). In the same way, citizensourcing will work only once governments have undertaken the necessary initiatives that will yield a comprehensive framework for collecting, storing, retrieving, and making sense of citizen input. This will include policies and incentive structures, hardware and software platforms, and staffing and organizational capacities.

There are several levels at which governments must work to become more citizen-centric in the networked society. One is at the "street" level, transforming the ways citizens experience and interact with government. The second level is at the level of policy and strategy, meaning the frameworks that shape the scope and quality of governance programs. Third is the infrastructure that enables efficient, effective citizen-government communication as well as government-government communication. Innovation must take place at all three levels to create a truly vibrant and secure environment for citizensourcing.

To advance governance in the networked society, we feel there are at least three citizen-facing innovations that the Government Services Administration, which operates the Office of Citizen Services and Communication—which oversees USA.gov, our target for these reforms—can undertake in the short term. These are the development of a "consultation portal," the establishment of a government information personalization service which, as a placeholder, we call "My.gov," and the creation of an executive "Office of the e-Envoy."

Consult.gov

At the present, few federal agencies regularly "consult" the public on various matters related to policy and program development and evaluation. Only a handful of very outstanding efforts, like the National Cancer Institute's ncilistens.cancer.gov, provide a consistent, high quality space for persistent government-citizen interaction online. For the most part, these efforts are very difficult to find and vary widely in their implementation. Consultations.gov is envisioned as a multi-layered approach to bringing greater visibility and standardization to the e-consultation process. We see three important iterations of this effort.

The first is a simple "windshield" that organizes up-to-date links to open consultations across government. The purpose of this feature— which could be implemented with a simple "consultations" tab on the USA.gov homepage that takes the user to a dynamically generated summary of live consultations—is to provide citizens with easy access to opportunities to engage agency managers around issues they care about.

The second iteration of Consultations.gov is a set of guidelines and standards for "best practices" in online consultation. This consultation "play book" would include guidance around when to seek public input, how to manage a consultation, and effective organization, management, interpretation, sharing, and reporting of data in ways that augment transparency and accountability while preserving the agencies' obligations for data privacy and security.

The third iteration of consultations.gov is as fulfledged, cross-agency platform for consultation. Any agency would adopt the architecture and design features of the software and create their own implementation. The infrastructure would allow for a consistent consultation experience across agency Web sites while enabling seamless data-sharing across agencies, providing opportunities to both reduce duplication and validate results.

My.gov

Most citizens are probably very interested in some of the things government does some of the time. Relatively few are actively engaged in tracking government activity all of the time. My.gov is envisioned as a platform for citizens to consolidate their interests in the activities of government into a single page. My.gov subscribers will be able to personalize their My.gov pages to display services they are interested in—for example tax filing and social security benefits—as well as information about policy activity—for example recent notices of comment in the Federal Register that deal with keywords individual users have identified.

A critical piece of work for My.gov to succeed is for agencies to adopt data standards and to make their content accessible across agency jurisdictions. This will enable users to interact within information through a single data architecture and design template and avoid the pitfalls of today's environment, in which users must hop from agency site to agency site as they seek out information.

Create an e-Democracy "Envoy"

Six months into his service as chief of homeland security, DHS Secretary Michael Chertoff appointed the nation's first "cybersecurity czar" when he created the position of assistant secretary for cyber and telecommunications security. In a similarly bold spirit, we should invigorate our democratic imagination by appointing a cabinet-level position responsible for transforming the way agencies and the legislature engage citizens. This does not need to be a permanent post, though it should have sufficient powers, resources and duration to push through important reforms across agencies.

The U.K. Cabinet Office of the e-Envoy is perhaps the best model for such a position, which existed for only a short period within Prime Minister Tony Blair's Service Delivery and Reform team based in the Cabinet Office. According to archived information about the temporary position, the e-Envoy was "responsible for ensuring that all government services are available electronically by 2005 with key services achieving high levels of use" (Cabinet Office, 2003). This effort resulted in such transformations to e-Gov information and service delivery in the United Kingdom as the development of direct.gov.uk, Downing Street's "supersite" for public access to government. Among the site's exemplary features are links directly to local government councils as well as a directory of open consultations across government (Directgov, 2005).

CONCLUSION

Crowdsourcing provides a powerful metaphor for networked governance that draws on some important lessons from success in the private sector. The opportunities to involve citizens in public problem solving that have been created through the spread of personal computers connected to the internet is unprecedented. At AmericaSpeaks, we've learned through experience that citizens across the country want to be engaged in meaningful opportunities to solve public problems—from health care reform to transportation planning, social security reform to municipal budgeting. Through our 21stCTM we have been able to tap "the wisdom of crowds" to bring the experience, knowledge, and creativity to bear on urgent public problems.

Today, while the federal agencies are using information technology to improve information and service delivery and legislators have expanded their tool sets to communicate with the public, government is falling behind in its mandate to foster an active and engaged citizenry. Citizensourcing provides the beginning of a conceptual framework for transforming government's relationship with the public: away from an understanding of citizens as "users and choosers" of government programs and services to "makers and shapers" of policies and decisions that affect their lives. While this is not a demand for "direct democracy," it is a strong call for invigorated thinking about the role of citizens in a networked society and an examination of the policies, programs, human resources, and infrastructure necessary to involve citizens in governance.

NOTES

1. Your Health Care Your Say.
2. EU Web site Meeting of Minds.
3. The Web site www.katrinalist.net is no longer available online, though a comprehensive description of the effort can be accessed at http://www.wiki-pedia.org
4. Visit Vice-presdident Wallstrom's site at http://ec.europa.eu/commission_barroso/wallstrom/index_en.htm for an introduction to the breadth of engagement initiatives being undertaken within the EU framework. Figures come from an e-mail exchange with a spokesperson for Institutional Relations and Communications Strategy.

REFERENCES

Boutin, P. (2006, July 13). *Crowdsourcing: Consumers as creators.* Retrieved December 28, 2006, from http://www.businessweek.com/innovate/content/jul2006/id20060713_755844.htm

Cabinet Office. (2003). *Office of the e-envoy.* Retrieved January 14, 2007, from http://archive.cabinetoffice.gov.uk/e-envoy/index-content.htm

Cornwall, A., & Gaventa, J. (2001). *From users and choosers to makers and shapers: Repositioning participation in social policy* (Working papers 127). Brighton, United Kingdom: Institute for Development Studies.

Directgov. (2005). *Public consultations.* Retrieved January 14, 2007, from http://www.direct.gov.uk/Dl1/Directories/PublicConsultations/fs/en

The Economist. (2005, April 21). *The future of journalism.* Retrieved June 6, 2007 from http://www.economist.com/business/displaystory.cfm?story_id=E1_PRJGDPJ

Facebook. (2007). *Facebook platform.* Retrieved June 6, 2007, from http://developers .facebook.com/

Fung, A. (2003). Survey article: Recipes for public spheres: Eight institutional design choices and their consequences. *Journal of Political Philosophy, 11*(3), 338-367

Gahran, A. (2006, November 30). *Gannet 'information centers:' Good for daily journalism?* Retrieved January 14, 2007, from http://www.poynter.org/column.asp?id =31&aid=113411

Howe, J. (2006a, June). *The rise of crowdsourcing.* Retrieved December 28, 2006, from http://www.wired.com/wired/archive/14.06/crowds.html

Howe, J. (2006b, November 30). *A message brought to you by the crowd.* Retrieved June 6, 2007, from http://crowdsourcing.typepad.com/cs/2006/11/a_message_broug.html

Institute for Politics, Democracy and the Internet. (2006). *Person-to-person-to-person: Harnessing the political power of online social networks and user-generated content.* Washington, DC: George Washington University.

Knight Foundation. (2006, September 18). *Knight Foundation competition will award millions to innovative community news experiments.* Retrieved June 11, 2007, from http://www.knightfdn.org/default.asp?story=news_at_knight/releases/2006/ 2006_09_18_newschallenge.html

Philanthropy News Digest. (2006). *Rockefeller foundation launches 'innovation initiative' to address global development challenges.* Retrieved December 28, 2006, from http://foundationcenter.org/pnd/news/story.jhtml?id=165000029

Leckart, S. (2006, January). *When the shoot hits the fans.* Retrieved December 28, 2006, from http://www.wired.com/wired/archive/15.01/play.html?pg=3

Li, C. (2007, April 6). *Kudos to Chevy Tahoe: It takes guts to brand with social computing.* Retrieved June 6, 2007, from http://blogs.forrester.com/charleneli/2006/ 04/kudos_to_chevy_.html

Louis, T. (2007, January 5). *Running the numbers on Second Life.* Retrieved June 1, 2007, from http://www.tnl.net/blog/2007/01/05/running-the-numbers-on-second-life/

Marketocracy. (2006). *About Marketocracy.* Retrieved June 6, 2007 http://www .marketocracy.com/cgi-bin/WebObjects/Portfolio.woa/ps/AboutOverviewPage/ bfix=1

Omidyar Network. (2007). *Welcome to the Omidyar.net community.* Retrieved June 6, 2007, from http://www.omidyar.net/home

Schatz, A. (2007, May 26). *BO, U R So Gr8.* Retrieved June 6, 2007, from http:// online.wsj.com/public/article/SB118011947223614895-iSeQ_ DC8SbZxiNLhtHwJyIftJN0_20070625.html

Sifry, M. (2006, October 9). *RNC vs. DNC Online: Precinct-Walking or Social-Networking?* Retrieved January 13, 2007, from http://www.personaldemocracy.com/ node/1036

Tapscott, D., & Williams, A. (2006) *Wikinomics: How mass collaboration changes everything.* New York: Penguin

Von Hippel, E. (2005). *Democratizing innovation.* Cambridge, MA: The MIT Press.

PART III

THE INTERNET AND CIVIC ENGAGEMENT

CHAPTER 10

DOES INTERNET USE REALLY FACILITATE CIVIC ENGAGEMENT?

Empirical Evidence From the American National Election Studies

Hun Myoung Park and James L. Perry

Civic engagement is known to catalyze government reform and participatory democracy. Informed and empowered citizens are able to facilitate good governance by making all levels of government more efficient, transparent, and accountable. Civic engagement and trust in government and politics, however, have declined for the past 5 decades in the United States (Putnam, 2000; Skocpol, 2003). In modern networked societies, civic engagement may be evolving to take different forms and styles. In particular, Internet use and online engagement are expected to provide a promising avenue for revitalizing democracy in the digital era.

Beginning in the mid-1990s, the Internet and World Wide Web have transformed the ways people do business. People can purchase products through electronic commerce, renew vehicle registrations and pay taxes

Civic Engagement in a Network Society
pp. 237–269
Copyright © 2008 by Information Age Publishing
All rights of reproduction in any form reserved.

through electronic government (e-government), donate money through Web sites for political parties and candidates, and educate themselves using Web-based teaching and learning applications. Online broadcasting has enabled citizens to acquire information previously available only on television, radio, magazines, and newspapers. To put it simply, the Internet is changing society by facilitating access to information and exchange relationships.

As citizens embrace the use of information technologies, scholars have turned their attention to the impact of the Internet on various aspects of society. One stream of research investigates how Internet use affects public service delivery, government reform, and democracy; another examines the impact on social capital and communities, digital inequality (digital divide), and cultural changes (Bimber 2001, 2003; DiMaggio, Hargittai, Neuman, & Robinson, 2001; Katz & Rice, 2002; Norris, 2001; Rheingold, 1993; Robbin, Courtright, & Davis, 2004; Selnow, 1998). Relatively little is known, however, about the relationship between Internet use and civic engagement.

Internet enthusiasts argue that the Internet will facilitate deliberative and participatory democracy (Browning, 2002; Grossman, 1995; Morris, 1999; Rheingold, 1993). Studies of the political use of the Internet suggest that the Internet is less likely to mobilize citizens and more likely to reinforce their power status (Davis, 1999; Norris, 2001). Bimber (2001, 2003) and Delli Carpini and Keeter (2003) report little evidence to support a significant relationship between Internet use and civic engagement. How do we reconcile the conflicting evidence about the impact of the Internet on civic engagement? Does Internet use matter for civic engagement in a networked society?

This chapter attempts to solve the puzzle. It begins by defining different forms of civic engagement and suggests the necessity to distinguish one form from another. The existing research on Internet use and civic engagement is then reviewed from three different perspectives. We next describe the American National Election Studies and explain the propensity score matching method and the recursive bivariate probit model we use to analyze the data. The analysis presents the results for the two methods, focusing on the average effect and discrete change of Internet use for political information. Finally, we discuss the findings and their implications for theories and methods in this field.

DEFINING CIVIC ENGAGEMENT

Civic engagement refers to citizens' individual and collective involvement in public affairs. This engagement differs from an administrative-centric perspective of citizen involvement in that the former is voluntary and the latter is "initiated and controlled by government" (Langton, 1978; Yang & Callahan 2005).[1] Civic engagement encompasses a variety of forms of political and nonpolitical activities. Conventional forms of civic engagement include: voting; working in election campaigns for political parties; contributing to political causes and candidates; contacting public officials; attending public meetings, political rallies, protests or speeches; signing petitions; serving local organizations; and writing articles for mass media (Verba, Scholzman, & Brady 1995; Putnam 2000; Ramakrishnan & Baldassare 2004; Weissberg 2005).

There are many theoretical and practical problems in defining and measuring civic engagement and political participation (Robbin et al., 2004; Weissberg, 2005). Weissberg (2005) argues that conventional inquiries on political participation are conceptually vague and thus fail to capture the variety of engagement in the real world. He claims that existing literature tends to focus on political activities that are easy to measure and treats all activities equally. Jennings and Zeitner (2003) criticize survey methodology because it focuses on limited numbers of civic engagement indicators and provides insufficient evidence for generalization. Weissberg (2005) also points out that most research takes the election-centered approach and excludes unsavory and idiosyncratic behavior such as violence and bribery, and that the unit of analysis is the individual's reported "act," not "activity" that they want to study.

Verba, Scholzman, and Brady (1995) differentiate political activities according to the capacity to convey information (or messages), strength of pressures, and required resources. Financial contributions to a political party and candidate can send many strong messages to politicians but in turn require more resources—money in particular. Serving local organizations and participating in protests may also convey strong messages to politicians and public officials. However, the required resources for these activities are not material resources like money but time and skills that enthusiasts are willing to spare. Voting conveys a few weak messages. A person is given only one ballot regardless of wealth, occupation, and education, and the likelihood that his or her ballot makes a difference in outcomes is very low. The voting cost is relatively low. Voting is, from the view of Verba et al. (1995), *sui genesis*.

Civic engagement may be electoral or nonelectoral. *Electoral engagement* involves elections and campaigns, while *nonelectoral engagement* is related to participation in general (nonpartisan) politics, government policies, or community issues. Some civic engagements are deliberative in a sense that they accompany exchange of information and opinions among citizens. This *deliberative engagement* is sensitive to the quality of information and communication because of its collective nature. *Action-oriented*

Table 10.1.   A Classification of Civic Engagement

	Deliberative Engagement	*Action-oriented Engagement*
Electoral Engagement	• Talk to people and try to show why they should vote for or against	• Attend rallies and speeches • Give money to a candidate or party
Nonelectoral Engagement	• Talk about politics with family or friends	• Contact government officials to express personal views on public issues • Work with other people to deal with community issues

engagement is going out to do something rather than debating public issues. Internet use appears to influence deliberative civic engagement more than action-oriented engagement.

This study examines four types of civic engagement (Table 10.1).[2] An example of electoral deliberative engagement occurs when people talk to any people and show why they should vote for or against a candidate. Talking about politics with family or friends is a nonelectoral deliberative engagement that is not necessarily related to election and partisan activities. These activities look similar, but differ in that pressing others to vote for or against a particular candidate or party is partisan and involves position taking and partisanship. Deliberative engagement involves information exchange among people in personal networks where citizens as opinion leaders exert personal influence on others (Katz & Lazarsfeld 1964).[3] Among electoral action-oriented engagement activities are attending political meetings, rallies, speeches, or dinners and giving money to a political party and candidate. Nonelectoral action-oriented engagement includes contacting government officials to express personal views on public issues and working with other people to deal with community issues.

LITERATURE REVIEW

This section discusses two aspects of extant research about Internet use and civic engagement. The first aspect is how research conceives the relationship between the Internet and society. Understanding broad differences in the perceived relationships provides some coherence for our analysis. A second but related aspect of the research is the methods used to model hypothesized relationships between Internet use and society—civic engagement in particular.

Relationship Between Internet Use and Society

DiMaggio et al. (2001) review five research domains for the Internet and society: digital inequality, community and social capital, political participation, organizational impact, and cultural impact. More recently, Robbin et al. (2004) provide a summary of research on the impact of information and communication technology (e.g., e-government and e-democracy) on political life. Arguments in the literature reflect three perspectives about the relationship between Internet use and society: optimism, pessimism, and skepticism (Arterton, 1987; Bimber, 2003; DiMaggio et al. 2001; Katz & Rice, 2002; Norris. 2001).

Internet enthusiasts have a utopian view that the Internet will get people more involved in public life, facilitate formation of social networks (social capital), and contribute to participatory and deliberative democracy (Browning, 2002; Corrado, 1996; Foot & Schneider, 2006; Grossman, 1995; Morris, 1999; Rheingold, 1993; Ward, Gibson, & Nixon, 2003;).[4] Cyber-optimists emphasize that information technology reduces the costs of information and communication and thus allows citizens to obtain and disseminate political information in an efficient and timely manner. This cost reduction, in particular, provides minority and marginalized groups with opportunities to have their voices heard in the public sphere (Rheingold, 1993). Two-way communication enriches connections between citizens and public officials in policy processes and improves transparency and accountability of government. Foot and Schneider (2006) analyze practices of informing, involving, connecting, and mobilizing of "Web spheres" and conclude Web campaigns have profound effects on electoral and political processes. Thus, the Internet and related technologies are viewed as a vehicle for mobilizing constituents, reinventing government, and revitalizing democracy.

The pessimists argue that the Internet reinforces rather than transforms existing power relationships and patterns of political participation (Davis, 1999, 2005; Kavanaugh, 2002; Norris, 2001). Davis (1999, 2005), from the reinforcement view, argues that the Internet tends to be dominated by those who are young, well educated, affluent, and powerful. The Internet facilitates the civic engagement of people who are already informed and motivated, but it does not change the involvement level of people who are disenfranchised (Kavanaugh, 2002; Norris, 2001). The Internet is less likely to mobilize the disengaged and more likely to reinforce established political actors who can take greater advantage of using political information on the network, and thus deepens the digital divide between the information haves and have-nots (Norris, 2001).

Finally, the skeptics caution that the Internet, despite its potential, does not necessarily facilitate or destroy civic engagement, but reflects "politics

**Table 10.2.   Perspectives on the
Relationship Between Internet Use and Society**

	Key Arguments	*Role of the Internet*
Optimism	Mobilization, transformation, participatory and deliberative democracy	Determinant (positive)
Pessimism	Reinforcement, digital inequality (digital divide), "engaging the engaged"	Determinant (negative)
Skepticism	Normalization, reflection (mirroring), displacement, complement, "Politics as usual"	Reflected and socially-shaped

as usual" (Bimber, 2003; Chadwick, 2006; Davis, Elin, & Reeher, 2002; Kamarck, 2002; Margolis & Resnick, 2000; Uslaner, 2004). Bimber (2001) argues that the Internet may reduce the cost of obtaining information and thus improve availability of information; however, the cost reduction and availability are not necessarily related to voting and political engagement. Bimber (2001) reported a marginally significant relationship only between the Internet and financial contributions to parties and candidates. Delli Carpini and Keeter (2003) also found little evidence to support a significant relationship between the use of the Internet and civic engagement. More recently, Uslaner (2004) concludes that the Internet is not transforming but looks much like the real world and that the Internet does not make up for the decline in civic engagement, nor does it facilitate social capital. Putnam (2000) argues that the Internet tends to displace face-to-face engagement and thus does not necessarily improve social capital.[5] This normalization thesis suggests that cyberspace is taking on the characteristics of ordinary life (Margolis & Resnick, 2000). Table 10.2 summarizes the three perspectives on the impact of Internet use on society.

Modeling the Relationship

Existing research employs various methods to examine the relationship between Internet use and civic engagement. Many studies envisage a unidirectional relationship between Internet use and society. This relationship is often criticized as a misspecification because of the nebulous causal relationship between the two variables (Arterton, 1987; Bimber, 2001; DiMaggio et al. 2001). Internet use and engagement may be iterative and interactive in the virtuous circle that exerts a positive impact on democracy (Norris, 2000). Most quantitative research relies on univariate and descriptive methods and seldom considers carefully the key issues, such as endogeneity and the missing data problem, when modeling Internet use and civic engagement.

Since 2000, West (2005) has annually conducted content analysis to investigate electronic services available on the Web sites of federal and state governments with special attention to the public outreach features of e-government. Norris (2001) depends largely on descriptive methods to examine three types of digital divide. Bimber (2001, 2003) employs the binary logit model to analyze the American National Election Studies data in 1998 and 2000. Bimber and Davis (2003) combine telephone surveys, content analysis, and interviews, but their approach is descriptive and narrative. Jennings and Zeitner (2003) conduct linear regression analyses using longitudinal survey data and find an insignificant association between the political use of the Internet and civic engagement. Uslaner (2004) employs two-stage least squares to fit the model of social capital (trust in people). More recently, Scott (2006) performs a content analysis to measure the extent that municipal government websites provide information and services to improve public involvement. He develops public involvement indices and then applies an ANOVA to compare group means of the indices.

Descriptive methods and content analysis tend to be biased toward supply of Internet services without considering how citizens use the Internet. Univariate methods implicitly assume a unidirectional causal relationship between Internet use and engagement; that is, the former influences the latter in some way. But the causal structure is not always clear and varies across specific engagement activities.[6] The relationship between Internet use and civic engagement may be reciprocal and jointly determined simultaneously. This causal structure should be carefully examined regardless of whether research is quantitative or qualitative. Internet use is endogenous in some civic engagements, but not in others. The missing data problem is common in nationwide surveys because randomized experiments tend to be costly, infeasible, and/or undesirable.[7] These issues are rarely addressed in traditional approaches.

DATA: AMERICAN NATIONAL ELECTION STUDIES

This study analyzes nationwide survey data from the American National Election Studies (ANES) collected in election years of 1996, 1998, 2000, and 2004. The question of Internet use for political information appears only in these four years. The data set was extracted from the cumulative data file of ANES from 1948 through 2004. Some key variables, such as contact with government officials and personal income, were separately drawn from individual survey data and then merged into the final data

Table 10.3. Summary of Categorical Variables (*N* = 6,014)

	Yes (1)	No (0)	Missing
Talk about voting	1,762 (29.30)	3,672 (61.06)	580 (9.64)
Talk about politics	3,796 (63.12)	1,632 (27.14)	586 (9.74)
Attend a campaign rally	328 (5.45)	5,106 (84.90)	580 (9.64)
Give money to a candidate	526 (8.75)	4,907 (81.59)	581 (9.66)
Contact officials (2000, 2004)	543 (17.99)	2,076 (68.76)	400 (13.25)
Work for communities (2000, 2004)	713 (23.62)	1,906 (63.13)	400 (13.25)
Political mobilization	2,093 (34.80)	3,911 (65.03)	10 (.17)
Strong partisanship	1,897 (31.54)	4,078 (67.81)	39 (.65)
Education (college)	1,743 (28.98)	4,256 (70.77)	15 (.25)
Gender (male)	2,699 (44.88)	3,315 (55.12)	
Race (white)	4,414 (73.40)	1,538 (25.57)	62 (1.03)
Strong partisanship	1,897 (31.54)	4,078 (67.81)	39 (.65)
Internet use	1,189 (19.77)	4,238 (70.47)	587 (9.76)
Media exposure (radio)	2,040 (33.92)	3,395 (56.45)	579 (9.63)

*Percentage in parentheses.

set. This data set is not, however, a panel data set because respondents are not necessarily the same across election years.

Table 10.3 summarizes categorical dependent and independent variables. The first six variables are dependent variables that are classified in Table 10.1. A respondent is coded as 1 if he or she talked about politics with family and friends at least once in the past week and 0 otherwise. Political mobilization is set to 1 if a respondent was mobilized by a political party or others. Partisanship is coded as 1 only if a respondent had strong partisanship. Note that contacts with government officials and work with others to deal with community issues are included only in 2000 and 2004 data sets (*N* = 3,019). See the appendix for detailed questions.

Table 10.4 presents descriptive statistics for interval independent variables. Individual questions were summed so that their output variable has a range from 0 to 1. For example, values 1 through 4 of political interest were respectively recoded as 0, .33, .67, and 1. Political efficacy is the mean of four questions whose 1 through 3 were recoded as 0, .5. and 1, respectively. Personal income is drawn by taking the midpoint of each income range and then transformed to the square root of the income. Poststratified sample weight was applied in analysis.

Table 10.4. Summary of Interval Variables (*N* = 6,014)

	N	*Mean*	*Std. Dev.*	*Min*	*Median*	*Max*
Political interest	5,418	.590	.319	.000	.670	1.000
Political knowledge	5,436	.631	.306	.000	.750	1.000
Trust in government	5,418	.345	.224	.000	.293	1.000
Social capital	5,600	.537	.425	.000	.500	1.000
Political efficacy	5,610	.504	.290	.000	.500	1.000
Personal income	5,586	4.915	2.434	1.225	4.848	14.663
Age	5,987	47.007	17.199	18.000	45.000	97.000

METHODS

The diversity of civic engagements suggests that Internet use may not influence each type of engagement in the same way. Therefore, civic engagements need to be differentiated from one another in analysis. Internet use and some civic engagement may be reciprocal or determined jointly at one time.[8] Internet use may be an endogenous variable for some civic engagements and exogenous for other types of engagement. If endogeneity comes from regressors that are correlated with omitted variables (disturbances), an instrumental variable (IV) approach (i.e., two-stage least squares) may work. But other sources of endogeneity such as simultaneity require different approaches. The "missing data problem" is pervasive in observational studies, but is seldom taken into account in existing research, which may lead to reporting biased and unreliable estimates of effects.[9] This study employs the propensity score matching method and the recursive bivariate probit model to deal with the missing data problem, endogeneity, and simultaneity.

Propensity Score Matching Method

Since the seminal work of Rosenbaum and Rubin (1983), propensity score matching (PSM) has increasingly been used in policy analysis and evaluations such as studies on job training programs (Angrist, 1998; Dehejia & Wahba, 1999; Heckman, Ichimura, & Todd, 1997; Lalonde, 1986). PSM is a nonexperimental method of sampling to produce a control group whose distribution of covariates is similar to that of the treated group. Conditioning many covariates produces a so called "curse of dimensionality" that calls for a method of "dimension reduction" (Hahn

1998, p. 317). PSM employs one-dimensional propensity scores, predicted probabilities of falling into a treated group, to summarize multi-dimensional covariates (D'Agostino & Rubin, 2000).

PSM is based on the "strongly ignorable treatment assignment" assumption that the treatment assignment d and outcomes of y_0 and y_1 are conditionally independent given covariates w (Rosenbaum & Rubin 1983).[10] Theorem 3 says that "if the treatment assignment is strongly ignorable given w, then it is also strongly ignorable given any balancing score $b(w)$" (p. 45). This theorem implies that "if treatment assignment is strongly ignorable, then adjustment for a balancing score b(w) is sufficient to produce unbiased estimates of the average treatment effect" (pp. 44-45). Under these assumptions, the unobservable $E\{y_0|b(w), d = 1\}$ is drawn from the observable $E\{y_0|b(w), d = 0\}$ given propensity scores $b(w)$.

$$E\{y_1|b(w), d = 1\} = E\{y_1|b(w), d = 0\} = E\{y_1|b(w)\}$$

$$E\{y_0|b(w), d = 1\} = E\{y_0|b(w), d = 0\} = E\{y_0|b(w)\}$$

The "expected difference in observed responses to the two treatments at $b(w)$ is equal to the average treatment effect at $b(w)$," if treatment assignment is strongly ignorable (Theorem 4) (p. 46). Thus, PSM makes it possible to estimate the average treatment effect on the treated as follows.

$$E\{y_1 - y_0 \,|b(w)\} = E\{y_1|b(w), d = 1\} - E\{y_0|b(w), d = 1\}$$

$$= E\{y_1|b(w), d = 1\} - E\{y_0|b(w), d = 0\}$$

The PSM method consists of four steps: (1) estimating propensity scores; (2) checking the balance of covariates; (3) matching (pair matching or subclassification); and (4) calculating average treatment effects (Becker & Ichino, 2002; Dehejia & Wahba, 1999; Rosenbaum & Rubin, 1984). This study employs the binary probit model to estimate propensity scores and applies one-to-one pair matching without replacement to match control and treated observations. Covariates include political and social factor (i.e., political interest, knowledge, and social capital), demographics (i.e., personal income, education, age, gender, and race), media exposure (radio), and three dummies for election years.[11]

PSM can produce robust estimators of effects without assuming any functional form or probability distribution. This method relies on the quality of covariates and usually requires a large sample size. PSM cannot control all biases that come from the unobserved because this method considers observed covariates only (Shadish, Cook, & Campbell 2002).

Recursive Bivariate Probit Model

The recursive bivariate probit model (RBPM) was proposed by Maddala and Lee (1976) and Maddala (1983), and later developed by Greene (1998, 2003). RBPM is a bivariate probit model in which one equation includes the binary dependent variable of the other equation as an endogenous independent variable. Its functional form is

$$y_1^* = \beta_1' x_1 + \gamma y_2 + \varepsilon_1, \qquad y_1 = 1 \text{ if } y_1^* > 0, \ 0 \text{ otherwise,}$$

$$y_2^* = \beta_2' x_2 + \varepsilon_2, \qquad\qquad y_2 = 1 \text{ if } y_2^* > 0, \ 0 \text{ otherwise,}$$

where y_1 is a binary dependent variable of interest in equation 1, y_2 is a binary dependent variable of equation 2 that is included in the first equation as an endogenous variable, and x_1 and x_2 are the regressor vectors of two regression equations. x_1 includes demographics (i.e., personal income, education, age, gender, and race), Internet use for political information, and political and social factors such as political interest, knowledge, mobilization, efficacy, social capital, trust in government, and political partisanship. x_2 is the same as covariates used in PSM. This equation system is identified if disturbances are independent or there is at least one exogenous variable in x_2 that is not included in x_1 (Maddala 1983). The bivariate standard normal probability distribution is defined as

$$\Phi_2(y_1, y_2, \rho) = \frac{1}{2\pi\sqrt{1-\rho^2}} \int_{-\infty}^{y_2} \int_{-\infty}^{y_1} \exp\left[\frac{-1}{2(1-\rho^2)}(y_1^2 + y_2^2 - 2\rho y_1 y_2)\right] dy_1 dy_2$$

where ρ is the correlation coefficient of disturbances of two equations.

The correlation coefficient between the disturbances measures the effect of y_2 on y_1 after the influence of the endogenous variable y_2 is accounted for in the first equation (Greene, 2003). The key null hypothesis is that the disturbances ε_1 and ε_1 are not correlated: $\rho = 0$. If the null hypothesis is not rejected, the two equations may be estimated separately by either the binary logit or probit model with y_2 as an exogenous variable.

Like the simultaneous equation model (SEM), RBPM assumes that the disturbances are correlated. Unlike SEM, RBPM is estimated by the full information maximum likelihood (FIML) method, not by ordinary least squares (OLS). Interestingly, the endogenous nature of y_2 in the first equation can be ignored in formulating the likelihood function (Greene 2003); y_2 can be used as an endogenous variable in the first equation as if there is no simultaneity problem because two dependent variables are jointly determined (Greene, 1998, 2003).

Because RBPM is nonlinear, its parameter estimates should be interpreted with special caution. The impact of an independent variable on predicted probabilities is not constant but depends on the values of the variable and other independent variables. Therefore, simply reporting parameter estimates and their significance is not helpful for understanding the effects of independent variables in nonlinear models. Marginal effects and discrete changes are often used to evaluate the effects of independent variables in logit and probit models (Greene, 2003; Long, 1997). In RBPM, conditional predicted probabilities, predicted probabilities given $y_2 = 1$, are used to evaluate the impact of the endogenous independent variable (i.e., Internet use in this study).[12] The reference points of marginal effects and discrete changes are the means of continuous variables and 1 for binary variables.

FINDINGS

Internet use for political information generally has a positive impact on civic engagement, but its pattern varies across individual engagements. PSM, RBPM, and the binary probit model report consistent results as a whole.

Deliberative Civic Engagement

The one-to-one pair matching suggests that Internet use influences both electoral and nonelectoral deliberative civic engagement significantly (Table 10.5). Citizens who have used the Internet to get political information are about 10% more likely than nonusers to talk to any people and show why they should vote for or against one of the parties or candidates. Internet users talk about politics with family and friends 10 percent more than nonusers.[13] These average effects of PSM are less than half of the corresponding effect sizes of independent sample t test. This

Table 10.5.   Average Effects on Deliberative Civic Engagement

Civic Engagement	Pairs*	Treated	Control	Effect	S.E.	T	P-value
Talk about voting	1,091	.4931	.3932	.0999	.0212	4.7191	<.0000
Talk about politics	1,091	.8671	.7663	.1008	.0164	6.1356	<.0000

*PSM matches 1,091 pairs of observations that have similar propensity scores.

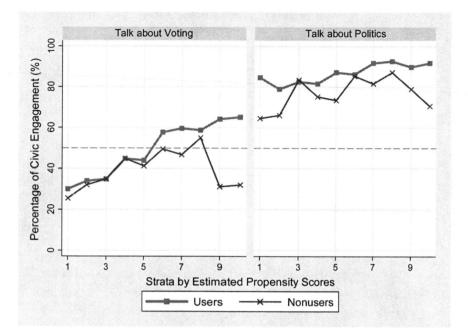

Figure 10.1.   Average effects on deliberative civic engagement.

result indicates that citizens who are willing to use the Internet may have a higher level of deliberative civic engagement than those who are not. Failure to take this correlation into account would result in overestimation of the average effect of Internet use.

Figure 10.1 illustrates the average effects of Internet use on these deliberative engagements. The distance between two engagements lines at a stratum indicates the average effect of Internet use at the stratum.[14] Citizens who get information about an election campaign on the Internet show a higher level of deliberative engagement than nonusers in most strata. The more likely citizens are to see political information on the Internet, the more likely they are to talk to any people and show why they should vote for or against a candidate (left plot in Figure 10.1). The likelihood of using the Internet appears to influence talking about politics moderately (right plot in Figure 10.1).

The RBPMs for deliberative engagement have significant endogeneity. The correlation of disturbances is −.523 for talking about why they should vote for or against and −.299 for talking about politics with family or friends (Table 10.6). Internet use and deliberative engagement appear to be jointly determined simultaneously with a causal relationship. Thus, it is

Table 10.6.   Impact of Internet Use on Deliberative Civic Engagement

	Talk About Voting		Talk About Politics	
	Engagement	Internet Use	Engagement	Internet Use
Political interest	.793 (.080)**	.554 (.092)**	1.188 (.088)**	.592 (.093)**
Political knowledge	.065 (.078)	.460 (.098)**	.330 (.079)**	.478 (.101)**
Social capital	-.015 (.055)	.280 (.065)**	.184 (.061)**	.276 (.067)**
Trust in government	-.262 (.102)**		-.196 (.112)+	
Political efficacy	.010 (.085)		.148 (.092)	
Political mobilization	.337 (.043)**		.185 (.048)**	
Partisanship	.255 (.045)**		.194 (.052)**	
Personal income	.036 (.010)**	.060 (.012)**	.022 (.012)+	.064 (.012)**
Education (college)	-.135 (.052)**	.411 (.057)**	.126 (.062)*	.416 (.058)**
Age	-.003 (.001)*	-.030 (.002)**	-.010 (.002)**	-.031 (.002)**
Gender (male)	.086 (.045)+	-.038 (.054)	-.166 (.048)**	-.041 (.055)
Race (white)	.019 (.052)	.116 (.062)+	.090 (.053)+	.107 (.063)+
Internet use	1.082 (.083)**		.866 (.171)**	
Media exposure		.258 (.052)**		.262 (.058)**
Dummy 1996		-1.176 (.076)**		-1.258 (.085)**
Dummy 1998		-.939 (.071)**		-.929 (.074)**
Dummy 2004		.617 (.064)**		.492 (.083)**
Intercept	-1.406 (.096)**	-.605 (.108)**	-.390 (.098)**	-.581 (.110)**
Rho (correlation)		-.523 (.048)**		-.299 (.108)**
Log Likelihood	-4471.1236		-4347.9477	
Wald test (Model)	1860.87**		1576.21**	
N	4960		4956	

*Standard errors in parentheses. $^+p < .10$. $^*p < .05$. $^{**}p < .01$.

necessary to take both direct and indirect effects of Internet use into account in order to assess its overall impact on deliberative engagement correctly.

Internet use for political information positively influences both deliberative engagements; its parameter estimates in two RBPMs are positive and statistically significant (Table 10.6). Figure 10.2 illustrates the conditional predicted probabilities that people will talk about voting and politics at different levels of political interest. The gap between two curves is

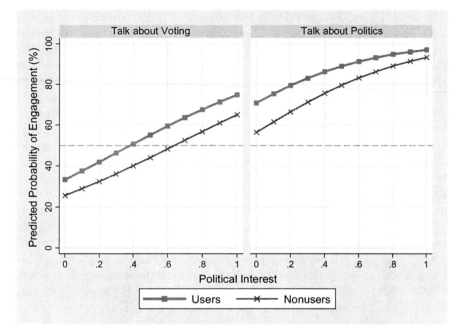

Figure 10.2.   Conditional predicted probability of deliberative civic engagement.

the discrete change of Internet use, which depicts the impact of Internet use on deliberative civic engagement. Discrete changes of Internet use in RBPM are comparable to the average effects in PSM presented in Table 10.5. Internet users who are intermediately interested are 11% more likely than nonusers to talk to any people and show why they should vote for or against, holding all other variables at their reference points (left plot in Figure 10.2). Two engagement curves appear to be parallel lines with a gap of 8-11%. The conditional predicted probability that intermediately interested Internet users will talk about politics with family or friends is about 9.5% higher than that of nonusers (right plot in Figure 10.2). The gap between the two curves for talking about politics ranges from 4% for the most interested to 14% for the least interested; the impact of Internet use becomes smaller as citizens are more interested in politics.

In the RBPM of talking about voting, political interest, knowledge, mobilization, partisanship, personal income, and media exposure (radio) have positive effects, whereas trust in government and age negatively affect this engagement. Political interest is a most influential indicator with a slope of .425; for a .1 increase from its mean, the conditional predicted probability will increase by 4.25%, holding other variables at their reference points (left plot in Figure 10.2). Political knowledge does not have a significant direct effect and instead affects this deliberative engagement indirectly by facilitating Internet use for political information; its overall marginal effect is 9.8%. Social capital has a negative direct impact but significantly influences Internet use to produce an overall effect of 3.6%. Mobilized Internet users are 14.8% more likely to talk about voting than those who are not. The discrete change of political partisanship is 11.2%. Personal income influences this engagement positively; for a $10,000 increase in income, Internet users are 2.4% more likely to talk about voting for or against. The marginal effect of trust in government and age are respectively −11.3 and −.6%, holding other variables at their reference points. Younger generations are more likely to use the Internet for political information and this indirect effect appears to dominate the overall impact of age. College education has negative direct and positive indirect effects that cancel out each other to make its overall impact negligible. The binary probit model would mistakenly report an insignificant effect of political knowledge and a significant negative effect of education. Social capital, political efficacy, gender, and race do not significantly influence talking about voting.

In the model of talking about politics with family or friends, political interest, knowledge, social capital, mobilization, partisanship, income, and education have significant positive effects. The marginal effects of political interest and knowledge are respectively .216 and .070 at the reference points (right plot in Figure 10.2). Social capital significantly influences this deliberative engagement; for a .1 increase in social capital, the conditional predicted probability of talking about politics will increase by .4%, holding other variables at their reference points. Political mobilization and partisanship boost the likelihood of engagement by about 4%, but their effects are smaller than those in talking about voting for or against. The marginal effect of personal income is significant but smaller than in electoral deliberative engagement. Internet users who attended a college are 4.0% more likely to discuss politics than those who did not. Young generations and female tend to talk about politics with family and friends more often than their counterparts. Trust in government, political efficacy, and race do not influence this engagement substantially.

Internet use itself is positively affected by political interest, knowledge, social capital, income, college education, and media exposure (radio), but it is negatively influenced by age. For a .1 increase in political interest, knowledge, and social capital, we can expect increase in the likelihood of using the Internet by 2.4%, 1.9%, and 1.1%, respectively. A $10,000 increase in personal income will increase the likelihood by 2.6%, holding other variable at their reference points. Internet users who attended a college are 14.9% more likely to use the Internet for political information than those who did not. Younger generations tend to use the Internet more than elder generations. Putnam (2000) suggests a displacement effect, but media exposure (radio) influences Internet use positively; they appear to supplement each other. There is no substantial inequality on gender and race. Significant parameter estimates of three dummy variables imply that Internet penetration and diffusion substantially vary across election years and thus affect accessibility of the Internet and availability of online political information. Smaller discrete changes of these dummies in talking about politics with family and friends indicate that not-electoral deliberative engagement less likely to change much over time than electoral engagement.

Action-Oriented Civic Engagement

Internet use for political information positively influences action-oriented civic engagement (Tables 10.7 and 10.8). The one-to-one pair matching suggests that citizens who have seen political information on the Internet are 4-5% more likely than nonusers to attend a rally and give money to a candidate.[15] Internet users contact government officials 12.6% more than nonusers. The average effect of Internet use is 11.0% for working with other people to deal with community issues.[16] Internet use appears to be more influential for nonelectoral action-oriented engagement than for the electoral counterpart.

In Figure 10.3, Internet users show a higher level of electoral action-oriented civic engagement than nonusers in most strata. But the narrow gap between two engagement lines implies a marginal average effect of Internet use on attendance at a rally and financial contributions. The likelihood of using the Internet for political information does not appear to

Table 10.7.   Average Effects on Action-Oriented Civic Engagement

Civic Engagement	Pairs	Treated	Control	Effect	S.E.	T	P Value
Attend a campaign rally	1,090	.1083	.0615	.0468	.0119	3.9317	<.0000
Give money	1,090	.1495	.1055	.0440	.0143	3.0874	<.0010
Contact officials*	872	.2993	.1732	.1261	.0201	6.2670	<.0000
Work for communities*	872	.3624	.2523	.1101	.0220	5.0152	<.0000

*The binary probit models for nonelectoral action-oriented engagement used 2000 and 2004 data only.

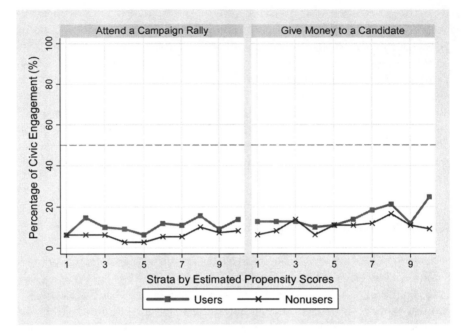

Figure 10.3.   Average effects on electoral action-oriented civic engagement.

matter much. Figure 10.4 illustrates the average effect of Internet use on non-electoral action-oriented engagement: contacts with government officials and work with others to deal with community issues. Internet users show a higher likelihood of participation in this engagement than nonusers in most strata. The gap between two non-electoral engagement lines is larger than that of the electoral counterpart shown in Figure 10.3. Nonelectoral engagement appears to be positively related to the likelihood of using the Internet.

All RBPMs of action-oriented engagement do not have significant correlations between disturbances. The correlation coefficient ranges from -.03 for work with other people to deal with community issues to .12 for contacts with government officials. Endogeneity does not appear significant in action-oriented engagement; Internet use for political information is exogenous and has only a direct effect on this type of engagement. Therefore, the binary probit model is used to estimate the impact of Internet use on action-oriented civic engagement.

Binary probit models suggest that Internet use for political information positively influences electoral action-oriented engagement: attendance at a campaign rally and financial contributions (first two columns

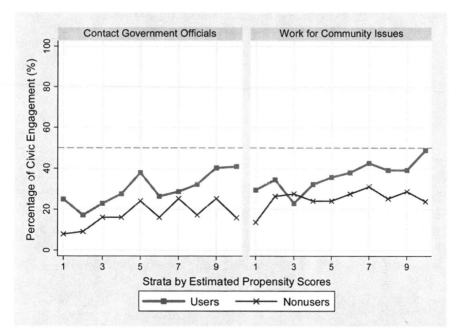

Figure 10.4.   Average effects on nonelectoral action-oriented civic engagement.

of Table 10.7). As illustrated in Figures 10.3 and 10.5, however, the impact of Internet use on these electoral engagements is not as large as expected. Internet users with an average political interest are 5.3% more likely than nonusers to attend a rally, holding other variables at their reference points (left plot in Figure 10.5). Similarly, the predicted probability that Internet users will give money to a political party or candidate is 5.4% higher than that of nonusers (right plot in Figure 10.5). The Internet, in particular, campaign Web sites, provides a variety of information and services but does not appear to elevate the level of electoral action-oriented engagement substantially.

The electoral action-oriented engagements are largely influenced by political factors such as political interest, mobilization, and partisanship (Table 10.8). The more interested, mobilized, strongly affiliated with major parties citizens are, the more likely they are to attend a rally and give money to a candidate. For a .1 increase in political interest from its mean, the predicted probability of attending a rally and giving money will increase respectively by 1.9% and 2.5%, holding other variables at their reference points (Figure 10.5). Engagement curves of Internet users and nonusers look like almost parallel lines with a gap of about 5% at the

Table 10.8. Impact of Internet Use on Action-Oriented Civic Engagement

	Electoral Engagement		Nonelectoral Engagement	
	Attend a Rally	Give Money	Contact Officials	Work for Comm.
Political interest	.718 (.137)**	.867 (.117)**	.734 (.135)**	.500 (.128)**
Political knowledge	.206 (.128)	.169 (.123)	.443 (.134)**	-.124 (.130)
Social capital	-.030 (.089)	.106 (.079)	.271 (.092)**	.345 (.088)**
Trust in government	.374 (.168)*	.009 (.156)	-.501 (.175)**	-.163 (.159)
Political efficacy	.024 (.134)	.185 (.133)	-.034 (.143)	.069 (.129)
Political mobilization	.486 (.069)**	.364 (.063)**	.320 (.072)**	.372 (.069)**
Partisanship	.364 (.069)**	.376 (.063)**	-.001 (.071)	-.020 (.070)
Personal income	.013 (.016)	.067 (.014)**	.009 (.015)	.041 (.014)**
Education (college)	.121 (.077)	.229 (.068)**	.253 (.079)**	.335 (.075)**
Age	-.004 (.002)*	.013 (.002)**	.001 (.002)	-.004 (.002)
Gender (male)	.043 (.074)	-.104 (.064)	-.016 (.073)	-.071 (.071)
Race (white)	.028 (.083)	.154 (.086)+	.079 (.089)	-.222 (.081)**
Internet use	.223 (.076)**	.203 (.075)**	.308 (.076)**	.240 (.073)**
Intercept	-2.711 (.145)**	-3.747 (.183)**	-2.070 (.159)**	-1.300 (.141)**
Log Likelihood	-949.102	-1189.146	-957.740	-1168.672
Wald test (Model)	227.98**	390.84**	235.18**	205.15**
Pseudo R^2	.122	.193	.125	.092
N	4959	4959	2291	2291

*Standard errors in parentheses; $^+p < .10$, $^*p < .05$, and $^{**}p < .01$.

intermediate level of political interest. Motivated Internet users are 10% more likely to attend a rally and 9% more likely to give money than those who are not. Strong partisanship increases the likelihood of attendance at a rally and financial contributions by 8% and 9%, respectively. Political knowledge, political efficacy, social capita, and trust in government do not make any substantial difference in electoral action-oriented engagement.

For attendance at a campaign rally, political interest, mobilization, and partisanship have significant effect, while personal income, education, and age are influential indicators of financial contributions. For a $10,000

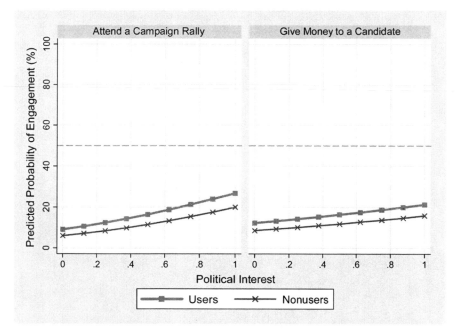

Figure 10.5.   Predicted probability of electoral action-oriented civic engagement.

increase in personal income from its mean, the predicted probability of giving money to a candidate will increase by about 2%, holding other variables at their reference points. Internet users who went to a college are 6.0% more likely to give money than those who did not. As citizens get older, they are, probably due to large disposable income and high opportunity cost, less likely attend a rally but more likely to donate money; a 10 year increase from the average age will increase the likelihood of this engagement by 3.9%. Gender and race do not have a significant effect on financial contributions.

Internet use for political information also positively affects nonelectoral action-oriented engagement (last two columns of Table 10.8). Internet users with the intermediate level of social capital are 9-11% more likely than nonusers to contact government officials and work with other people to deal with for community issues, holding other variables at their reference points (Figure 10.6). These discrete changes of Internet use are comparable to the average effect of 11-13% in Table 10.7. Internet use appears more influential for nonelectoral action-oriented engagement than for the electoral counterpart.

Nonelectoral engagement is influenced by social capital, political interest, mobilization, and education. A .1 increase of social capital will

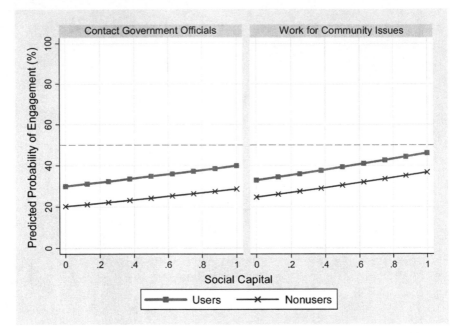

Figure 10.6.   Predicted probability of nonelectoral action-oriented civic engagement.

increase the predicted probability that Internet users contact government officials and work with other people respectively by 1.0% and 1.3%, holding other variables at their reference points. For a .1 increase in political interest from its mean, the likelihood of these nonelectoral engagements will increase by 2.7% and 1.9%, respectively. Internet users with strong partisanship are 11.0% and 13.4% more likely to contact government officials and work for community issues than those without. The discrete change of college education is 8.8 for contacts with government officials and 12.2 for work with other people. This nonelectoral engagement is not significantly influenced by political efficacy and partisanship.

Contacts with government officials require political knowledge and skills, which are closely related to education. For a .1 increase in knowledge from its mean, the predicted probability that Internet users contact officials will increase by 1.6%, holding other variables at their reference points. Trust in government negatively affects contacts with government officials; a .1 increase in trust will decrease this engagement by 1.9%. Personal income, age, gender, and race do not make a significant difference. In working with other people to deal with community issues, social capital, personal income, and race are influential predictors. The marginal effect of social capital is 13.3%. A $10,000 increase in personal income will increase the likelihood of this engagement by 1.6%, holding other variables at their reference points. White Internet users are 8.7% less likely to take part in working with other people for community issues. However, political knowledge, efficacy, trust in government, partisanship, age, and gender do not influence significantly this engagement.

Summary of Findings

The propensity score matching method, the recursive bivariate probit model, and the binary probit model consistently suggest that Internet use for political information has a positive influence on civic engagement in the public sphere. Its impact is not, however, the same for all forms of engagements. Deliberative and nonelectoral action-oriented engagements are substantially influenced by Internet use for political information. However, Internet use, despite its statistical significance, does not make a big difference in electoral action-oriented engagement. As a dominant information and communication technology, the Internet appears to facilitate citizen deliberation and nonelectoral activities rather than mobilize citizens to take part in electoral action-oriented activities, such as financial contributions and attendance at a campaign rally. Endogeneity matters in deliberative engagement but not much in action-oriented engagement. Deliberative engagement and Internet use appear reciprocal and jointly determined rather than one causing the other.

DISCUSSION AND IMPLICATIONS

Civic engagement encompasses a variety of voluntary activities such as voting, attending public meetings, discussing political and policy issues, and serving community organizations. Some activities are deliberative and others are action-oriented. Some engagements are based on individual choices, while others involve collective actions. Some engagements are electoral and others are more related to general politics and community issues. Individual engagements require different resources, convey different messages, and exert pressures to different degrees on government officials and politicians (Verba et al., 1995). Thus, different types of civic engagement need to be distinguished from one another. Empirical analysis in this study suggests that Internet use for political information influences civic engagement differently depending on the type of engagement. The Internet use is more influential for deliberative engagement and nonpartisan action-oriented engagement than for partisan action-oriented engagement. Similarly, Uslaner (2000, 2004) suggests that the Internet positively influences public deliberation and information exchange within personal networks. This positive effect of Internet use appears to support the transformation theory that the Internet is able to mobilize citizens to participate politically.

Deliberative engagement and Internet use may be reciprocal and jointly determined at one time with some causality. The virtuous circle of iterative reciprocity was not, however, investigated explicitly in this study. Internet use for political information is endogenous in the model of deliberative engagement such as talking about politics with family and friends. Internet use accounts for the deliberative engagement, but there must be some other variation in this engagement that is still left over. In addition to political factors and demographics, researchers should take into account information technology factors regarding how citizens use the Internet. Both direct and indirect effects need to be considered to estimate correctly the overall impact of the Internet on this type of engagement, which involves information exchange among citizens through personal networks. A single equation model such as the binary probit model could not reflect the indirect effects and thus would report a misleading result.

Deliberative engagement is not a product of individual choices, but is based on collective action. This implies that the Internet, in general, may be able to contribute to public deliberation by reducing the costs of information, facilitating information exchange, and minimizing collective action problems (Rheingold, 2002). At the same time, the Internet, due to its sensitivity to the quality of information and communication, may degrade or destroy deliberation when it suffers from misinformation, disinformation, flaming, and the like.[17] In this vein, the key issue is not what the Internet will do to us, but what we will do with it and how (Putnam, 2000).

Endogeneity does not appear to matter much in action-oriented civic engagement such as attendance at a rally, financial contributions, and contacts with government officials. The Internet is an exogenous variable of this type of engagement and appears to supplement traditional means of engagement (mobilization) and helps citizens make their personal decisions. Campaign websites, for instance, mobilize party members and supporters to volunteer, attend rallies and speeches, and give money by providing relevant information and convenient ways to participate—financial contributions in particular.[18] Action-oriented engagement is less likely to involve two-way communications among citizens, government officials, and politicians, but is more likely determined by the individual decisions of those who are already mobilized. This electoral engagement is influenced by political partisanship rather than social capital. In fact, candidates and parties do not tend to have a strong incentive to get enthusiastically involved in online public deliberation (Stromer-Galley, 2000).

Like Bimber (2003), this study suggests that as an exogenous variable Internet use has a positive effect on financial contributions. However, its impact is not as large as expected by Internet enthusiasts. This is because this electoral action-oriented engagement tends to be based on individualized decision making of a particular group (i.e., party members and supporters) who tend to have strong partisanship. College education appears to be related to personal income and thus influences financial contributions positively. This finding supports the reinforcement theory and the normalization theory rather than the transformation (mobilization) theory in that the Internet mobilizes mainly the engaged without changing the level of civic engagement significantly.

Nonelectoral action-oriented civic engagement does not involve endogeneity, but is influenced substantially by Internet use for political information. This result implies great potential of the Internet for nonelectoral and nonpartisan engagements such as contacts with government officials and work with others to deal with community issues. These voluntary activities differ from citizen involvement initiated by government or electoral action-oriented engagement mobilized by political parties and candidates. Citizens actively express their policy preferences to exert explicit influence on government officials and cooperate with neighbors to deal with their problems by themselves. Social capital appears to encourage these motivated and self-governing citizens to get involved in nonelectoral action-oriented engagement. The Internet appears to be a tool to facilitate and supplement their activities and then reinforce their motivation. This virtuous circle has implications for the general public, in particular, minority and disenfranchised citizens who are more likely to take advantage of the Internet than the rich and enfranchised groups such as major political parties and interest groups.[19]

Individual Internet applications have their own clients and purposes that are pursued in different settings. For instance, government portals are used by the general public, while campaign websites are visited largely by party members and supporters (Bimber & Davis 2003). Issue-based political Web sites provide political information that is different from what online newspapers and magazines do. Hence, use of these applications should be differentiated to illuminate their distinct implications for individual civic engagements (Bimber 2003; DiMaggio et al., 2001). The ANES data set, however, includes only a variable that asks if respondents have seen information about election campaigns on the Internet or World Wide Web. The variable does not distinguish a type of Internet use from the other. Due to this shortcoming of the data set, the findings in this chapter should be interpreted with caution.

An ambiguous and complicated causal structure makes it difficult to investigate the relationship between Internet use and civic engagement. Many studies explicitly or implicitly envisage a unidirectional relationship, but this notion has been criticized as a misspecification or a nebulous causal relationship (Arterton, 1987; Bimber, 2001; DiMaggio et al., 2001). The relationship may be reciprocal and may form a virtuous circle (DiMaggio et al. 2001; Norris, 2000, 2001). Internet use and some civic engagements are jointly determined simultaneously. There might be many compounding factors that make the relationship spurious but are not controlled properly. Truncation and self-selection may be involved in empirical research. Also, Internet use itself may be a part of civic engagement in some cases. For example, citizens may email civil servants to make policy suggestions, post messages to online forums, and run political blogs (weblogs). This problem calls for special caution when modeling the relationship. RBPM is employed in an attempt to deal with this complex causal structure of Internet use and deliberative engagement. PSM supplements RBPM and the binary probit model by producing consistent robust results.

CONCLUSION

This study investigates the impact of Internet use on civic engagement. The propensity score matching method and the recursive bivariate probit model were employed to analyze the longitudinal data of the American National Election Studies. The analysis suggests that Internet use for political information positively influences civic engagement in the public sphere, but its impact differs by the type of civic engagement. In deliberative engagement such as discussion of politics, Internet use is endogenous and jointly determined with the engagement. Both direct and indirect effects need to be considered to estimate overall effects precisely. Endogeneity does not, however, matter much in action-oriented engagement such as attendance at a rally and contacts with government officials. Internet use appears to be more influential for deliberative and nonelectoral action-oriented engagement than for electoral action-oriented engagement.

This study, however, has some limitations in the data set because it does not include various types of Internet use such as e-government and campaign websites. It is necessary to distinguish different uses of the Internet to examine their impact correctly. The data set does not include many information technology factors such as Internet experience and broadband use. Like other nationwide surveys, most questions in the ANES data are binary or categorical with missing values. These problems raise issues of specification and measurement error.

Considering the diversity of civic engagement, it is not surprising that models of Internet optimism, pessimism, and skepticism alone are not able to depict all the effects of the Internet comprehensively. Instead, each perspective may successfully reflect some aspects of society but not others. The impact of Internet use should be discussed in the context of a particular type of Internet use and civic engagement. More importantly, the Internet, like television and radio, is a tool of information processing and communications. Since the potential of the Internet is not automatically realized in daily life, the key question is how to effectively use the Internet in the networked society.

APPENDIX: SURVEY QUESTIONS

Variable	Questions and description
Talk about voting	Did you talk to any people and try to show them why they should vote for or against one of the parties or candidates? (0717)
Talk about politics	How many days in the past week did you talk about politics with your family or friends? (0733) Recoded as 1 for more than one times.
Attend a rally	Did you go to any political meetings, rallies, speeches, dinners, or things like that in support of a particular candidate? (0718)
Give money	Did you give money to an individual candidate or political party running for public office? (0721)
Contact officials	Have you telephoned, written a letter to, or visited a government official to express your views on a public issue? (001492, 045167)
Work for community	Have you worked with other people to deal with some issue facing your community? (001491, 045166)
Political interest	Would you say you follow what's going on in government and public affairs? (0313) 1 through 4 were recoded as 0, .33, .67, and 1, respectively.
Political Knowledge	-Do you happen to know which party had the most members in the House of Representatives in Washington before the elections this/last month? (0729) 1 and 2 was recoded as 0 and 1. -Do you happen to know which party had the most members in the U.S. Senate before the election this/last month? (9036) 2 through 8 were recoded as 0. -What job or political office does he now hold? Dennis Hastert, Dick Cheney Tony Blair, and William Rehnquist (year 2004); What U.S. state does he live in now? What is his religion? George Bush, Dick Cheney, Al Gore, and Joseph Lieberman (year 2000); What job or political office does he now hold? Al Gore, William Rehnquist, Boris Yeltsin, Newt Gingrich (year 1996, 2000)

Trust in government	• How much of the time do you think you can trust the government in Washington to do what is right? (0604) 1 through 4 were recoded as 0, .33, .67, and 1, respectively. • Would you say the government is pretty much run by a few big interests looking out for themselves or that it is run for the benefit of all the people? (0605) 1 and 2 were recoded as 0 and 1. • Do you think that people in government waste a lot of the money we pay in taxes, waste some of it, or don't waste very much of it? (0606) 1 through 3 were respectively recoded as 0, .5, and 1. • Do you think that quite a few of the people running the government are crooked, not very many are, or do you think hardly any of them are crooked? (0608) 1 through 3 were respectively recoded as 0, .5, and 1.
Social capital	• Would you say that most people can be trusted or that you can't be too careful in dealing with people? (0619)) 1 and 2 were recoded as 0 and 1. • Do you think most people would try to take advantage of you if they got the chance or would they try to be fair? (0621)) 1 and 2 were recoded as 0 and 1.
Political efficacy	• Public officials don't care much what people like me think (0609) 1, 2, and 3 were recoded as 0, 1 and .5. • People like me don't have any say about what the government does (0613). 1, 2, and 3 were recoded as 0, 1 and .5. • How much attention do you feel the government pays to what people think when it decides what to do? (0622) 1, 2, and 3 were recoded as 0. .5 and 1. • How much do you feel that having elections makes the government pay attention to what the people think? (0624) 1, 2, and 3 were recoded as 0. .5 and 1.
Political mobilization	• Did anyone from one of the political call you up or come around and talk to you about the campaign this year? (9030a) 2 was recoded as 0. • Other than someone from the two major parties, did anyone else call you up or come around and talk to you about supporting specific candidates in this last election? (9031) 5 was recoded as 0.
Partisanship	Strength of partisanship (0305) Recoded as 1 for strong partisan
Personal income	Personal income (960702, 980653, 000997, 043294). Midpoint was taken and then transformed to the square root of the income ($1,000).
Education	College education (0110): 1 for college or advanced degree
Age	Age (0101)
Gender	Gender (0104): 1 for male
Race	Race (0106a): 1 for white citizens
Internet use	Have you seen any information about this election campaign on the Internet or Web? (0745)
Media: radio	Do you ever listen to political talk radio programs of this type? (961155, 980207, 001430, 045154)
Media: TV	Did you watch any programs about the campaign on television? (001202, 045002)

| Media: maga- zine | Did you read about the campaign in any magazines or newspaper? (000336, 045004) |
| Sample weight | Poststratified sample weight (0009a) |

NOTES

1. Cooper (2005) defines civic engagement as "participating together for deliberation and collective action within an array of interests, institutions and networks, developing civic identity, and involving people in governance processes" and distinguishes it from citizen participation "contrived by governments to provide opportunities for citizens to have input into the public policy process" (pp. 534-535).

2. Some civic engagements in this 2×2 typology may be difficult to be clearly classified since they lie between electoral and nonelectoral engagement and/or between deliberative and action-oriented engagement.

3. These examples of deliberative engagements are private in character, but as important as those in public deliberation spaces, such as Citizens Jury, Issue Forums, 21st Century Town Meeting, Neighborhood America, online consultation, online dialogue or forum, and others described in Lukensmeyer and Torres (2006).

4. Corrado (1996) argues, however, that citizens need to be willing to use the emerging technology (i.e., the Internet) for political participation and have fair and equitable access to the Internet in order to realize various prospects of a revitalized democracy that he envisages.

5. This is largely due to social inequality (digital divide) of access to cyberspace, inability to transmit as much nonverbal and in-depth information as face-to-face communication, "cyberbalkanization" against diversity and heterogeneous communications, and limited abilities to complement face-to-face-communications.

6. Bimber's (2001) binary logit model of voting fits the data well. Given the uniqueness of voting, this simple causal structure appears doubtful.

7. If an individual receives the treatment, we cannot observe what the outcome would have been had he or she been assigned to the control group. That is, a citizen is either an Internet user or nonuser, not both.

8. Reciprocity or iterative process is difficult to be examined without well-organized longitudinal data and sophisticated methods such as a dynamic model.

9. Like endogeneity, the missing data problem comes from a couple of sources such as self-selection.

10. Let y_1 denote civic engagement of an individual who has used the Internet for political information and y_0 be the engagement without Internet use.

11. The baseline year is 2000 when citizens used the Internet for political information more than 1996 and 1998 but less than 2004.

12. RBPM was estimated using the .biprobit command in Stata. Marginal effects and discrete changes in conditional predicted probabilities were

manually computed using Stata. In the binary probit model, marginal effects and discrete changes were analyzed using the Long and Freese's SPost module.

13. Independent sample t test reports a mean difference of .2095 (p < .0000) for talking about voting and .2097 (p < .0000) for talking about politics. This t test does not deal with the missing data problem and thus overestimates the impact of Internet use substantially.

14. A low stratum number means a low likelihood that citizens will see political information on the Internet.

15. Independent sample t test reports a mean difference of .0595 (p < .0000) for attendance at a rally and .0634 (p < .0000) for financial contributions.

16. Independent sample t test reports a mean difference of .1439 (p < .0000) for contacts with government officials and .1464 (p < .0000) for work with other people to deal with community issues.

17. Flaming is the act of posting messages on the Internet (Usenet and online forums) that are deliberately hostile and insulting in the social context. Flamers are those people who post such messages called flames (http://en.wikipedia.org/wiki/Flaming). Also see Putnam (2000, p. 176).

18. Bimber and Davis (2003) found that the target client of campaign Web sites is supporters who are frequent visitors to the Web sites.

19. Some examples include Jesse Ventura in the Minnesota gubernational election of 1998 and Nosamo, an online political advocacy organization that supported South Korea presidential candidate Roh Moo-hyun in the 2002 election to achieve a dramatic victory over the most likely counterpart. For more on Nosamo, see Kim, Moon, and Yang (2004). Rheingold (2002) illustrates how effectively "smart mobs" use the Internet and telecommunication technologies to minimize collective action problems and improve public goods (social network capital).

REFERENCES

Angrist, Joshua D. 1998. "Estimating the Labor Market Impact of Voluntary Military Service Using Social Security Data on Military Applicants. *Econometrica*, 66(2): 249-288.

Arterton, F. Christopher. 1987. *Teledemocracy: Can Technology Protect Democracy?* Beverly Hills, CA: Sage Publications.

Becker, Sascha O., and Andrea Ichino. 2002. "Estimation of Average Treatment Effects Based on Propensity Scores. *STATA Journal*, 2(4): 358-377.

Bimber, Bruce, and Richard Davis. 2003. *Campaigning Online: the Internet in U.S. Elections*. New York: Oxford University Press.

Bimber, Bruce. 2001. "Information and Political Engagement in America: The Search for Effects of Information Technology at the Individual Level. *Political Research Quarterly*, 54(1): 53-67.

Bimber, Bruce. 2003. *Information and American Democracy: Technology in the Evolution of Political Power*. New York: Cambridge University Press.

Browning, Graeme. 2002. *Electronic Democracy: Using the Internet to Transform American Politics*, 2nd ed. Medford, NJ: CyberAge Books.

Chadwick, Andrew. 2006. *Internet Politics: States, Citizens, and New Communication Technologies*. New York: Oxford University Press.

Cooper, Terry L. 2005. "Civic Engagement in the Twenty-First Century: Toward a Scholarly and Practical Agenda. *Public Administration Review*, 65(5): 534-535.

Corrado, Anthony. 1996. "Elections in Cyberspace: Prospects and Problems. In Anthony Corrado and Charles M. Firestone, eds. *Elections in Cyberspace: Toward a New Era in American Politics*. Washington, D.C.: Aspen Institute, 1-31.

D'Agostino, Ralph B., Jr., and Donald B. Rubin. 2000. "Estimating and Using Propensity Scores with Partially Missing Data. *Journal of the American Statistical Association*, 95(451): 749-759.

Davis, Richard. 1999. *The Web of Politics: The Internet's Impact on the American Political System*. New York: Oxford University Press.

Davis, Richard. 2005. *Politics Online: Blogs, Chatrooms, and Discussion Groups in American Democracy*. New York: Routledge.

Davis, Steve, Larry Elin, and Grant Reeher. 2002. *Click on Democracy: The Internet's Power to Change Political Apathy into Civic Action*. Boulder, CO: Westview Press.

Dehejia, Rajeev H., and Sadek Wahba. 1999. "Causal Effects in Nonexperimental Studies: Reevaluating the Evaluation of Training Programs. *Journal of the American Statistical Association*, 94(448): 1053-1062.

Delli Carpini, Michael X., and Scott Keeter. 2003. "The Internet and an Informed Citizenry. In Michael Cornfield, and David M. Anderson, eds. *The Civic Web: Online Politics and Democratic Values*. Lanham, MD: Rowman & Littlefield Publishers, 129-153.

DiMaggio, Paul, Eszter Hargittai, W. Russell Neuman, and John P. Robinson. 2001. "Social Implications of the Internet. *Annual Review of Sociology*, 27(1): 307-336.

Foot, Kirsten A., and Steven M. Schneider. 2006. *Web Campaigning*. Cambridge, MA: MIT Press.

Greene, William H. 1998. "Gender Economics Courses in Liberal Arts Colleges: Further Results. *Journal of Economic Education*, 29(4): 291-300.

Greene, William H. 2003. *Econometric Analysis, 5th ed.* Upper Saddle River, NJ: Prentice Hall.

Grossman, Lawrence K. 1995. *The Electronic Republic: Reshaping Democracy in the Information Age*. New York: Viking Penguin.

Hahn, Jinyong. 1998. "On the Role of the Propensity Score in Efficient Semiparametric Estimation of Average Treatment Effects. *Econometrica*, 66(2): 315-331.

Heckman, James J., Hidehiko Ichimura, and Petra E. Todd. 1997. "Matching as an Econometric Evaluation Estimator: Evidence from Evaluating a Job Training Programme. *Review of Economic Studies*, 64(4): 605-654.

Jennings, M. Kent, and Vicki Zeitner. 2003. "Internet Use and Civic Engagement. *Public Opinion Quarterly*, 67(3): 311-334.

Kamarck, Elaine Ciulla. 2002. "Political Campaigning on the Internet: Business as Usual? In Elaine Ciulla Kamarck and Joseph S. Nye, Jr., eds. *Governance.com: Democracy in the Information Age*. Washington D.C.: Brookings Institution Press, 81-103.

Katz, Elihu, and Paul F. Lazarsfeld. 1964. *Personal Influence: the Part Played by People in the Flow of Mass Communications*. New Brunswick, NJ : Transaction Publishers.

Katz, James E., and Ronald E. Rice. 2002. *Social Consequences of Internet Use: Access, Involvement, and Interaction*. Cambridge, MA: MIT Press.

Kavanaugh, Andrea L. 2002. "Community Networks and Civic Engagement: A Social Network Approach. *The Good Society*, 11(3): 17-24.

Kim, Heekyung Hellen, Jae Yun Moon, and Shinkyu Yang. 2004. "Broadband Penetration and Participatory Politics: South Korea Case." Proceedings of the 37th Hawaii International Conference on System Sciences (HICSS-38) in Hawaii, p. 50117b.

LaLonde, Robert J. 1986. "Evaluating the Econometric Evaluations of Training Programs with Experimental Data. *American Economic Review*, 76(4): 604-620.

Langton, Stuart. 1978. *Citizen Participation in America: Essays on the State of the Art*. Lexington, MA: Lexington Books.

Long, J. Scott. 1997. *Regression Models for Categorical and Limited Dependent Variables. Advanced Quantitative Techniques in the Social Sciences*. Sage Publications.

Lukensmeyer, Carolyn J., and Lars Hasselblad Torres. 2006. *Public Deliberation: A Manager's Guide to Citizen Engagement*. IBM Center for The Business to Government. http://www.businessofgovernment.org/

Maddala, G. S. 1983. *Limited Dependent and Qualitative Variables in Econometrics*. New York: Cambridge University Press.

Maddala, G.S., and Lung-Fei Lee. 1976. "Recursive Models with Qualitative Endogenous Variables. *Annals of Economic and Social Measurement*, 5(4): 525-545.

Margolis, Michael, and David Resnick. 2000. *Politics As Usual: The Cyberspace*. Thousand Oaks, CA: Sage Publications.

Morris, Dick. 1999. *Vote.com*. Los, Angeles, CA.: Renaissance Books.

Norris, Pippa. 2000. *A Virtuous Circle: Political Communication in Post-Industrial Democracies*. New York: Cambridge University Press.

Norris, Pippa. 2001. *The Digital Divide: Civic Engagement, Information Poverty and the Internet Worldwide*. New York: Cambridge University Press.

Putnam, Robert D. 2000. *Bowling Alone: The Collapse and Revival of American Community*. New York: Simon & Schuster.

Ramakrishnan, S. Karthick, and Mark Baldassare. 2004. *The Ties That Bind: Changing Demographics and Civic Engagement in California*. San Francisco, CA: Public Policy Institute of California.

Rheingold, Howard. 1993. *The Virtual Community*. Addison-Wesley Publishing.

Rheingold, Howard. 2002. *Smart Mobs: The Next Social Revolution*. Cambridge, MA: Basic Books.

Robbin, Alice, Christina Courtright, and Leah Davis. 2004. "ICTs and Political Life. *Annual Review of Information Science and Technology*, 38:411-481.

Rosenbaum, Paul R., and Donald B. Rubin. 1983. "The Central Role of the Propensity Score in Observational Studies for Causal Effects. *Biometrika*, 70(1): 41-55.

Rosenbaum, Paul R., and Donald B. Rubin. 1984. "Reducing Bias in Observational Studies Using Subclassification on the Propensity Score. *Journal of the American Statistical Association*, 79(387): 516-524.

Scott, James K. 2006. "'E' the People: Do U.S. Municipal Government Web Sites Support Public Involvement? *Public Administration Review*, 66(3): 341-353.

Selnow, Gary W. 1998. *Electronic Whistle-Stops: The Impact of the Internet on American Politics*. Westport, CT: Praeger.

Shadish, William R., Thomas D. Cook, and Donald T. Campbell. 2002. *Experimental and Quasi-experimental Designs for Generalized Causal Inference*. Boston, MA: Houghton Mifflin.

Skocpol, Theda. 2003. *Diminished Democracy: From Membership to Management in American Civic Life*. Norman: University of Oklahoma Press.

Stromer-Galley, J. 2000. "On-Line Interaction and Why Candidates Avoid It." *Journal of Communication*, 50(1): 111-132.

Uslaner, Eric M. 2000. "Social Capital and Net. *Communications of the ACM*, 43(12): 60-64.

Uslaner, Eric M. 2004. "Trust, Civic Engagement, and the Internet. *Political Communication*, 21(2): 223-242.

Verba, Sidney, Kay Schlozman, and Henry E. Brady. 1995. *Voice and Equality: Civic Voluntarism in American Politics*. Cambridge, MA: Harvard University Press.

Ward, Stephen, Rachel Gibson, and Paul Nixon. 2003. "Parties and the Internet: An Overview." In Rachel Gibson, Paul Nixon, and Stephen Ward, eds. *Political Parties and the Internet: Net Gain?* New York: Routledge, 11-38.

Weissberg, Robert. 2005. *The Limits of Civic Activism: Cautionary Tales on the Use of Politics*. New Brunswick, NJ: Transaction Publishers.

West, Darrell M. 2005. *Digital Government: Technology and Public Sector Performance*. Princeton, NJ: Princeton University Press.

Yang, Kaifeng, and Kathe Callahan. 2005. "Assessing Citizen Involvement Efforts by Local Governments," *Public Performance and Management Review*, 29(2): 191-216.

CHAPTER 11

SOMETHING RICH
AND STRANGE

Participation, Engagement,
and the Tempest of Online Politics

Jason MacDonald and Caroline Tolbert

Can online communication reverse long-term reductions in social capital? Early research suggested a negative conclusion and even suggested that Internet use could exacerbate this grim trend (e.g., Davis & Owen 1998; Margolis & Resnick, 2000; Putnam 2000). In the landmark book *Bowling Alone,* Robert Putnam finds that "respondents who say that they rely primarily on the Internet for news are *less* likely than other Americans to volunteer, to spend time with friends, to trust one another" (Putnam, 2000, 479). This finding, however, relies on data collected immediately after the initial explosion of Internet usage during the late 1990s, and may mischaracterize the Internet's effect on political and civic life.

Other research, however, suggests a positive link between Internet use and engagement. Research on the link between the Internet and a separate phenomenon, political participation, documents that Internet use is associated with higher levels of participation, based on the medium's abil-

Civic Engagement in a Network Society
pp. 271–297
Copyright © 2008 by Information Age Publishing
All rights of reproduction in any form reserved.

ity to provide additional information to the electorate. This research suggests that online communication increases political participation generally (Bimber, 2003; Graf & Darr, 2004; Tolbert & McNeal, 2003), voter turnout (Bimber, 2003; Tolbert & McNeal, 2003), campaign contributions (Bimber, 2001, 2003; Graf & Darr, 2004), and citizen-initiated contact with government (Bimber, 1999; Thomas & Streib, 2003). Additionally, some evidence suggests that Internet use encourages engagement with society. For example, Jennings and Zeitner (2003) employ panel data to show that individuals who became Internet users in the 1990s demonstrated greater increases in civic engagement between 1982 and 1997 than individuals who did not embrace the Internet. Additionally, Kim, Jung, Cohen, and Ball-Rokeach (2004) find that Internet use was positively and significantly associated with political and civic activities in response to the terrorist attacks of September 11, 2001. Likewise, Uslaner (2004) shows that Internet use is positively associated with social interaction and Shah, Kwak, and Holbert (2001) demonstrate that individuals who use the Internet to obtain information are more likely to evince higher levels of social capital.

Given the potential benefit of the Internet for democracy, we follow these studies to investigate the relationship between Internet use and civic engagement, hypothesizing that the online consumption of political information increases engagement. Specifically, we examine a wide array of phenomena, hypothesizing that consuming political information online helps citizens obtain higher levels of political knowledge, become more interested in politics, and deliberate with their fellow citizens about politics more frequently. In doing so, we analyze previously unexamined data that is particularly well suited to allowing us to assess these hypotheses.

In addition to examining various types of civic engagement, our research tackles an empirical issue not addressed by prior studies: the potential endogeneity of Internet use to civic engagement. Individuals who possess high levels of civic engagement may use the Internet more often because their engagement with society propels them to acquire information, as is found on the Internet, to enrich their participation in civic activities. In this scenario, there is a positive association between Internet use and civic engagement; however, this relationship is not due to Internet use spurring civic engagement. Rather, preexisting engagement on the part of individuals leads to their use of the Internet. Therefore, prior studies that do not control for this endogeneity risk overstating the degree to which Internet use fosters civic engagement. In the analysis below, we account for the difficulty that such endogeneity introduces into the ability to assess the effect of Internet use on engagement using two staged estimation procedures.

If the consumption of online political information increases sophistication, stimulates interest, and fuels discussion, it may serve to, in part, counteract a 3-decade trend of declining civic engagement (Abramson & Aldrich, 1982; Putnam, 2000; Verba, Schlozman, & Brady 1995). Of course, this hopeful view is not to assert that the Internet is a panacea for all that ails American democracy; rather, it is to emphasize that a major element of contemporary modernization is a help—not a hindrance—to civic engagement.

THE INTERNET AS A HURDLE TO CIVIC ENGAGEMENT?

Before proceeding to our analysis, we consider the theoretical bases for these competing views. Early findings about the link between Internet use and civic engagement ranged from neutral to ominous. Discouragingly, once researchers controlled for levels of educational attainment, Internet users were indistinguishable from nonusers on civic engagement measures (Aspden & Katz, 1997; Bimber, 1999; Pew Research Center for the People and the Press, 1998; Putnam, 2000). More discouragingly, based on analysis of DDB Needham Life Style 1996-1998 surveys, Putnam found that online news consumers volunteered, trusted, and spent time with friends at lower rates than other Americans, leading him to dismiss the hope that online communication could foster increased engagement (2000, p. 221).[1]

This finding led Putnam and others to consider why the consumption of political information online may diminish civic engagement. One explanation notes that computer discussions may depersonalize communication and psychologically weaken social cues (Nie & Erbring, 2000). Eye contact, gestures, nods, body language, seating arrangements or even hesitation are omitted in online discourse. Hence, computer-mediated communication masks the nonverbal communication of face-to-face encounters, which otherwise enhance trust (Putnam, 2000, p. 176). Therefore, the absence of social cues in computer-mediated communication may undermine civic engagement.

Online inequality is also a hurdle to the enhancement of engagement. Scholars have observed a "digital divide" in that race, ethnicity, age, income, and education influence whether an individual has access to the Internet (Lenhart, 2003; Neu, Anderson, & Bikson, 1999; Norris, 2001; Mossberger, Tolbert, & Stansbury 2003; Warshauer, 2003; Wilhelm, 2000; 2004). Individuals least likely to have technology access (a home computer, home Internet access, or an email address) tend to be poorer, less educated, older, and/or Latino or African American (Lenhart, 2003; Mossberger et al., 2003). The poor and less educated are also less likely to use online political information, including e-government (Mossberger & Tolbert, 2006; Thomas & Streib, 2003), and are less likely to vote in an election online or support online voting or voter registration (Alvarez & Hall, 2004; McNeal & Tolbert, 2004). Moreover, these inequalities can affect who participates politically (Alvarez & Hall, 2003; Bimber, 2003; Norris, 2001). To the extent that computers and the Internet offer tools for civic engagement, the price of unequal technology use and skills may be the widening of existing disparities in political participation. Worse yet, to the extent that such technology becomes vital to civic participation, those without access to such technology and/or the skills necessary to use it, that is, the poor and racial minorities, may become even less likely to participate.[2]

Finally, Sunstein (2001) argues that the Internet may limit the scope of one's discourse to others who share one's views, reducing exposure to, and tolerance of, other groups and ideas. Such "cyberbalkanization," occurs when individuals purposefully communicate only with others who share their beliefs, screening out information that challenges their predispositions (Putnam, 2000, p. 178). Whereas real world interactions and print and TV media often force individuals to confront diversity, the virtual world may be more homogeneous, quashing deliberation.

In spite of these arguments, there are good empirical reasons to believe that the consumption of online political information facilitates engagement. First, although the evidence from "digital divide" research is discouraging, the presence of a divide says nothing about whether, once individuals are exposed to information, they will become more/less engaged. Second, there is evidence that the "cyberbalkanization" argument is overdrawn. Contrary to this hypothesis, Internet users have greater overall exposure to political arguments, including those that challenge their candidate preferences and their policy positions (Pew Research Center for the People and the Press, 2004b). Internet users also have greater political sophistication than those using television, radio or even print media as their major source of political information (Pew, 2004a). This evidence, although based on descriptive statistics, suggests that exposure to online information may foster engagement.

Third, there are good theoretical reasons to believe that the character of online discourse (including frequent repetition as well as interpersonal and small-group communication), overall, transcends the impediments itemized above, making the consumption of political information online an effective method of enhancing engagement. The Internet's interactivity, diversity, flexibility, speed, convenience, low-cost and information capacity potentially allow the public to become more knowledgeable about politics and government, a first step toward greater participation (Norris, 2001). There may also be unique advantages to online political discussions that are important for civic engagement. Research has shown that online discussions are more frank and egalitarian than face-to-face meetings. Women, for example, are less likely to be interrupted in cyberspace discussions (Putnam, 2000, p. 173; Sproul & Kiesler, 1991).

Fifth, research has shown the content of online news tends to be more diverse and ideologically extreme than mainstream media, such as television and newsprint (Pew Research Center for the People and the Press, 2004a). Examples from the left include truthout.org, the largest online news service in the world, or on the right, freeprepublic.com. Much of the in depth news online is only partially covered by mainstream media outlets, or never receives airing via the mainstream media. Examples are so numerous that it has become common knowledge, with scholars such as Robert McChesney (1999) arguing that waves of media mergers and acquisitions have created a television media monopoly that no longer provides citizens with the information they need to participate in a democracy. Evidence of this is that credibility ratings for the major broadcast and cable television outlets have fallen in recent years, due in large part to increased cynicism toward the media on the part of conservatives (Pew Research Center for the People and the Press, 2004c). From 1996 to 2002, CNN was viewed as the most believable broadcast or cable outlet, but its ratings have fallen gradually over time. As of 2006, 28% of respondents to a PEW survey noted "they can believe all or most of what they see" on CNN (the network was still trusted most by respondents), a figured that dropped from 37% in 2002, 39% in 2000, and a high of 42% in 1998 (Pew Research Center for the People and the Press, 2006).

As trust in traditional news sources declines, readership of online news has become increasingly important. The population of online news users has grown dramatically in the last decade with 29% of Americans regularly going online for news in 2004 (Pew Research Center for the People and the Press, 2004c), while two thirds of Americans (66%) say they go online to access the Internet or to send and receive email, the latter often including political content. Given this growth, we may now be approaching a critical tipping point in which use of online news affects elections and engagement.

As mentioned above, the diversity and partisan nature of news online has led to concerns about the dangers of limiting the scope of discourse (Sunstein, 2001). But the flip side of this argument is that sources of information on the Internet may be more emotional, richer and more likely to mobilize engagement in the political process than other sources (The informational and emotional content of online media are discussed in greater detail below). For all these reasons, if Internet news sources differ from traditional sources, as the research suggests, what is the effect on citizen behavior? It is to this question which we now turn.

THE EFFECT OF CONSUMING ONLINE POLITICAL INFORMATION
ON POLITICAL KNOWLEDGE, DISCOURSE, AND INTEREST

The consumption of political information from media sources enhances civic engagement by increasing citizens' knowledge about politics (Brians & Wattenberg, 1996; Delli Carpini & Keeter, 1996; Tan, 1980). With regard to the specific mechanisms through which individuals accrue knowledge, McLeod and McDonald (1985) find that viewing television news and reading newspapers increases individuals' political knowledge and efficacy, while Brians and Wattengber (1996) find that citizens learn about candidates from campaign ads. More specifically, voters acquire information on candidate traits (Weaver, 1996) and issue positions (Chaffee & Kanihan, 1997; Weaver & Drew 1993) through the consumption of news. Campaign spending enhances voters' knowledge about candidates (Coleman, 2001; Coleman & Manna, 2000) through the political communication it purchases. Voter awareness about the importance of issues in Senate elections is enhanced by the degree to which the issues are discussed by candidates and the media (Kahn & Kinney, 2001). A growing literature documents the added value of more information on civic engagement and participation, showing citizens exposed to salient ballot measures (initiatives and referenda) have increased political knowledge (Smith, 2002; Smith & Tolbert, 2004). Finally, television advertising increases levels of knowledge among voters (Freedman, Franz, & Goldstein, 2004; Brians & Wattenberg, 1996), especially those with low levels of information (Freedman, Franz, & Goldstein, 2004).[3]

Given this evidence, that consuming information online increases knowledge seems uncontroversial. Nevertheless, it has not been empirically demonstrated in the literature even though there is good reason to believe that online consumption is particularly likely to increase knowledge. Like reading newspapers, reading news on the Internet constitutes literacy-intensive consumption (Mossberger et al., 2003; Warchauser, 2003). As such, reading facilitates literacy skills, engendering higher information-processing skills, including those related to memory (Healy & McNamara, 1996; Kyllonen & Christal, 1990). This fact is consistent with the finding that more learning occurs from reading about politics in newspapers than watching television (Smith, 1989). Therefore, there is good reason theoretically to expect that consuming political information online, a literacy intensive action, should enhance knowledge.[2] Finally, though based on descriptive statistics, recent Pew data support this assertion in that individuals who consumed news online had higher levels of knowledge/recall about the 2004 elections than those who relied on traditional media, just as television and newspapers (Pew Research Center for the People and the Press, 2004a). In summary, these considerations lead us to hypothesize that consumption of online political news should increase citizens' knowledge about politics.

For two reasons, the Internet should also stimulate civic engagement by engendering political discussion. First, like other forms of media, it provides individuals with information that facilitates discussion: research shows that information obtained from the media helps foster political dialogue (e.g., Beck, 1991; Chaffee & McLeod, 1973; Huckfeldt & Sprauge, 1991; Mondak, 1995). Further still, Chaffee and McLeod (1973, p. 243) found that individuals seek media to provide political information for partisan arguments to help support their positions during interpersonal discourse. Likewise, Mondak (1995) found that individuals invoke information obtained from the media to support their positions. Second, unlike other forms of media, the Internet creates immediate opportunities for convenient, flexible and inexpensive interpersonal communication through email, listservs and chat rooms. Growing opportunities for communication made possible by email communication should encourage greater political discourse (see Thomas & Strieb, 2003, on email contacting). In summary, since the consumption of political information online constitutes media consumption, which we know facilitates discussion in general, and since it uniquely offers interactive opportunities for participation, we hypothesize those individuals who use the Internet as a source of political information should discuss politics at higher levels. We stress that, although this hypothesis is consistent with the literature on the consumption of political information, no previous research has proposed or established this relationship between the consumption of online political information and discourse.

How should the Internet, a tool for individuals to learn about and participate in politics, affect citizen interest in politics, possibly the most important of the three forms of engagement analyzed here? Can salient and controversial online news spark a general interest in politics, one of the most important predictors of sustained political engagement? Research has found citizens exposed to ballot measures (and media campaigns related to these controversial policies) express a greater interest in politics overall (Smith & Tolbert, 2004). The literature documents the value added of information (often through ballot measure campaigns) on civic engagement (Smith, 2002; Smith & Tolbert, 2004).

As discussed earlier, online political information tends to be more partisan than traditional newsprint and television (Sustein, 2001), conveying information with an emotional coating. Harold Lasswell argued that issues with a "triple appeal"—those appealing to an individual's passions, rational reason and morality—will likely lead to action (Lasswell, 1932). Online news is rarely presented in dispassionate, emotionally neutral terms. Rather, the emails and news stories are often emotionally rich; provoking diverse responses ranging from anger and fear to sympathy. As a result, online news may facilitate use of the likeability heuristic, by which people make informational inferences on the basis of their likes and dislikes (Sniderman, Brody, & Tetlock, 1991).

In short, due to the cognitive and emotional content of Internet political information we would expect online news to produce citizens who are both more informed about politics, more interested in the election, and more engaged in political debates. These hypotheses are consistent with Freedman et al. (2004) who find support for an informational hypothesis that exposure to information during a campaign (in the form of thirty second advertisements on television) enhances knowledge, and, by extension, fosters civic engagement by increasing the probability of voting. Similarly, we propose an engagement hypothesis that exposure information on the internet fosters knowledge. Although Freedman et al. (2004) conceptualize knowledge separately from engagement, since knowledge leads to engagement, we understand the internet to be a tool that can promote engagement by promoting a factor, political knowledge, that leads to engagement. Indeed, the link between knowledge and engagement is so close that prior studies have conceptualized knowledge as a form of engagement (Smith & Tolbert, 2004). In summary, we hypothesize that citizens using online political information are more likely to be knowledgeable about politics, interested in politics, as well as discuss it more frequently. That is we propose that the sum of the hypotheses itemized above constitute an *Internet engagement hypothesis*, that is, this feature of modernization fosters civic engagement.

DATA AND METHODS

To assess these hypotheses, we analyze data from the 2000 American National Election Studies (NES) survey, a 2002 Pew Internet and American Life Daily Tracking survey, and a 2004 Pew Research Center for the People and the Press survey.[4] Data from the 2000 NES allow us to assess the effect of consuming political information online on respondents' political engagement, political knowledge, and political interest. Data from the 2002 and 2004 Pew studies allow us to assess the impact of consuming political information online on respondents' political interest (2002 and 2004) and political knowledge (2004).

We measured respondents' political engagement by employing their responses to the 2000 NES's question asking them about the number of days (0 to 7) during the previous week that they discussed politics with friends or family. To measure respondents' political knowledge, we created count variables indicating the number of factual questions they answered correctly in the 2000 NES and the 2004 Pew survey. These count variables range from 0 to 6 for the 2000 NES and 0 to 2 for the 2004 Pew survey.[5] To measure respondents' interest in politics, we created ordinal variables indicating their level of interest. For the 2000 NES analysis, this variable is coded 1 for respondents who were *not very interested*, 3 for respondents who were *interested*, and 5 for respondents who were *very interested* in the 2000 election. The dependent variables measuring interest in the 2002 and 2004 Pew surveys are coded similarly, with higher values indicating that respondents followed the 2002 midterm elections and the 2004 Democratic presidential nomination more closely: 1 = *not at all closely*, 2 = *not too closely*, 3 = *fairly closely*, and 4 = *very closely*.

To measure consumption of political information online, we employed a question posed to respondents in all of the surveys that asked about whether they had read news about elections from online sources. If the respondent read election news online they were coded 1; 0 otherwise. Unfortunately, this blunt measure does not allow us to observe how frequently respondents read about politics online or how important they considered online sources relative to traditional sources.[6] Importantly, however, measuring online readership of political information in this way provides for conservative tests of the hypotheses. By collapsing individuals who read about politics online habitually with those who do so infrequently, and those who consider online news sources as gospel with those who view it skeptically, we are less likely to observe a relationship between online readership and forms of political engagement even if there is one. If we do observe a relationship, then, it should demarcate the lower bounds of the effect of reading about politics online on engagement.

In the analyses, we control for a host of attitudinal and demographic characteristics of respondents. For the 2000 NES data, we control for the following demographics: (1) educational attainment using a 7-point scale on which higher values indicate higher attainment levels; (2) gender using a dummy variable assuming the value of 1 for female respondents; (3) race using dummy variables indicating that respondents were African American, Asian American, and Latino (1 if yes; 0 otherwise) with non-Hispanic Whites as the reference group; (4) age using respondents' age in years; and (5) income using a 22-point scale on which higher values indicate higher incomes. To control for the likelihood that partisans discuss politics more frequently than nonpartisans, we created a dummy variable assuming the value of 1 if individuals were strong Democrats or Republicans; 0 otherwise.[7] We control for the degree to which respondents consume information about politics from traditional media sources by including a variable indicating the number of days during the previous week during which respondents read the newspaper or watched the national nightly news. We control for external political efficacy by summing the scores from two 5-point scales that range from *strongly disagree* to *strongly agree* with the statements, "People don't have say in government," and "Public officials don't care about people like me," creating a 2-10 scale. Finally, in the separate analyses of discourse, knowledge and interest using the 2000 NES data, we control for each dependent variable as an independent variable, such as, in estimating discourse, we control for knowledge and interest as independent variables. We identify the NES descriptions of all of the variables employed in the analyses from the 2000 NES data in Appendix A.

For the 2002 and 2004 Pew analyses, we controlled for respondents demographic characteristics as follows: (1) education using 7-point scale with larger values indicating higher levels of education completed on the part of respondents; (2) income using an 8-point scale on which higher values indicate higher family income levels; (3) race using a series of dummy variables measuring whether respondents were African American, Asian American and Latino (1 = yes; 0 otherwise) with non-Latino Whites serving as the reference group; (4) gender using a dummy variable assuming the value of 1 for female respondents; and (5) age using respondents' age in years. For both 2002 and 2004, we controlled for respondents' partisanship by creating a two dummy variables, each assuming the value of 1 if respondents were Democrats and Republicans; 0 otherwise (Independents as reference category). For the 2002 data, we controlled for respondents' propensity to obtain news by creating two dummy variables assuming the value of 1 if respondents had (1) read the newspaper or (2) watched a national TV news program the day prior to being surveyed; 0 otherwise. For the 2004 data, we controlled for this propensity by creating two dummy variables indicating whether respondents obtained most of their news about the presidential campaign from (1) newspapers (1 = yes; 0 otherwise) and (2) television (1 = yes; 0 otherwise). Finally, for the 2004 analysis of knowledge (interest), we controlled for respondents' political interest (knowledge); however, since there was no variable measuring respondents' knowledge in the 2002 data, we could not control for it in the 2002 analysis of interest.

One modeling hurdle to assessing the hypotheses that consuming political information online increases these forms of engagement is that the consumption of online news is positively related to control variables in our analysis, such as education. Therefore, we needed to account for this endogeniety to avoid overstating the influence of reading about politics online on the dependent variables. To do so, we employed two-staged estimation procedures for limited dependent variables employed in previous research (Alverez, 1998; Alvarez & Bedolla, 2004; Alvarez & Butterfield, 2000; Alvarez & Glasgow, 2000). We employed the logit estimator to estimate the reduced form equations of online news readership, obtaining predicted values of whether respondents read political news online.[8] We then substituted these values for the endogenous variables when estimating the second-stage models.

In the second-stage models, we employ Poisson regression to estimate the frequency respondents discussed politics during the prior week and the level of political knowledge respondents possessed. To estimate the second stage model of respondents' political interest, we employ the ordered logit estimator. Since political interest is a variable in the first stage models, the two models in which we estimate it are recursive.

FINDINGS

The coefficients reported below and in appendix tables are second-stage estimates of the effect of online election news on civic engagement.[9] In the first model reported in Appendix B, Table 11.B1 the dependent variable is coded so that higher scores are associated with increased frequency of political discussion. Since the dependent variable (discuss politics) represents a count, Poisson regression coefficients are reported. The data suggests that viewing Internet election news is positively associated with the frequency of political discussion, after controlling for traditional media consumption and individual level factors, including socioeconomic status. This suggests the Internet may promote political discussion by providing supplementary information (measured by Internet news). That is, the Internet may shape political discussion through providing individuals with information to foster discussion.

In the model, political interest and knowledge are also positively linked to discussion, supporting previous research showing that the three variables are interrelated (Weaver, 1996). Both newspaper usage and television news were found to be a significant predictor of political discussion, suggesting that news in general helps to foster political discussion through providing information to fuel discussion.

Since political knowledge is a count of the number of six questions correctly answered, Poisson regression coefficients are also reported in the second column of appendix Table 11.B1. Again, viewing online political news is positively related to increased political sophistication. This suggests the use of the Internet for political information is important in increasing citizen political knowledge, consistent with recent Pew reports based on descriptive statistics (Pew Research Center for the People and the Press, 2004a). This finding corroborates the result that Internet news is related to discussion. Also, the model shows that both television and newspaper news are positively related to enhanced political knowledge

(Delli Carpini & Keeter, 1996), contrary to previous research (Smith, 1989). The finding that Internet news is positively related to political knowledge, even after controlling for television news and newsprint, suggests that the Internet may be providing different sources of information above and beyond what can be gathered from traditional media forms (see Pew Research Center for the People and the Press, 2004a).

Since we measure political interest on an ordinal scale, we employ ordered logistic regression to estimate the effect of consuming political information online on interest. We report coefficients of this relationship in Appendix B, Table 11.B1 (2000 NES survey), Table 11.B2 (2002 Pew survey) and Table 11.B3 (2004 Pew survey). Again, the data suggest consuming political information online increases individuals' interest in politics, holding other factors constant, and the relationship is significant over time (2000, 2002 and 2004). This is in contrast to the findings for newspapers. In all three tables, viewing television news was positively associated with heightened political interest while newspaper consumption was significantly in only one (2004). Use of this new medium not only may foster civic engagement in terms of political discussion and knowledge, but also may engage the disengaged in politics (cf. Graf & Darr, 2004). The strong statistical relationship repeated in three surveys over a 4-year period lends confidence to the finding that consumption of online news does indeed increase a general interest in politics.

Finally, as recently as 2004 we find evidence for the pattern of consumption of online political news associated with increased civic engagement. In Appendix B, Table 11.B4, consuming online election news was associated with increased political knowledge, using the two-stage model to control for endogeneity and holding other demographic and attitudinal factors constant. This finding confirms similar patterns based on the 2000 NES data (Table 11.B1) and descriptive data reported by Pew Research Center for the People and the Press (2004a) that did not control for overlapping factors, such as income, education and media consumption. Together, the multiple year analysis provides strong evidence that respondents using the Internet for news have increased political sophistication, interest in politics and propensity to discuss politics, three critical ingredients in an informed and sustained democratic electorate.

Table 11.1 provides a summary of the findings, indicating consumption of online political news is associated with increased political discussion, knowledge and interest, and that the impact of online news on engagement is consistent over time. The results suggest the Internet may have a positive impact on a critical set of factors that mobilize new citizens to be involved in politics. Expected probabilities show that the magnitude of the online news consumption on civic engagement is dramatic, with online news users 20% more likely to engage in political discussion each

Table 11.1.   The Effect of Online News Consumption on Political Discussion, Knowledge, and Interest

	Discussion (2000)	Knowledge (2000)	Interest (2000)	Interest (2002)	Knowledge (2004)
Online News Consumption (predicted probability)	.179** (.075)	.306** (.109)	3.03*** (.322)	13.724*** (.639)	.556** (.252)

Estimated News Consumption	Prob. Number of Discussions	Prob. Number of Correct Answers	Prob. Very Interested	Prob. Very Interested	Prob. Number of Correct Answers
High	4.18 (.261)	2.03 (.181)	.786 (.040)	1.00 (.000)	.77 (.181)
Mean	3.69 (.087)	1.63 (.055)	.316 (.022)	.62 (.036)	.48 (.066)
Low	3.49 (.106)	1.48 (.067)	.154 (.019)	.15 (.021)	.43 (.064)
High-Low (Absolute Change)	0.69	0.55	.632	.85	.34
High-Low (Relative % Change)	19.77%	37.16%	410.39%	566.67%	79.07%

*$p < .05$. **$p < .01$. ***$p < .001$. Cell entries are ordered logit or Poisson regression coefficients with standard errors in parentheses. Simulations of political interest in 2004 not reported due to space constraints. See Appendix B for full models and details on estimation.

Predicted probabilities estimated with Clarify. Numbers in parentheses are standard errors for the predicted probabilities. "High" and "low" Internet use represents changes from the maximum (1) of the predicted probability of reading online news to the mean (baseline) to the minimum (0) for this variable. For the 2000 NES data, we hold age, income, efficacy, political knowledge, television and newspaper consumption and education to their means. Political interest was set at its median. Gender was set at female and race/ethnicity at White. Simulations estimated for not strong partisans. For the 2002 and 2004 Pew surveys we hold age, income, and education at their means. Political interest was set at its median, and gender at female and race/ethnicity at White. Television and newspaper consumption as primary media for following the elections was set at yes (1). Simulations estimated for nonpartisans.

week, almost 40% more knowledgeable about politics in the 2000 elections and almost 400% more likely to express interest in politics in 2000. Parallel findings are found using the Pew data, with online news users 80 percent more knowledgeable about the 2004 primary elections and significantly more interested in 2002 midterm elections, ceteris paribus. The findings provide additional evidence that the relationship between the Internet and political participation is empirically grounded.

ENGAGING THE YOUNG ONLINE

In less then 10 years, the Internet has become a more important source of election news for all Americans, but young people continue to go online for election news at higher rates than older Americans. Nearly a third (3 in 10) of those age 18-29 say they got most of their election news online in 2004, up from 22% in November 2000. That compares with 21% of those age 30-49, and smaller percentages of older people, who get most of their election news from the Internet (Pew Research Center for the People and the Press, 2004c). Given that the young are more likely to use online election news, they may become politically engaged via online communication (Lupia & Baird 2003).

We test this hypothesis with an interaction term of age multiplied by the predicted probability of reading online news. These conditional effects models are reported in the second column of Tables 11.B2-11.B4 for the Pew 2002 and 2004 data, and discussed in the text for the NES data. We find support for the hypothesis that the effect of online news consumption on knowledge is contingent on age and that younger people using this medium are more politically sophisticated (See second column of Table 11.B4). The inverse and statistically significant interaction term for the Pew 2004 data indicates young people who use online news are more likely to be politically sophisticated than older people who read online news. This may be because the young use the Internet for intensively (Mossberger et al., 2003) and for a broader range of activities (Horrigan, 2004). In general political knowledge increases over time, so online news may have a greater effect in increasing the political sophistication of the young. Since the young have more to learn, the effect of exposure to information may be greater.

Analysis of the 2000 NES data (not reported due to space constraints) indicates than the young who use online news are more knowledgeable than other age groups using the same medium. Since our hypothesis is directional, the lower threshold of a one-tailed t test used to test this hypothesis for the NES data is appropriate. Analysis of the two surveys conducted four years apart confirm the same pattern, but the results are more pronounced in 2004, reflecting the increased Internet use for news by the young over time.

However, the impact of reading news online on political interest does not appear to be contingent on age. Young people who read news online are not more interested in politics, as evidenced by the nonstatistically significant interaction terms in both the 2002 and 2004 Pew survey analysis (see second column of Tables 11.B2 and 11.B3). This suggests that while online news may interact with age to improve political sophistication, it does not condition political interest. Consumption of online news appears to have a similar impact in engaging both the young and old in politics.

INCREASING CIVIC ENGAGEMENT THROUGH CONSUMING POLITICAL INFORMATION ONLINE

In this chapter we offer a theoretical account for why a major feature of modernization, the Internet, should foster civic engagement and find support for this engagement hypothesis. This findings provide evidence to support one set of claims that the Internet enhances engagement and participation in politics. It builds on previous research showing that use of online news can increase voter turnout and political participation (Bimber, 2003; Tolbert & McNeal, 2003), by extending the findings to civic engagement, necessary for sustained participation in politics. The findings also run counter to other influential explanations on the effect of the Internet on engagement (Putnam, 2000) and democracy (Norris, 2001; Sunstein, 2001). Despite arguments that new online forms of communication offer little hope of reversing, and may even exacerbate, long-term reductions in social capital (Putnam, 2000), our findings suggest otherwise. We find support for our *Internet engagement hypothesis* as it related online news consumption. That is, individuals who consume political information online are more likely to participate in political discussions, have higher levels of political knowledge, and demonstrate greater political awareness measured by political interest. Additionally, since we observe this relationship even though we employ a blunt measure of the consumption of online news that masks variance in the frequency and importance that individuals prescribe to online sources of political information, we view these findings as particularly compelling. With more precise measures of online news consumption, the relationship we find should be even more pronounced. We view these findings as significant, and less prosaically, hopeful in light of declining civic engagement in American politics over the past 3 decades. At least with respect to these characteristics of citizens' engagement with politics, we find that Internet use promotes engagement.

The analyses based on survey data demonstrate a causal relationship between Internet use for news and civic engagement. By reducing individual costs and increasing the benefits of political participation, as well as providing alternative information than mainstream media, we hypothesized that the Internet is positively related to increased civic engagement. The research findings suggest the Internet provides additional sources of information and communication fostering civic engagement, above and beyond traditional media, such as television and newsprint. The research is consistent with a growing body of literature on the importance of infor-mation in participation and civic engagement beyond traditional media (Alvarez, 1998; Bowler & Donovan, 1998; Grofman, 1995; Lassen, 1995; Lupia, 1994; Luskin, 1987, 1990; Lupia & McCubbins, 1998; Popkin, 1991).

The young—a demographic group with the lowest civic and political participation—are the most likely to seek online political news and be active in politics online. Because the young are more likely to have tech-nology access, and to use online news (Lupia & Baird 2003; Mossberger et al., 2003; Lenhart, 2003), the consequences for sustained engagement of future generations are significant. Our study found important evidence (measured with an interaction term) that online news may be especially important to the young, leading to increased political sophistication among this age group.

As noted above, we view this relationship in a hopeful light. We find that the Internet, as well as television, has a positive effect on civic engagement. The online consumption of political information increases political knowledge, fosters political discourse, and engages political interest. These findings are consistent over a 4-year period. Moreover, the rate at which individuals consume political information online has been increasing and continues to increase, especially by the young. Since the young will one day get older, they may become politically engaged via online communication (Lupia & Baird, 2003). And they will be replaced with new younger people who will also use the Internet. Our findings are consistent with Verba, Schlozman, and Brady (1995) who note that skill acts increase participation and engagement. We find the interactivity of the Internet enhances the skills that foster participation/engagement. Therefore, the Internet, as the major feature of modernization in the early twenty-first century, fosters—not impedes, as Putnam's work sug-gests—civic engagement.

In Shakespeare's *The Tempest*, Arial sings to Ferdinand of transforming his father, Alonso, the King of Naples, into something "rich and strange" with "pearls" for eyes and "coral" for bones, so that "Sea nymphs hourly ring his knell." In considering the effect of modernization on humanity, T.S. Eliot references this change ominously in several passages of *The Wasteland*. For Eliot, then, modernization represented a threat to the well-being of humanity. We believe our findings about the effect of the Inter-net on civic engagement warrant a more hopeful view of this form of con-temporary modernization.

APPENDIX A:
2000 NES POSTELECTION DATA (ICPSR SURVEY #3137)

Dependent Variable Question Wording

Frequency of Discussion: NES v001205.
Political Information: NES v001446-v001457; v001356 and v001357.
Political Interest: NES v001201.

Independent Variable Question Coding

Internet Election News (for first stage): NES v001434
Internet Access: NES v001433.
Newspaper Reading: NES v000335.
Television Watching: NES v000329.
Partisan Strength: NES v000523.
Age: NES v000908.
Sex: NES v001029.
Race: NES v001006.
Latino Origin: NES v001012.
Education: NES v000913.
Income: NES v000994.
Efficacy: Combining NES v001529 and v001527.

APPENDIX B

Table 11.B1.   Impact of Online News Consumption on Political Discussion, Knowledge and Interest (2000): Second-Stage Estimates

	Political Discussion		Political Knowledge		Political Interest	
	Coef. (S.E.)	P > |z|	Coef. (S.E.)	P > |z|	Coef. (S.E.)	P > |z|
Media						
Predicted Probability of online election news consumption[1]	.179 (.075)	.017	.306 (.109)	.005	3.03 (.322)	.000
Newspaper Consumption	.022 (.005)	.000	.023 (.007)	.002	-.014 (.022)	.532
Television (National) Consumption	.018 (.005)	.000	.021 (.007)	.003	.146 (.023)	.000
Controls						
Strong Partisan	.069 (.029)	.019	.122 (.040)	.003	.606 (.135)	.000
Age	-.003 (.001)	.001	.006 (001)	.000	.032 (005)	.000
Female	.063 (.029)	.030	-.315 (.040)	.000	.127 (.124)	.307
Latino	.016 (.055)	.769	-.286 (.091)	.002	.475 (.236)	.044
African American	-.131 (.050)	.009	-.286 (.078)	.000	.809 (.204)	.000
Asian American	-.067 (.104)	.515	.005 (.131)	.969	-1.375 (.441)	.002
Education	.014 (.011)	.211	.133 (015)	.000	-.120 (.048)	.013
Income	.016 (.004)	.000	.005 (.005)	.307	-.022 (.018)	.234
Political Efficacy	.018 (.006)	.004	-.023 (.009)	.013	-.060 (.028)	.030
Political Knowledge	.044 (.010)	.000			.228 (.044)	.000
Political Discussion			.033 (.008)	.000	.239 (.024)	.000
Political Interest	.164 (.012)	.000	.098 (.018)	.000		
Constant	.367 (.092)	.000	-.702 (.132)	.000		
Cut 1					1.230 (.375)	
Cut 2					4.232 (.397)	
Pseudo R^2	.0966		.1565		.2234	
LR Chi^2	674.14	.000	794.08	.000	590.53	
Number	1309		1309		1309	

Source: 2000 American National Election Survey, Postelection study. Unstandardized Poisson regression coefficients with standard errors in parentheses for models estimating political discussion and knowledge. Unstandardized ordered logistic regression coefficients with standard errors in parentheses for political interest. Reported probabilities are based on two-tailed test. Statistically significant coefficients at .05 or less in bold. Endogeneous models for discussion and knowledge. Recursive model for interest. Note, no constant reported for ordered logistic regression models.

Note: 1. The predicted probability for reading online political news was constructed from a logistic regression model where reading online political news was the dependent variable and independent variables included female, national television news consumption, newspaper consumption, age, education, income, Internet access, strong partisan, efficacy, political interest, African American, Asian American, and Latino.

**Table 11.B2.   Impact of Online News Consumption
on Political Interest (2002): Second-Stage Estimates**

	Political Interest		*Conditional Effects Model*	
	Coef. (S. E.)	*P> |z|*	*Coef. (S. E.)*	*P> |z|*
Media				
Predicted Probability of online election news consumption[1]	**13.724 (.639)**	**.000**	**11.775 (1.619)**	**.000**
Newspaper Consumption	.108 (.129)	.402	.112 (.129)	.385
Television (National) Consumption	**.400 (.124)**	**.001**	**.399 (.123)**	**.001**
Control Variables				
Democrat	.115 (.150)	.442	.129 (.150)	.390
Republican	.167 (.146)	.252	.173 (.146)	.236
Age	**.068 (.004)**	**.000**	**.064 (.004)**	**.000**
Female	**.458 (.119)**	**.000**	**.445 (.119)**	**.000**
Latino	.263 (.222)	.235	.265 (.221)	.230
African American	.325 (.207)	.117	.310 (.207)	.134
Asian American	-.322 (.391)	.410	-.311 (.392)	.427
Education	**-.160 (.042)**	**.000**	**-.162 (.042)**	**.000**
Income	**-.117 (.032)**	**.000**	**-.124 (.032)**	**.000**
Age*Online News Consumption			.049 (.038)	.200
Cut 1	-.742 (.291)		-.873 (.313)	
Cut 2	3.734 (.305)		3.566 (.330)	
Cut 3	4.030 (.307)		3.861 (.332)	
Pseudo R^2	.3424		.3428	
LR chi2	1210.65	.000	1212.30	.000
Number	1867		1867	

Source: The Internet and American Life Daily Tracking Survey, October-November 2002, Pew Research Center for the People and the Press. Unstandardized ordered logistic regression coefficients with standard errors in parentheses. Statistically significant coefficients at .05 or less in bold.

Note: 1. The predicted probability for reading online political news was constructed from a logistic regression model reported in Table 11.B5 where reading online political news was the dependent variable and explanatory variables included female, national television news consumption, newspaper consumption, age, education, income, Internet access, Democrat, Republican, political interest, African American, Asian American, and Latino.

Table 11.B3. Impact of Online News Consumption on Political Interest (2004): Second-Stage Estimates

	Political Interest		Conditional Effects Model	
	Coef. (S. E.)	P>|z|	Coef. (S. E.)	P>|z|
Media				
Predicted Probability of online election news consumption[1]	**11.096 (.519)**	**.000**	**12.211 (1.029)**	**.000**
Newspaper Consumption	**1.298 (.212)**	**.000**	**1.319 (1.029)**	**.000**
Television (National) Consumption	**2.343 (.193)**	**.000**	**2.358 (.193)**	**.000**
Control Variables				
Democrat	**.772 (.144)**	**.000**	**.777 (.144)**	**.000**
Republican	**.695 (.142)**	**.000**	**.663 (.142)**	**.000**
Age	**.051 (.004)**	**.000**	**.054 (.005)**	**.000**
Female	**.423 (.123)**	**.001**	**.428 (.123)**	**.001**
Latino	**1.055 (.243)**	**.000**	**1.082 (.244)**	**.000**
African American	**.409 (.203)**	**.045**	**.405 (.203)**	**.047**
Asian American	-.706 (.478)	.112	-.783 (.479)	.102
Education	**-.354 (.045)**	**.000**	**-.340 (.045)**	**.000**
Income	.009 (.029)	.755	.014 (.029)	.616
Age*Online News Consumption			-.0272 (.021)	.204
Cut 1	2.873 (.345)		3.090 (.386)	
Cut 2	5.062 (.367)		5.289 (.410)	
Cut 3	8.128 (.413)		8.350 (.450)	
Pseudo R^2	.2792		.2797	
LR chi2	925.64	.000	927.24	.000
Number	1241		1241	

Source: Cable and Internet Loom Large in Fragmented Political News Universe Survey, January 11, 2004. Pew Research Center for the People and the Press. Unstandardized ordered logistics regression coefficients with standard errors in parentheses.
Reported probabilities are based on two-tailed test. Statistically significant coefficients at .05 or less in bold.

Note: 1. The predicted probability for reading online political news was constructed from a logistic regression model reported in Table 11.B5 where reading online political news was the dependent variable and explanatory variables included female, national television news consumption, newspaper consumption, age, education, income, Internet access, Democrat, Republican, political interest, African American, Asian American, and Latino.

Table 11.B4.   Impact of Online News Consumption on Political Knowledge (2004): Second-Stage Estimates

	Political Knowledge		Conditional Effects Model	
	Coef. (S.E.)	P > |z|	Coef. (S.E.)	P > |z|
Media				
Predicted Probability of online election news consumption[1]	**.537 (.244)**	**.028**	**1.886 (.514)**	**.000**
Newspaper Consumption	-.114 (.112)	.309	-.067 (.114)	.552
Television (National) Consumption	-.110 (.107)	.303	-.052 (.110)	.635
Control Variables				
Democrat	-.050 (.086)	.558	-.039 (.086)	.648
Republican	-.021 (.086)	.800	-.013 (.086)	.877
Age	**.019 (.002)**	**.000**	**.025 (.003)**	**.000**
Female	**-.366 (.075)**	**.000**	**-.435 (.076)**	**.000**
Latino	**-.053 (.224)**	**.025**	**-.435 (.225)**	**.054**
African American	**-.458 (.159)**	**.004**	**-.457 (.159)**	**.004**
Asian American	-.225 (.338)	.506	-.280 (.339)	.409
Education	**.144 (.028)**	**.000**	**.148 (.027)**	**.000**
Income	**.087 (.017)**	**.000**	**.095 (.017)**	**.000**
Political Interest	**.327 (.053)**	**.000**	**.304 (.053)**	**.000**
Age* Online News Consumption			-.0269 (.009)	.003
Constant	**-3.556 (.219)**	**.000**	**-3.931 (.256)**	**.000**
Pseudo R^2	.1679		.1679	
LR χ^2	463.90	.000	463.92	.000
Number	1241		1241	

Source: Cable and Internet Loom Large in Fragmented Political News Universe Survey, January 11, 2004. Pew Research Center for the People and the Press. Unstandardized ordered logistic regression coefficients with standard errors in parentheses. Reported probabilities are based on two-tailed test. Statistically significant coefficients at .05 or less in bold.

Note: 1. The predicted probability for reading online political news was constructed from a logistic regression model reported in Table B5 where reading online political news was the dependent variable and explanatory variables included female, national television news consumption, newspaper consumption, age, education, income, Internet access, Democrat, Republican, political interest, African American, Asian American and Latino.

Table 11B5.   Online News Consumption: First-Stage Estimates

	2000 NES		2002 PEW		2004 PEW	
	Coef. (S.E.)	P > |z|	Coef. (S.E.)	P > |z|	Coef. (S.E.)	P > |z|
Media						
Newspaper Consumption	.040 (.005)	.168	.336 (.158)	.034	-.426 (.036)	.036
Television (National) Consumption	-.009 (.031)	.776	.185 (.163)	.257	-1.278 (.164)	.000
Controls						
Strong Partisan	.379 (.169)	.025				
Democrat			.220 (.240)	.282	-.289 (.166)	.081
Republican			.347 (.183)	.057	-.469 (.168)	.005
Age	-.041 (.006)	.000	-.032 (006)	.000	-.020 (005)	.000
Female	-.398 (.029)	.009	-.419 (.150)	.005	-.543 (.138)	.000
Latino	.012 (.297)	.968	-.182 (.305)	.550	-.877 (.274)	.001
African American	-.101 (.297)	.734	-.189 (.309)	.542	-.126 (.217)	.562
Asian American	.320 (.551)	.561	-.205 (.542)	.705	.314 (.437)	.473
Education	.221 (.056)	.000	.177 (054)	.001	.272 (.048)	.000
Income	-.016 (.611)	.434	.093 (.042)	.027	.069 (.034)	.045
Political Efficacy	-.031 (.036)	.390				
Political Interest	.314 (.061)	.000	.918 (.091)	.000	1.109 (.086)	.000
Internet Access	20.593 (172)	.990	19.368 (151)	.990	19.513 (120)	.987
Constant	-20.820 (172)	.990	-24.313 (151)	.987	-22.985 (120)	.985
-2 Log Likelihood	1044.471		1159.336		1445.987	
Nagelkerke R^2	.511		.400		.460	
LR χ^2	599.220	.000	501.633	.000	808.017	.000
Number	1333		1863		1241	

Source: 2000 American National Election Survey, Postelection study. Source 2002 Model: *The Internet and American Life Daily Tracking Survey, October-November 2002,* Pew Research Center for the People and the Press. Source 2004 Model: *Cable and Internet Loom Large in Fragmented Political News Universe Survey,* January 11, 2004. Pew Research Center for the People and the Press.

Note: Unstandardized logistic regression coefficients with standard errors in parentheses. Reported probabilities are based on two-tailed test. Statistically significant coefficients at .05 or less in bold.

NOTES

1. The "Life Style" survey was developed to assess how individuals' life styles affect their consumption of goods and services. See Wells and Prensky (1996)
2. We thank an anonymous reader for making this observation.
3. That the media has been found to increase political knowledge does not negate other important predictors of political sophistication. What an individual receives can also be determined by their background level of knowledge and mediated by education. Price and Zaller (1993) suggest that background political knowledge, not media use, is the strongest and most consistent predictor of current news story recall across a wide range of topics. Of course, online political information is transmitted to consumers through a combination of means—not merely through print. As with television and/or radio, individuals can consume news on the Internet through audio-streamed speeches, steaming video and webcam images. Nevertheless, Internet news is largely a print-driven format, and at any rate, all forms of media can increase political knowledge (Delli Carpini & Keeter 1996).
4. We are not using the 2002 NES because it did not ask respondents about Internet use for political information
5. (5) "Which party had a majority in the House before the election?"; and (6) "Which party held a majority in the Senate before the election?" In the 2004 Pew survey, respondents were asked: "Do you happen to know which of the Democratic presidential candidates ..." (1) "... Served as an Army general?"; (2) "... Served as the Majority Leader in the House of Representatives?"
6. In the 2000 NES, respondents were asked: (1) "What position does Trent Lott hold?; (2) "What position does William Rehnquist hold?"; (3) "What position does Tony Blair hold?"; (4) "What position does Janet Reno hold?";
7. The survey questions used in this analysis measure obtaining news online, rather than participating in an email, chat, blog, or online forum. The analysis is constrained by the availability of the data in the 2000 NES. While more detailed questions regarding online news are available for the Pew surveys, we focus on consumption of online news for consistency between the 2000 NES and 2002 and 2004 Pew surveys. Establishing a general pattern of the impact of the Internet on civic engagement is the aim of this research. We also acknowledge the significant diversity in online news content, such as *The New York Times* versus the *Drudge Report*. The national survey instruments are not refined enough to measure this type of variation. In future research we hope to use a more refined measure of online news consumption.
8. We created this variable from the NES's 7-point measure of partisanship. See Appendix A.
9. As with any two-stage model, we made some identification assumptions in the structural models. We hypothesized that demographic factors, such as

gender, race, age, education, and income would effect online consumption of election news, as well as home Internet access, given the research on the digital divide (Bimber, 2003; Mossberger et al., 2003; Norris, 2001). We hypothesized that political interest would be one of the most

10.   In straightforward one-stage models reading online news was a positive and statistically significant predictor of all three forms of civic engagement (knowledge, interest, discussion) using both the NES and Pew surveys. Table 11.B5 of Appendix B also includes the first-stage models for the 2000 NES, 2002 Pew, and 2004 Pew survey

REFERENCES

Abramson, P. R., & Aldrich, J. H. (1982). The Decline of Participation in America. *American Political Science Review* 76: 502-21.

Alvarez, M. (1998). *Information and elections*. Ann Arbor: University of Michigan Press.

Alvarez, M., & Bedolla, L. (2004). The Revolution against affirmative action in California: Racism, economics, and Proposition 209. *State Politics and Policy Quarterly, 4*, 1-17.

Alvarez, M., & Butterfield, T. (2000). The Resurgence of nativism in California? The Case of Proposition 187 and illegal immigration. *Social Science Quarterly, 81*, 167-79.

Alvarez, M., & Hall, T. (2004). *Point, click and vote: The future of Internet voting.* Washington, DC: Brookings Institute Press.

Alverez, M., & Glasgow, G. (2000). Two-stage estimation of nonrecursive choice models. *Political Analysis, 8*, 147-65.

Aspden, P., & Katz, J. E. (1997). A nation of strangers? *Communications of the ACM* 40, 81-86.

Beck, P. A. (1991). Voters' intermediation environments in the 1988 president contest. *Public Opinion Quarterly, 55*, 371-94.

Bimber, B. (1999). The Internet and citizen communication with government: Does the medium matter? *Political Communication, 16*, 409-428.

Bimber, B. (2001). Information and political engagement in America: The search for effects of information technology at the individual level. *Political Research Quarterly, 54*, 53-67.

Bimber, B. (2003). *The Internet and American democracy.* New York: Cambridge University Press.

Bowler, S., & Donovan, T. (1998). *Demanding choices: Opinion, voting and direct Democracy.* Ann Arbor: University of Michigan Press.

Brians, C., & Wattenberg, M. (1996). Campaign issue knowledge and salience: Comparing reception from TV commercials, TV news, and newspapers. *American Journal of Political Science, 40*, 172-193.

Chaffee, S., & McLeon, J. (1973). Individual vs. social predictors of information-Seeking. *Journalism Quarterly, 50*, 95-120.

Chaffee, S., & Kanihan, S. (1997). Learning about politics from the media. *Political Communication, 14*, 421-430.

Coleman, J. (2001). The distribution of campaign spending benefits across groups. *Journal of Politics, 63*, 916-934.

Coleman, J., & Manna, P. (2000). Congressional campaign spending and the quality of democracy. *Journal of Politics, 62*, 757-789.

Davis, R., & Owen, D. (1998). *New media and American politics.* New York: Oxford University Press.

Delli Carpini, M., & Keeter, S. (1993). Measuring political knowledge: Putting first things first. *American Journal of Political Science, 37*, 1179-1206.

Delli Carpini, M., & Keeter, S. (1996). *What Americans know about politics and why it matters.* New Haven, CT: Yale University Press.

Freedman, P., Franz, M., & Goldstein, K. (2004). Campaign advertising and democratic citizenship. *American Journal of Political Science, 48*, 723-741.

Graf, J., & Darr, C. (2004, February 5). *Political influentials online in the 2004 presidential election.* Retrieved September 8, 2006, from Institute for Politics, Democracy and the Internet Web site: http://www.ipdi.org

Grofman, B. (Ed.). (1995). *Information, participation and choice: An economic theory of democracy in perspective.* Ann Arbor: University of Michigan Press.

Healy, A., & McNamara, D. (1996). Verbal learning and memory: Does the modal model still work? In J. Spense, J. Darley, & D. Foss (Eds.) *Annual review of psychology* (Vol. 47, pp. 143-172). Palo Alto, CA: Annual Reviews.

Horrigan, J. (2004, April 19). *Broadband penetration on the upswing* (Pew Internet and American Life Project). Retrieved September 8, 2006, from http://www.pewinternet.org

Huckfeldt, R., & Sprague, J. (1991). Discussant effects on vote choice: Intimacy, structure, and interdependence. *Journal of Politics, 53*, 122-158.

Jennings, M. K., & Zeitner, V. (2003). Internet use and civic engagement: A longitudinal analysis. *Public Opinion Quarterly, 67*, 311-334.

Kahn, K., & Kenney, P. (2001). The importance of issues in senate campaigns: Citizens' reception of issue messages. *Legislative Studies Quarterly, 26*, 573-597.

Kim, Y. C., Jung, J., Cohen, E., & Ball-Rokeach, S. J. (2004). Internet connectedness before and after September 11, 2001. *New Media and Society, 6*, 612-632.

Kyllonen, P., & Christal, R. (1990). Reasoning ability is (little more than) working-memory capacity? *Intelligence, 14*, 389-433.

Lassen, D. (2005). The effect of information on voter turnout: Evidence from a natural experiment. *American Journal of Political Science, 49*, 103-118.

Lasswell, H. (1932). The triple-appeal principle: A contribution of psychoanalysis to political science and social science. *American Journal of Sociology, 37*, 523-538.

Lenhart, A. (2003, July 15). *The ever-shifting Internet population: A new look at Internet access and the digital divide* [Pew Internet and American Life Project]. Retrieved September 8, 2006, from http://www.pewinternet.org

Lupia, A. (1994). Shortcuts versus Encyclopedias: Information and voting behavior in California insurance reform elections. *American Political Science Review, 88*, 63-76.

Lupia. A., & Baird, Z. (2003). Can Web sites change citizens? Implications of web white and blue 2000. *PS: Political Science and Politics, 37*, 77-82.

Lupia, A., & McCubbins, M. (1998). *The Democratic dilemma: Can citizens learn what they need to know?* New York: Cambridge University Press.

Luskin, R. (1987). Measuring political sophistication. *American Journal of Political Science, 31*, 856-899.

Luskin, R. (1990). Explaining Political Sophistication. *Political Behavior, 12*, 331-361.

Margois, M., & Resnick, D. (2000). *Politics as usual: The cyberspace "revolution."* Thousand Oaks, CA: Sage.

McChesney, R. (1999). Rich media, poor democracy: Communication politics in dubious times. Urbana: University of Illinois Press.

McLeod, J., & McDonald, D. (1985). Beyond simple exposure: Media orientations and their impact on the political process. *Communication Research, 12*, 3-34

McNeal, R., & Tolbert, C. (2004). Support for online voting in the United States. In N. Kersting & H. Baldersheim (Eds.), *Electronic voting and democracy* (pp. 000-00). Basingstoke, United Kingdom: Palgrave-Macmillan.

Mondak. J. (1995). Media exposure and political discussion in U.S. elections. *Journal of Politics, 57*, 62-85.

Mossberger, K., & Tolbert, C. (2006). The effects of e-government on trust and confidence in government. *Public Administration Review, 66*, 354-369.

Mossberger, K., Tolbert, C., & Stansbury, M. (2003). *Virtual inequality: Beyond the digital divide.* Washington, DC: Georgetown University Press.

Neu, C., Anderson, R., & Bikson, T. (1999). *Sending your government a message: Email communication between citizens and government.* Santa Monica, CA: Rand.

Nie, N., & Erbring, L. (2000). *Internet and society: A preliminary report.* Stanford, CA: Stanford Institute for the Quantitative Study of Society, Stanford University.

Norris, P. (2001). *Digital divide: Civic engagement, information poverty, and the Internet worldwide.* New York: Cambridge University Press.

Pew Research Center for the People and the Press. (1998). *Internet takes off* (biennial news consumption survey). Retrieved September 8, 2006, from http://www.people-press.org/med98rpt.htm

Pew Research Center for the People and the Press. (2004a, January 11). *Cable and Internet loom large in fragmented political news universe.* Retrieved September 8, 2006, from http://www.people-press.org

Pew Research Center for the People and the Press. (2004b, October 27). *The Internet and democratic debate: Wired Americans hear more points of view about candidates and key issues than other citizens. They are not using the internet to screen out ideas with which they disagree.* Retrieved September 8, 2006, from http://www.people-press.org

Pew Research Center for the People and the Press. (2004c, June 8). News audiences increasingly politicized: Online news audiences larger, more diverse. Retrieved September 8, 2006, from http://www.people-press.org

Pew Research Center for the People and the Press. (2006, July 30). Maturing internet audience—Broader than deep. Retrieved September 8, 2006, from http:www.people-press.org

Price, V., & J. Zaller. (1993). Who gets the news? Alternative measures of news reception and their implications for research. *Public Opinion Quarterly, 57*, 133-64.

Popkin, S. (1991). *The reasoning voter.* Chicago: University of Chicago Press.

Putnam, R. (2000). *Bowling alone: The collapse and revival of American community.* New York: Simon & Schuster.

Shah, D., Kwak, N., & Holbert, R. (2001). "Connecting" and "disconnecting" with civic life: Patterns of Internet use and the production of social capital. *Political Communication, 18,* 141-162.

Smith, E. (1989). *The unchanging American voter.* Berkeley: University of California Press.

Smith, M. (2002). Ballot initiatives and the democratic citizen. *Journal of Politics, 64,* 892-903.

Smith, D., & Tolbert, C. (2004). *Educated by initiative: The effects of direct democracy on citizens and political organizations in the American states.* Ann Arbor: University of Michigan Press.

Smith, E. (1989). *The unchanging American voter.* Berkeley: University of California Press.

Smith, M. (2002). Ballot initiatives and the democratic citizen. *Journal of Politics, 64,* 892-903.

Sniderman, P., Brody, R., & Tetlock, P. (1991). *Reasoning and choice: Explorations in political psychology.* New York: Cambridge University Press.

Sproul, L., & S. Kiesler, (1991). *Connections: New ways of working in the networked organization.* Cambridge, MA: MIT Press.

Sunstein, C. (2001). Freedom of expression in the United States: The future. In T. Hensley (Ed.), *The boundaries of freedom of expression and order in American democracy* (pp. 000-000). Kent, OH: Kent State University Press.

Tan, A. S. (1980). Mass media use, issue knowledge and political involvement. *Public Opinion Quarterly, 44,* 241-248.

Thomas, J., & Streib, G. (2003). The new face of government: Citizen-initiated contacts in the era of e-government. *Journal of Public Administration Research and Theory, 13,* 83-102.

Tolbert, C., & McNeal, R. (2003). Unraveling the effects of the Internet on political participation. *Political Research Quarterly, 56,* 175-185.

Uslaner, E. (2004). Trust, civic engagement, and the Internet. *Political Communication, 21,* 223-242.

Verba, S., Schlozman, K., & Brady, H. (1995). *Voice and equality: Civic voluntarism in American politics.* Cambridge, MA: Harvard University Press.

Warschauer, M. (2003). *Technology and social inclusion: Rethinking the digital divide.* Cambridge, MA: MIT Press.

Weaver, D. H. (1996, July). What voters learn from media. *Annual of the AAPSS,* 34-47.

Weaver, D. H., & Drew, D. (1993). Voter learning in the 1990 off-year election: Did the media matter? *Journalism Quarterly, 70,* 356-368.

Wells, W. D., & Prensky, J. (1996). *Consumer behavior.* New York: John Wiley & Sons.

Wilhelm, A. (2000). *Democracy in the digital age: Challenges to political life in cyberspace.* New York: Routledge.

Wilhelm, A. (2004). *Digital nation.* Cambridge, MA: M.I.T Press.

CHAPTER 12

OPPORTUNITIES FOR CIVIC ENGAGEMENT

An Online Assessment of Worldwide Municipal Web Sites

Marc Holzer and Aroon Manoharan

INTRODUCTION

The following chapter highlights the results of an international survey conducted in the fall of 2005 that evaluated the practice of e-governance in large municipalities and examined their emphasis on citizen participation. A similar study in 2003 (Holzer & Kim, 2004; Melitski, Holzer, Kim, Kim, & Rhoal, 2005) resulted in one of the most exhaustive studies of municipal e-governance ever conducted. The survey was replicated in 2005 through a collaboration between the E-Governance Institute at Rutgers-Newark and the Global e-Policy e-Government Institute at Sungkyunkwan University in Seoul. This joint study ranked municipalities worldwide based on their scores in five e-governance categories of security and privacy, usability, content, services and citizen participation. In this chapter the results of that study are examined specifically with regard

Civic Engagement in a Network Society
pp. 299–318
Copyright © 2008 by Information Age Publishing
All rights of reproduction in any form reserved.

to citizen participation practices in these municipalities over the last 2 years, and their overall commitment to e-democracy and civic engagement is assessed.

LITERATURE REVIEW

The growth of information and communication technology (ICT) has led to an increasing effort to computerize government services around the globe.

> E-government, the application of ICT within public administration to optimise its internal and external functions, provides government, the citizen and business with a set of tools that can potentially transform the way in which interactions take place, services are delivered,... and citizens participate in governance. (United Nations Department of Economic and Social Affairs, 2003, p. 1).

E-governance refers to both digital government (delivery of public service) and digital democracy (citizen participation in governance). Thus, e-government is associated with the infrastructure and physical attributes, while e-governance involves the overall governing process of which e-democracy is an essential component. E-Democracy refers to citizen interaction with government and their participation in decision making on policy issues. "It seeks to engage the citizens with governments and legislatures through the use of new information and communication technologies (ICTs)" (Riley, 2003, p. 3). According to Riley, "e-democracy concerns those aspects of e-governance that engage the public in electronically-mediated consultation and participation, whether these occur during elections (electronic voting), in the midst of the process of policy formulation (electronic "town-hall meetings"), or subsequently during program implementation (on-line feedback and fine-tuning of regulations)" (Sheridan & Rileys, in press).

The Internet is a convenient mechanism for citizen-users and advocacy groups to engage their government, with the potential to decentralize decision making. Numerous researchers have highlighted this potential for e-governance. During the early stages of the technology-democracy link, the emphasis was dominated by cable television and telephone conferencing (Arterton, 1987, 1988; Becker, 1993; Christopher 1987, McLean, 1989). However, the Internet has taken over from earlier phenomena (Bellamy & Taylor, 1998; Gattiker 2001; Kamarck & Nye, 1999, 2003; Loader, 1997; Westen, 1998, 2000; Wilhelm 1998; Witschge 2002). Computers, unlike other mediums, enable citizens to be able to demand and obtain desired information when online (Browning, 2002).

Korac-Kakabadse and Korac-Kakabadse (1999) further note that ICTs provide the possibility for e-democracy on a larger scale. According to them, e-democracy is the capacity for ICTs to enhance the degree and quality of public participation in government. E-democracy will also allow for greater government transparency and openness, which leads to a better-informed citizenry. The openness of government can lead to increased accountability and reduced government corruption. The case of Seoul's Online Procedures Enhancement for Civil Application (OPEN) system has demonstrated a successful practice of transparency and decreased corruption in government via the use of the Internet (Holzer & Kim, 2004).

Many scholars and practitioners of e-government have expressed confidence in its potential for e-democracy and the practice of citizen participation online. However governments, when providing services online, sometimes tend to neglect initiatives that foster citizen involvement. There are three stages in introducing e-government: (1) publishing, where government information is published online and disseminated electronically; (2) interacting, where ICTs are used to encourage civic participation in government decision making and (3) transacting, where government services are accessed online (Center for Democracy and Technolog & infoDev, 2002). E-government initiatives, specifically the Internet, need to adopt a more "intentions-based" design that enables citizens to utilize Web portals more effectively (Howard, 2001).

It is important to study where governments, especially municipalities, stand in regard to transforming to e-government and how they address the demand for providing channels for citizen participation online. International studies are critical contributions to the overall literature on digital governance. Thus, a global study of municipal e-governance would help to understand this phenomenon, and the Rutgers-SKKU Municipal E-Governance Survey is one such study. More importantly, regional studies provide benchmarks and best practices that allow for increased performance in digital governance over time, especially for those municipalities still in the earliest stages of development.

RUTGERS-SKKU MUNICIPAL E-GOVERNANCE SURVEY

The chapter is based on two international surveys conducted in the 2003 and 2005, both of which evaluated the practice of digital governance in large municipalities. Overall, the surveys analyzed five different categories—security, usability, and content of Web sites, the type of online services currently being offered, and citizen response and participation through Web sites established by city governments. This chapter focuses on the results of the surveys in the area of citizen participation and analyzes the emphasis placed by municipal governments on citizen participation when introducing e-government.

The survey instrument used for the municipal e-governance study is one of the most thorough in practice for e-governance research today. With 98 measures and five distinct categorical areas of e-governance research, the performance index differs quite significantly from other survey instruments. Compared to our 2003 survey, we have strengthened our survey instrument in the area of citizen participation and once again found that the potential for online citizen participation is still in its early stages of development. Very few public agencies offer online opportunities for civic engagement when switching to e-government. Our analysis looked at several ways public agencies at the local level are involving citizens. For example, do municipal Web sites allow users to provide online comments or feedback to individual agencies or elected officials?

Our analysis examined whether local governments offer current information about municipal governance online or through an online newsletter or e-mail listserv. The analysis also examined the use of Internet-based polls about specific local issues. In addition, we examined whether communities allow users to participate and view the results of citizen satisfaction surveys online. For example, some municipalities used their Web sites to measure performance and published the results of performance measurement activities online.

Still other municipalities used online bulletin boards or other chat capabilities for gathering input on public issues. Most often, online bulletin boards offer citizens the opportunity to post ideas, comments, or opinions without specific discussion topics. In some cases agencies attempt to structure online discussions around policy issues or specific agencies. Our research looked for municipal use of the Internet to foster civic engagement and citizen participation in government.

In this research, the main city homepage is defined as the official Web site where information about city administration and online services are provided by the city. The city Web site includes sections about the city council, mayor and executive branch of the city. If there are separate homepages for agencies, departments, or the city council, evaluators examined whether these sites were linked to the menu on the main city homepage. If the Web site was not linked, it was excluded from evaluation.

METHODOLOGY

This study focused on cities throughout the world based on their population size, the total number of individuals using the Internet and the percentage of individuals using the Internet. The top 100 municipalities were selected using data from the International Telecommunication

Union (ITU), an organization affiliated with the United Nations (UN). Of 196 countries for which telecommunications data was reported, those with a total online population over 160,000 were identified. As a result, the most populated cities in 98 countries were selected to be surveyed. The survey was conducted between August and November of 2005.[1] Of the 100 cities, 81 were included in the overall rankings, excluding the 19 municipalities where no official Web site was obtainable.

The survey instrument of the 2005 survey of municipal Web sites throughout the world is based on the Rutgers-SKKU E-Governance Performance Index. The instrument consisted of five components: 1. Security and Privacy; 2. Usability; 3. Content; 4. Services; and 5. Citizen Participation. For each of those five components, our research applied 18-20 measures, and each measure was coded on a scale of four-points (0, 1, 2, 3) or a dichotomy of two-points (0, 3 or 0, 1). To ensure reliability, each municipal Web site was assessed in the native language by two evaluators, and in cases where significant variation (+ or − 10%) existed on the adjusted score between evaluators, Web sites were analyzed a third time. Moreover, an example for each measure indicated how to score the variable. Evaluators were given comprehensive written instructions for assessing the Web sites. The performance measures and the description of their scores are provided in Table 12.1 and Table 12.2.

Table 12.1.   E-Governance Performance Measures

E-governance Category	Key Concepts	Raw Score	Weighted Score	Keywords
Security/ Privacy	18	25	20	Privacy policies, authentication, encryption, data management, and use of cookies
Usability	20	32	20	User-friendly design, branding, length of homepage, targeted audience links or channels, and site search capabilities
Content	20	48	20	Access to current accurate information, public documents, reports, publications, and multimedia materials
Service	20	59	20	Transactional services involving purchase or register, interaction between citizens, businesses and government
Citizen Participation	20	55	20	Online civic engagement, internet based policy deliberation, and citizen based performance measurement
Total	98	219	100	

Table 12.2.   E-Governance Scale

Scale	Description
0	Information about a given topic does not exist on the Web site
1	Information about a given topic exists on the Web site (including links to other information and e-mail addresses)
2	Downloadable items are available on the Web site (forms, audio, video, and other one-way transactions, popup boxes)
3	Services, transactions, or interactions can take place completely online (credit card transactions, applications for permits, searchable databases, use of cookies, digital signatures, restricted access)

OVERALL RESULTS

Based on worldwide evaluation of 81 municipal Web sites, during 2005, the top 20 cities based on overall scores are provided in Table 12.3. These overall scores reflect the combined total of each municipality's score in the five categories. Seoul with a score of 81.70 was the highest ranked city Web site for 2005. Seoul's Web site was also the highest ranked in 2003 with a score of 73.48. New York City had the second highest ranked municipal Web site, with a score 72.71. New York City moved up two places from its fourth place ranking in 2003. Similarly, Shanghai, China moved up two places in ranking since 2003, with the third ranked score of 63.93 in 2005. Hong Kong and Sydney, Australia complete the top five ranked municipal Web sites with scores of 61.51 and 60.82, respectively. Hong Kong was also ranked in the top five in 2003; however, Sydney significantly increased in score and in ranking from 2003 (ranked 19th with a score of 37.41). Table 12.3 shows the overall scores of the top 20 ranked municipalities.

COMPARISON OF WEB SITE PERFORMANCE AMONG CATEGORIES

The overall average score for municipalities surveyed has increased from 28.49 in 2003 to an average of 33.11 in 2005 (Figure 12.1). The Web sites' average scores have also increased in each of the five categories, and this would be the expectation for municipalities increasingly seeking ways to utilize technology to increase effectiveness and efficiency. However the increases have been recorded in different proportions as shown in Table 12.4. The most significant improvement in average score is in the area of privacy and security. Municipalities have recognized Web site security and citizen privacy as key components to effective and efficient Web sites. The

Table 12.3.   Overall E-Governance Rankings (2005)

Ranking	City	Country	Score
1	Seoul	Republic of Korea	81.70
2	New York	United States	72.71
3	Shanghai	China	63.93
4	Hong Kong	Hong Kong	61.51
5	Sydney	Australia	60.82
6	Singapore	Singapore	60.22
7	Tokyo	Japan	59.24
8	Zurich	Switzerland	55.99
9	Toronto	Canada	55.10
10	Riga	Latvia	53.95
11	Warsaw	Poland	53.26
12	Reykjavik	Iceland	52.24
13	Sofia	Bulgaria	49.11
14	Prague	Czech Rep.	47.27
15	Luxembourg	Luxembourg	46.58
16	Amsterdam	Netherlands	46.44
17	Paris	France	45.49
18	Macao	Macao	45.48
19	Dublin	Ireland	44.10
20	Bratislava	Slovak Republic	43.65

categories with the smallest increases in average score are usability and citizen participation. Many municipalities are yet to recognize that citizen participation in government is a critical component for online functions. Table 12.4 and Figure 12.1 highlight these findings.

The average score in the category of citizen participation is 3.57, an increase from a score of 3.26 in 2003, and these results can also be attributed, in part, to the lack of support for such online practices.

COMPARISON OF CITIZEN PARTICIPATION AND OVERALL SCORES

When compared to the overall results, the results for citizen participation indicate a different story—only one of the top overall cities, Seoul, is among the top five in citizen participation. Table 12.5 provides the results of the top 20 cities in the category of citizen participation, which indicate

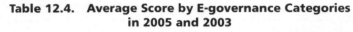

**Table 12.4.   Average Score by E-governance Categories
in 2005 and 2003**

	Average	Usability	Content	Service	Privacy & Security	Citizen Participation
2005 Average Scores	33.11	12.42	7.63	5.32	4.17	3.57
2003 Average Scores	28.49	11.45	6.43	4.82	2.53	3.26
% Increase in Scores	16.21	8.47	18.66	10.37	64.82	9.5

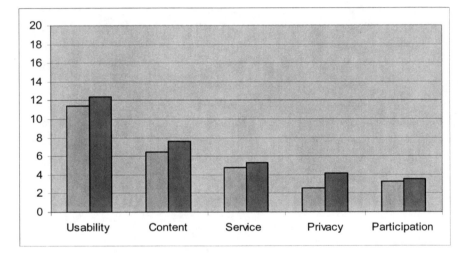

Figure 12.1.   Average score by E-governance categories in 2003 and 2005.

that Seoul, Warsaw, Bratislava, London, and Prague are top ranked cities in that order. Warsaw was ranked 74th overall in 2003 with a score of 0.00, but has improved to second overall with a score of 12.55 in 2005. Bratislava was not ranked in 2003, but has received a third overall ranking with a score of 10.91 in 2005. London was ranked 51st in 2003 with a score of 1.54, but has improved to fourth overall with a score of 10.55 in 2005. Prague was not ranked in 2003 but received a fifth overall ranking with a score of 10.18 in 2005.

When comparing the overall scores and the citizen participation scores for the top 20 ranked cities (overall), it is observed that two sets of scores do not seem to correlate with each other. Figure 12.2 compares the trends of these two scores.

Table 12.5.   Results in Citizen Participation (2005)

Ranking	City	Country	Score
1	Seoul	Republic of Korea	13.64
2	Warsaw	Poland	12.55
3	Bratislava	Slovak Republic	10.91
4	London	United Kingdom	10.55
5	Prague	Czech Rep.	10.18
6	Riga	Latvia	9.45
7	Sofia	Bulgaria	8.55
7	Toronto	Canada	8.55
9	Shanghai	China	8.36
10	Tokyo	Japan	8.36
11	Amsterdam	Netherlands	7.82
12	Singapore	Singapore	7.64
13	New York	United States	7.09
14	Tegucigalpa	Honduras	6.73
15	Budapest	Hungary	6.55
16	Bangkok	Thailand	5.64
17	Jakarta	Indonesia	5.45
18	Cape Town	South Africa	5.09
19	Belgrade	Serbia & Montenegro	4.91
20	Luxembourg city	Luxembourg	4.91

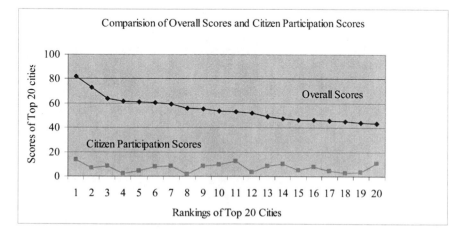

Figure 12.2.   Comparison of overall scores and citizen participation scores for top 20 municipalities (2005).

CONTINENT-WISE ANALYSIS OF CITIZEN PARTICIPATION

Table 12.6 represents the average score in citizen participation by continent. Overall, cities in Europe ranked the highest among the continents with a score of 4.39, while cities in South America scored only 0.69 in this category. Oceania was replaced by Europe as the continent with the highest average. South America replaced Africa as the continent with lowest average score. Africa increased its score of 1.41 in 2003 to a score of 2.68 in 2005. Cities in OECD countries scored an average of 5.18, while cities in nonmember countries scored only 2.63 in this category. This result indicates that cities in economically advanced countries continue to have more emphasis on citizen participation than do cities in less developed countries. Figures 12.3 and 12.4 illustrate the data presented in Table 12.6.

Table 12.6.   Average Score in Citizen Participation by Continent and OECD Member and Nonmember Countries (2005)

	Europe	Oceania	Asia	Average	North America	Africa	South America
OECD	4.76	4.09	8.79	5.18	5.33	—	—
Citizen Participation	4.39	4.09	3.65	3.57	3.41	2.68	0.69
Non-OECD	3.71	—	2.92	2.63	2.25	2.68	0.69

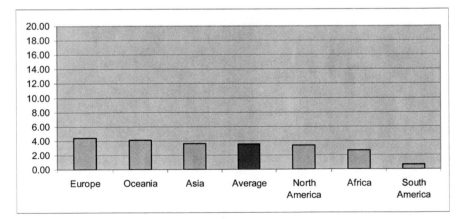

Figure 12.3.   Average score in citizen participation by continent (2005).

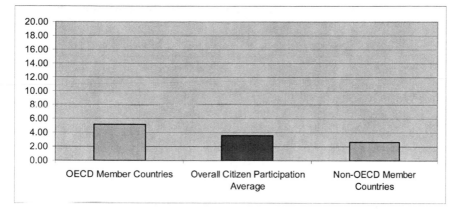

Figure 12.4.   Average score in citizen participation by OECD member and non-member countries (2005).

BREAKDOWN OF CITIZEN PARTICIPATION

Table 12.7 indicates the results of key aspects selected for the category of citizen participation by continent. In terms of evaluating if the Web sites allow users to provide comments or feedback to individual departments/agencies through online forms, 31% of municipalities provide a mechanism allowing comments or feedback through online forms. Fifty percent of cities in Oceania and Africa provide such an online feedback form. With respect to online bulletin board or chat capabilities for gathering citizen input on public issues (online bulletin board or chat capabilities refer to that component of the city Web site where citizens can post ideas, comments, or opinions without specific discussion topics), more than 32% do have these capabilities. More than 38% of cities in Oceania and 25% of cities in Asia provide online bulletin board or chat capabilities. With regard to online discussion forums on policy issues, 25% of municipalities evaluated do have a site containing an online discussion forum. In addition, the results of citywide performance measurement systems are provided by only 10% of municipal Web sites evaluated. North American and African cities lead the way with 25% of their cities currently offering such services. Table 12.7 shows the results for key aspects of citizen participation.

Table 12.8 represents the results of key aspects selected in the category of Citizen Participation by OECD membership. In terms of evaluating if the Web sites allow users to provide comments or feedback to individual departments/agencies through online forms, 47% of municipalities in

Table 12.7.   Results for Citizen Participation by Continent (2005)

	Oceania	Europe	Ave	Asia	North America	South America	Africa
Feedback Form	50%	44%	31%	29%	0%	0%	50%
Bulletin Board	0%	44%	32%	42%	13%	0%	0%
Policy Forum	0%	38%	25%	25%	13%	0%	0%
Performance Measurement	0%	9%	10%	8%	25%	0%	25%

Table 12.8.   Results for Citizen Participation by OECD Member and Nonmember Countries (2005)

	OECD	Average	Non-OECD
Feedback Form	47%	31%	22%
Bulletin Board	37%	32%	29%
Policy Forum	37%	25%	18%
Performance Measurement	20%	10%	4%

OECD countries provide a mechanism allowing comments or feedback through online forms. About 22% of municipalities in non-OECD countries provide a mechanism allowing comments or feedback through online forms. 37% of municipalities in OECD countries provide online bulletin board or chat capabilities for gathering citizen input on public issues. Only 29% of municipalities in non-OECD countries provide online bulletin board or chat capabilities. 37% of municipalities in OECD countries have a site containing an online discussion forum on policy issues. Only 18% of municipalities in non-OECD countries, however, have a site containing an online discussion forum. The results of citywide performance measurement systems are provided by 20% of municipalities in OECD countries, while only 4% of municipalities in non-OECD countries have performance measurement systems online. Figure 12.5 illustrates the overall presence of online policy forums.

EFFECTIVE STRATEGIES FOR ONLINE CITIZEN PARTICIPATION

As the survey results have indicated, the e-government strategies adopted by municipal governments worldwide tend to neglect the category of citizen participation and civic engagement. To enable the Internet to achieve

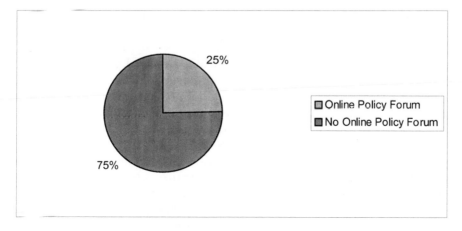

Figure 12.5.   Online policy forums (2005).

e-democracy, these Web sites need to adopt various online initiatives to engage the public in online decision making. Moreover, citizen groups also need to embrace the ICTs that would facilitate better communication within and with the government. ICTs facilitate organizations to "do research on the Web, build links with online communities, host their own Web sites to post reports, and make use of email to connect with their peers" (Bridges.org, 2002).

Contrary to popular belief, many proponents of wider citizen participation do not readily shun technology. Instead, many tend to view technology as a significant means to achieve greater participation. The Internet is yet another technological tool that has not lived up to its promise of citizen empowerment (Ferber, Foltz, & Pugliese, 2005). For the Internet to significantly enhance citizen participation, the e-government portal needs to be sufficiently equipped with tools like bulletin boards, feedback forms, policy forums and performance reporting systems. These initiatives are elaborated in the following section. Many of these initiatives are developed based on the citizen participation criteria measured by the Rutgers-SKKU Performance Index.

ONLINE POLICY FORUM

An important facilitator of citizen participation through Web sites is by providing online discussion forums on policy issues. An online discussion forum refers to that component of the city Web site where the city arranges public consultation on policy issues and citizens participate in discussing those specific topics. In cases where online forums are not provided, the site should at least post a notice with regard to gathering citizens' opinion about policy issues through e-mail, fax, or telephone. Online discussion forums should also include results of previous forums.

Based on survey findings, Seoul consolidates its #1 rank from the 2003 evaluation and continues to excel in all five e-governance categories, especially in citizen participation. One of the unique features of its municipal Web site was the Cyber Policy Forum, established in 2003, that represents the municipality's efforts toward enhancing online citizen participation. Seoul provides citizens with opportunities to participate in governmental processes, including well-organized and systematic opportunities to submit their ideas and suggestions on proposed policies via policy forums in which citizens can freely suggest policy ideas and agendas to public servants. The Cyber Policy Forum aims to "provide citizens with opportunities to understand policy issues and to facilitate discussions; to encourage citizen participation in public administration and to obtain feedback about policy issues; and to reflect citizens' opinions in city policies and produce more tailored policy solutions for citizens" (Holzer & Kim, 2005, p. 87).

BULLETIN BOARDS

The concept of e-bulletin boards has enabled a wide scope of discussion among citizens ranging from formal to informal methods (Garson, 2005). In order for government Web sites to encourage citizen participation, they need to be more interactive. In a study of interactivity by Ferber et al. (2005), bulletin boards form a major component of enhancing the interactivity of a government Web site. The municipal Web site should have online bulletin board or chat capabilities for gathering citizen input on public issues. These online bulletin boards or chat capabilities refer to that component of the city Web site where any citizens can post ideas, comments, or opinions without requiring specific discussion topics. The bulletin board should be user-friendly especially for first time users, and search mechanisms and proper keywords need to be provided on the site. The Web site should also provide support for users to provide their comments directly to elected officials. Additionally, the elected officials should have the email addresses posted online. Again the forum should be more than just a one-way channel for communication. It should include public participants, experts and an active forum moderator.

The city of Indianapolis offers an online bulletin board on which citizens can provide comments specifically on city emergency management plans and transportation plans. To post a message on the city bulletin board, citizens need to register themselves onto the forum, which is free of charge. Forums are controlled by moderators who, along with creating new topics, can also edit or delete any posts in their forums. After a particular period of time, a forum is closed for discussion and is stored in the archives as read-only (IndyGov, 2007).

E-MEETINGS

The online forum should follow a regular schedule for e-meetings or discussions. E-meetings refer to the real-time discussions that occur at specific timings in a synchronized way so that participants can exchange opinions at the same time. These e-meetings need to be scheduled in such a manner that it allows for elaborate discussions between the citizens and public officials, and the results of these meetings need to be posted on the site.

E-PETITION

E-petition refers to the formal request to a city council or a government agency, signed by a number of citizens online, to raise issues of concern. One of the successful e-petition initiatives launched was by the Council of The Royal Borough of Kingston upon Thames in south-west London. The council established the online petitioning system to enable citizens to raise issues by filing an e-petition and collecting signatures that are then published on the borough's official Web site. The main objectives of this system are to enable citizens to report any local problems to the city council, show their support or opposition to any decision of the council, and also recall any decision issued by the council within a particular period of time. Although the e-petitions were primarily meant to report on decisions under the influence of the council, citizens could also file e-petitions concerning other organizations, which the council may decide on in terms of offering support to the citizens' demands. Interestingly, e-petitions on the council's Web site are open to anyone having a stake in the development of the borough and not just to those residing in the borough, e.g., apart from its citizens, even outsiders who own business, visitors, shoppers can also file e-petitions. And there are no age restrictions. Thus according to the council, "petitioning is one way that individuals, community groups and organizations can participate in the democratic process, by raising issues of public concern with the council and allowing councilors to consider the need for change either within the borough or on a wider scale" (Royal Kingston, 2006).

E-CITIZEN JURIES, E-REFERENDA

Along with the above mentioned tools, citizen participation should also involve channels for online decision making such as e-citizen juries and e-referenda. Electronic citizen juries consist of a group of representative citizens who take evidence about issues over an extended period, deliberate online and recommend conclusions to government. E-referenda or online referenda involve asking the whole population to vote online on issues, thereby introducing or amending policies.

ONLINE CITIZEN SATISFACTION SURVEYS

Citizen satisfaction surveys are effective means of gauging citizen feedback on administrative actions. When conducted on a regular basis, with similar questions, these surveys can detect community problems over time (Webb & Hatry, 1973). Providing survey mechanisms online is an effective strategy to institutionalize surveys to obtain regular feedback from citizens on the state of their governments. These surveys should be clearly visible to users on the webpage along with clear instructions for participation. In some cases, citizens would prefer to complete them at their convenience while offline. Hence, to accommodate citizens' preferences, the webpage should enable users to download surveys and also provide information for the completed surveys to be returned back by fax, mail or through email. Citizen survey results should be regularly posted on the webpage and previous results should be searchable on an online database.

The Web site should also offer polls for specific issues affecting the city. These polls need to be accompanied with real time results as well as results of previous polls. To create a visible impact through citizen participation, typically there should be a minimum of three polls per year.

PERFORMANCE REPORTING

Public reporting is an act by the government to ensure an informed citizenry. According to Lee, public reporting is "the management activity intended to cover systematically and regularly information about government operations, in order to promote an informed citizenry in a democracy and accountability to public opinion" (Lee, 2004). And he further states that, "public reporting is characterized by being effectively communicative to citizens." In the past decades, interest in public reporting has been rekindled. The growing emphasis of citizen participation and citizen engagement has rejuvenated the phenomenon of public reporting, especially public performance reporting (Caddy & Vergez, 2004). Thus, public reporting is essential for establishing the democratic criteria of communicating to citizens and enhancing public control (Lee, 2004).

To achieve this purpose of effectively communicating to citizens, municipalities should maximize the use of their Web sites by regularly publishing results of the performance measurement systems. The performance measures, standards, or benchmarks also need to be published on the Web site and for each of these measures proper explanation needs to be provided. Moreover, these results should be in a searchable database online and downloadable from the Web site, and the site should offer contact information for obtaining results of performance measurement.

NEWSLETTERS

Apart from performance reports, the municipal Web site should also provide a link for updates on community events via newsletters or periodic reports. This report should be in a downloadable format as a .doc or .pdf file and options should also be provided for subscribing and unsubscribing to the newsletter and other mail groups. Such measures would encourage effective citizen participation and engage the public in local level decision making.

CONCLUSION

The study of municipal citizen participation practices throughout the world is an area that clearly requires ongoing research. Our studies in 2003 and 2005 have produced findings that contribute to the e-governance literature on citizen participation along with privacy/security, usability, content, and services. The 2005 study highlights the increased attention spent on privacy and security and the contrasting attitude to citizen participation via municipal Web sites. Among the five categories, citizen participation recorded one of the smallest percentage increases between 2003 and 2005.

The results clearly indicate that municipalities do not place much emphasis on citizen participation practices online while simultaneously upgrading other features of e-government. When comparing the overall scores and the citizen participation scores for the top 20 ranked cities (overall), only one municipality (Seoul) among the top five overall rankings figures in the top five rankings for citizen participation. Additionally, there exists a significant gap between OECD and non-OECD member countries in citizen participation scores since 2003. Therefore we recommend developing a comprehensive e-government policy that also considers transitioning to citizen participation online. For e-government to transform into e-governance, effective two-way communications need to exist, communications that facilitate citizen participation. Apart from capacity building for municipalities, including information infrastructure, the comprehensive policy should also emphasize providing access for individuals and citizen groups.

With the growing research and development of e-governance emerging throughout the world, as well as the importance of ICTs, we expect that the municipalities involved in e-government will try to close the gap in citizen participation. The continued study of municipalities worldwide, with a third evaluation in 2007, will further provide insight into the direction of e-governance, in general, and the practice of online citizen participation, in particular, throughout regions of the world. The second study of worldwide digital governance in 2005 has allowed for initial assessments in the direction of e-governance performance via a 2-year comparison. With forthcoming studies, already in process, the data will become critical in evaluating whether these gaps as highlighted continue to increase. Although the 2005 study highlights increases in e-governance performance throughout the world, continuous improvement should be the norm for every municipality.

Acknowledgements

We are grateful for the assistance of research staff members in the E-Governance Institute/National Center for Public Productivity at Rutgers, the State University of New Jersey, Campus at Newark and the Global e-Policy e-Government Institute at Sungkyunkwan University. We would also like to express our deepest thanks to the evaluators who participated in this project.

NOTE

1. Although the majority of municipal Web sites were evaluated during the stated time period, a few Web sites were evaluated or revaluated as late as January 2006 for this most recent study.

REFERENCES

Arterton, F. C. (1987). *Can technology protect democracy?* Newbury Park, CA: Sage Publications.

Arterton, F. C. (1988). Political participation and teledemocracy. *PS: Political Science and Politics, 21*(3), 620-626.

Becker, T. (1993). Teledemocracy: Gathering momentum in state and local governance. Spectrum: *The Journal of State and Government, 66*(2), 14-19.

Bellamy, C., & Taylor, J. A. (1998). *Governing in the information age*. Buckingham, England: Open University Press.

Bridges.org. 2002. *Taking stock and looking ahead: Digital divide assessment of the city of Cape Town, 2002*. Retrieved: March 16, 2004, from http://www.bridges.org/capetown.

Browning, G. (2002). *Electronic democracy: Using the Internet to transform American politics* (2nd ed.). Medford, NJ: CyberAge Books.

Caddy, J., & Vergez, C. (2004). *Citizens as partners: Information, consultation and public participation in policy-making*. Paris: Organisation for Economic Co-operation and Development.

Center for Democracy and Technology & infoDev. (2002). *E-Government handbook for developing countries*. Retrieved March 16, 2004, from http://www.cdt.org/egov/handbook/

Christopher, A. F. (1987). *Teledemocracy: Can technology protect democracy?* Newbury Park, CA: SAGE Publications.

Ferber, P., Foltz, F., & Pugliese, R. (2005). Interactivity versus interaction: What really matters for state legislature websites. *Bulletin of Science Technology Society Sites, 25*(5), 402-411.

Gattiker, U. E. (2001). *The Internet as a diverse community: Cultural, organizational, and political issues*. Mahwah, NJ: Erlbaum.

Garson, G. D. (2005). E-Government: A research perspective. *International Journal of Public Administration, 28*(7/8), 547-552.

Holzer, M., & Kim, S. -T. (2004). *Digital governance in municipalities worldwide*. Newark, NJ: National Center for Public Productivity. Retrieved March 5, 2007, from http://www.andromeda.rutgers.edu/~egovinst/Website/PDFs/Report%20-%20Egov.pdf

Holzer, M., & Kim, S. -T. (2005). *Digital governance in municipalities worldwide*. Newark, NJ: National Center for Public Productivity. Retrieved March 5, 2007, http://www.andromeda.rutgers.edu/~egovinst/Website/PDFs/100%20City%20Report%202005%20--%20Final.pdf

Howard, M. (2001, August). e-Government across the globe: How will "e" change government? *Government Finance Review*, 6-9.

IndyGov. (2007). *Office of the mayor, Indianapolis*. Retrieved March 17, 2007, from http://www.indygov.org/eGov/Mayor/PR/2002/4/20020401c.htm

Kamarck, E. C. & Nye, J. S., Jr., (Eds.), (1999). *Democracy.com? Governance in a Networked World*. Hollis: Hollis Publishing.

Kamarck, E. C. & Nye, J. S. Jr., (Eds.). (2003). *Governance.com: Democracy in the information age*. Washington, DC: Brookings Institution Press.

Korac-Kakabadse, A., & Korac-Kakabadse, N. (1999). Information technology's impact on the quality of democracy: Reinventing the "democratic vessel." In R. Heeks (Ed.), *Reinventing government in the information age: International practice in IT-enabled public sector reform* (pp. 211-228). London: Routledge.

Lee, M. (2004). Public reporting: A neglected aspect of nonprofit accountability. *Nonprofit Management & Leadership, 15*(2), 169.

Loader, B. D. (Ed.). (1997). *The governance of cyberspace: Politics, technology and global restructuring.* London: Routledge.

McLean, I. (1989). *Democracy and the new technology.* Cambridge, England: Polity Press.

Melitski, J., Holzer, M., Kim, S. -T., Kim, C.-G., & Rho, S. Y. (2005). Digital government worldwide: An e-Government Assessment of Municipal Web-sites. *International Journal of E-Government Research*, 1(1), 1-19.

Sheridan, W., & Riley, T. (in press). *Bringing growth and success through e-governance: Case studies in Cyprus and Malta.* Ottawa, Ontario, Canada: Commonwealth Centre for e-Governance.

Riley, C. G. (2003). *The changing role of the citizen in the e-governance and e-democracy equation.* Retrieved April 25, 2007 from http://www.rileyis.com/publications/research_papers/cgr_thesis.pdf

Royal Kingston. (2006). *E-petitions guidelines.* Retrieved March 17, 2007, from http://www.kingston.gov.uk/information/your_council/epetitions/petitions_guidance.html

United Nations Department of Economic and Social Affairs. (2003). *e-Government readiness assessment survey.* Retrieved: March 16, 2007, from http://www.cabinet.gov.jm/docs/pdf/eGov_Readiness_Intro.pdf.

Webb, K., & Hatry, H. (1973). *Obtaining citizen feedback: The application of citizen surveys to local governments.* Washington, DC: The Urban Institute.

Westen, T. (1998). Can technology save democracy? *National Civic Review, 87*(1), 47-56.

Westen, T. (2000). E-democracy: Ready or not, here it comes. *National Civic Review, 89*(3), 217-227.

Wilhelm, A. G. (1998). Virtual sounding boards: How deliberative is on-line political discussion. *Information, Communication & Society*, 1(3), 313-338.

Witschge, T. (2002, September). *Online deliberation: Possibilities of the internet for deliberation.* Paper presented at the Prospects for Electronic Democracy Conference, Carnegie Mellon University, Pittsburgh, Pennsylvania.

ABOUT THE AUTHORS

Annika Agger is an assistant professor in public administration at Roskilde University in Denmark, and a member of Centre of Democratic Network Governance. She has worked as a facilitator and advisor in various collaborative and participatory citizen participation projects. She has written articles and contributions to books on how to create institutional settings for public deliberations.

Robert Agranoff is professor emeritus in the Indiana University—Bloomington School of Public and Environmental Affairs, and since 1990, he has been affiliated with the Instituto Universitario Ortega y Gasset in madrid. He is coauthor of *Collaborative Public Management: New Strategies for Local Governments*, which earned the 2003 Louis Brownlow Book Award from the National Academy of Public Administration and author of *Managing Within Networks*. He has recently completed a book on local governments under Spain's federal arrangements.

Erik Bergrud is director of the International Center for Civic Engagement, and special assistant to the president for university projects on civic engagement at Park University. Bergrud returned to Park University in 2005 following 7 years of service to the American Society for Public Administration where, among other responsibilities, he was their liaison to the United Nations Online Network in Public Administration and Finance.

David E. Booher is the senior policy advisor at the Center for Collaborative Policy and adjunct faculty member of the Department of Public Policy and Administration at California State University Sacramento. He is also a visiting scholar at the Institute of Urban and Regional Development at the University of California Berkeley.

Jean Hillier is a professor of town and country planning at Newcastle University and managing editor of *Planning Theory*. Research includes developing poststructuralist planning theory and discursive, relational analyses of planning decision making. Recent publications include *Shadows of Power* (2002), *Stretching Beyond the Horizon* (2007), three volumes of *Critical Essays in Planning Theory* (with Patsy Healey, 2008) and *Conceptual Challenges in Planning Theory* (2009).

Marc Holzer, dean of the Rutgers School of Public Affairs and Administration, is a leading expert in performance measurement, public management and e-governance. Dr. Holzer is the founder and director of the National Center for Public Performance, a research and public service organization devoted to improving performance in the public sector. He also developed the E-Governance Institute, created to explore the ongoing impact of the internet and other information technologies on the productivity and performance of the public sector, and how e-government fosters new and deeper citizen involvement within the governing process.

Shunsaku Komatzuzaki is currently a graduate student in the PhD program in the School of Public Affairs and Administration at Rutgers, the State University of New Jersey. He is also a research fellow in the Civil Engineering Department at the University of Tokyo.

Carolyn J. Lukensmeyer, PhD, is the founder and president of America-Speaks, and has made her mark as an innovator in deliberative democracy, public administration, and organizational development. Prior to founding AmericaSpeaks, Dr. Lukensmeyer served as consultant to the White House chief of staff from November 1993 through June 1994. She also served as the deputy project director for management of the National Performance Review, Vice President Al Gore's reinventing government task force. From 1986 to 1991, Lukensmeyer served as chief of staff to Governor Richard F. Celeste of Ohio. Lukensmeyer also led her own successful organizational development and management consulting firm for 14 years.

Jason A. MacDonald is an assistant professor of political science at Kent State University. His research examines how institutions affect public policy and political behavior. His research has appeared in *Legislative Studies Quarterly, Political Research Quarterly* and *American Politics Research*.

Myrna P. Mandell, PhD, is professor emeritus at California State University, Northridge and an adjunct faculty at the School of Mangement at Queensland University of Technology in Brisbane, Australia. She is recognized as a researcher and consultant in the fields of collaboration through networks and network structures and intergovernmental management in the public sector. She has recently published a booklet, with Paul Vandeventer, on best practices for networks. She has published numerous articles and book chapters on managing and operating networks. In addition she has done work on the new role for nonprofits working with government and others; performance measures for networks; and leadership in networks.

Aroon Manoharan is currently pursuing his doctoral studies in public administration at the Rutgers School of Public Affairs and Administration. His research focuses on performance measurement/reporting, e-governance, public transit issues and comparative public administration. He is currently the associate director of the E-Governance Institute, Rutgers University-Newark.

Hun Myoung Park, PhD in public policy, is a statistical software analyst at the University Information Technology Services (UITS) Center for Statistical and Mathematical Computing, Indiana University. His research interests include policy analysis and evaluation, public management information systems, and econometric data analysis.

James L. Perry is chancellor's professor, School of Public and Environmental Affairs, Indiana University, Bloomington. His most recent books are *Civic Service: What Difference Does It Make?* and *Quick Hits for Educating Citizens.*

Hindy Lauer Schachter is a professor of management at New Jersey Institute of Technology. Her research interests include citizen participation and public-administration history. Dr. Schachter is the author of *Reinventing Government or Reinventing Ourselves: The Role of Citizen Owners in Making a Better Government* and *Frederick Taylor and the Public Administration Community: A Reevaluation.*

Eva Sørensen is a professor of public administration at Roskilde University in Denmark, and vice-director of Centre of Democratic Network Governance. She has written several books and articles on democracy, public administration and new forms of governance. Her latest book is *Theories of Democratic Network Governance* coedited with Jacob Torfing and *Public Administration in Transition* coedited with Gunnar Gjelstrup.

Caroline J. Tolbert is an associate professor of political science at the University of Iowa. She is coauthor of *Digital Citizenship: The Internet, Society and Participation* and *Virtual Inequality: Beyond the Digital Divide*. She is also coauthor of *Educated by Initiative: The Effects of Direct Democracy on Citizens and Political Organizations in the American States* and coeditor of *Citizens as Legislators: Direct Democracy in the United States*. She has published numerous articles on voting, elections and representation and technology in the United States.

Jacob Torfing is a professor in politics and institutions at Roskilde University in Denmark, and director of the Centre of Democratic Network Governance. He is currently working on democratic network governance, discourse theory and employment policy. His latest books include: *Democratic Network Governance in Europe*, coedited with Martin Marcussen and *Theories of Democratic Network Governance*, coedited with Eva Sørensen.

Lars Hasselblad Torres, staff researcher at AmericaSpeaks from 2001-2007, was responsible for coordinating many of AmericaSpeaks' investigations carried out through the Democracy Lab for Research and Innovation. Lars' activities focused on four primary areas of inquiry: the civic benefits of deliberation, policy and institutional impact, the state of practice, and online innovation in citizen engagement. Lars is the editor of the *Deliberative Democracy Consortium's eBulletin* (www.deliberative-democracy.net), a freelance writer, and the founder and coordinator of the Global Peace Tiles Project (www.peacetiles.net).

Joris Van Wezemael is a research associate at the Centre for Cultural Studies in Architecture, Zurich; reader in urban geography at the Economic Geography Division, University of Zurich, and he is the managing director of the Swiss foundation Research Design Competitions. His main focus of research is on decision making and social complexity in urban development and planning. He can be contacted at: joris.vanwezemael@arch.ethz.ch

Eran Vigoda-Gadot, professor, is the head of the Division of Public Administration and Policy and the head of the Center for Public Management and Policy (CPMP), University of Haifa, Israel. Vigoda-Gadot is the author and coauthor of more than 70 articles and book chapters, 8 books and symposiums, as well as many other scholarly presentations and working papers in the field of public administration, management, and organizational behavior.

Kaifeng Yang is an assistant professor at the Askew School of Public Administration and Policy, Florida State University. He studies civic engagement, performance measurement, and public management. His recent edited books include *International Handbook of Practice-Based Performance Measurement* and *Handbook of Research Methods for Public Administration*.

Printed in the United States
133298LV00002B/9/P

9 781593 115579